LaTeX

Line by Line

Second Edition

Tips and Techniques for Document Processing

Antoni Diller
University of Birmingham

JOHN WILEY & SONS
Chichester · New York · Weinheim · Brisbane · Singapore · Toronto

Copyright © 1993, 1999 by Antoni Diller
Published in 1999 by John Wiley & Sons Ltd,
Baffins Lane, Chichester,
West Sussex PO19 1UD, England

National   01243 779777
International (+44) 1243 779777
e-mail (for orders and customer service enquiries): cs-books@wiley.co.uk
Visit our Home Page on http://www.wiley.co.uk
or http://www.wiley.com

First edition 1993
Reprinted 1993, 1994, 1995
Second edition 1999

Other Wiley Editorial Offices

John Wiley & Sons, Inc., 605 Third Avenue,
New York, NY 10158-0012, USA

WILEY-VCH Verlag GmbH, Pappelallee 3,
D-69469 Weinheim, Germany

Jacaranda Wiley Ltd, 33 Park Road, Milton,
Queensland 4064, Australia

John Wiley & Sons (Asia) Pte Ltd, 2 Clementi Loop #02-01,
Jin Xing Distripark, Singapore 129 809

John Wiley & Sons (Canada) Ltd, 22 Worcester Road,
Rexdale, Ontario M9W 1L1, Canada

British Library Cataloguing in Publication Data
A catalogue record for this book is available from the British Library.

ISBN 0 471 97918 X second edition
(ISBN 0 471 93471 2 first edition)

Produced from Camera Ready Copy supplied by the author.
Printed and bound in Great Britain by Redwood Books, Trowbridge, Wiltshire.
This book is printed on acid-free paper responsibly manufactured from sustainable forestry, in which at least two trees are planted for each one used for paper production.

Contents

Preface to the Second Edition   vii

Acknowledgements   xv

1 Why Use It?   1
  1.1 Introduction 1
  1.2 Quality of Output 1
  1.3 Producing Mathematical Formulas 2
  1.4 Producing Unusual Material 3
  1.5 Decreasing Drudgery 4

2 Getting Started   7
  2.1 Introduction 7
  2.2 LaTeX Commands 9
  2.3 General Structure of an Input File 12
  2.4 Modes 14
  2.5 Altering the Size of the Output Page 16
  2.6 Defining your own Commands 16
  2.7 Coping with Errors 17

3 Fancy Prose   21
  3.1 Accents and Non-English Letters 21
  3.2 Type-changing Declarations and Commands 22
  3.3 Declarations that Change the Size of Type 25
  3.4 Punctuation Marks 26
  3.5 Footnotes 29

4 List-like Environments   31
  4.1 Introduction 31
  4.2 The `quote` Environment 31
  4.3 The `quotation` Environment 32
  4.4 The `verse` Environment 33
  4.5 The `flushright`, `center` and `flushleft` Environments 34
  4.6 The `itemize` Environment 35
  4.7 The `enumerate` Environment 36

4.8   The `description` Environment 38
4.9   The `thebibliography` Environment 39
4.10 The `\newtheorem` Command 41
4.11 The `list` and `trivlist` Environments 44
4.12 Environment Definition 46

5   **Boxes and Tables**   **49**
5.1   Boxes 49
5.2   The `minipage` Environment and `\parbox` 51
5.3   The `tabular` Environment 52
5.4   Floats 58
5.5   The `tabbing` Environment 63
5.6   The `verbatim` Environment 65

6   **Making Bibliographies**   **67**
6.1   Introduction 67
6.2   The Structure of a `bib` File 67
6.3   Authors, Titles and Abbreviations 73
6.4   Producing the Bibliography 75
6.5   The `harvard` Package 77

7   **Making Indexes**   **79**
7.1   The Hard Way 79
7.2   The Easy Way 80
7.3   Some Glossary Commands 82

8   **Standard Document Classes**   **83**
8.1   The `article` Document Class 83
8.2   The `report` Document Class 89
8.3   The `book` Document Class 94
8.4   The `letter` Document Class 95
8.5   The `slides` Document Class 98

9   **Basic Mathematical Formatting**   **101**
9.1   Introduction 101
9.2   Decorating Expressions 102
9.3   Framing Formulas 107
9.4   Delimiters 108
9.5   Spacing in Mathematical Formulas 112

10 **More Mathematical Formatting**   **117**
10.1 The `array` Environment 117
10.2 Equation Arrays 125

11 Introducing $\mathcal{A}_{\mathcal{M}}\mathcal{S}$-LaTeX   **129**
   11.1 Some Deficiencies of Basic LaTeX 129
   11.2 The `align` and `align*` Environments 130
   11.3 Non-numerical Labels 133
   11.4 Explanatory Notes in Aligned Equations 134
   11.5 Definition by Cases 135
   11.6 Fraction-like Structures 136
   11.7 Commutative Diagrams 138

12 Simple Diagrams   **143**
   12.1 Introduction 143
   12.2 Straight Lines 147
   12.3 Disks and Circles 148
   12.4 Arrows and Ovals 150
   12.5 Saving and Reusing Boxes 152
   12.6 Contract Bridge Diagrams 154
   12.7 Bézier Curves 155

A Mathematical Symbols   **157**
   A.1 Introduction 157
   A.2 Ordinary Symbols 157
   A.3 Unary Operators 162
   A.4 Binary Operators 164
   A.5 Binary Relation Symbols 165
   A.6 Opening and Closing Symbols 169
   A.7 Punctuation Symbols 170

B Useful Notions   **171**
   B.1 Lengths and Length Parameters 171
   B.2 Environments 173
   B.3 Counters and Current `\ref` Values 173
   B.4 Moving Arguments and Fragile Commands 174

C Glossary   **177**

D When Things go Wrong   **269**
   D.1 Introduction 269
   D.2 LaTeX Error Messages 269
   D.3 TeX Error Messages 270
   D.4 LaTeX Warning Messages 271
   D.5 TeX Warning Messages 271
   D.6 When all else Fails 272

E Differences   **273**
    E.1 Introduction . . . . `.` 273
    E.2 Type-changing Declaration 274
    E.3 Increased Functionality 275
    E.4 Entirely New Commands 276

Bibliography   **279**

Index   **283**

Preface to the Second Edition

LaTeX

LaTeX is a document preparation system which can be used to typeset a wide variety of documents, but you do not need to know very much about typesetting in order to use it. This is because it is possible, in using LaTeX, to concentrate on the logical structure of the document that you are writing rather than on how each page of the finished result is going to look. For example, there is a command in LaTeX which tells the system that a particular phrase is the name of a first-level heading, but in using this command you do not need to concern yourself about the size and style of type that is going to be used to produce the heading in your output. All this is taken care of behind the scenes (though you can alter what LaTeX does if you so wish). Part of the LaTeX philosophy is that users should use, as much as possible, such high-level commands which describe the logical structure of their documents rather than low-level commands which might, for example, tell the system to use a 16 point, roman, bold, upright typeface for a first-level heading, followed by one inch of white space before the first paragraph appears, the first line of which is not indented from the left-hand edge of the page. Obviously, LaTeX makes use of such low-level commands, but most users need never concern themselves with this fine detail. In the case of LaTeX, these low-level commands are typesetting commands belonging to TeX, the low-level language into which LaTeX is translated.

TeX is both a computer program and a programming language. The language contains about 300 so-called *primitive* commands. In terms of these primitives about 600 further commands have been defined and these constitute *plain* TeX. Donald Knuth wrote the program, designed the language and defined plain TeX: the program is explained in Knuth (1986b), the language and plain TeX are described in Knuth (1986a). LaTeX is a collection of TeX macros and it was designed by Leslie Lamport to be used as a markup language. The first version is now known as *LaTeX 2.09* and it is described in Lamport (1986); the second version is called *LaTeX 2_ε* and it is explained in Lamport (1994). The logo 'LaTeX' without qualification refers these days to LaTeX 2_ε. This book is a thorough introduction to this new version. LaTeX 2_ε is updated on a regular basis, but as these new issues are (or should be!) backwards compatible the information contained in this book applies to any release whose date is the first of December 1995 or later and virtually all of it is correct for earlier issues as well. (This book also contains a full description of BibTeX and the *MakeIndex* program.) People who have previously used LaTeX 2.09 are advised to read Appendix E where the main differences between the two versions of LaTeX are given. People who only have access to LaTeX 2.09 will still be able to learn LaTeX from this book; they too should start by reading Appendix E. Note that if you process a LaTeX 2.09 input file using LaTeX 2_ε, it enters *compatibility mode* and your file is processed as it would be had you used LaTeX 2.09.

One of the characteristic features of LaTeX is its ability to be extended by including or loading so-called *packages*. These provide commands for specific typesetting tasks. In this book I use the phrase *basic LaTeX* to refer to all those commands that are available to you when no packages have been loaded. (In LaTeX 2.09 packages were called *style files* and *basic LaTeX 2.09* is the system in its pure state which makes no use of any of these.) It is important to know whether a command belongs to basic LaTeX or whether it is only defined in a specific package, because most packages are not included in the standard LaTeX distribution. (They can be obtained from CTAN as explained below.) Most users, however, do not need to know whether a command is a primitive TeX command, a plain TeX command or a LaTeX command. I have tried to be accurate in my description, since this information is useful to more advanced users. In addition, I have only mentioned TeX commands in this book which fit into the LaTeX philosophy (or which you need to know about in order to understand some common error messages). Several packages are described in this book; the most important of these belong to the $\mathcal{AMS}$-LaTeX distribution, as one of LaTeX's greatest strengths is its ability to typeset complicated mathematics properly (most of the time). What I say in this book applies to any release of version 1.2 of $\mathcal{AMS}$-LaTeX whose date is the 23rd of February 1995 or later, though virtually everything I say applies to all releases of that version.

Audience

This book is written for someone who wants to use LaTeX to produce a document and whose main interest is in the subject-matter of what they are writing about rather than in computerized typesetting. Furthermore, I assume that the reader of this book has access to a computer system on which LaTeX has been installed; this book contains no information about how you can install LaTeX, though I do say something about how you can obtain some of the many packages that are available and which extend LaTeX's functionality in various ways. (Some information about installing LaTeX can be found in the book by Kopka and Daly (1995), section D.4, pp. 386–387.) One of the distinguishing features of this book is that it is written from the user's point of view. I imagine the reader sitting at a computer terminal with this book close at hand. Groups of LaTeX commands that are usually used together will be found conveniently located near to each other. Emphasis is placed on how LaTeX is characteristically used, rather than on the principles used in its design and internal organization. This book can, therefore, be read by someone who has no previous knowledge of either LaTeX or TeX. Chapter 2 explains simply and concisely exactly what you have to do in order to produce an article using LaTeX. For some people this will be all the information they need, but succeeding chapters explain how a wide variety of specialist material can be produced. I have included numerous examples of formatting tasks; in particular, many of the mathematical formulas that are used as examples come from published books and articles in computer science or mathematics. In all such cases a reference is given to the source of the example: not because I expect the reader to look up the original, but because I want to stress the genuineness of the illustrations used. I have tried to make all the examples realistic, even the made-up ones, and a further advantage of this book is that it contains no silly examples involving gnus. The examples of typesetting that are contained here can be used as templates, recipes or skeletons by the user to format his or her own material by making only minor adjustments to the commands given. These templates, furthermore, are clearly explained so that the interested reader can easily learn the principles involved in their construction. To find them look in the index under 'examples of typesetting'; the relevant code is always nearby.

Another distinguishing feature of this book is the widespread use of locally defined commands in order to improve the structure of LaTeX input so that it is easy to understand. Using such commands sensibly also decreases the chances of your code being incorrect. They are introduced in section 2.6 and used throughout the entire book. In Chapter 11 two techniques, both of which use locally defined commands, are introduced that can be used in order to solve complicated typesetting problems: one is based on the principle of abstraction formulated by MacLennan (1987), p. 53, and the other is an application of the well-known method of program design known as top-down stepwise development. These techniques are used to produce the code that generates Ramanujan's formula displayed on p. 2 and Frege's schema shown on p. 4, respectively.

Organization

In the first chapter of this book, entitled 'Why Use It?', I mention some of the distinctive features of LaTeX. Because there are several poor-quality computerized typesetting systems available, some people may assume that TeX and LaTeX share the deficiencies and limitations of those systems. For example, in a recently published *Dictionary of Printing and Publishing* (Collin 1997, p. 173) you can read, 'Ligatures are less commonly used now, because it is difficult to keyboard them on personal computers, which are frequently used by authors to supply text to publishers'. The difficulty lies not in the limitations of keyboards, but in those of the programmers who wrote the systems used. TeX by contrast, does produce English ligatures (though it is possible to get it to produce ligatures belonging to other languages). Without mentioning any other typesetting systems by name, this and several other ways in which TeX and LaTeX are better than their rivals are mentioned in Chapter 1.

Chapter 2 describes how LaTeX is used in order to produce a small document like an article; in addition, the main concepts that you need in order to understand how LaTeX works are explained. If you seriously intend to use LaTeX, then it is essential that you read this chapter and understand the fundamental principles that it contains.

Chapter 3 shows how a variety of accents and unusual letters and characters can be produced in LaTeX, together with information about how you can get LaTeX to produce different styles of typeface in various sizes.

Chapter 4 describes LaTeX's list-like environments. These make it easy to produce things like quotations, lists of various sorts, glossaries, do-it-yourself bibliographies and so-called proclamations (the theorem-like structures often used by mathematicians). In Chapter 5 I explain how to produce boxes and tables, Chapter 6 contains information about how to use BibTeX in order to produce a bibliography and Chapter 7 explains how you can get LaTeX to produce an index for you. You can either do this yourself (the hard way) or get help from the *MakeIndex* program (the easy way).

Chapter 8 describes LaTeX's five standard document classes. These are `article`, `report` and `book` (used for producing documents of various lengths), `letter` (used for producing, not surprisingly, letters) and `slides` (used for producing the transparencies or foils that are placed on top of overhead projectors).

One of LaTeX's great strengths is its ability to typeset mathematics properly (most of the time) and Chapters 9, 10 and 11 illustrate how it does this. The first two of these chapters concentrate on features available in basic LaTeX and Chapter 11 is an introduction to $\mathcal{AMS}$-LaTeX. I do not provide a comprehensive account of the packages in this distribution, but hope to whet the reader's appetite so that he or she wants to find out more. The book by Grätzer (1996) provides a full treatment of $\mathcal{AMS}$-LaTeX.

The main part of the book ends with Chapter 12 in which I explain the `picture` environment; this can be used for producing simple line diagrams. If you want to do more sophisticated graphics, then you should get hold of *The LaTeX Graphics Companion* by Goossens, Rahtz and Mittelbach (1997).

There are five appendices to this book. The first presents the mathematical symbols that LaTeX can produce. The material is displayed in a way that I have not seen in any other book on LaTeX. What is characteristically done in those other books, if they do not restrict themselves to describing the standard LaTeX distribution, is to present a table of symbols available in basic LaTeX (and maybe the `latexsym` package) followed by a table of symbols belonging to the same category available in the `amssymb` package. For example, in Goossens, Mittelbach and Samarin (1994) on p. 218 you find a list of binary operators available either in basic LaTeX or in the `latexsym` package (Table 8.4) and then on p. 222 you see a list of binary operators available in the `amssymb` package (Table 8.19). This is unsatisfactory because the two lists of symbols are separated by several pages; this means that symbols which are conceptually closely related are physically distant from each other. This problem is not solved even if the two lists occur on the same page as in Grätzer (1996), p. 350. My solution is to merge the various lists of symbols belonging to the same category in such a way that related symbols are close to each other physically. Thus, Appendix A is divided into several sections; each of these presents all the symbols belonging to a single category. In each section the various symbols are displayed in a logical order. In this appendix it is also explained how you can define your own mathematical symbols.

Appendix B contains information about a number of important ideas involved in LaTeX. Appendix C is a glossary of every basic LaTeX 2_ε command (except those that produce mathematical symbols) and a selection of other commands that have been discussed somewhere in the book. This is the main reference section of the book. In Appendix D some of the error and warning messages that you get when your input cannot be processed correctly are explained and in Appendix E the main differences between the old and new versions of LaTeX are outlined. The book ends with a list of references and a comprehensive index.

Differences from the First Edition

The main difference between this book and the first edition is that this edition explains LaTeX 2_ε, whereas the first described LaTeX 2.09. This has necessitated making very many changes as the functionality of many commands has been increased in LaTeX 2_ε and a large number of entirely new commands have been added. Furthermore, the arrangement of material in this edition has been altered quite considerably (especially in the later chapters) in order to make the organization more logical. Much completely new material has been added; this has replaced obsolete information. Some of the typesetting examples found in the first edition have been removed or shortened in order to make room for more interesting information. In addition, this edition says practically nothing about TeX and very few TeX commands are used. This is because LaTeX 2_ε is a vast improvement over LaTeX 2.09 and most of the deficiencies and limitations of LaTeX 2.09 that led me to devote a lot of space to TeX in the first edition have been remedied. The old TeX material has been replaced with an introduction to the widely used packages available in the $\mathcal{AMS}$-LaTeX distribution.

The first edition of this book contained a glossary of every basic LaTeX 2.09 command; in this edition this is no longer the case. In order to make room for more interesting material the glossary does not contain commands that produce mathematical symbols; every other basic LaTeX 2_ε command is included, however.

Notational Conventions

In this book typewriter font is used for a variety of purposes; what unites all of them is that they all relate to information that is either input to a computer or is output by a computer. Thus, the material that can appear inside a LaTeX input file is represented in typewriter font. This is true of commands like `\begin{document}` and `\itshape` and also of textual input like `Once upon a time` or `'Tis the middle of night by the castle clock`. It is also true of the names of packages like `makeidx` or `amsmath`, since these can occur inside the argument of the `\usepackage` command in an input file. As typewriter font is used for the names of packages in an input file it makes sense to use the same font for file names. This is because the commands defined in a package like `makeidx` are stored externally in a file called `makeidx.sty`. As external package names appear in typewriter font it is logical for all external file names to appear in this font. File names sometimes occur as the arguments to operating system commands and so it is again sensible that these too should occur in typewriter font. Sometimes the issuing of an operating system command results in messages being written to your terminal and these also appear in typewriter font in this book.

Although typewriter font is used for LATEX commands, when the general format of these is given, italic type is used to indicate a place-holder for material that can vary from one use of the command to another. For example, the general format of the \author command is \author{*text*}. This tells you that this command takes a single argument, namely *text*, which is the name of the person who wrote the document in question. Inside an input file you will actually find something like \author{Antoni Diller} or \author{Paul Feyerabend}.

This book contains many examples of the output that LATEX produces. As the book itself was produced using LATEX there is sometimes the possibility that this output may be confused with the explanatory text that surrounds it. To prevent this happening horizontal rules are used. For example, the following is an example of a paragraph produced by LATEX which is not left-justified:

Time-travel is impossible and yet science fiction writers from H.G. Wells onwards have been fascinated by the idea. One narrative paradigm that has had several incarnations involves the time-traveller being an art historian who is interested in discovering more about a famous artist—in some versions a painter and in others a sculptor—who ...

The above paragraph, the one that appears between the horizontal rules, was produced by means of these commands:

```
\begin{flushright}
Time-travel is impossible and yet science fiction writers
from H.G.~Wells onwards have been fascinated by the idea.
One narrative paradigm that has had several incarnations
involves the time-traveller being an art historian who is
interested in discovering more about a famous artist---in
some versions a painter and in others a sculptor---who \ldots
\end{flushright}
```

Horizontal rules are also sometimes used to help in the comprehension of displayed material that appears in a table or figure.

Accessing CTAN

CTAN is an acronym for the Comprehensive TEX Archive Network and the main CTAN sites are the following:

UK	ftp.tex.ac.uk
USA	ctan.tug.org
Germany	ftp.dante.de

All of the packages mentioned in this book are available from these sites as is a lot of other useful material. In order to make use of CTAN you need to have access to the Internet and some file transfer software. This is often invoked by an `ftp` (file transfer protocol) command. So, to make contact with the UK CTAN site you would issue a command like `ftp ftp.tex.ac.uk` and then you will be asked for your name and password. In response to the name request type `anonymous` and in response to the password request type your email address. Say, you want to get the `proof.sty` package, written by Makoto Tatsuta, which is useful for drawing diagrams of proof trees. You first have to move to the CTAN directory, so issue the `cd ctan:` command and now you need to find out the location of the `proof.sty` package, so give the following command:

```
quote site index proof.sty
```

The last time I did this (on Wednesday, the 22nd of April 1998) I got the following reply:

```
200-index proof.sty
200-NOTE. This index shows at most 20 lines. for a full list of
200-files, retrieve /pub/archive/FILES.byname
200-1997/03/06 |
          9379 | macros/latex/contrib/other/proof/proof.sty
200-1996/03/29 |
          1501 | macros/latex/contrib/supported/piff/newproof.sty
200    (end of 'index proof.sty')
```

The first file mentioned is the correct one. The archive lives in another directory, so you have to give the following command to get there:

```
cd macros/latex/contrib/other/proof
```

To copy the required package to your own computer you should issue the command `get proof.sty` and to leave the system you need the `bye` command. Note that quite a few packages in CTAN have the extension `dtx`; to obtain a `sty` file from such a file just process it using LaTeX.

In order to make use of the $\mathcal{AMS}$-LaTeX distribution you need to get the contents of the following two directories:

```
/tex-archive/macros/latex/packages/amslatex
/tex-archive/fonts/amsfonts
```

(The command `mget_*` copies all the files in a directory.) Put these somewhere sensible and follow any instructions contained in them. More information about file transfer can be found in Chapter 11 of Bride (1995). Appendix G of Grätzer (1996) and Appendix B of Goossens et al. (1994) contain further specific information about how to get files from the CTAN sites.

There are now several web sites from which you can access CTAN. The current URLs for these are:

```
http://www.tex.ac.uk/
http://tug2.cs.umb.edu/
```

These also contain a lot of information about TeX and LaTeX.

Getting Further Information

There are many sources of information about TeX and LaTeX. For example, you can access the Internet newsgroup `comp.text.tex` or contact the web site of the TeX Users Group at `http://www.tug.org` or you can reach them by email at `tug@mail.tug.org` or by ordinary mail at 1466 NW Front Avenue, Suite 3141, Portland, OR 97209-2820, USA; but be aware that their address changes periodically. In the UK you can send an email message to `uktug-enquiries@tex.ac.uk` which goes to the UK TeX Users Group. My email address is `A.R.Diller@cs.bham.ac.uk` and my web site is at `http://www.cs.bham.ac.uk/~ard` where some of the examples contained in this book can be found. I am very keen to hear what users of this book think of it and any suggestions on how it can be improved for a third edition will be very welcome.

Antoni Diller
Birmingham
December 1998

Acknowledgements

The following trademarks are used in this book: 'PostScript' is a trademark of Adobe Systems Incorporated. 'TeX' is a trademark of the American Mathematical Society. 'Unix' is a trademark of AT&T Bell Laboratories.

Frege's schema, which occurs on p. 4 in Fig. 1.2 and on p. 141, is reproduced by permission of Blackwell Publishers, Oxford, from p. 63 of Gottlob Frege, *Philosophical and Mathematical Correspondence*, which appears in the bibliography as Frege (1980).

Lots of people have helped me to understand TeX and LaTeX; in particular, I would like to mention Rachid Anane, who read through early drafts of some of the chapters of the first edition and made several helpful suggestions, and Donald Peterson, with whom I have had many conversations about LaTeX especially concerning the best way in which to organize information about it. David Stevens drew my attention to a number of mistakes in the first edition and corrections to these have been incorporated in this edition. Debra Barton read through several chapters of the second edition and saved me from making a number of mistakes; for this I am very grateful.

Chapter 1

Why Use It?

1.1 Introduction

I have used LaTeX extensively for several years and these are the main reasons why:

- The overall quality of the output that it produces is of a very high standard. In fact, a growing number of books nowadays are being produced from LaTeX output.

- It is very good at typesetting mathematical formulas.

- It is relatively straightforward to get it to produce non-standard effects like the mouse's tale from *Alice in Wonderland*, reproduced in Fig. 1.1 on p. 3, and the diagram that Frege included in one of his letters, reproduced in Fig. 1.2 on p. 4.

- If you are using it to typeset a book or some other kind of large document, then it can be used to take the drudgery out of many of the necessary tasks that are involved in the composition of this kind of text. For example, it can produce a table of contents for you and it can help in the compilation of the index.

- LaTeX is great fun to use.

The remainder of this chapter elaborates and illustrates the first four of these points and, hopefully, the whole book conveys the fun of using LaTeX.

1.2 Quality of Output

Although TeX, the system on which LaTeX is based, was designed to computerize the typesetting of mathematical formulas, it is also very good at typesetting ordinary prose. When writing prose your input will largely consist of letters and punctuation marks, but the output that TeX produces will contain ligatures where appropriate and kerning will also be done automatically. A ligature is a symbol made up by joining two or three letters. The English ligatures are ff, fi, fl, ffi and ffl. Note that ligatures vary from language to language and by default TeX produces English ligatures. It is also possible to get TEX to produce the vowel ligatures æ, œ, Æ and Œ, but these are not produced automatically as they are only used in special circumstances. Kerning refers to the amount of space that is placed between letters in a single word. Compare, for example, 'TAVERN' with 'TAVERN': the second of these has not been kerned.

In addition, TEX will neither introduce too much nor too little inter-word space and it will not produce paragraphs with rivers of space running through them. Hyphenation will be done sensibly and the traditional stock of punctuation marks will appear as they should. For example, unlike some documents produced by computer, TEX has both single and double opening and closing quotation marks available to enclose 'words' and "phrases".

1.3   Producing Mathematical Formulas

One of the most important features of LATEX is its ability to produce complicated mathematical formulas. As an example consider the following equation, due to Ramanujan, which is displayed in Hofstadter (1979), p. 563:

$$\cfrac{1}{1+\cfrac{e^{-2\pi\sqrt{5}}}{1+\cfrac{e^{-4\pi\sqrt{5}}}{1+\cfrac{e^{-6\pi\sqrt{5}}}{1+\cdots}}}} = \left(\frac{\sqrt{5}}{1+\sqrt[5]{5^{3/4}\left(\frac{\sqrt{5}-1}{2}\right)^{5/2}-1}} - \frac{\sqrt{5}+1}{2}\right) e^{2\pi/\sqrt{5}}.$$

In order to get LATEX to produce this equation you simply need to tell it the logical structure of the formula and it will typeset it. The actual commands needed are explained on p. 138 below. Some formulas have to be hand-tweaked, but most do not. It is not surprising that LATEX is good at typesetting mathematics as TEX, the system on which it is based, was commissioned by the American Mathematical Society for the very purpose of producing mathematical formulas by computer, and Donald Knuth, TEX's creator, has done a very good job indeed.

As well as typesetting mathematical formulas LATEX, if told to do so, will also number them automatically and allow you to refer to them. Thus, if you write an article containing 20 numbered formulas and then realize that you need to add an extra numbered formula between formulas (3) and (4), LATEX will automatically renumber all the formulas from (4) to (20) and will also alter all your cross-references automatically. Such an operation, if done manually, is highly error-prone. Similarly, if you are writing a book or paper with various numbered theorems, definitions, lemmas, propositions and so on, then LATEX will number them automatically for you (and you can tell it to do the numbering in a variety of ways). Furthermore, if you realize at some stage that you have inadvertently left out a numbered definition or lemma, say, near the beginning of your book or paper, then when you insert it LATEX will automatically renumber all the other definitions and lemmas accordingly.

Fury said to a
mouse, That
he met
in the
house,
'Let us
both go
to law:
I will
prosecute
you.—
Come, I'll
take no
denial;
We must
have a
trial:
For really
this morning
I've nothing
to do.'
Said the
mouse to
the cur,
'Such a
trial
dear sir,
With no
jury or
judge
would be
wasting
our breath
'I'll be
judge,
I'll be
jury,'
Said
cunning
old Fury:
'I'll try
the whole
cause
and
condemn
you
to
death.'

Figure 1.1: The mouse's tale from *Alice in Wonderland*.

1.4   Producing Unusual Material

Quite a few books contain unusual, non-standard or one-off typesetting requirements. One example of this is emblematic or figured verse. A famous example of such verse is the mouse's tale from Chapter III, entitled 'A Caucus-race and a Long Tale', of Lewis Carroll's *Alice in Wonderland*. If you look in various editions of *Alice*, you will find that it is typeset in a variety of ways. That shown in Fig. 1.1 is different from all the ones known to me. Although the production of the mouse's tale involves considerable input from the user, it makes use of standard LaTeX ideas and features and it is easy to

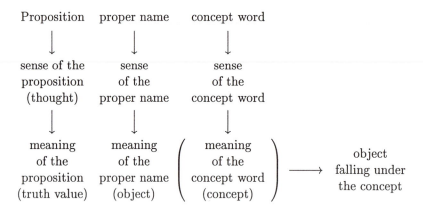

Figure 1.2: Frege's schema.

understand conceptually what is involved. This will become apparent when I explain how it was achieved on p. 25 below.

Another example of a one-off typesetting problem is found in the published version of Frege's letter to Husserl dated the 24th of May 1891, found in Frege (1980), p. 63, and reproduced in Fig. 1.2. This is again produced using standard ideas and techniques, though it is more difficult to achieve than more usual typesetting structures such as quotations or enumerated lists. There are probably several ways of producing Frege's schema. The method I have adopted involves using commands that were devised for the typesetting of commutative diagrams in mathematics and it is explained in section 11.7 below.

Whereas the mouse's tale from *Alice in Wonderland* and Frege's schema present one-off typesetting problems, a book on contract bridge is likely to contain several diagrams similar to that shown in Fig. 1.3. It is time-consuming and expensive to typeset such diagrams in the traditional way, but using LaTeX to produce them takes very little time and is no more expensive than typesetting ordinary prose. In section 12.6 below I explain how the diagram that occurs in Fig. 1.3 was produced.

1.5   Decreasing Drudgery

When the creative part of writing a book (and this is especially true of non-fiction books) is finished or is nearing completion, then a number of necessary, but tedious, tasks have to be done. For example, a table of contents needs to be prepared and if your book contains a significant number of tables or figures or both, then it is desirable to have a list of figures or a list of tables or both. LaTeX will generate these automatically for you (as explained in section 8.2.2 below).

LaTeX automatically generates chapter and section numbers, although this can be suppressed if desired, and if you decide to alter the structure of your book by moving chapters or sections, then LaTeX will automatically renumber all the chapters

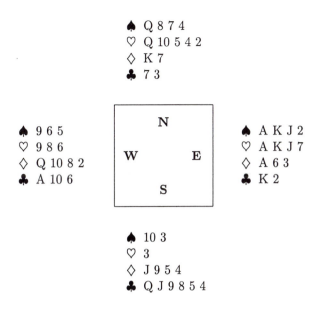

Figure 1.3: A contract bridge diagram.

and sections appropriately and produce an updated and correct table of contents. In addition, if your book contains cross-references to chapters, sections or pages, then all this cross-referencing information will be automatically updated as well. Similarly, LATEX automatically numbers footnotes consecutively with Arabic numerals, although it is possible to alter this default handling of footnotes if so desired. Furthermore, if you decide to add or delete a few footnotes, when your book is nearing completion, then LATEX will automatically renumber all the others.

LATEX also helps with the production of an index, but this is not fully automated in the basic system. The facilities available in basic LATEX, nevertheless, take much of the drudgery out of producing an index and additional packages are widely available that fully automate the process. All this is fully explained in Chapter 7 below.

Chapter 2

Getting Started

2.1 Introduction

This chapter begins by explaining the overall process of document production using LaTeX. This is quite different from standard word-processing systems as LaTeX is definitely not a WYSIWYG system. You start by creating a text or ASCII file using your favourite text editor. Apart from end-of-line and space characters (and an end-of-file character inserted by the operating system), this will only contain visible characters drawn from the following list:

```
a b c d e f g h i j k l m n o p q r s t u v w x y z
A B C D E F G H I J K L M N O P Q R S T U V W X Y Z
0 1 2 3 4 5 6 7 8 9
! " # $ % & ' ( ) * + , - . / :
; < = > ? @ [ \ ] ^ _ ` { | } ~
```

An example of the content of such a LaTeX *input* file is shown in Fig. 2.1 on p. 8. In many operating systems names of files consist of two parts, namely a *base name* and a *file extension*, which are separated by a full stop or period. (Sometimes the base name is called a *first name* or a *root name* (Kopka and Daly 1995, p. 13) and the file extension is known as a *suffix*.) For example, the file that contains what is shown in Fig. 2.1 is called `vamp.tex` with `vamp` being the base name and `tex` the file extension. If you are reading this book near to a computer terminal, it would be a good idea for you to create a file called `vamp.tex` containing what is shown in Fig. 2.1. The meaning of the various commands appearing in that file will be explained in due course. The main issue to highlight at this stage is the overall process of how you use LaTeX to produce a document.

The way you indicate to TeX that you want to start a new paragraph is by leaving one or more blank lines in your input file. TeX treats any number of consecutive spaces as a single space and a single carriage return (or end-of-line character) is treated like an ordinary space. Thus, the way your input file is organized into lines bears little relation to the way in which the output is organized into lines. Having created the file `vamp.tex` you then need to process it or run LaTeX on it. The way you do this

```
\documentclass[11pt]{article}
\title{The Historical Dracula?}
\author{Antoni Diller}
\begin{document}
\maketitle
\noindent
There is growing evidence that Bram Stoker's Count Dracula
was based on the historical figure of Vlad III \c{T}epe\c{s}
(1431--1476) of Wallachia, which is south-east of
Transylvania.  This prince is more commonly known as Vlad the
Impaler, because of a penchant for a particularly unpleasant
form of capital punishment whose precise details are perhaps
best left to the reader's imagination.  In present-day
Romania he is revered as a national hero.

Vlad's father was a member of the Order of the Dragon---one
of several semi-military and religious orders of knights then
in existence---and came to be called 'Dracul'.  The word
\textit{drac} in Romanian means \textit{dragon} (but it can
also mean \textit{devil}) and the ending \textit{ul} is
simply the definite article.  Vlad the Impaler thus came to
be called 'Dracula'.  The final letter {\itshape a\/} in
{\itshape dracula\/} is a diminutive and the whole thing just
means {\itshape son of dracul}.
\end{document}
```

Figure 2.1: The contents of the input file `vamp.tex`.

may vary from one operating system to another, but on many systems you issue the operating system command `latex vamp` or `latex vamp.tex`. LaTeX input files usually have the extension `tex` and some operating systems will assume this if you just type your input file's base name. (Note that LaTeX input files can have any extension. If this is not `tex`, however, then it has to be explicitly mentioned when you invoke LaTeX.) Various messages will be written to your terminal and, assuming that LaTeX discovered no errors when processing your file, you will find that when LaTeX has completed its processing it will have created three additional files, namely `vamp.aux`, `vamp.dvi` and `vamp.log`. (On some systems the transcript file has the extension `lis`, `list` or `texlog`.) The `aux` (or auxiliary) file contains various cross-referencing information and the `log` (or transcript) file contains everything that appeared on your terminal when you ran LaTeX and additional information as well. The `dvi` (or device independent) file is the most important one. In order to produce a document you need to run another program

The Historical Dracula?

Antoni Diller

April 1, 1998

There is growing evidence that Bram Stoker's Count Dracula was based on the historical figure of Vlad III Țepeș (1431–1476) of Wallachia, which is south-east of Transylvania. This prince is more commonly known as Vlad the Impaler, because of a penchant for a particularly unpleasant form of capital punishment whose precise details are perhaps best left to the reader's imagination. In present-day Romania he is revered as a national hero.

Vlad's father was a member of the Order of the Dragon—one of several semi-military and religious orders of knights then in existence—and came to be called 'Dracul'. The word *drac* in Romanian means *dragon* (but it can also mean *devil*) and the ending *ul* is simply the definite article. Vlad the Impaler thus came to be called 'Dracula'. The final letter *a* in *dracula* is a diminutive and the whole thing just means *son of dracul*.

Figure 2.2: 'The Historical Dracula?'

---

on the `dvi` file. For example, if the printer you are using understands PostScript, then you need to run a program which converts the `dvi` file into a PostScript file. Such a program is often called something like `dvi2ps`, `dvitops` or `dvips`. Once you have a PostScript file, this can then be sent to the printer which will produce the final output. Hopefully, this will look something like what is shown in Fig. 2.2. The date shown on your output will, however, be different.

2.2 LATEX Commands

2.2.1 Special Characters and Control Sequences

TEX treats the following ten characters as special characters:

> # $ % & \ ^ _ { } ~

(This is a complete list of such characters.) The character %, for example, signals that everything that follows it on the line on which it occurs is a comment. Everything that occurs between the character % and the next occurring end-of-line character (including that end-of-line character) is ignored by TEX and does not appear in the final document produced by LATEX. The two characters { and } are used for grouping purposes and they should always be matched. The character \ is the escape character. (This has nothing to do with the escape *key* on a computer terminal.)

The meaning of the other special characters will be explained in their appropriate contexts. (If you want to include one of these special characters—except the backslash, hat and tilde symbols—in your output document, then you have to precede it with the escape character. Thus, to produce & you type \& and to produce $ you type \$. To produce the backslash, however, you need to type $\backslash$, to produce the hat you need \^{} and to produce the tilde you need either \~{} or $\sim$: the former produces ˜ and the latter ∼.)

Every LaTeX command starts with the escape character and is followed by either one or more letters or by a single non-alphanumeric character. Such commands are known, in TeX, as *control sequences*. Control sequences consisting of the escape character followed by one or more letters are known as *control words* and control sequences consisting of the escape character followed by a single non-alphanumeric character are known as *control symbols*. For example, \noindent, \textit and \c are control words and \/ is a control symbol. Note that TeX is case-sensitive. So \eg and \Eg, for example, are two different control words. Note that in a control word *only* letters can occur and not also numerals. Control words are terminated either by a space or by any character which is not a letter. If terminated by a space, then that space is ignored; TeX does not treat it as a real space. Furthermore, TeX treats a sequence of any number of spaces as a single space.

2.2.2   Environments

In Fig. 2.1 on p. 8 one instance of the **document** environment occurs. The command \begin{document} is used to open the **document** environment and the command \end{document} is used to close it. The **document** environment is slightly unusual in that only *one* instance of it can occur in any input file; normally, several instances of the same environment can occur in an input file and they can also be nested within other environments. A simple example of an environment is the **quotation** environment which is used for including quotations in your documents. For example, the commands:

```
\begin{quotation}
In the past two centuries there have been five points where
empiricism has taken a turn for the better.  The first is
the shift from ideas to words.  The second is the shift of
semantic focus from terms to sentences.  The third is the
shift of semantic focus from sentences to systems of
sentences.  The fourth is, in Morton White's phrase,
methodological monism: abandonment of the analytic-synthetic
dualism.  The fifth is naturalism: abandonment of the goal
of a first philosophy prior to natural science.
\end{quotation}
```

produce the following piece of indented text (which is from Quine (1981), p. 67):

> In the past two centuries there have been five points where empiricism
> has taken a turn for the better. The first is the shift from ideas to words.
> The second is the shift of semantic focus from terms to sentences. The third
> is the shift of semantic focus from sentences to systems of sentences. The
> fourth is, in Morton White's phrase, methodological monism: abandonment
> of the analytic-synthetic dualism. The fifth is naturalism: abandonment of
> the goal of a first philosophy prior to natural science.

By default the first line inside the `quotation` environment is indented, but this indentation can be inhibited by the use of a `\noindent` command. The general format of an environment is:

> `\begin{`*env*`}` *env-body* `\end{`*env*`}`

In describing the general structure of LATEX commands words and symbols which appear in typewriter-style type represent characters that can actually occur in an input file. Character-strings which appear in italics, however, are parameters or place-holders for the text, LATEX commands or constructs which can be substituted for them as appropriate. For example, in the general format of an environment shown above *env* must be replaced by the name of an environment, such as `document` or `quotation`, and *env-body* can be replaced by a sensible combination of LATEX commands and text input. Names of environments normally consist entirely of letters, though some environment names end in an asterisk. Environment names cannot contain any characters other than letters and the asterisk. Associated with some environments there are a number of commands that can only be used inside those environments and some commands, such as `\item`, have different meanings in different environments.

2.2.3 Declarations

A *declaration* in LATEX is a command which does not produce any output, but it affects the appearance of the output in some way. For example, in the input shown in Fig. 2.1 on p. 8 there are several occurrences of the `\itshape` declaration. This declaration tells LATEX to process what follows it in such a way that it will appear in the output in *italic* type. The *scope* of a local declaration, like the `\itshape` declaration, begins with the declaration itself and is ended by the first right brace `}` or `\end` command whose matching left brace `{` or `\begin` command precedes the declaration. Note that the scope of a local declaration is further delimited in certain environments, such as `array` and `tabular`, by an ampersand or `\\` command. (LATEX contains a small number of *global* declarations whose scope is not delimited by braces or environments. Look in the index under 'global declaration' for a list of all the global declarations available in basic LATEX.)

In Fig. 2.1 note the presence of the *italic correction* control symbol `\/` when italic type is followed by upright type. This control symbol adds additional inter-word space. To see why this is needed compare '*dead* beat' with '*dead* beat'; the first was produced by the input {\itshape dead} beat in which no italic correction was present, whereas the second quoted expression was produced by the input {\itshape dead\/} beat in which italic correction was present. Note that there is no need to add any italic correction when the italicized word or phrase is followed by a full stop or a comma, though it is needed when the following punctuation mark is a colon or a semicolon. It is also needed when the italicized passage is followed by a quotation mark, em-dash, exclamation mark or question mark.

The parameterized command \textit{*text*} also produces *text* in italics, but it has the advantage that there is no need to explicitly tell LaTeX to add some italic correction as this is done automatically for you.

2.3 General Structure of an Input File

Every LaTeX input file has the following general form:

```
        prologue
\documentclass[opt-list]{doc-class}[date]
        preamble
\begin{document}
        doc-body
\end{document}
```

The *prologue* is usually empty. Only a very small number of commands can occur in it. Among them are \batchmode, \errorstopmode, \nonstopmode and \scrollmode. (These run mode commands are explained in the glossary contained in Appendix C.) The filecontents and filecontents* environments can also occur in the prologue. As the prologue is usually empty, the first command in a LaTeX input file is normally a \documentclass command. This is the case in the input file vamp.tex:

```
\documentclass[11pt]{article}
```

This means that the document you are producing will be typeset using the article document class. The class chosen governs the appearance of many aspects of the final output. (This is explained in Chapter 8 below.) The standard alternatives to article are report, book, letter and slides; but additional ones may be available on your system. One and only one of these can take the place of *doc-class*.

The argument *date*, if present, must have the format *year/month/day*, where *year* consists of four digits and both *month* and *day* consist of two digits each. An example of the *date* argument is 1998/03/11. (Square brackets in LaTeX indicate the presence of an optional argument and they are omitted if the argument is not present.) A warning message will be printed if the date of the class file specified is earlier than this.

In the first command in the file vamp.tex the 11pt option has been chosen. This relates to the size of the type that will appear in the final document. The letters pt here are short for 'point', which is a unit of length. One inch is equal to 72.27 points. A large number of units are used in TeX and LaTeX, but the important ones are point (pt), inch (in) and millimetre (mm). All of the length units recognized by TeX are discussed in section B.1. Other standard options are 10pt, 12pt, letterpaper, legalpaper, executivepaper, a4paper, a5paper, b5paper, final, draft, oneside, twoside, onecolumn, twocolumn, notitlepage, titlepage, openright, openany, landscape, openbib, leqno, fleqn and clock. (There are, however, certain restrictions on which combinations of these options are allowed and not all of them are available in every document class. The entries on the standard document classes contained in the glossary in Appendix C state which options are available for that document class.) If no options are chosen, then you also leave out the square brackets like this:

```
\documentclass{article}
```

Usually in LaTeX mandatory arguments to commands are enclosed in braces, whereas optional arguments are enclosed in square brackets; the major exceptions to this occur in some commands relating to the picture environment. You can have two or more options, but if you do, the options you choose must be separated by commas. Be careful, however, not to include any spaces inside the square brackets as this will cause strange things to happen. In other words, *opt-list* is a sequence of one or more options separated by commas and not containing any spaces. If you make a copy of the file vamp.tex and call the copy vamp2.tex and then change the first command in that file to the following:

```
\documentclass[11pt,twocolumn]{article}
```

and also include the command \newpage before the blank line and just after the concluding words of the first paragraph and then process it as explained in section 2.1 above, then the result will look something like what is shown in Fig. 2.3 on p. 14.

The part of a LaTeX input file that occurs between the \documentclass command and the opening of the document environment is known as the *preamble*. What follows the \documentclass command in the preamble is a (possibly empty) sequence of declarations that affect the final appearance of the output document. In the case of the file vamp.tex the preamble contains the two declarations:

```
\title{The Historical Dracula?}
\author{Antoni Diller}
```

These, by themselves, do not produce any output; the first of them declares The Historical Dracula? to be the title of the article and the second declares Antoni Diller to be the author of the article. The actual title of the article, and also the name of the author and the date, are produced by the \maketitle command occurring within the document environment. Note that LaTeX automatically inserts the date on which your input file was processed into the output it produces. If you want a different date to appear on your document, then use the \date declaration. This takes a single argument. For example, putting \date{10 July 1953} into the preamble will result in '10 July 1953' appearing on the document produced.

The Historical Dracula?

Antoni Diller

April 1, 1998

There is growing evidence that Bram Stoker's Count Dracula was based on the historical figure of Vlad III Ţepeş (1431–1476) of Wallachia, which is south-east of Transylvania. This prince is more commonly known as Vlad the Impaler, because of a penchant for a particularly unpleasant form of capital punishment whose precise details are perhaps best left to the reader's imagination. In present-day Romania he is revered as a national hero.

Vlad's father was a member of the Order of the Dragon—one of several semi-military and religious orders of knights then in existence—and came to be called 'Dracul'. The word *drac* in Romanian means *dragon* (but it can also mean *devil*) and the ending *ul* is simply the definite article. Vlad the Impaler thus came to be called 'Dracula'. The final letter *a* in *dracula* is a diminutive and the whole thing just means *son of dracul.*

Figure 2.3: 'The Historical Dracula?' in two columns.

2.4   Modes

When processing an input file LaTeX is in one of three modes, namely paragraph mode, mathematics mode or LR mode (left-to-right mode). If you ever use the `picture` environment, then picture mode is used, but this is just a restricted form of LR mode.

2.4.1   Paragraph Mode

LaTeX is in *paragraph mode* when it is processing ordinary prose. To start a new paragraph leave one or more blank lines in your input file; alternatively, the command `\par` opens a new paragraph. By default, paragraphs are indicated in output produced by TeX by being indented slightly from the left margin. The amount of indentation is stored in the *length parameter* `\parindent` and can be changed to half an inch, say, by the declaration `\setlength{\parindent}{0.5in}`, which can occur anywhere in your input file, but is best placed in the preamble. To prevent TeX from indenting the first line of a paragraph use the command `\noindent`. The amount of vertical space that TeX inserts between paragraphs, in addition to the normal amout of vertical space that it puts between lines, is stored in the length parameter `\parskip`. (Section B.1 contains more information about length parameters.)

2.4.2 Mathematics Mode

The great advantage of both TeX and LaTeX over comparable programs is in typesetting mathematics. To produce a mathematical formula as part of a paragraph you are writing enclose it in dollar signs. So, `$x - y > 3$` results in $x - y > 3$. There are two alternative ways of producing this in LaTeX, namely `\(x - y > 3\)` and `\begin{math}x - y > 3\end{math}`, but it is difficult to think of a sensible reason to ever use these since they are more complicated that the straightforward dollar signs. Between the single dollar signs TeX is in *maths mode* (and it processes any formulas there in text style). Spacing inside maths mode is done differently from how it is done in paragraph mode (see section 9.5 for more information) and the inclusion of spaces in maths mode does not affect what TeX does. The only place where they have to occur is after a control word that is followed by a letter, that is to say, to indicate the ending of a control word.

If you want a mathematical formula to be displayed, then put the control symbol `\[` before it and the control symbol `\]` after it. Thus, the input `\[x - y > 3\]` results in the displayed formula:

$$x - y > 3.$$

The same result can be obtained by using the `displaymath` environment like this:

```
\begin{displaymath}
x - y > 3
\end{displaymath}
```

Inside the `displaymath` environment and between the commands `\[` and `\]` TeX is in *maths mode* (and it processes the formulas that occur there in display style). Normally, displayed formulas are centred on the page, but if you choose the `fleqn` option to the `\documentclass` command they will not be centred. What will happen is that they will be indented slightly from the left margin. The distance that they are indented is kept in the `\mathindent` rigid length parameter.

When writing mathematics do not forget to include the correct punctuation! (One of the most annoying things about many books, especially those written by some computer scientists, is their incorrect punctuation of mathematical formulas.) There are a large number of mathematical symbols available in LaTeX; see Appendix A for more information. Chapters 9, 10 and 11 contain a lot of information about how to do mathematical typesetting using LaTeX.

2.4.3 LR Mode

LR mode is basically a way of keeping a piece of text together on one line. Some people, for example, do not want names of computer programs hyphenated. In order to ensure that they are not enclose them like this `\mbox{ProgramName}`. This is also useful to ensure that mathematical formulas or expressions are not broken across lines. For example, writing `\mbox{$x - y > 3$}` will ensure that the formula $x - y > 3$ will appear on a single line. Inside the argument to the `\mbox` command LaTeX is in LR mode. The `\mbox` (make box) command produces a *box*, which in TeXese is a block of material that is treated as a unit and which will not under any circumstances be broken up into its constituents.

2.5 Altering the Size of the Output Page

When producing a page of output LaTeX can place text in three distinct regions on the page, namely the head, the body and the foot. If running heads are being produced, then they and the current page number go into the head region; but if running heads are not being produced, then the page number is placed in the centre of the foot region. Note that footnotes, if present, go into the *body* region of the output page. There are commands to position the body of the text differently on the physical page and also to alter its size. The distance, for example, from the top edge of the physical piece of paper to the top of the head region is one inch plus the value of the LaTeX rigid length parameter \topmargin. This can be altered by means of a declaration like

```
\setlength{\topmargin}{0.25in}
```

Note that altering the value of \topmargin has the result of shifting the head, body and foot regions either up or down, since they are regarded as a unit. The distance from the left edge of the physical piece of paper to the left-hand edge of the body region is one inch plus the value of the rigid length parameter \oddsidemargin. Note that the article document class is a *one-sided* class. In one-sided document classes all pages are (conceptually) right-handed and odd-numbered ones. This means that the head, body and foot of both odd- and even-numbered pages are positioned in the same place on the physical piece of paper relative to the left and top edges of the paper. When two-sided printing is in effect the length parameter \oddsidemargin affects the width of the left-hand margin on odd-numbered pages and the length parameter \evensidemargin affects the width of the left-hand margin on even-numbered pages; when one-sided printing is in effect only \oddsidemargin has any effect.

You can also alter the size of the body of the text by changing the values of the LaTeX length parameters \textheight and \textwidth. The following declarations are examples of how this can be done:

```
\setlength{\textheight}{8.5in}
\setlength{\textwidth}{6in}
```

These declarations do not alter the left-hand margin or the top margin. Note that the lengths used in these declarations are for illustrative purposes only and are not meant to be meaningful. (There are several other length parameters that affect the appearance of the output page. Most of them are shown in Fig. C.4 on p. 260.)

2.6 Defining your own Commands

According to Spivak (1986), p. 120, one reason to define your own commands, also known in TeXese as *macros*, is to save yourself some typing. This is not as useful as it may at first sight appear, but I do use the following definitions:

```
\newcommand*{\eg}{for example}
\newcommand*{\Eg}{For example}
\newcommand*{\ie}{that is to say}
\newcommand*{\Ie}{That is to say}
```

With these in force, an occurrence of \ie, for example, in your input file produces 'that is to say' in the output document. Note that \newcommand* checks to see if the command you are trying to define already exists; if it does, then your attempted definition is rejected. (The way in which you redefine already existing commands in LaTeX is by using the \renewcommand* command.)

Definitions introduced by either \newcommand* or \renewcommand* can occur anywhere in your input file, but if you intend to use LaTeX regularly, it would be a good idea to set up your own package. This can have any first or base name, but its extension must be sty. For illustrative purposes I shall assume that your package is called own.sty. In this you should put all your global definitions. To ensure that these definitions are loaded when you use LaTeX you should include a \usepackage command in your input file with the first or base name of your package as its argument. This must occur in the preamble and it must come after the \documentclass command. In other words, you should include the following in the preamble of your input file:

```
\usepackage{own}
```

Whereas any commands that you define in your input file must have names consisting entirely of letters, names of commands defined in a package can also include the commercial at-sign @; thus, \@lqq and \@rqq are acceptable as names of commands defined in a package. Such commands cannot, however, be used outside of a package, though such a command defined in one package can be used in another.

Any commands defined in the preamble of an input file or in any package that you use are global. It is, however, possible to define commands in LaTeX that are local to an environment. For example, let us assume that \serial is a command that has not been globally defined and that the following occurs in your input file inside the document environment:

```
\begin{quotation}
\newcommand*{\serial}{Ted Bundy}
\serial\ killed over thirty people.
\end{quotation}
```

The command \serial can only be used inside the quotation environment in which it is defined. If you were to try to use it outside that environment, you would get an error message.

2.7   Coping with Errors

When people first start to use LaTeX one of the commonest mistakes is to incorrectly input the name of some command. To show you what happens when you do this,

change the command \maketitle in the file vamp.tex to \maketitel and then process
it using LaTeX; the processing of your file will be aborted and something like the
following will appear on your terminal:

```
This is TeX, Version 3.1415 (C version 6.1)
(vamp.tex
LaTeX2e <1995/12/01>
(/bham/pd/lib/tex/inputs/latex2e/base/article.cls
Document Class:
   article 1995/11/30 v1.3p Standard LaTeX document class
(/bham/pd/lib/tex/inputs/latex2e/base/size11.clo)) (vamp.aux)
! Undefined control sequence.
l.5 \maketitel

?
```

(You will not see exactly this because some of the information it contains is peculiar to
the system on which I use LaTeX, in particular the path names of the files article.cls
and size11.clo.) If you now type a lowercase letter e in response to the question-
mark prompt, you should find yourself in a text editor with the cursor positioned at
the start of the line in which the misspelt command name occurs. You can also type
h in response to the prompt and then LaTeX or TeX will usually give you additional
information about what went wrong. Sometimes you may experience difficulties in
exiting LaTeX; in this case inputting i\stop in response to the prompt should get you
out. There are quite a few TeX and LaTeX error messages that you might get, but
most of them are self-explanatory and so do not merit any additional explanation. If
you want to know what they are consult Chapter 8 of Lamport (1994).

Something else which frequently happens when processing LaTeX files is that you
get an Overfull \hbox warning message. To illustrate this, add the declaration

```
\setlength{\textwidth}{4.5in}
```

to the preamble of the file vamp.tex, after changing \maketitel back to \maketitle,
and then run LaTeX on it. You will see something like the following:

```
This is TeX, Version 3.1415 (C version 6.1)
(vamp.tex
LaTeX2e <1995/12/01>
(/bham/pd/lib/tex/inputs/latex2e/base/article.cls
Document Class:
   article 1995/11/30 v1.3p Standard LaTeX document class
(/bham/pd/lib/tex/inputs/latex2e/base/size11.clo)) (vamp.aux)
Overfull \hbox (6.54004pt too wide) in paragraph at lines 17--26
\OT1/cmr/m/n/10.95 sev-eral semi-military and re-li-gious
or-ders of knights then in existence---
[1] (vamp.aux) )
```

```
(see the transcript file for additional information)
Output written on vamp.dvi (1 page, 1632 bytes).
Transcript written on vamp.log.
```

This warning message means that some text sticks out into the right-hand margin of the page. The best way to resolve this problem is to rewrite the sentence that caused the problem. Alternatively, you could tell TEX explicitly where it can insert a hyphen. Part of the above message is:

```
\OT1/cmr/m/n/10.95 sev-eral semi-military and re-li-gious
or-ders of knights then in existence---
```

The command \OT1/cmr/m/n/10.95 indicates simply that TEX is producing (almost) 11 point roman, medium, upright type output; what follows this is the actual line whose end juts out into the right-hand margin. The single hyphens in this are the places where TEX can hyphenate a word. The control sequence \- is known as the *discretionary hyphen* and it allows TEX to hyphenate a word where it occurs; the hyphen only appears if the word is broken across lines. You could try to remedy the problem under discussion by changing existence in vamp.tex into exis\-tence and seeing what happens when you process your input using LATEX. The commands \hyphenation, \sloppy and \linebreak can also be used to try and resolve this problem; they are all explained in the glossary in Appendix C. Appendix D contains more information about error and warning messages and in section D.5 the meaning of the various components in a command like \OT1/cmr/m/n/10.95 are explained.

Chapter 3

Fancy Prose

3.1 Accents and Non-English Letters

In the file `vamp.tex` shown in Fig. 2.1 on p. 8 the input `\c{T}epe\c{s}` produces as output the word 'Ţepeş'. This illustrates one of LaTeX's commands for making accents. All of these are shown in the following table, in which the name of the accent is given in the final column:

á	`\'{a}`	acute
b̆	`\u{b}`	breve
c̊	`\r{c}`	circle
d̂	`\^{d}`	circumflex
ë	`\"{e}`	diaeresis (umlaut)
f̋	`\H{f}`	Hungarian umlaut
ġ	`\.{g}`	dot
h̀	`\`{h}`	grave
ǐ	`\v{\i}`	háček
j̄	`\={\j}`	macron
k̃	`\~{k}`	tilde
l̲	`\b{l}`	bar-under
m̧	`\c{m}`	cedilla
ṇ	`\d{n}`	dot-under
o͡p	`\t{op}`	tie-after accent

All of these commands, except `\t`, produce an accent either over or under the next character; hence, there is no need to enclose that character in braces, although there is no harm in doing so. Note that the commands `\i` and `\j` produce a dotless 'i' and 'j', respectively, which are used when an accent is to be placed over either the letter 'i' or the letter 'j'.

LaTeX can also produce a number of non-English letters and vowel ligatures. The following table shows the relevant commands and the characters that they produce:

| å | \aa | æ | \ae | ł | \l | ø | \o | œ | \oe | ß | \ss |
| Å | \AA | Æ | \AE | Ł | \L | Ø | \O | Œ | \OE | SS | \SS |

There are two ways of producing the non-English punctuation marks ¡ and ¿ and they are shown in the following table:

| ¡ | !` | \textexclamdown |
| ¿ | ?` | \textquestiondown |

3.2 Type-changing Declarations and Commands

There are several declarations in LaTeX that alter the style of type produced. A type style has three components, namely family, series and shape. There are three declarations that can be used to control the family of a type style and they are \rmfamily, \sffamily and \ttfamily. The two declarations that affect the series of a type style are \bfseries and \mdseries and the four declarations that select the shape of a type style are \itshape, \scshape, \slshape and \upshape. The default type style used by LaTeX is determined by the document class chosen. For the **article**, **report**, **book** and **letter** classes the default is a roman, medium, upright typeface. If you use the \itshape declaration, for example, this only alters the shape of the type style being used. It has no effect on the family or series components of that type style. In order to illustrate the effect of these commands I show how they can be used to typeset the phrase 'Once upon a time ...' in different ways. To begin the command \Once is defined as follows:

```
\newcommand*{\Once}{Once upon a time \ldots}
```

(The LaTeX command \ldots produces an ellipsis consisting of three full stops.) The effect of the declarations already mentioned is shown in the following table:

result	command	name
Once upon a time ...	{\rmfamily \Once}	roman
Once upon a time ...	{\sffamily \Once}	sans serif
Once upon a time ...	{\ttfamily \Once}	typewriter
Once upon a time ...	{\bfseries \Once}	bold
Once upon a time ...	{\mdseries \Once}	medium
Once upon a time ...	{\itshape \Once}	italic
ONCE UPON A TIME ...	{\scshape \Once}	small capitals
Once upon a time ...	{\slshape \Once}	slanted
Once upon a time ...	{\upshape \Once}	upright

There are three occurrences of the \itshape declaration in the input file **vamp.tex** shown in Fig. 2.1 on p. 8:

```
The final letter {\itshape a\/} in {\itshape dracula\/}
is a diminutive and the whole thing just means {\itshape
son of dracul}.
```

Note the presence of the control symbol \/ inside the scope of the first two occurrences of \itshape. This control symbol is the so-called *italic correction*. It should always be included when italic or slanted type is followed by type that is neither italic nor slanted. This principle does not apply, however, when the italicized passage is followed by a full stop or a comma, but it does apply when the following punctutaion mark is a colon, semicolon or em-dash. Italic correction is also needed if the italicized passage is followed by a quotation mark, exclamation mark or question mark.

Corresponding to each of the type-changing declarations already mentioned there is a command that takes a single argument that has (almost) the same effect. These commands are illustrated in the following table:

result	command	name
Once upon a time ...	\textrm{\Once}	roman
Once upon a time ...	\textsf{\Once}	sans serif
Once upon a time ...	\texttt{\Once}	typewriter
Once upon a time ...	\textbf{\Once}	bold
Once upon a time ...	\textmd{\Once}	medium
Once upon a time ...	\textit{\Once}	italic
ONCE UPON A TIME ...	\textsc{\Once}	small capitals
Once upon a time ...	\textsl{\Once}	slanted
Once upon a time ...	\textup{\Once}	upright

The reason that these commands have *almost* the same effect as their corresponding declarations is because there is one very significant difference between them and that is that there is no need to add the italic correction control symbol when using them. The italic correction is automatically added for you.

The three components of a type style are independent of each other and so a command which affects the shape of a type style can be combined, for example, with one that controls the series of a type style. Not all such combinations are available, but here are examples of a few that should be available on your system:

Once upon a time ...	\textbf{\textit{\Once}}
Once upon a time ...	\textbf{\textsf{\Once}}
ONCE UPON A TIME ...	\textsc{\texttt{\Once}}
Once upon a time ...	\textit{\textsf{\Once}}

In theory, it is possible to alter the shape, the series and the family of a type style to give, for example, a slanted, bold, sans serif type style, but you would have to check if such a type style exists on your system.

LATEX also contains the declaration `\normalfont`. This ensures that everything in its scope is typeset using the default values of the three components of the type style determined by the document class being used. Corresponding to the declaration `\normalfont` is the parameterized command `\textnormal{text}`. This typesets its argument *text* using the default values of the main text font of the document being processed.

All the type-changing declarations and commands mentioned so far in this section are new to LATEX 2ε. The old type-changing declarations `\bf`, `\it`, `\rm`, `\sc`, `\sf`, `\sl` and `\tt` are still available, though their use is not encouraged. Unlike their newer counterparts, these declarations select a particular font rather than changing only one component of a type style. The following table shows the correspondence between the old and the new declaration:

`\bf`	`\normalfont\bfseries`
`\it`	`\normalfont\itshape`
`\rm`	`\normalfont\rmfamily`
`\sc`	`\normalfont\scshape`
`\sf`	`\normalfont\sffamily`
`\sl`	`\normalfont\slshape`
`\tt`	`\normalfont\ttfamily`

There is a further type-changing declaration that behaves differently from those already discussed and that is `\em`. This declaration causes the text in its scope to be emphasized. There is also a command that takes a single argument called `\emph` which has (almost) the same effect as the declaration `\em`. The effect of the declaration `\em` and the command `\emph` depends on the context in which it occurs. I will illustrate this context-dependence using the command `\emph`:

output	input
I *hate* you.	`\textrm{I \emph{hate} you.}`
I *hate* you.	`\textsf{I \emph{hate} you.}`
I *hate* you.	`\texttt{I \emph{hate} you.}`
I *hate* you.	`\textbf{I \emph{hate} you.}`
I *hate* you.	`\textmd{I \emph{hate} you.}`
I hate *you.*	`\textit{I \emph{hate} you.}`
I *hate* YOU.	`\textsc{I \emph{hate} you.}`
I hate *you.*	`\textsl{I \emph{hate} you.}`
I *hate* you.	`\textup{I \emph{hate} you.}`

If you use the declaration `\em` rather than the command `\emph`, then italic correction must be included when italic or slanted type is followed by type that is neither italic nor slanted; if you are not sure what `\em` will do, then put in the italic correction as it has no effect unless italic or slanted type is followed by type that is neither.

3.3   Declarations that Change the Size of Type

There are ten declarations in LaTeX for altering the size of type being used and these are shown in order, with the smallest coming first, in the table that follows:

output	input
Once upon a time ...	`{\tiny\Once}`
Once upon a time ...	`{\scriptsize\Once}`
Once upon a time ...	`{\footnotesize\Once}`
Once upon a time ...	`{\small\Once}`
Once upon a time ...	`{\normalsize\Once}`
Once upon a time ...	`{\large\Once}`
Once upon a time ...	`{\Large\Once}`
Once upon a time ...	`{\LARGE\Once}`
Once upon a time ...	`{\huge\Once}`
Once upon a time ...	`{\Huge\Once}`

Some of these commands were used in order to produce the mouse's tale from *Alice in Wonderland* displayed in Fig. 1.1 on p. 3: I will not show here all the commands needed to produce the mouse's tale, but the beginning is produced by the following commands:

```
{\setlength{\parskip}{-1.5pt}

{\large
\setlength{\parindent}{1in}              Fury said to
\addtolength{\parindent}{1em}\par        a mouse, That
\addtolength{\parindent}{4em}\par        he met
\addtolength{\parindent}{0.5em}\par      in the
\addtolength{\parindent}{0.5em}\par      house,\par}

{\normalsize
\setlength{\parindent}{2.05in}           'Let us
\addtolength{\parindent}{-1.5em}\par     both go
\addtolength{\parindent}{-0.5em}\par     to law:
\addtolength{\parindent}{-1em}\par       {\itshape I\/} will
\addtolength{\parindent}{-1em}\par       prosecute
\addtolength{\parindent}{-0.5em}\par     {\itshape you\/}.---\par}}
```

There are probably other and better ways of doing this in TeX and LaTeX, but in this method each line is in a paragraph all by itself. The length parameter `\parskip` is the addditional vertical space that TeX puts between paragraphs; additional, that is to say, to `\baselineskip` which is the normal distance between base lines. (The *base line* in TeX is the imaginary line on which letters 'sit'. Some letters, like 'g' and 'y', have parts that descend below the base line on which they 'sit'.) The length parameter \parindent is the amount of indentation that marks the first line of every paragraph. The command \setlength{*cmd*}{*len*} assigns the length *len* to *cmd*, which must begin with an initial backslash. The command \addtolength{*cmd*}{*len*} adds *len* to the current value of *cmd* and puts the result in *cmd*. In both \setlength and \addtolength *len* can be any valid TeX length or it can be another length parameter (or user-defined length command) which can be multiplied by some floating-point number, thus \addtolength{\parindent}{-1.5\parindent} is a valid use of the \addtolength command.

3.4   Punctuation Marks

Dashes

Four distinct types of dashes are used by typesetters, namely the em-dash, the en-dash, the hyphen and the minus sign. (The em- and en-dashes are sometimes known as the em- and en-*rules*.) If you include $x - y$ in your input file, for example, then the hyphen becomes a minus sign and you get '$x - y$'. The minus sign in this expression is a binary operator and more information about the behaviour of such operators can be found in section A.4 starting on p. 164. Note that if you put -5.3 in your input file, you will get '-5.3'; there is less space following the minus sign because it indicates a negative quantity and does not stand for a binary operation. In this section I will look in detail at the three other kinds of dashes, namely the em-dash (—), the en-dash (–) and the hyphen (-).

The Em-dash   To produce the em-dash you need three consecutive hyphens in LR or paragraph mode. Alternatively, it can be produced by using the command \textemdash. Em-dashes are often used in pairs to indicate that the text that occurs between them is to be read parenthetically. The following sentence, from Amis (1985), p. 206, is an example of this: 'I grew up—or got bigger—out here, out here in the US of A.' This was produced by means of the following commands:

```
I grew up---or got bigger---out here, out here in the US of A\@.
```

(The meaning of the control symbol \@ is explained on p. 28 below.)

The En-dash   To produce the en-dash use two consecutive hyphens in LR or paragraph mode. Alternatively, it can be produced by using the command \textendash. It is used in number ranges, like 'pp. 33–35' or 'the 1939–1945 holocaust', between place names that are linked in some way, for example, 'the Rome–Berlin axis' and between names of joint authors to avoid confusion with double-barrelled names, for example, 'the Church–Rosser theorem'. It is also used instead of a hyphen in a compound adjective at least one of whose components consists of a hyphenated word or of two words. For example, 'the New York–Amsterdam flight' and 'a quasi-public–quasi-judicial body'.

Hyphen The dash that occurs in hyphenated words, like 'semi-standard', is produced by typing a single hyphen in LR or paragraph mode.

Quotation Marks

To enclose a word or phrase in single quotation marks enclose it with an apostrophe and quotation mark. So, 'death' is produced by typing `'death'`. A single opening quotation mark can also be produced by means of the command `\textquoteleft` and a single closing one by using the command `\textquoteright`. To enclose a word or phrase in double quotation marks enclose it in two apostrophes and two quotation marks. So, "death" is produced by typing `''death''`. Double opening quotation marks can also be produced by means of the command `\textquotedblleft` and double closing ones by using `\textquotedblright`.

Books and articles published in Britain use, on the whole, single quotation marks for direct speech and for mentioning words and phrase, whereas American books usually use double quotation marks. (More information about this topic can be found in Quirk, Greenbaum, Leech and Svartvik (1985), pp. 1630–1631.) The following table illustrates this:

	output	input
American	"I heard 'Go away' being shouted," she said.	`''I heard 'Go away' being shouted,'' she said.`
British	'I heard "Go away" being shouted,' she said.	`'I heard ''Go away'' being shouted,' she said.`

If nested closing quotation marks occur next to each other, then a thin amount of space (produced by the command `\,`) should follow a single quotation mark if it is followed by double quotation marks, but there is no need to insert this amount of space if double quotation marks are followed by a single quotation mark (Knuth 1986a, p. 5):

	output	input
American	John said, "James said, 'Janet said, "Yes."'"	`John said, ''James said, 'Janet said, ''Yes.''{}'\,''`
British	John said, 'James said, "Janet said, 'Yes.'"'	`John said, 'James said, ''Janet said, 'Yes.'\,''{}'`

In the case of nested opening quotation marks the general rule in TeX is that a thin amount of space should follow double quotation marks when they are followed by a single quotation mark, but it is wrong to include this amount of space if a single quotation mark is followed by double quotation marks (Knuth 1986a, p. 305); as Knuth goes on to say, 'Left and right are opposites.' Thus, use `''\,'` and `'{}''` as appropriate.

The thin space introduced here is also useful in other contexts. According to Knuth (1986a), pp. 311 and 409, a Biblical reference like 'Isaiah 30 : 22' is produced by the input `Isaiah~30\,:\,22` and a musical reference like 'Op. 59' is produced by the input `Op.\,59`. Note that the tilde ~ just produces an inter-word space, but TEX will never break a line at the place in your input file where it occurs.

A further difference between American and British English emerges in the way that quotation marks, used to indicate the title of books, articles, films, plays and so on, interact with punctuation marks:

	output	input
American	Coppola has directed the films "Apocalypse Now," "The Conversation," "The Godfather," "One from the Heart" and others.	`Coppola has directed the films ''Apocalypse Now,'' ''The Conversation,'' ''The Godfather,'' ''One from the Heart'' and others.`
British	Coppola has directed the films 'Apocalypse Now', 'The Conversation', 'The Godfather', 'One from the Heart' and others.	`Coppola has directed the films 'Apocalypse Now', 'The Conversation', 'The Godfather', 'One from the Heart' and others.`

Spacing

By default TEX puts more space after a colon, full stop, question mark and exclamation mark than it normally puts between words, except when any of these follow a capital letter (Lamport 1994, p. 15). This creates two problems. The first occurs when one of these punctuation marks is preceded by a capital letter when it ends a sentence. The second occurs when one of these punctuation marks does not end a sentence and yet it is not preceded by a capital letter. These problems are resolved as follows:

output	input
Warner Bros. is a film production company.	`Warner Bros.\ is a film production company.`
He was from the UK. In fact, he was born in Wales.	`He was from the UK\@. In fact, he was born in Wales.`

The control symbol \␣ inserts normal inter-word space where it occurs. When placed before a colon, full stop, exclamation mark or question mark, the control symbol \@ has the effect of putting more space after the punctuation mark involved. Note that more space is placed after a colon, full stop, exclamation mark and question mark even if these are followed by quotation marks or parentheses; the above redemies work in these cases as well. If you want TeX to treat the space following a colon, full stop, exclamation mark and question mark as normal inter-word space throughout an entire document, then you should use the \frenchspacing declaration.

3.5 Footnotes

Footnotes are produced by means of the \footnote{*text*} command; this places *text* at the bottom of the page with a number as the footnote mark and the same footnote mark is placed in the body of the page as a superscript. Footnotes are numbered automatically by LaTeX with the first one being numbered 1; the counter footnote is used for this purpose. (A *counter* in LaTeX is an integer-valued variable; for more information about counters see section B.3.) The footnote counter is initialized to zero at the start of each chapter in the report and book document classes and at the beginning of the document in the article document class. Note that the counter is incremented before the footnote mark is produced. (Inside the minipage environment alphabetical footnote marks are produced starting with *a* and the counter used is mpfootnote.)

There are certain contexts in which the \footnote command will not work, namely those that produce a box. (The only exception to this is inside the minipage environment.) There you should use \footnotemark inside the box-making command to produce the footnote mark in the text as a superscript and just outside the box-making command you should use a \footnotetext{*text*} command to place *text* as a footnote at the bottom of the page; note that the \footnotemark command increments the footnote counter. (These commands can all take an additional optional argument whose effect is explained in the glossary contained in Appendix C.)

Chapter 4

List-like Environments

4.1 Introduction

In this chapter LaTeX's list-like environments are explained. These are the environments: `quote`, `quotation`, `verse`, `flushright`, `center`, `flushleft`, `itemize`, `enumerate`, `description` and `thebibliography`. These are all defined by means of either the general-purpose `list` environment or its restricted `trivlist` version; both of these are explained in section 4.11 below. In this chapter the `\newtheorem` global declaration is also described, because this is used to produce a list-like environment, and at the very end of the chapter I show how you can define your own environments.

4.2 The `quote` Environment

The `quote` environment is used for short quotations. The following quotation, for example, is from Popper (1975, p. 266):

> Whenever a theory appears to you as the only possible one, take this as a sign that you have neither understood the theory nor the problem which it was intended to solve.

This short quotation from Popper was produced by means of the following LaTeX commands:

```
\begin{quote}
Whenever a theory appears to you as the only possible one,
take this as a sign that you have neither understood the theory
nor the problem which it was intended to solve.
\end{quote}
```

The first line of the output produced by the `quote` environment is not indented and the first lines of subsequent paragraphs, if any, are not indented either, although a small amount of extra vertical space is inserted between paragraphs.

4.3   The `quotation` Environment

The `quote` environment is used for including short quotations in your document; for longer quotations LATEX provides the `quotation` environment. Consider, for example, the following quotation (which is from Carroll (1988), p. 161, where he quotes Heath (1981), p. 136):

> The plot of a typical narrative movie is a set of transformations which operate on a series of disequilibriums with the net result that some sort of narrative equilibrium emerges. Heath writes:
>
> > A narrative action is a series of elements held in a relation of transformation such that their consecution—the movement of the transformation from the ones to the others—determines a state S' different to an initial state S ...
>
> One of Heath's presiding metaphors in describing the work of movie narrative is 'getting things back into place.'

This quotation was produced by means of the following commands:

```
\begin{quotation}
\noindent
The plot of a typical narrative movie is a set of transformations
which operate on a series of disequilibriums with the net result
that some sort of narrative equilibrium emerges.  Heath writes:
\begin{quotation}
\noindent
A narrative action is a series of elements held in a relation of
transformation such that their consecution---the movement of the
transformation from the ones to the others---determines a state
$S'$ different to an initial state $S$ \ldots
\end{quotation}

One of Heath's presiding metaphors in describing the work of
movie narrative is 'getting things back into place.'
\end{quotation}
```

The first line of every paragraph produced by the `quotation` environment is indented, but this indentation can be suppressed by using a \noindent command. The first line of the paragraph that follows an instance of the `quotation` environment is also indented by default, but this can also be suppressed by using a \noindent command.

4.4 The verse Environment

The verse environment is used for typesetting poetry. Coleridge's poem *Christabel* begins with the following lines:

'Tis the middle of night by the castle clock,
And the owls have awakened the crowing cock;
Tu-u-whoo! Tu-u-whoo!
And hark, again! the crowing cock,
How drowsily it crew.

Sir Leoline, the Baron rich,
Hath a toothless mastiff bitch;
From her kennel beneath the rock
She makes answer to the clock,
Four for the quarters, and twelve for the hour;
Ever and aye, moonshine or shower,
Sixteen short howls, not over loud;
Some say, she sees my lady's shroud.

These opening lines were produced by means of the following commands:

```
\begin{verse}
'Tis the middle of night by the castle clock, \\
And the owls have awakened the crowing cock; \\
Tu-u-whoo! Tu-u-whoo! \\
And hark, again! the crowing cock, \\
How drowsily it crew.

Sir Leoline, the Baron rich, \\
Hath a toothless mastiff bitch; \\
From her kennel beneath the rock \\
She makes answer to the clock, \\
Four for the quarters, and twelve for the hour; \\
Ever and aye, moonshine or shower, \\
Sixteen short howls, not over loud; \\
Some say, she sees my lady's shroud.
\end{verse}
```

The control symbol \\ is used to mark the end of a line in the verse environment and one or more blank lines are used to mark the end of a stanza. Do not, however, put the control symbol \\ at the end of the final line inside the verse environment and do not add any blank lines after the final line inside the environment. If you do either of these things, then extra vertical space will be added between the displayed poem and the following text.

4.5   The `flushright`, `center` and `flushleft` Environments

Consider the following piece of text:

Time-travel is impossible and yet science fiction writers from H.G. Wells onwards
have been fascinated by the idea. One narrative paradigm that has had several
incarnations involves the time-traveller being an art historian who is interested in
discovering more about a famous artist—in some versions a painter and in others a
sculptor—who ...

The above passage was produced by means of the following input:

```
\begin{flushright}
Time-travel is impossible and yet science fiction writers
from H.G.~Wells onwards have been fascinated by the idea.
One narrative paradigm that has had several incarnations
involves the time-traveller being an art historian who is
interested in discovering more about a famous artist---in
some versions a painter and in others a sculptor---who \ldots
\end{flushright}
```

Changing the environment from `flushright` to `center` produces:

Time-travel is impossible and yet science fiction writers from H.G. Wells onwards
have been fascinated by the idea. One narrative paradigm that has had several
incarnations involves the time-traveller being an art historian who is interested in
discovering more about a famous artist—in some versions a painter and in others a
sculptor—who ...

Changing the environment from `flushright` to `flushleft` produces:

Time-travel is impossible and yet science fiction writers from H.G. Wells onwards
have been fascinated by the idea. One narrative paradigm that has had several
incarnations involves the time-traveller being an art historian who is interested in
discovering more about a famous artist—in some versions a painter and in others a
sculptor—who ...

In each of these environments it is possible to use an end-of-line command \\ in order
to force the termination of a line. Do not confuse the end-of-line command \\ with
the end-of-line or carriage return character that ends lines in your input file and which
TeX treats as an ordinary space.

It is possible to use the \raggedright declaration instead of the flushleft environment, the \centering declaration instead of the center environment and the \raggedleft declaration instead of the flushright environment. One difference, however, is that when an environment is used LaTeX inserts a certain amount of additional vertical space between the output of the environment and the preceding text. This is not inserted if the above declarations are used. If neither a blank line nor a \par command precedes the environment, then the amount of vertical space added is given by the sum of the values of the length parameters \topsep and \parskip. If either a blank line or a \par command does precede the use of the environment, then the amount of vertical space added is given by the sum of the values of the three length parameters \topsep, \parskip and \partopsep. In fact, this amount of space is inserted before all the list-like environments described in this chapter. The same amount of space is added between the end of the text produced by a list-like environment and the following material. The diagram that appears in Fig. C.3 on p. 225 illustrates these remarks graphically.

4.6   The `itemize` Environment

An itemized list in LaTeX looks like this:

- Computer science is the mathematical study of algorithms.

- A programming language is a notation for expressing algorithms.

- The way in which programming languages are studied is based on the way in which logical systems are studied.

- Axiomatic semantics is the application of proof theory to the study of programming languages.

This list was produced by means of the following commands:

```
\begin{itemize}
\item
Computer science is the mathematical study of algorithms.
\item
A programming language is a notation for expressing algorithms.
\item
The way in which programming languages are studied is based
on the way in which logical systems are studied.
\item
Axiomatic semantics is the application of proof theory
to the study of programming languages.
\end{itemize}
```

The command \item is used to indicate the start of a new entry in the list. It is possible to have different labels at the same level of nesting by giving an argument to the \item command inside the itemize environment. Such an optional argument must be enclosed in square brackets. Only four levels of nesting are permitted and by default the labels are the symbols: •, −, ∗ and ·. These symbols are 'stored' in the four commands \labelitemi, \labelitemii, \labelitemiii and \labelitemiv, respectively. So, if you want to use ♠, for example, instead of • as a label at the top level you have to redefine the \labelitemi command.

4.7   The enumerate Environment

Enumerated lists in LaTeX look like this:

---

1. Show that the following hold in the classical propositional calculus:

   (a) $Q \Rightarrow R \vdash (P \lor Q) \Rightarrow (P \lor R)$.
   (b) $\vdash ((P \Rightarrow Q) \Rightarrow P) \Rightarrow P$.

2. Show that the following hold in classical first-order logic:

   (a) $(\forall x)(Px \Rightarrow Qx) \vdash (\forall x)Px \Rightarrow (\forall x)Qx$.
   (b) $(\exists x)(\forall y)Pxy \vdash (\forall y)(\exists x)Pxy$.

This list was produced by the following commands:

```
\begin{enumerate}
\item
Show that the following hold in the classical
propositional calculus:
\begin{enumerate}
\item
$Q \implies R \vdash (P \lor Q) \implies (P \lor R)$.
\item \label{PEIRCE}
$\vdash ((P \implies Q) \implies P) \implies P$.
\end{enumerate}
\item
Show that the following hold in classical first-order logic:
\begin{enumerate}
\item
$(\forall x) (Px \implies Qx)
\vdash (\forall x) Px \implies (\forall x) Qx$.
\item
$(\exists x)(\forall y) Pxy \vdash (\forall y)(\exists x) Pxy$.
\end{enumerate}
\end{enumerate}
```

The command \implies used here is defined as follows:

    \newcommand*{\implies}{\mathbin{\Rightarrow}}

By default, \Rightarrow produces a symbol for a binary relation, but this definition makes \implies into a binary operator. The command \mathbin is further explained in section A.4.

Only four levels of nesting of the enumerate environment are allowed. The outer-most items are labelled 1., 2., and so on; items in the next level of nesting are labelled as (a), (b), and so on; in the next level they are i., ii., and so on; and in the fourth level the labels appear as A., B., and so on. The labels are generated automatically and the four counters enumi, enumii, enumiii and enumiv are used for this purpose. (A *counter* in LaTeX is an integer-valued variable; for more information about counters see section B.3.)

It is possible to use a \label command inside an enumerate environment, as the above example illustrates, and the command \ref{PEIRCE} yields '1b'. (The formula $((P \Rightarrow Q) \Rightarrow P) \Rightarrow P$ is known as Peirce's law.) If you want to refer to the page on which this occurrence of Peirce's law appears, then you need to use the command \pageref{PEIRCE}. Thus, the input p.~\pageref{PEIRCE} yields 'p. 36'. Note the use of the tilde which prevents a line break happening at the point where it occurs.

It is also possible to give optional arguments to the \item commands that occur inside an enumerate environment. Consider, for example, the following commands:

    \begin{enumerate}
    \item[(1)]
    $Q \implies R \vdash (P \lor Q) \implies (P \lor R)$.
    \item[(2)]
    $\vdash ((P \implies Q) \implies P) \implies P$.
    \item[(3)]
    $(P \implies Q) \land R \vdash (P \land R) \implies (P \land Q)$.
    \item[(4)]
    $P \land (Q \implies R) \vdash (P \land Q) \implies (P \land R)$.
    \end{enumerate}

These commands produce the following enumerated list:

---

(1) $Q \Rightarrow R \vdash (P \lor Q) \Rightarrow (P \lor R)$.

(2) $\vdash ((P \Rightarrow Q) \Rightarrow P) \Rightarrow P$.

(3) $(P \Rightarrow Q) \land R \vdash (P \land R) \Rightarrow (P \land Q)$.

(4) $P \land (Q \Rightarrow R) \vdash (P \land Q) \Rightarrow (P \land R)$.

If an optional argument is given to the \item command, then this also has the effect that the relevant counter is not incremented.

4.8   The description **Environment**

The description environment can be used to produce glossaries. Consider, for example, the following commands:

```
\begin{description}
\item[lamplighter]
A provider of such support services as surveillance and minding.
\item[finger man]
An agent whose job it is to kill specified people.
\item[wrangler]
An operative whose job it is to break codes.
\end{description}
```

The above commands produce the following mini-glossary of some of the jargon that John le Carré uses in his novels:

---

lamplighter A provider of such support services as surveillance and minding.

finger man An agent whose job it is to kill specified people.

wrangler An operative whose job it is to break codes.

Note that although the words being defined are given as optional arguments to the \item commands, if they are omitted, the result produced by LaTeX will look very odd. By default the optional argument to the \item command appears in bold type in the output, but this can be altered by including type-changing declarations inside the square brackets. The following commands illustrate this:

```
\begin{description}
\item[\mdseries\ttfamily lamplighter]
A provider of such support services
as surveillance and minding.
\item[\sffamily finger man]
An agent whose job it is to kill specified people.
\item[\mdseries\slshape wrangler]
An operative whose job it is to break codes.
\end{description}
```

These commands produce the following result:

---

lamplighter A provider of such support services as surveillance and minding.

finger man An agent whose job it is to kill specified people.

wrangler An operative whose job it is to break codes.

```
\begin{thebibliography}{7}
\bibitem{hal:towards}
Michael Hallett,
`Towards a Theory of Mathematical Research Programmes (I)',
{\itshape British Journal for the Philosophy of Science},
vol.~30 (1979), pp.~1--25.
\bibitem{lak:proofs}
Imre Lakatos,
{\itshape Proofs and Refutations:
The Logic of Mathematical Discovery},
[Cambridge, Cambridge University Press, 1976].
\end{thebibliography}
```

References

[1] Michael Hallett, 'Towards a Theory of Mathematical Research Programmes (I)', *British Journal for the Philosophy of Science*, vol. 30
(1979), pp. 1–25.

[2] Imre Lakatos, *Proofs and Refutations: The Logic of Mathematical Discovery*, [Cambridge, Cambridge University Press, 1976].

Figure 4.1: Using the thebibibliography environment.

4.9   The thebibliography Environment

The thebibliography environment can be used to produce a bibliography or list of
references in a document generated by LATEX. Its general format is:

```
\begin{thebibliography}{text}
    entry-list
\end{thebibliography}
```

The opening command of the thebibliography environment requires a mandatory
argument *text* which is used to determine the appearance of the output produced.
The argument *text* does not appear in the finished document; only its width, after
processing, is important to LATEX. It should be at least as large as the largest label
produced by the \bibitem commands in *entry-list*. For example, if you are going
to use \bibitem commands without giving them optional arguments, then what you
replace *text* with will depend on how many entries occur in *entry-list*. If it contains
less than 10 things, then use a single numeral for this argument; if it contains more
than 9 items but less than 100, then use two numerals for this argument; and so on.

```
\begin{thebibliography}{Lakatos 76}
\bibitem[Hallett 79]{hal:towards}
Michael Hallett,
'Towards a Theory of Mathematical Research Programmes (I)',
{\itshape British Journal for the Philosophy of Science},
vol.~30 (1979), pp.~1--25.
\bibitem[Lakatos 76]{lak:proofs}
Imre Lakatos,
{\itshape Proofs and Refutations:
The Logic of Mathematical Discovery},
[Cambridge, Cambridge University Press, 1976].
\end{thebibliography}
```

References

[Hallett 79]   Michael Hallett, 'Towards a Theory of Mathematical Research Programmes (I)', *British Journal for the Philosophy of Science*, vol. 30 (1979), pp. 1–25.

[Lakatos 76]   Imre Lakatos, *Proofs and Refutations: The Logic of Mathematical Discovery*, [Cambridge, Cambridge University Press, 1976].

Figure 4.2: The optional argument to the \bibitem command.

(All the numerals have the same width, namely half an em in the current font, so it does not matter which you use.)

An example of the use of the thebibliography environment is shown in the top part of Fig. 4.1 and the output that it produces after being processed by LaTeX is shown in the bottom part of Fig. 4.1. When used in the article document class, the bibliography is placed in a section called 'References'. If you want a different heading to be used, then redefine the \refname command. When used in either the report or book document classes, however, the bibliography is put into a chapter headed 'Bibliography'. If you want a different heading to be used, then redefine the \bibname command.

Inside the thebibliography environment entries are introduced by means of a \bibitem{*key*} command. The argument *key* is made up out of letters, numerals and punctuation characters other than the comma. To refer to an item in the bibliography you have to use a \cite command. LaTeX automatically generates numerical cross-referencing labels. Thus, given the input shown in the top part of Fig. 4.1, \cite{lak:proofs} generates [2] and \cite{hal:towards} generates [1].

However, you need to run LaTeX at least twice in order to get the cross-referencing information into your output. The first time you run LaTeX the information in the `thebibliography` environment is written to the `aux` file and the next time you run LaTeX this information is used to generate the labels that appear in the output. The general form of the \cite command is \cite[*text*]{*key-list*}, where *key-list* is a sequence of one or more keys (if more than one is present, then they should be separated by commas) and *text* is an optional annotation. For example, the input \cite{lak:proofs,hal:towards} generates [2, 1] and the output [2, pp. 1–8] is generated by the input \cite[pp.~1--8]{lak:proofs}.

The \bibitem command can have an optional argument as shown in the top part of Fig. 4.2. This is used as the label to the reference throughout the document. In this case the 'width' argument to the `thebibliography` environment should be the widest optional argument to the \bibitem command used within that argument. In this case \cite{lak:proofs} generates [Lakatos 76] and \cite{hal:towards} generates [Hallett 79].

4.10   The \newtheorem **Command**

Ever since Euclid wrote the *Elements* around 300 BC the axiomatic presentation of results has been very popular, not only with mathematicians, but also with logicians, scientists and philosophers. The \newtheorem declaration allows you to carry on writing in this tradition. For example, the declaration

```
\newtheorem{definition}{Definition}
```

defines two things, namely a new environment called `definition` and also a counter with the same name. This declaration can go anywhere in your input file, but it makes most sense to either put it in the preamble or in your own package. The `definition` environment created by the above declaration is used like any other built-in environment. Thus the commands

```
\begin{definition}
A \textup{\textbf{point}} is that which has no part.
\end{definition}
```

which the reader will recognize to be Euclid's first definition in the *Elements*—Euclid (1956), p. 153—produce:

Definition 1 *A* **point** *is that which has no part.*

If we wanted to include Euclid's 5th definition out of sequence, we would need the following commands:

```
\setcounter{definition}{4}
\begin{definition}
```

```
A \textup{\textbf{surface}} is that which
has length and breadth only.
\end{definition}
```

These produce the following, from Euclid (1956), p. 153:

Definition 5 *A* **surface** *is that which has length and breadth only.*

It is possible to define several new environments in the same input file with the \newtheorem declaration. In addition to the definition environment already mentioned we could create a common environment for common notions and a prop environment for propositions:

```
\newtheorem{common}
   {\normalfont\scshape Common notion}
\newtheorem{post}{Postulate}
\newtheorem{prop}{Proposition}
```

If we did this, then the first time we used the common environment the common notion produced would be labelled 1 and the second time we used it the common notion produced would be labelled 2 and so on. Similarly, with the prop environment. For example, the commands

```
\setcounter{common}{4}
\begin{common}
The whole is greater than the part.
\end{common}
```

produce the following common notion, from Euclid (1956), p. 155:

COMMON NOTION 5 *The whole is greater than the part.*

Furthermore, the commands

```
\setcounter{post}{4}
\begin{post}
\upshape
That, if a straight line falling on two straight lines
make the interior angles on the same side less than two
right angles, the two straight lines, if produced indefinitely,
meet on that side on which are the angles less than the two
right angles.
\end{post}
```

produce the following postulate, also from Euclid (1956), p. 155:

Postulate 5 That, if a straight line falling on two straight lines make the interior angles on the same side less than two right angles, the two straight lines, if produced indefinitely, meet on that side on which are the angles less than the two right angles.

In addition, the commands

```
\setcounter{prop}{4}
\begin{prop}
\upshape
In isosceles triangles the angles at the base are equal to one
another, and, if the equal straight lines be produced further,
the angles under the base will be equal to one another.
\end{prop}
```

produce the following proposition, from Euclid (1956), p. 251:

Proposition 5 In isosceles triangles the angles at the base are equal to one another, and, if the equal straight lines be produced further, the angles under the base will be equal to one another.

The numbering of definitions, common notions and propositions would normally be entirely independent of one another. Sometimes, however, we might like to have our definitions, common notions and propositions all numbered consecutively in the same sequence. This would be achieved by means of the following declarations:

```
\newtheorem{definition}{Definition}
\newtheorem{common}[definition]
   {\normalfont\scshape Common notion}
\newtheorem{prop}[definition]{Proposition}
```

By default when environments created by the \newtheorem declaration are used then the numbering is continuous throughout the entire document that is produced. Thus, if you are using the \newtheorem declaration in a book to define a definition environment, then if the last use of this environment in the first chapter generated the number 15, then the first use of this environment in the second chapter will generate the number 16. You can, however, have your definitions numbered consecutively within chapters. This is achieved by giving the \newtheorem declaration an additional parameter which is the name of the sectional unit within which you want definitions, for example, to be numbered. For example, the declaration

```
\newtheorem{definition}{Definition}[chapter]
```

would, in the situation described earlier, result in the first definition of Chapter 2 being numbered 2.1. The two optional arguments can be combined like this:

```
\newtheorem{definition}{Definition}[chapter]
\newtheorem{common}[definition]
   {\normalfont\scshape Common notions}
```

It is not possible, however, for both optional arguments to be present together.

The environments created by the `\newtheorem` declaration can take an optional argument as the following example—from Euclid (1956), p. 349—shows:

Proposition 47 (Pythagoras) *In right-angled triangles the square on the side subtending the right angle is equal to the squares on the sides containing the right angle.*

This was produced by means of these commands:

```
\setcounter{prop}{46}
\begin{prop}[Pythagoras]
In right-angled triangles the square on the side subtending
the right angle is equal to the squares on the sides
containing the right angle.
\end{prop}
```

4.11   The `list` and `trivlist` Environments

LaTeX's `list` environment is a flexible mechanism for displaying information sequentially with the option of labelling each individual piece of information in a variety of ways. Several of LaTeX's list-like environments are defined by means of it, namely `quote`, `quotation`, `verse`, `flushright`, `center`, `flushleft`, `itemize`, `enumerate`, `description` and `thebibliography`. Its general format is:

$$\text{\textbackslash begin\{list\}\{}text_1\text{\}\{}dec\text{-}list\text{\}}\quad text_2 \quad \text{\textbackslash end\{list\}}$$

The argument $text_1$ is what will be generated by an `\item` command which does not have an optional argument. The argument *dec-list* is a sequence of assignments to some of the length parameters that determine the appearance of the list to be produced. What these parameters do is shown in Fig. C.3 on p. 225. Any length parameter that is not given a value in this way is initialized by an assignment in one of the `@listi`, ..., `@listv` or `@listvi` commands (the choice depends on the level of nesting) and these are carried out before the assignments in *dec-list*. The argument $text_2$ is the information to be displayed. One or more `\item` commands can occur in $text_2$.

The `trivlist` environment is a restricted version of the `list` environment. It inherits the values of all parameters in force when the environment opens, except that `\leftmargin`, `\labelwidth` and `\itemindent` are set to zero inches and `\parsep` is set to the current value of `\parskip`.

To illustrate the use of the list environment I will explain how Fig. 4.2 on p. 40 was produced in this book. It was obtained by means of the following commands:

```
\begin{minipage}{360pt}
\begin{flushleft}
{\Large\bfseries References}
\end{flushleft}
\settowidth{\dd}{[Lakatos 76]}
\begin{list}{}%
{\setlength{\labelwidth}{\dd}%
\setlength{\leftmargin}{\dd}%
\addtolength{\leftmargin}{\labelsep}}
\item[{\rmfamily [Hallett 79]}\hfill]
Michael Hallett,
'Towards a Theory of Mathematical Research Programmes (I)',
{\itshape British Journal for the Philosophy of Science},
vol.~30 (1979), pp.~1--25.
\item[{\rmfamily [Lakatos 76]}]
Imre Lakatos,
{\itshape Proofs and Refutations:
The Logic of Mathematical Discovery},
[Cambridge, Cambridge University Press, 1976].
\end{list}
\end{minipage}
```

The minipage environment used here is explained in section 5.2 below. It produces a box of width 360 points which is the default value of the \textwidth parameter if you use the letterpaper option to the \documentclass command. The length command \dd is used to give values to some of the length parameters that affect the appearance of the list being produced; this was introduced earlier in the input file by means of a \newlength{\dd} global declaration. The \settowidth{*cmd*}{*text*} command assigns to the length command *cmd* the natural width of the result of processing *text* in LR mode and the \setlength{*cmd*}{*len*} command assigns to the length command *cmd* the value *len*. The function of an \addtolength{*cmd*}{*len*} command is to assign to the length command *cmd* the result of adding *len* to its current value. The command \hfill inserts horizontal space where it occurs that expands to fill all the available space. Its effect here is to push the 'label' '[Hallett 79]' to the left, making it flush with the left-hand edge of the enclosing box.

If you want the list produced to be numbered automatically in some way by LaTeX, then you need to define a counter and employ the \usecounter command. This is illustrated in the following example which presents the commands used in order to produce Fig. 4.1 on p. 39:

```
\begin{minipage}{360pt}
\begin{flushleft}
{\Large\bfseries References}
```

```
\end{flushleft}
\settowidth{\dd}{[1]}
\begin{list}%
{[\arabic{ddd}]}%
{\usecounter{ddd}%
\setlength{\labelwidth}{\dd}%
\setlength{\leftmargin}{\dd}%
\addtolength{\leftmargin}{\labelsep}}
\item
Michael Hallett,
'Towards a Theory of Mathematical Research Programmes (I)',
{\itshape British Journal for the Philosophy of Science},
vol.~30 (1979), pp.~1--25.
\item
Imre Lakatos,
{\itshape Proofs and Refutations:
The Logic of Mathematical Discovery},
[Cambridge, Cambridge University Press, 1976].
\end{list}
\end{minipage}
```

The counter `ddd` used here was introduced earlier in the input file by means of a `\newcounter{ddd}` global declaration.

4.12   Environment Definition

Some books have quotations at the start of a chapter or section that look like this:

It was said of Jordan's writings that if he had 4 things on the same footing (as a, b, c, d) they would appear as a, M'_3, ϵ_2 and $\Pi''_{1,2}$.

Littlewood (1986), p. 60.

This could be produced by means of the following commands:

```
\begin{list}{}{\setlength{\leftmargin}{7em}
\setlength{\rightmargin}{0em}}\item[]
It was said of Jordan's writings that if he had 4 things
on the same footing (as $a$, $b$, $c$, $d$) they would appear
as $a$, $M'_3$, $\epsilon_2$ and $\Pi''_{1,2}$.
\begin{flushright}
Littlewood (1986), p.~60.
\end{flushright}
\end{list}
```

However, if you are planning on beginning several chapters or sections in a book with a quotation like this, then it would be a good idea to make the structure into an environment by using the \newenvironment* local declaration. The following achieves this:

```
\newenvironment*{popper}
{\begin{list}{}{\setlength{\leftmargin}{7em}
\setlength{\rightmargin}{0em}}\item[]}
{\end{list}}
```

(This environment is called popper after the philosopher Karl Popper because I first saw this kind of quotation in his book *The Open Society and its Enemies*.) You start this defined environment with the command \begin{popper} and close it with the command \end{popper} as for the built-in environments. The following commands, therefore, would also produce the quotation displayed near the beginning of this section:

```
\begin{popper}
It was said of Jordan's writings that if he had 4 things
on the same footing (as $a$, $b$, $c$, $d$) they would appear
as $a$, $M'_3$, $\epsilon_2$ and $\Pi''_{1,2}$.
\begin{flushright}
Littlewood (1986), p.~60.
\end{flushright}
\end{popper}
```

The general formats of the \newenvironment* and \newenvironment local declarations are explained in the glossary as are the local declarations \renewenvironment* and \renewenvironment which are used for redefining existing environments.

Chapter 5

Boxes and Tables

5.1 Boxes

A *box* is something that TeX treats as a unit and it will not, therefore, be broken across lines or pages. In this section the \framebox, \makebox and \savebox box-making commands are described. There are two versions of each of these; one that can only be used inside the picture environment and one that can be used anywhere else. In this section the versions available outside the picture environment are described.

The \framebox command produces a box with a frame, made out of horizontal and vertical rules, drawn around it. For example, \framebox{*text*} produces ⎢*text*⎢, in which *text* has been processed in LR mode. (The value of the length parameter \fboxrule gives the width of the rules that make up the frame.) The general format of the \framebox command is:

> \framebox[*len*][*pos*]{*text*}

The optional argument *len* is a rigid length parameter. If it is present, it determines the width of the box that is produced. Its default value is the width of *text* after processing plus twice the value of the length parameter \fboxsep, which is the amount of space that separates the frame from the result of processing *text*. The optional argument *pos* can be replaced by either c, l, r or s. Its default value is c. The effect of this optional argument is shown in Fig. 5.1. The effect of the option s is, however, more complicated than what appears in Fig. 5.1. If the argument *text* contains stretchable space, when the option s has been chosen, then *text* is stretched to fill the available space determined by the *len* argument. Inter-word space is stretchable and so the command \framebox[3in][s]{To be or not to be} produces ⎢To   be   or   not   to   be⎢. Alternatively, you could put a rubber length command in *text* or a command like \hfill, \dotfill or \hrulefill.

Normally, the argument *len* is replaced with a rigid length like 3in or 10cm, but the commands \depth, \height, \totalheight and \width can also occur inside *len*. The value of \depth is the depth of the box that is produced when *text* has been processed, that is to say, it is the distance from the base line to the bottom of that box. The value of \height is the height of the box that is produced when *text* has

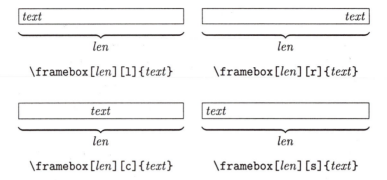

Figure 5.1: The effect of the *pos* argument in the \framebox command.

been processed, that is to say, it is the distance from the base line to the top of that box. The value of \totalheight is the sum of the values of the commands \depth and \height. The value of \width is the width of the box that is produced when *text* has been processed. For example, \framebox[3\width]{*text*} produces ⬚ *text* ⬚.

The \makebox command is similar to the \framebox command except that no frame is drawn around the result of processing *text*. Its general format is:

   \makebox[*len*][*pos*]{*text*}

where the arguments *len*, *pos* and *text* have exactly the same meaning as in the \framebox command.

The \savebox command is similar to the \makebox command except that no output is produced. The box produced is rather placed in a *storage bin* and the \usebox command can then be used to output the stored box. This is particularly useful for things that you want to include several times in a document and which take a lot of processing; using the commands \savebox and \usebox ensures that the processing only takes place once. The general format of these two commands is:

   \savebox{*cmd*}[*len*][*pos*]{*text*}
   \usebox{*cmd*}

In the \savebox command the arguments *len*, *pos* and *text* have exactly the same meaning as they do for the \makebox command. The argument *cmd*, in both commands, is the name of a storage bin which must start with an initial backslash and which must previously have been introduced by means of a \newsavebox{*cmd*} global declaration.

The commands \fbox, \mbox and \sbox are variants of the commands \framebox, \makebox and \savebox, respectively. Unlike \framebox, \makebox and \savebox, the commands \fbox, \mbox and \sbox do not have any optional arguments. The correspondence between the two groups of commands is shown in the following table:

\framebox{*text*}	\fbox{*text*}
\makebox{*text*}	\mbox{*text*}
\savebox{*cmd*}{*text*}	\sbox{*cmd*}{*text*}

5.2   The minipage Environment and \parbox

Whereas the \framebox, \makebox and \savebox commands process their *text* argument in LR mode, the minipage environment and the \parbox command process their *text* argument in paragraph mode. The boxes they produce are, thus, known as *parboxes*. Consider, for example, the following commands:

```
\begin{center}
\begin{minipage}{4in}
Time-travel is impossible and yet science fiction writers
from H.G.~Wells onwards have been fascinated by the idea the
fecundity of which has once again been shown by the recent
success of the \textit{Back to the Future} and the
\textit{Terminator} series of films.\footnote{For more
information about time-travel see Lem's 'The Time-travel
Story' and Gardner's 'Time Travel'.}

One narrative paradigm that has had several incarnations
involves the time-traveller being an art historian who is
interested in discovering more about a famous artist---in some
versions a painter and in others a sculptor---who \ldots
\end{minipage}
\end{center}
```

These commands produce the following output:

Time-travel is impossible and yet science fiction writers from
H.G. Wells onwards have been fascinated by the idea the
fecundity of which has once again been shown by the recent
success of the *Back to the Future* and the *Terminator* series
of films.[a]
One narrative paradigm that has had several incarnations
involves the time-traveller being an art historian who is interested in discovering more about a famous artist—in some
versions a painter and in others a sculptor—who . . .

---

[a]For more information about time-travel see Lem's 'The Time-travel
Story' and Gardner's 'Time Travel'.

Note that paragraphs are not indented in the output produced by the minipage environment, but slightly more vertical space than that which is normally placed between lines is inserted between paragraphs. The general format of the minipage environment is as follows:

```
\begin{minipage}[pos₁][len₂][pos₂]{len₁}
    text
\end{minipage}
```

The rigid length argument len_1 determines the width of the parbox that is produced. It is the only mandatory argument required by the `minipage` environment. The optional argument pos_1 determines the alignment of the parbox produced with respect to the context in which it occurs: a `t` option aligns the base line of the first line with the base line of the current line, a `b` option aligns the base line of the last line with the base line of the current line and the default is to centre the parbox vertically. You can use the option `c` to emphasize the default placement. The rigid length argument len_2 determines the height of the box that is produced and pos_2 determines where in the box of height len_2 the result of processing *text* is to be positioned: a `t` option puts *text* at the top of the box, a `b` option puts it at the bottom, a `c` option centres it and an `s` option allows *text* to be stretched vertically. If pos_2 is absent, then the value of pos_1 is used. Note that the commands \depth, \height, \totalheight and \width can occur in the argument len_2.

The \parbox command has a similar effect to the `minipage` environment. Its general format is:

\parbox[pos_1][len_2][pos_2]{len_1}{*text*}

The meanings of the arguments len_1, pos_1, len_2, pos_2 and *text* are the same as for the `minipage` environment. The main difference between the \parbox command and the `minipage` environment is that neither the `tabular` nor the `tabbing` environments nor any of the list-like environments described in Chapter 4 can occur in the *text* argument of the \parbox command.

5.3 The `tabular` Environment

5.3.1 Basic Principles

LaTeX's `tabular` environment is used to produce the following sort of table:

Category	Intuitive meaning	Typical element
Nml	numerals	N
UnOps	unary operators	α
BinOps	binary operators	ω
Ide	identifiers	I
Exp	expressions	E
Cmd	commands	C

In fact, the above table was produced by the following commands:

```
\begin{center}
\begin{tabular}{|c|c|c|} \hline
Category           & Intuitive meaning & Typical
                                         element  \\ \hline
                                                  \hline
$\mathit{Nml}$     & numerals          & $N$     \\ \hline
```

```
$\mathit{UnOps}$   & unary operators   & $\alpha$  \\ \hline
$\mathit{BinOps}$  & binary operators  & $\omega$  \\ \hline
$\mathit{Ide}$     & identifiers       & $I$       \\ \hline
$\mathit{Exp}$     & expressions       & $E$       \\ \hline
$\mathit{Cmd}$     & commands          & $C$       \\ \hline
\end{tabular}
\end{center}
```

The enclosing `center` environment is just used to centre the resulting table on the page; if it was absent, then the table would be set (almost) flush left on the page. If the first item in the preamble of the `tabular` environment is neither | nor an @-expression, then the table is not set flush left on the page; horizontal blank space equal to the value of the length parameter `\tabcolsep` is inserted before the box produced. The same amount of space is inserted after the box produced if the preamble does not end with | or an @-expression. If this space causes any problems use @{} at the start or end of the preamble to remove it.

The `tabular` environment can occur in any mode and its general format is:

`\begin{tabular}`[*pos*]`{`*preamble*`}` *row-list* `\end{tabular}`

The optional *pos* argument controls the vertical positioning of the box produced. By default alignment is on the centre of the box, but a `t` option aligns on the top row and a `b` option aligns on the bottom row. The *preamble* specifies how the columns of the table are going to be formatted. In the example just given the *preamble* is |c|c|c|. The three occurrences of the letter `c` indicate that this table will consist of three columns and that the material in each column will be centred in that column. (The `c` comes from 'centre' and not 'column'.) Instead of a `c` you can use `l` for left-aligning items or `r` for right-aligning them. A line | in the *preamble* causes a vertical line to be produced; usually this extends from the top to the bottom of the resulting box. You can have two or more lines next to one another in the *preamble*, like ||. This causes two vertical lines to be produced. The distance between the two vertical lines is given by the rigid length parameter `\doublerulesep`. The width of the lines produced is given by the rigid length parameter `\arrayrulewidth`. To change either of these you need to include commands like `\setlength{\doublerulesep}{5mm}` or `\setlength{\arrayrulewidth}{2pt}` in your input file. The *preamble* |c|c|c| has exactly the same effect as the *preamble* |*{3}{c|}. The element *{*i*}{*pre*} is equivalent to *i* copies of *pre* where *i* is any positive whole number and *pre* is any valid preamble. In fact, *pre* can itself contain *-expressions.

Following the opening of the environment in the above example there is a `\hline` command. This causes a horizontal line to be produced across the entire width of the resulting box.

The *row-list* element in a `tabular` environment consists of one or more *row* components which are separated by \\ commands. Each *row* will usually contain $i - 1$ ampersands where i is the number of columns that the table contains. (Note that if a row contains some `\multicolumn` commands, then fewer ampersands may be required.) Following a \\ command you can include one or more `\hline` commands. If two \hline commands occur next to one another, then the vertical space separating them is given by the rigid length parameter \doublerulesep. Note that vertical lines produced by | expressions in the *preamble* do not appear in the space between the horizontal lines produced by two adjacent \hline commands. If you want a line to appear at the bottom of your table, then the final \hline command must be preceded by a \\ command; but the \\ command should be left out if not followed by a \hline command.

5.3.2 The \multicolumn Command

The following table contains information about the classification of natural deduction inference rules as given by Prawitz (1965), pp. 16–21:

inference rules	
proper	improper
∧-introduction	
∧-elimination	
∨-introduction	∨-elimination
⇒-elimination	⇒-introduction
¬-elimination	¬-introduction
¬¬-elimination	
#-elimination	
∀-elimination	∀-introduction
∃-introduction	∃-elimination

The above table was produced by the following commands:

```
\begin{center}
\begin{tabular}{|c|c|} \hline
\multicolumn{2}{|c|}{inference rules}        \\ \hline\hline
proper                  & improper           \\ \hline\hline
$\land$-introduction    &                    \\
$\land$-elimination     &                    \\
$\lor$-introduction     & $\lor$-elimination \\
$\implies$-elimination & $\implies$-introduction \\
$\neg$-elimination      & $\neg$-introduction \\
$\neg\neg$-elimination &                     \\
$\#$-elimination        &                    \\
$\forall$-elimination   & $\forall$-introduction \\
$\exists$-introduction & $\exists$-elimination \\ \hline
\end{tabular}
\end{center}
```

The **tabular** environment here again occurs inside a **center** environment. One new feature of the **tabular** environment is introduced here and that is the \multicolumn command whose general format is \multicolumn{*i*}{*pre*}{*text*}, where *i* is a positive whole number, *pre* is similar to the preamble of the tabular environment except that fewer expressions are allowed to appear in it and *text* is what is to appear. The argument *pre* must contain one and only one occurrence of either l, r or c; it can contain, but does not have to, one or more @-expressions and it can contain, but does not have to, one or more vertical line characters. A \multicolumn command must either begin a *row* or immediately follow an ampersand. In the example given there occurs \multicolumn{2}{|c|}{inference rules}. This means that the *text* inference rules is to span two columns of the table produced and |c| means that it will be centred with vertical lines occurring at the start of the first column and at the end of the second column. The presence of a \multicolumn command suppresses any vertical lines or positioning expressions which occur in the tabular environment's *preamble*. (The command \implies used in the above example is defined on p. 37 above.)

5.3.3   Using the \shortstack **Command**

The following table presents the results, in frames, between four snooker players:

	Davis	Hendry	Parrott	White
Steve Davis	×	23	19	0
Stephen Hendry	34	×	0	4
John Parrott	22	0	×	18
Jimmy White	0	10	11	×

To produce the above table you need the following commands:

```
\begin{center}
\newcommand*{\temp}[1]{\multicolumn{1}{|r|}{#1}}
\begin{tabular}{r|c|c|c|c|} \cline{2-5}
 & \shortstack{D\\a\\v\\i\\s}
 & \shortstack{H\\e\\n\\d\\r\\y}
 & \shortstack{\rule{0mm}{1mm}\\P\\a\\r\\r\\o\\t\\t}
 & \shortstack{W\\h\\i\\t\\e} \\ \hline
\temp{Steve Davis}     & $\times$ & 23 & 19 &  0 \\ \hline
\temp{Stephen Hendry} & 34 & $\times$ &  0 &  4 \\ \hline
\temp{John Parrott}   & 22 &  0 & $\times$ & 18 \\ \hline
\temp{Jimmy White}    &  0 & 10 & 11 & $\times$ \\ \hline
\end{tabular}
\end{center}
```

Several new ideas are introduced here. The first is the command \cline{2-5} which is similar to \hline, except that the horizontal rule that is produced only extends

	Atypical vampire story	*Invasion of the Body Snatchers* (1956, Siegel)
onset	A mysterious stranger arrives in a small town and both the mortality rate and the number of anaemia cases goes up.	The doctor in a small community notices that some of its members are behaving strangely.
discovery	The heroine begins to suspect that there is a vampire about, but no one believes her—not even her fiancé.	He stumbles across a pod and realises that people are being replaced by aliens, but he never manages to get absolute proof.
confirmation	The heroine's fiancé becomes anaemic and the local doctor and priest see the characteristic puncture marks of the nosferatu on his throat and believe.	A truck carrying pods out of the community provides the required proof.
confrontation	The priest, the heroine, her fiancé and his doctor seek out the vampire's coffin, drive a stake through her heart and cut off her head.	Absent.

Table 5.1: The confrontation plot structure.

```
\begin{center}
\newcommand*{\temphead}{Atypical vampire story}
\newcommand*{\tempon}{A mysterious stranger arrives in a small
town and both the mortality rate and the number of anaemia
cases goes up.}
\newcommand*{\tempdisc}{The heroine begins to suspect that
there is a vampire about, but no one believes her---not even
her fianc\'{e}.}
\newcommand*{\tempfirm}{The heroine's fianc\'{e} becomes anaemic
and the local doctor and priest see the characteristic puncture
marks of the nosferatu on his throat and believe.}
\newcommand*{\tempfront}{The priest, the heroine, her fianc\'{e}
and his doctor seek out the vampire's coffin, drive a stake
through her heart and cut off her head.}

\newcommand*{\TempHead}{{\itshape Invasion of the Body
Snatchers\/} (1956, Siegel)}
\newcommand*{\TempOn}{The doctor in a small community notices
that some of its members are behaving strangely.}
\newcommand*{\TempDisc}{He stumbles across a pod and realises
that people are being replaced by aliens, but he never manages
to get absolute proof.}
\newcommand*{\TempFirm}{A truck carrying pods out of the
community provides the required proof.}
\newcommand*{\TempFront}{Absent.}

\setlength{\tabcolsep}{4mm}
\renewcommand*{\arraystretch}{2.5}

\begin{tabular}{lp{4.4cm}p{4.4cm}}
                            & \temphead  & \TempHead \\
\bfseries onset             & \tempon    & \TempOn \\
\bfseries discovery         & \tempdisc  & \TempDisc \\
\bfseries confirmation      & \tempfirm  & \TempFirm \\
\bfseries confrontation     & \tempfront & \TempFront
\end{tabular}
\end{center}
```

Figure 5.2: Commands used for producing Table 5.1.

between columns 2 to 5 inclusive; the \cline command can occur anywhere that the \hline command can occur. It is possible to use the \cline command to draw a horizontal rule spanning just a single column, but you still need two column numbers and a hyphen; thus, the command \cline{*i-i*} draws a line spanning the *i*th column.

The \shortstack command is a bit like a single-column tabular environment and is used, as its name suggests, for stacking letters or other material. There is less inter-row space, however, than if a tabular environment had been used. The \rule command is usually used to produce rectangular blobs of ink, but here it is used to produce an invisible strut whose purpose is to ensure that the topmost horizontal rule is not too close vertically to the letter 'P' of 'Parrott'.

Note that the scope of the command \temp is delimited by the center environment, that is to say, it is a command local to that environment. This is, in fact, true in general; definitions that occur inside environments are local to those environments.

5.3.4   Including Parboxes

To produce the spatial arrangement of text displayed in Table 5.1 on p. 56 you need to include the commands shown in Fig. 5.2 on p. 57. (The structure of complex discovery plots used in this example is that described in Chapter 3 of Carroll (1990).) The rigid length parameter \tabcolsep is half the amount of horizontal space left between the columns produced by a tabular (or tabular*) environment. The command \arraystretch has a value which is a floating-point number. It controls the amount of vertical space that occurs between the rows produced in a tabular (or tabular* or array) environment by multiplying the default width. Its default value is 1 and changing it to 1.25, say, by means of the \renewcommand* declaration makes the rows produced one and a quarter times further apart.

The *preamble* of the tabular environment in Fig. 5.2 is lp{4.4cm}p{4.4cm}. This means that the resulting table will have three columns; the material in the first column will be placed flush with the left-hand edge of the column. The text in the next two columns will be treated similarly to each other; what occurs in an entry in the tabular environment will be typeset in a parbox of width 4.4 centimetres; in effect, each such entry will be typeset as if it were the argument *text* of a \parbox[t]{4.4cm}{*text*} command.

5.4   Floats

5.4.1   One-column Output

A *float* in LaTeX is a box, the relative position of whose input is not usually mirrored in the relative position of its output. Two environments produce floats and those are the figure and the table ones. (There are also *-versions of these two environments, namely figure* and table*, but they behave exactly like the figure and table environments, respectively, except when the twocolumn option to the \documentclass command has been chosen.) The general formats of the figure and table environments are as follows:

```
\begin{figure}[pos]    text    \end{figure}
\begin{table}[pos]     text    \end{table}
```

The only difference between these appears when you include a \caption command inside them: in the case of the figure environment the word 'Figure' is produced by LaTeX and in the case of the table environment the word 'Table' is automatically generated by LaTeX. (If you want some other words or phrases to be automatically generated by LaTeX, then you need to redefine either the \figurename or the \tablename command.) The *text* argument is processed in paragraph mode and a parbox of width \textwidth is produced. The optional parameter *pos* is a sequence of between one and four different letters chosen from b, h, p and t. It affects the position where the float may appear as follows:

b The float may appear at the bottom of a text page.

h The float may be placed in the output in the same relative position to its neighbours as it occurs in the input.

p The float may appear on a floats-only page.

t The float may appear at the top of a text page.

The default value of *pos* is tbp. The character ! can also occur in the *pos* argument. This tells LaTeX to place the float as close as it can to the place where the environment that produced it occurs, but taking the other components of the *pos* argument into account. The \suppressfloats[pos] command ensures that no floats are placed on the current page. The optional argument *pos* can be either b or t. If it is b, then no floats will be placed at the bottom of the current page; and if it is t, then no floats will be placed at the top of the current page. If you use the ! character in the *pos* argument of either the figure or table environment, then that overrides the effect of any \suppressfloats command.

To see how the table environment works look at Table 5.2 on p. 60 which was produced by the following commands:

```
\begin{table}
\begin{center}
\begin{tabular}{cp{2in}p{2in}}
& \multicolumn{1}{c}{\itshape ponens}
& \multicolumn{1}{c}{\itshape tollens} \\
\itshape ponendo &
If Jack snores, then Maxine hallucinates;
but Jack does snore;
{\itshape therefore}, Maxine hallucinates. &
It is not the case that both
Jack snores and Maxine hallucinates;
but Jack does snore;
{\itshape therefore}, Maxine does not hallucinate. \\
```

	ponens	*tollens*
ponendo	If Jack snores, then Maxine hallucinates; but Jack does snore; *therefore*, Maxine hallucinates.	It is not the case that both Jack snores and Maxine hallucinates; but Jack does snore; *therefore*, Maxine does not hallucinate.
tollendo	Either Jack snores or Maxine hallucinates; but Maxine does not hallucinate; *therefore*, Jack snores.	If Jack snores, then Maxine hallucinates; but Maxine does not hallucinate; *therefore*, Jack does not snore.

Table 5.2: The family *modus*.

```
\itshape tollendo &
Either Jack snores or Maxine hallucinates;
but Maxine does not hallucinate;
{\itshape therefore}, Jack snores. &
If Jack snores, then Maxine hallucinates;
but Maxine does not hallucinate;
{\itshape therefore}, Jack does not snore.
\end{tabular}
\end{center}
\caption{The family {\itshape modus}.}
\label{MODUS}
\end{table}
```

The \caption command is used to produce a caption to the table or figure produced. Its general format is \caption[*entry*]{*heading*} and it produces a numbered caption. (If you want to refer to a captioned figure or table, then you need to include a \label command either somewhere in *heading* or else following the \caption command but within the body of the environment.) If a list of figures or a list of tables is produced by means of either the \listoffigures or the \listoftables command and *entry* is absent, then *heading* is the text that will appear in the list of figures or the list of tables produced. If the argument *entry* is present, then *entry* is the text that will appear in any list of figures or tables produced by a \listoffigures or a \listoftables command. In either case *heading* is used as the caption for the float produced.

There are a number of parameters that affect the placement of floats. First, I will look at the counters that affect the placement of floats:

topnumber is the maximum number of floats that can occur at the top of each page which contains both text and floats.

`bottomnumber` is the maximum number of floats that can occur at the bottom of each page which contains both text and floats.

`totalnumber` is the maximum number of floats that can occur on a page.

Next, I look at some parameters whose values are floating-point numbers between 0 and 1 that affect the placement of floats:

`\topfraction` is the fraction of each page that can be occupied by floats at its top (if it also contains text).

`\bottomfraction` is the fraction of the page that can be occupied by floats at its bottom (if it also contains text).

`\textfraction` is the minimum fraction of a page, containing both text and floats, that has to be occupied by text.

`\floatpagefraction` is the minimum fraction of a floats-only page that can be taken up by floats.

Finally, I look at some rubber length parameters that affect the appearance of floats:

`\floatsep` is the amount of vertical space left between floats that appear on the same text page.

`\intextsep` is the amount of vertical space placed above and below a float that occurs in the middle of a text page because the h location option has been chosen.

`\textfloatsep` is the amount of vertical space left between a float and the text either below or above it, if the float appears at either the top or the bottom of a page that contains both text and floats.

5.4.2 Two-column Output

In order to produce a document that has two columns of text on every page you need to choose the `twocolumn` option to the `\documentclass` command. Most LaTeX commands have the same meaning in two-column output as they do in one-column output; one of the consequences, however, of choosing the `twocolumn` option is that various length parameters are initialized to values that are different from what they would have been initialized to otherwise. For example, paragraph indentation is different and the indentation of list-like environments is also different.

If you just want part of your document to be typeset in the two-column format, then you can use the `\twocolumn` declaration to achieve this; the `\onecolumn` declaration reverts the output back to the one-column format. Both the declarations `\onecolumn` and `\twocolumn` force a new page to be started. An important difference between the `twocolumn` option and the `\twocolumn` declaration is that the latter does not alter the values of any length parameters as the former does.

There are a few commands which behave differently when the `twocolumn` option is chosen, in particular `\pagebreak`, `\newpage` and `\marginpar`. The `\pagebreak` and

`\newpage` commands start new columns rather than new pages, but the `\clearpage` and `\cleardoublepage` commands continue to terminate the current page. The command `\marginpar` places marginal notes in the nearest margin, that is to say, in the right-hand margin if the `\marginpar` command occurs in the right-hand column and in the left-hand margin if the `\marginpar` command occurs in the left-hand column. Whether one-sided or two-sided printing is in force has no effect on the placement of such marginal notes.

The value of the length parameter `\columnsep` is the width of the gap that separates the two columns of text and the value of `\columnseprule` is the width of the vertical rule that is placed in the gap between the two columns; the default value of this is zero inches. The value of the rigid length parameter `\columnwidth` is the width of a single column of text. It is calculated by LaTeX from the values of `\textwidth` and `\columnsep`. It should only be used in order to determine the values of other length commands and it should not be altered.

The greatest differences between one-column and two-column output, however, are in the treatment of floats. In two-column output both one-column and two-column wide floats are available. The `figure` and `table` environments produce floats one-column wide; whereas the `figure*` and `table*` environments produce floats that are two-columns wide. There are a number of parameters that affect the placement and appearance of floats; first, I look at the effects of the following counters:

topnumber is the maximum number of floats that can occur at the top of each column which contains both text and floats.

bottomnumber is the maximum number of floats that can occur at the bottom of each column which contains both text and floats.

totalnumber is the maximum number of floats that can occur in a single column.

dbltopnumber is the maximum number of two-column floats that can occur at the top of a page that contains text as well as floats.

Note that two-column wide floats cannot be placed at the bottom of the page. Next, I explain how the meanings of those parameters whose values are floating-point numbers are affected by the choice of the `twocolumn` option:

`\topfraction` is the amount of each column that can be occupied by floats at its top (if it also contains text).

`\bottomfraction` is the amount of the column that can be occupied by floats at its bottom (if it also contains text).

`\textfraction` is the minimum amount of text that can appear in a column.

`\floatpagefraction` is the minimum amount of a floats-only column that has to be taken up by floats.

`\dbltopfraction` is the amount of each page that can be occupied by two-column wide floats at its top (if it also contains text).

\dblfloatpagefraction is the minimum amount of a floats-only page that has to be taken up by two-column wide floats.

Finally, I look at those rubber length parameters that affect the appearance of floats:

\floatsep is the amount of vertical space left between single-column floats on a page that contains both text and floats.

\intextsep is the amount of vertical space placed above and below a float that occurs in the middle of a text page because the h location option has been chosen.

\textfloatsep is the amount of vertical space left between a single-column wide float and the text either below or above it.

\dblfloatsep is the amount of vertical space that is placed between two two-column wide floats on a page that contains both text and floats.

\dbltextfloatsep is the amount of vertical space left between a double-column float and the text either below or above it.

5.5 The tabbing Environment

The tabbing environment is used to present information in which certain items are aligned vertically. The basic idea is conveyed by the following simple example:

```
                        \begin{tabbing}
                        123\=456\=789\=\kill
one                     \>        one \\
two                     \>        two \\
    three               \>\>      three \\
    four                \>\>      four \\
        five            \>\>\> five \\
        six             \>\>\> six \\
    seven               \>\>      seven \\
    eight               \>\>      eight \\
nine                    \>        nine
                        \end{tabbing}
```

The first line inside the tabbing environment in this example sets the tab positions, rather like tab positions on a typewriter, and the \kill command just tells LaTeX not to produce any output corresponding to this line. The \= commands set the tab positions. Note that outside the tabbing environment \= produces a macron accent; if you need a macron accent inside the tabbing environment use \a=. Note also that in the Computer Modern fonts designed by Knuth all the digits are half an em wide. The command \> moves the following text so that it is aligned on the next tab stop.

Inside the tabbing environment LaTeX maintains two variables, namely *next-tab-stop* and *left-margin-tab*, whose values are non-negative whole numbers. The tab positions are, in effect, imaginary vertical lines along which text is aligned; each such line is numbered starting with 0 and usually they are numbered consecutively as you move to the right. In the above example three tabs are set and they are numbered 0, 1 and 2. Initially, the value of *left-margin-tab* is set to 0 and it is positioned at the current left margin and initially the value of *next-tab-stop* is set to 1. The command \> aligns text on line i, if i is the value of *next-tab-stop*, and it increments *next-tab-stop* by 1. (Note that the end-of-line command \\ resets *next-tab-stop* to $1 +$ *left-margin-tab* as well as terminating the current line; it has no effect on *left-margin-tab*.)

The above output could also be produced in the following two ways:

```
\begin{tabbing}                \begin{tabbing}
123\=456\=789\=\kill           123\=456\=789\=\kill
\+ \\                          \+ \\
      one \\                         one \\
      two \\                         two \+ \\
\>    three \\                       three \\
\>    four \\                        four \+ \\
\>\> five \\                         five \\
\>\> six \\                          six \- \\
\>    seven \\                       seven \\
\>    eight \\                       eight \- \\
      nine                           nine
\end{tabbing}                  \end{tabbing}
```

The command \+ increments the value of *left-margin-tab* by 1 and \- decreases its value by 1. Note that outside the tabbing environment \- is the discretionary hyphen.

Some further features of the tabbing environment are illustrated by the following example:

```
                               \begin{minipage}{1.75in}
                               \begin{tabbing}
                               123\=456\=789\=\kill
                               \+ \\
one                            one \\
two                            two \+ \\
    three                      three \\
    four                       four \+ \\
  five                         five \' \\
        six                    six \- \\
            seven              \` seven \\
      eight                    eight \- \\
  nine                         nine
                               \end{tabbing}
                               \end{minipage}
```

The command \' is a little like \hfill except that it pushes text leftwards towards the imaginary alignment line numbered by the value of *left-margin-tab* leaving a distance between the line and the text which is given by the value of the rigid length parameter

`\tabbingsep`. The command `\'` is also similar to `\hfill` in that it pushes any text that follows it rightwards as far as the prevailing right margin. Note that outside the `tabbing` environment `\'` produces an acute accent and `\'` produces a grave accent; to get these inside the `tabbing` environment use `\a'` and `\a'`, respectively. The `minipage` environment is included here to show the effect of the `\'` command.

Some further commands available inside the `tabbing` environment are illustrated in the production of the following program fragment (which uses an Algol-like syntax):

$$a := 0;$$
$$b := 1;$$
$$i := 0;$$
$$\textbf{while } n \ne i \textbf{ do}$$
$$\quad (b := a + b;$$
$$\quad\;\; a := b - a;$$
$$\quad\;\; i := i + 1);$$
$$p := a$$

(This program, by the way, calculates Fibonacci numbers. On termination the variable p contains the value of fib(n).) The above was obtained by using the `tabbing` environment as follows:

```
\begin{tabbing}
$a\:$\=$:= 0$; \kill
$a$\>$:= 0$; \\
$b$\>$:= 1$; \\
$i$\>$:= 0$; \\
$\mathbf{while}\ n \ne i\ \mathbf{do}$ \\
\pushtabs
\hspace*{1em}\=$($\=$b\:$\=$:= a + b$; \kill
\>$($\>$b$\>$:= a + b$; \\
\>\>$a$\>$:= b - a$; \\
\>\>$i$\>$:= i + 1)$; \\
\poptabs
$p$\>$:= a$
\end{tabbing}
```

The first line here, the one terminated by `\kill`, sets the tab positions. The `\kill` command tells LaTeX that the characters occurring on that line are not to occur in the final output; but do *not* use an end-of-line command `\\` before the `\kill` command. The control symbol `\=` sets the tabs. In order to use the nth tab position you need n occurrences of the control symbol `\>`. The `\pushtabs` command stores the current tab settings and they are restored by the `\poptabs` command.

5.6 The `verbatim` Environment

When all else fails you can use the **verbatim** environment to output text exactly as it appears in your input file. For example, the input:

```
\begin{quote}
\begin{verbatim}
Jardine was one of the most controversial English cricket
captains that there has ever been.  Australians, especially,
usually regard him as the embodiment of the antithesis of
sportsmanship; but is this reputation deserved?
\end{verbatim}
\end{quote}
```

produces the following output, in typewriter style:

```
Jardine was one of the most controversial English cricket
captains that there has ever been.  Australians, especially,
usually regard him as the embodiment of the antithesis of
sportsmanship; but is this reputation deserved?
```

Note that in the ending of the environment `\end{verbatim}` no spaces can occur between `\end` and `{verbatim}`. A `verbatim` environment cannot occur in the argument to any other command, but it can occur inside another environment. The `verbatim*` environment is similar to `verbatim` except that spaces in the input file appear as '␣' in the output document. LaTeX also contains the commands `\verb` and `\verb*` for outputting short input exactly as it appears; see the glossary for more information.

Chapter 6

Making Bibliographies

6.1 Introduction

In section 4.9 above it was explained how you can include a bibliography in your document using the `thebibliography` environment. In this chapter I explain how you can use BibTeX to produce a bibliography. BibTeX is a widely available system used for producing bibliographies in conjunction with LaTeX; it was implemented by Oren Patashnik. In order to use it you first have to create a file with extension `bib` containing a sequence of entries (the structure of these is explained in the next section) and then in your LaTeX input file it is necessary to include, in addition to the standard `\cite` commands, some additional commands peculiar to BibTeX which tell it how to format the bibliography it produces and what the names of the `bib` files containing database entries are that it should use. These are explained in section 6.4 below.

6.2 The Structure of a `bib` File

A `bib` file contains one or more entries each of which looks something like this:

```
@book{il:pr:lmd,
   address    = "Cambridge",
   author     = "Imre Lakatos",
   isbn       = "0 521 21078 X (hard covers)
                 0 521 29038 4 (paperback)",
   note       = "Edited by John Worrall and Elie Zahar",
   publisher = "Cambridge University Press",
   title      = "Proofs and Refutations:
                 The Logic of Mathematical Discovery",
   year       = 1976}
```

The general form of such an entry is *publication-type{key, field-list}*. The available possibilities for *publication-type* are given in Table 6.1 together with a brief description of what sort of material each kind of entry should be used for. Unlike LaTeX much of BibTeX is not case sensitive. Thus, `@book` can appear as `@BOOK` or even as `@BooK`.

@article{*key*,*field-list*} is used for articles or papers that have been published in journals, periodicals or magazines.

@book{*key*,*field-list*} is used for books which have a named publisher.

@booklet{*key*,*field-list*} is used for a work that has been printed and bound, but which has no indication on it identifying who produced it.

@conference{*key*,*field-list*} is used for an article or paper that is published in the proceedings of some conference. (This kind of entry is exactly the same as the @inproceedings type.)

@inbook{*key*,*field-list*} is used for chapters, or other parts, of a book. It can even be used just for a collection of pages from a book.

@incollection{*key*,*field-list*} is used for chapters, or other parts, of a book which have their own titles. The book in question may have, for example, each chapter written by a different person.

@inproceedings{*key*,*field-list*} is used for an article or paper that is published in the proceedings of some conference. (This kind of entry is exactly the same as the @conference type.)

@manual{*key*,*field-list*} is used for manuals and similar kinds of technical documentation.

@mastersthesis{*key*,*field-list*} is used for a dissertation or thesis written for a Master's degree.

@misc{*key*,*field-list*} is used when something you want to refer to fits nowhere else.

@phdthesis{*key*,*field-list*} is used for a doctoral thesis or dissertation.

@proceedings{*key*,*field-list*} is used for the proceedings of a conference as distinct from a single paper in such a collection.

@techreport{*key*,*field-list*} is used for a research or technical report produced by an institution such as a school or department in a university or an industrial research laboratory.

@unpublished{*key*,*field-list*} is used for a document, such as a typescript, that has a title and an author but has not been published in any way. A samizdat document may belong in this category.

Table 6.1: Different kinds of *publication-type*.

Instead of using braces to enclose the *key* and *field-list* of an entry ordinary parentheses, that is to say, (and), can be used. If any braces occur inside these delimiters, then they must come in matching pairs and this applies even to \{ and \}.

The *key* is what will appear in any \cite commands that you use to refer to the publication in question. For example, to refer to Lakatos's *Proofs and Refutations* you would use the command \cite{il:pr:lmd}.

The *field-list* is separated from the key by a comma and it consists of a list of fields separated by commas. An example of a field is author = "Imre Lakatos" and here author is the name of the field and "Imre Lakatos" is the text of the field. Field-names are not case-sensitive, so author could appear as AUTHOR or even as AutHOr. The field-list is either enclosed in double quotation marks or an opening and closing brace. If a field-text consists *entirely* of numerals, such as 1976, then there is no need to enclose it in double quotation marks. (In the *key* and *field-list* multiple spaces around commas or equals signs make no difference to the output.) The following is a complete list of all the field-names that are currently recognized by BibTeX:

address This field is used to give the city or town where the publisher of the book has its main office. If the place is not well known, then it is a good idea to include more information in order to help any interested reader to locate the work.

annote Currently, this field is ignored by all standard bibliography styles, but it may be used by non-standard styles that produce an annotated bibliography. Hence, it should be used for such annotations.

author This field holds the name of the author of the work or their names if there is more than one. See section 6.3 for more information about how to use this field.

booktitle If only part of a book is being referred to, then its title should be included in this field.

chapter The number of a chapter or other sectional unit being referred to goes in this field.

crossref This field is used for the key of the database entry whose fields will be inherited by this entry if they are not explicitly included. (Included fields are used in preference.) An example of how you use the crossref field is shown in the file ide.bib displayed in Fig. 6.1. The reference to Kripke's paper *inherits* any fields that it is lacking from the entry with key mkm:ii. Note that the booktitle field is ignored if present in a @book entry; it is only included in the entry with key mkm:ii so that it can be inherited by other entries in the database. Furthermore, the cross-referenced entry, here the one with key mkm:ii, must come *after* any entries which reference it; in this example those with keys ml:ir and sk:in.

edition This field contains the edition of the work being referred to. For example, 7 or "Thirty-ninth". If a numeral is not used, then an ordinal with an initial uppercase letter should be used.

```
@incollection{ml:ir,
   author    = "Michael Lockwood",
   crossref  = "mkm:ii",
   pages     = "199--211",
   title     = "Identity and Reference"}

@incollection{sk:in,
   author    = "Saul Kripke",
   crossref  = "mkm:ii",
   pages     = "135--164",
   title     = "Identity and Necessity"}

@book{mkm:ii,
   address   = "New York",
   booktitle = "Identity and Individuation",
   editor    = "Milton K. Munitz",
   publisher = "New York University Press",
   title     = "Identity and Individuation",
   year      = 1971}
```

Figure 6.1: Contents of the BibTeX database file `ide.bib`.

editor This field holds the name of the editor of a book being referred to (or their names if there is more than one) or the name of the editor of a book, such as the proceedings of a conference, part of which is being referred to (or their names if there is more than one). See section 6.3 for more information about how to use thie field.

howpublished This field holds information about how the item in question was published. The text should start with an initial uppercase letter.

institution This field holds the name of the institution, for example, "Programming Research Group", under whose auspices the technical report being referred to was produced.

journal This field contains the name of the journal in which the article being referred to was published. Various abbreviations may be available on your system; check with someone who knows.

key You should not confuse this field-name with the *key* that is used in \cite commands. This field is used for sorting the entry when no other field usually used for sorting is present.

month Use one of the following abbreviations in this field: `jan`, `feb`, `mar`, `apr`, `may`, `jun`, `jul`, `aug`, `sep`, `oct`, `nov` or `dec`.

note Use this field for any additional information that you want to appear in the bibliography that is produced, such as `note = "Edited by John Worrall and Elie Zahar"`. Note that the first word should have an initial uppercase letter.

number This field contains the number of the work being referred to.

organization Use this field for the sponsors of a conference or the organization associated with a technical manual.

pages Use this field for a page number, a range of page numbers or several of these. For example, `"679--703"`, `"33--45, 60--63"` or `"35, 40--43, 70"`.

publisher This field holds the name of a publishing house. For example, `"Cambridge University Press"` or `"Springer"`.

school Use this field for the name of a department or school to which a thesis was submitted.

series Some books are published in a series; put the name of the series in this field.

title This field contains the title of an article, book or whatever. See section 6.3 for more information about how to use thie field.

type There are many varieties of technical reports; in this field you should state which one the work you are citing belongs to.

volume Use this field for the volume number of a journal or the volume number of a book or conference proceedings that is one of a series.

year This field holds the year associated with a work that you are referring to. Usually, something like 1976, but the standard BibTeX styles can handle text like `"Circa 1600"` whose last four non-punctuation characters are numerals.

Note that the field-name `isbn` that appears in the entry for Lakatos's *Proofs and Refutations* on p. 67 is not one that is (currently) recognized by BibTeX. It causes no error or warning message when processed and is included just for information; it does not appear in any bibliography produced.

Depending on which *publication-type* you are using different fields are either mandatory, optional or ignored. (The status of some fields is more complicated than this threefold classification as explained below.) For example, in producing a database entry for a book, like Lakatos's *Proofs and Refutations*, only the `publisher`, `title` and `year` fields have to be present. Furthermore, either the `author` or the `editor` field must be present (but not both) and at most one of the `volume` and `number` fields can be present (but both can be absent). The `address`, `crossref`, `edition`, `key`, `month`, `note` and `series` fields are all optional, that is to say, they are used if present; every other kind of field is simply ignored. In the table shown in Table 6.2 six different kinds

	@article	@book	@booklet	@conference	@inbook	@incollection	@inproceedings	@manual	@mastersthesis	@misc	@phdthesis	@proceedings	@techreport	@unpublished
address		O	O	O	O	O	O	O	O		O	O	O	
annote														
author	R	E	O	R	E	R	R	O	R	O	R		R	R
booktitle				R		R	R							
chapter					A	O								
crossref	O	O	O	O	O	O	O	O	O	O	O	O	O	O
edition		O			O	O		O						
editor		E		O	E	O	O					O		
howpublished		O								O				
institution													R	
journal	R													
key	O	O	O	O	O	O	O	O	O	O	O	O	O	O
month	O	O	O	O	O	O	O	O	O	O	O	O	O	O
note	O	O	O	O	O	O	O	O	O	O	O	O	O	R
number	O	V		V	V	V	V					V	O	
organization				O			O	O				O		
pages	O			O	A	O	O							
publisher		R		O	R	R	O					O		
school									R		R			
series		O		O	O	O	O					O		
title	R	R	R	R	R	R	R	R	R	O	R	R	R	R
type					O				O		O		O	
volume	O	V		V	V	V	V					V		
year	R	R	O	R	R	R	R	O	R	O	R	R	R	O

Table 6.2: Status of fields for different types of publication.

of field are shown. These are indicated by the five letters A, E, O, R and V and also by leaving a blank. These have the following meaning:

A When this occurs in the `@inbook` column, it means that you can include either a `chapter` field or a `pages` field or both in the *field-list* argument. If neither are present, then a warning is issued but the output produced looks okay.

E This is used in the `@book` and `@inbook` columns to indicate that either the `author` or the `editor` fields can be included. If both of these fields are present, then a warning message is issued when you run BIBTEX and the `editor` field is ignored. If neither of these fields is present, nor a `key` field, then you get a warning informing you that BIBTEX cannot sort this bibliographic entry. It does, however, appear in the bibliography that is produced.

O This means that the field in question is optional. That is to say, the information will be used if it is present, but no problems will be caused by its absence.

R This is used to indicate that the field in question is mandatory or required. If the field is left out, then an error message will be produced when you run BIBTEX and it is possible that the bibliography produced will not be formatted properly.

V This letter occurs in the columns for the following types of bibliographic entries: `@book`, `@conference`, `@inbook`, `@incollection`, `@inproceedings` and `@proceedings`. It is used to indicate that either the `volume` or `number` fields can be present. If both are present, you get a warning message and the `number` field is ignored. If just the `volume` field is present or both are absent, everything goes ahead smoothly. If the `number` field is present and the `series` field is absent, you get a warning message but the output looks okay.

␣ This indicates that the field, even if present, is simply ignored.

6.3 Authors, Titles and Abbreviations

The name of the author of a work goes into the `author` field. It is a good idea to give as much information as possible in a BIBTEX entry and this also applies to people's names. If the surname comes first, then it should be followed by a comma; thus, the following two fields are equivalent:

```
author = "Karl Raimund Popper",
author = "Popper, Karl Raimund",
```

How the name actually appears in the bibliography produced depends on several factors and often the given names will only appear as initials. Names which contain such 'auxiliary' words as 'von', 'tom' or 'le' pose no problem, but they should be entered in lowercase letters. For example:

```
editor = "T. tom Dieck",
editor = "tom Dieck, T.",
```

(Leave a space and do *not* put a tilde after initials.) Some people have surnames which consist of two words that are not hyphenated. These should be entered as follows:

```
author = "Brinch Hansen, Per",
```

That is to say, the entire surname should come before the comma.

If two or more people have written or edited a book, then their names should be separated by and and if a work has, say, more than six authors, you can terminate its text with the words and others which will appear as '*et al.*' when the bibliography is produced. The following are equivalent:

```
author = "Windy Dryden and Joseph Yankura",
author = "Windy Dryden and Yankura, Joseph",
```

If a name contains either a comma or the word 'and', then that should be enclosed in braces. In fact, anything enclosed in braces will not be processed by BibTeX in any way; it will simply be written to the bbl file without alteration. This is also useful in ensuring that the names of countries or people, say, that appear in titles do not occur in the bibliography that is produced with initial lowercase letters. For example,

```
title = "Ponsford and {Woodfull}: A Premier Partnership",
```

Note that the special function of and to separate names of multiple authors or editors only applies inside the text of an author or editor field. People disagree about which words should be capitalized in titles; the most important rule to follow is that of being consistent.

Mathematical expressions occur in the titles of some articles and this poses no problem for BibTeX. For example, the following database entry is perfectly acceptable:

```
@article{nha:ur,
    author    = "N. H. Abel",
    journal   = "Journal {f\"{u}r} Reine und
                 Argewandte Mathematik",
    pages     = "311--339",
    title     = "Untersuchungen {\"{u}ber} die Reihe
                 $\displaystyle 1 + \frac{m}{1} x
                 + \frac{m.(m-1)}{2} x^2
                 + \frac{m.(m-1)(m-2)}{2.3} x^3 \ldots$",
    volume    = 1,
    year      = 1826}
```

How this actually appears in any bibliography you produce would depend upon the style of references that you decide to employ and the bibliography style you adopt. The mathematical expressions involved, however, will be correctly typeset. The effect of the local declaration \displaystyle is to force everything in its scope to be typeset in display style.

If you are going to refer to several articles published in the same journal, then it would be a good idea to use an abbreviation for it as follows:

```
@string{bjps = "British Journal for the Philosophy of Science"}
```

This can occur anywhere in a `bib` file, but it must come before any use of it. Note that the case of letters in neither `@string` nor `bjps` is significant. Note also that abbreviations must begin with a letter and that they cannot contain any of the following characters:

```
"  #  %  '  (  )  ,  {  }
```

Abbreviations can take the place of the text part of any field, for example:

```
@article{mh:ttmrp:i,
   author  = "Michael Hallett",
   journal =  bjps,
   pages   = "1--25",
   title   = "Towards a Theory of Mathematical
              Research Programmes {(I)}",
   volume  =  30,
   year    =  1979}
```

6.4 Producing the Bibliography

In order to get BIBTEX to produce a bibliography for you it is necessary to include both a `\bibliographystyle` and a `\bibliography` command inside the `document` environment of your input file. The `\bibliographystyle` command usually comes immediately after the `\begin{document}` command, but it has to come before any `\cite` commands; and the `\bibliography` command usually comes close to the end of the `document` environment in the place where you want the bibliography produced to occur. These things are illustrated in Fig. 6.2 where the LATEX commands at the top produce the output at the bottom. Note that information about a work with key *key* is placed into the bibliography by BIBTEX *only* if at least one `\cite{key}` command occurs in your input file. If you want a work placed in the bibliography that you do not cite, but which occurs in one of your `bib` files, then you have to use a `\nocite{key}` command. A `\nocite{*}` command in your input file causes *every* work in the BIBTEX database files mentioned in the `\bibliography` command to appear in the bibliography produced.

The general format of the `\bibliography` command is:

```
\bibliography{bib-file-list}
```

The argument *bib-file-list* is a list of the first or base names of one or more `bib` files; if the list contains more than one member, then they should be separated by commas. In Fig. 6.2 the command `\bibligraphy{pom}` occurs. This assumes the existence of a file `pom.bib` which should contain, at least, the entries for Lakatos's book, shown on p. 67 above, and for Hallett's article, shown above.

The general format of the `\bibliographystyle` command is:

```
\documentclass[11pt]{article}
\begin{document}
\bibliographystyle{plain}
\noindent
Hallett \cite{mh:ttmrp:i} develops Lakatos's
views on the philosophy of mathematics presented,
for example, in \cite{il:pr:lmd}.
\bibliography{pom}
\end{document}
```

Hallett [1] develops Lakatos's views on the philosophy of mathematics presented, for example, in [2].

References

[1] Michael Hallett. Towards a theory of mathematical research programmes (I). *British Journal for the Philosophy of Science*, 30:1–25, 1979.

[2] Imre Lakatos. *Proofs and Refutations: The Logic of Mathematical Discovery*. Cambridge University Press, Cambridge, 1976. Edited by John Worrall and Elie Zahar.

Figure 6.2: Using BIBTEX.

```
\bibliographystyle{bib-style}
```

The standard possibilities for *bib-style* are plain, unsrt, abbrv and alpha. The style of bibliography produced if the plain option is chosen is shown in Fig. 6.2. The entries in the bibliography produced are sorted automatically by BIBTEX. They are arranged so that the names of authors and editors are ordered alphabetically. Works by the same author or editor appear sorted numerically by year and works by the same author or editor published in the same year are sorted alphabetically by title.

If the unsrt option is chosen instead, then the entries in the bibliography produced look exactly the same as if the plain option had been used *except* that they are not sorted; they appear in the bibliography produced in the order in which references to them occur in the input file.

If the abbrv option is chosen, then the order of the entries in the bibliography produced is exactly the same as if the plain option had been used; the only difference is that given names and certain other words are abbreviated.

If the alpha option is chosen, then the bibliography produced is sorted as if the `plain` option had been chosen, but it looks as follows:

References

[Hal79] Michael Hallett. Towards a theory of mathematical research programmes (I). *British Journal for the Philosophy of Science*, 30:1–25, 1979.

[Lak76] Imre Lakatos. *Proofs and Refutations: The Logic of Mathematical Discovery*. Cambridge University Press, Cambridge, 1976. Edited by John Worrall and Elie Zahar.

The command \cite{il:pr:lmd} produces the citation [Lak76] and the command \cite{mh:ttmrp:i} produces [Hal79]. That is to say, the labels produced automatically by LaTeX consist of the first three letters of a single author's name followed by the last two digits of the year of publication (all enclosed in square brackets).

To get LaTeX and BibTeX to generate and include a bibliography in the output corresponding to your input file you need to run both LaTeX and BibTeX on your input file: first of all you process your input file in the usual way by running LaTeX on it, then you process it using BibTeX—in many oprerating systems this is achieved by means of the command `bibtex` *file* where *file* is the base name of your input file—and then you run LaTeX twice on your input file. (In exceptional circumstances you may need to process your input file even more times than this.)

6.5 The harvard Package

In the Harvard or author–date system references are given by mentioning the author (or authors) and year of publication of a work. It is possible to get BibTeX to produce such references, but it is not part of basic LaTeX. In order to get BibTeX to produce references in the Harvard style you need to load the **harvard** package, which was implemented by Peter Williams, and then use either the **agsm**, **dcu** or **kluwer** option to the \bibliographystyle command. To illustrates some of these possibilities, consider the following LaTeX input file:

```
\documentclass[11pt]{article}
\usepackage{harvard}
\begin{document}
\bibliographystyle{agsm}
\noindent
Citations look like \citeasnoun{mh:ttmrp:i} or \cite{il:pr:lmd}.
\bibliography{pom}
\end{document}
```

The above input file produces the following output:

Citations look like Hallett (1979) or (Lakatos 1976).

References

Hallett, M. (1979), 'Towards a theory of mathematical research programmes (I)', *British Journal for the Philosophy of Science*, **30**, 1–25.

Lakatos, I. (1976), *Proofs and Refutations: The Logic of Mathematical Discovery*, Cambridge University Press, Cambridge. Edited by John Worrall and Elie Zahar.

The options agsm, dcu and kluwer produce slightly different bibliographies. Also available is a \citationstyle command which has two options, namely agsm (the default) or dcu. This affects the output produced by the \cite and \citeasnoun commands that occur in your input file. The differences between the two options to the \citationstyle command are shown in the following table:

agsm	dcu	
(Lakatos 1976)	(Lakatos, 1976)	\cite{il:pr:lmd}
(Lakatos 1976, Hallett 1979)	(Lakatos, 1976; Hallett, 1979)	\cite{il:pr:lmd, mh:ttmrp:i}
Lakatos (1976)	Lakatos (1976)	\citeasnoun{il:pr:lmd}
(Lakatos 1976, pp. 23–34)	(Lakatos, 1976, pp. 23–34)	\cite[pp. 23--34] {il:pr:lmd}
Lakatos (1976, pp. 23–34)	Lakatos (1976, pp. 23–34)	\citeasnoun [pp. 23--34]{il:pr:lmd}

Note that the \citeasnoun command *cannot* accept a list of keys as its argument; it only works for a single key.

Chapter 7

Making Indexes

7.1 The Hard Way

It is possible to make an index in LaTeX by using the `theindex` environment. The index that is produced is in a two-column format. Inside the `theindex` environment you can use the `\item`, `\subitem`, `\subsubitem` and `\indexspace` commands. The `\item` command begins an entry in the index produced, the `\subitem` command begins sub-entries which are slightly indented and what `\subsubitem` produces is indented still more than that. The `\indexspace` command is used to separate groups of entries. It produces a small amount of vertical space and it is often used to separate groups of entries beginning with different letters of the alphabet. The following example illustrates the effect of the `\item`, `\subitem` and `\subsubitem` commands:

serpigo, 3, 120	`\item serpigo, 3, 120`
set, 11	`\item set, 11`
free, 8, 35	`\subitem free, 8, 35`
in, 6, 8, 130	`\subitem in, 6, 8, 130`
hand, 5, 11	`\subsubitem hand, 5, 11`
off, 2	`\subitem off, 2`
shadow, 4	`\item shadow, 4`
box, 3, 88	`\subitem box, 3, 88`
shame, 13, 90	`\item shame, 13, 90`

If you are processing a document that uses the `article` document class, then the `theindex` environment starts a new section whose title is 'Index'. (The index that is produced also starts on a new page.) It is as if a `\section*{Index}` command had been encountered by LaTeX. If you are using either the `report` or the `book` document class, then the `theindex` environment starts a new chapter just as if LaTeX had encountered a `\chapter*{Index}` command. If you want the heading that LaTeX generates automatically to be something other than 'Index', then you need to redefine the `\indexname` command.

It is entirely straightforward to use the `theindex` environment in order to produce an index. The difficult part of producing an index is the task of putting the correct information into the `theindex` environment. This task is not fully automated in basic LaTeX, but some useful commands are available. You can get LaTeX to write an `idx` file which contains information about which words and phrases you want to appear in your index. In order to get LaTeX to write such an `idx` file you need to include a `\makeindex` command in the preamble of your input file and within the `document` environment you need to include some `\index{text}` commands. Any characters can occur in *text* (but all braces, including `\{` and `\}`, must come in matching pairs) unless the `\index` command occurs inside the argument of another command, such as the `\footnote` command, when *text* can only include letters, numerals and punctuation marks. When LaTeX is run on such an input file, an `idx` file with the same first or base name is written. (If an `idx` file exists, then it is overwritten; to prevent such overwriting you need to include a `\nofiles` command in the preamble of your input file.) This `idx` file contains commands of the form `\indexentry{text}{p}` where *p* was the value of the `page` counter when `\index{text}` was processed.

The problem with using LaTeX to make an index is getting the information in an `idx` file into a `theindex` environment. One way to accomplish this is to run LaTeX on the file `idx.tex`. When you do this you will get a prompt asking you for the name of a file. Say you input `lakatos.tex`; then a file called `idx.dvi` will be generated and if you print this off on a printer, it will tell you all the arguments to all the `\index` commands that occurred on page 1 and all the arguments of all the `\index` commands that occurred on page 2 and so on. You will then have to transform this information manually into the body of the `theindex` environment.

7.2   The Easy Way

The easy way to get LaTeX to produce an index for you is to use the `makeidx` package in conjunction with the *MakeIndex* program. In addition to loading the `makeidx` package, you also have to include the `\makeindex` command in the preamble of your input file and the command `\printindex` inside the `document` environment at the point where you want the index to appear. Normally, the index comes right at the end of a book or other document. Inside the `document` environment you need to put a number of `\index{text}` commands. The `makeidx` package gives a special meaning to a number of characters and pairs of characters inside the *text* argument to the `\index` command. These will be explained in due course, but first I will explain how an index is produced by means of the *MakeIndex* program. This involves the following stages:

(1) You process your input file by running LaTeX on it. This produces an `idx` file. For example, if your input file was called `therapy.tex`, then the `idx` file will be called `therapy.idx`.

(2) You process the `idx` file using *MakeIndex*. How this is done may vary from one operating system to another, but on many operating systems it will be achieved by issuing a command like `makeindex therapy`. Note that you do not have to give the full name of the file you are processing. *MakeIndex* reads the file `therapy.idx` and a style file with the extension `ist` and generates an `ind` file.

Continuing with the example already introduced, this would be `therapy.ind`. LaTeX will also generate a transcript file called `therapy.ilg`.

(3) You then have to process your input file for a second time by running LaTeX on it. The files `therapy.tex` and `therapy.ind` will be read in and an alphabetically sorted index will be produced at that place in your document corresponding to the `\printindex` command.

Unfortunately, in the index produced, if two words differ only in the fact that one begins with an uppercase letter whereas the other begins with the same letter but in lowercase, then the one beginning with the uppercase letter comes first. The advice in some books, however, is that the word beginning with the lowercase letter should come first. See, for example, Isaacs, Daintith and Martin (1991), p. 178, in the entry for 'indexing'.

As already mentioned, the `makeidx` package gives a special meaning to a number of characters and pairs of characters inside the *text* argument of the `\index{text}` command. It is now necessary to explain what these are and how they work:

`\index{text}` The index produced will contain an entry *text* together with a list of numbers corresponding to the pages where `\index{text}` occurred.

`\index{text|(}` If you want the index to contain a page range, such as 24–33, then put the command `\index{text|(}` at the beginning of the range and `\index{text|)}` at the end of the range.

`\index{text|)}` See the explanantion of `\index{text|(}` above.

`\index{text₁!text₂}` The index will contain an entry *text₁* with *text₂* as a sub-entry attached to it.

`\index{text₁!text₂!text₃}` The index will contain an entry *text₁* with *text₂* as a sub-entry attached to it and *text₃* will be a sub-sub-entry attached to *text₂*.

`\index{text₁@text₂}` LaTeX will use *text₁* when sorting the entries into alphabetical order, but *text₂* will actually occur in the index.

`\index{text₁|see{text₂}}` If you put the command `\index{set|see{class}}` into your input file, say, then the index produced will contain the line:

    set, *see* class

If you want some word other than '*see*' to appear in the index, then redefine the `\seename` command. In fact, a number of commands can follow the vertical line, though you have to leave off the initial backslash. For example, a command `\index{aggregate|textbf}` would produce a bold numeral corresponding to the page where this command occurred. The command `\see` is defined inside the `makeidx` package. In general, the command `\index{text|cmd}` will produce a page number of the form `\cmd{p}`, where *p* is the page number in question. See Goossens, Mittelbach and Samarin (1994, pp. 349–350) for more information.

7.3   Some Glossary Commands

LaTeX contains commands called `\makeglossary` and `\glossary` that work analogously to the `\makeindex` and `\index` commands. A file with extension `glo` is written or overwritten and this contains `\glossaryentry` commands which are analogous to `\indexentry` commands. The following table lists these analogies:

`\makeindex`	`\makeglossary`
`\index{`*text*`}`	`\glossary{`*text*`}`
`idx`	`glo`
`\indexentry{`*text*`}{`*p*`}`	`\glossaryentry{`*text*`}{`*p*`}`

Some people are misled by the word 'glossary' in these command names; they just mirror the index-producing commands. Note that there is no `theglossary` environment analogous to the `theindex` environment. The `description` environment explained in section 4.8 is best used for producing what most people think of as a glossary.

Chapter 8

Standard Document Classes

8.1 The `article` Document Class

8.1.1 Introduction

The overall structure of a LATEX input file has already been discussed in Chapter 2. In the case of articles this becomes:

> *prologue*
> \documentclass[*opt-list*]{article}[*date*]
> *preamble*
> \begin{document}
> *doc-body*
> \end{document}

In this section further commands which relate to the large-scale organization of an input file for producing articles are explained. The standard options to the `article` document class are: at most one of `10pt` (the default), `11pt` or `12pt`; at most one of `letterpaper` (the default), `legalpaper`, `executivepaper`, `a4paper`, `a5paper` or `b5paper`; at most one of `final` (the default) or `draft`; at most one of `oneside` (the default) or `twoside`; at most one of `onecolumn` (the default) or `twocolumn`; and at most one of `notitlepage` (the default) or `titlepage`. Furthermore, any or none of the following can occur in *opt-list*: `landscape`, `openbib`, `leqno` and `fleqn`.

By default one-sided 'printing' is automatically in operation, that is to say, all pages are (conceptually) right-handed and odd-numbered ones. This means, for example, that the head, body and foot regions of both odd- and even-numbered pages are positioned in the same place on the physical piece of paper relative to the left and top edges of the paper. The value of the rigid length parameter \evensidemargin, therefore, has no effect on the appearance of the output. To change this default choose the `twoside` option to the \documentclass command. (All the length parameters that affect the appearance of the page, and what they do, are shown in Fig. C.4 on p. 260.)

The default page style is `plain`, that is to say, the head region is empty and the page number appears in the centre of the foot region. In addition, the \raggedbottom

```
\documentclass[11pt]{article}
\usepackage{own}
\title{Lakatos's Philosophy of Mathematics}
\author{Antoni Diller}
\begin{document}
\bibliographystyle{plain}
\maketitle
\begin{abstract}
\noindent
In this paper I investigate the influence of Popper's
'evolutionary' epistemology on Lakatos's account of the
growth of mathematical knowledge by means of proofs and
refutations.
\end{abstract}
    text
\bibliography{pom}
\end{document}
```

Figure 8.1: The contents of the input file `lpm.tex`.

declaration is also in force; this means that inter-paragraph vertical space is kept constant and, so, the height of the text on each page may vary slightly. To force the height of material on each output page to be the same include the `\flushbottom` declaration in the preamble of your input file. (Note that if you use the `twoside` document-class option, the default becomes the `\flushbottom` declaration.)

8.1.2 Bibliography

It may seem strange to discuss bibliographies so early on in this chapter as they almost invariably come near the end of any work in which they occur. However, if you are using BibTeX to produce your bibliography, then you need to include a `\bibliographystyle` command soon after the start of the **document** environment and a `\bibliography` command near to the end of the **document** environment. Thus, your input file is going to look something like the one shown in Fig. 8.1. This assumes the existence of a personal package called `own.sty` and also the existence of a file containing BibTeX database entries called `pom.bib`. Note that the `\bibliography` command will automatically generate the unnumbered section heading 'References' when you process your input file. If you want your list of references to be called something other than 'References', then you need to redefine the `\refname` command. For example, if you want your list of references to be placed in a section called 'Bibliography', then place the following in the preamble of your input file:

```
\renewcommand*{\refname}{Bibliography}
```

If you are using the `thebibliography` environment to produce a bibliography, then this should come just before the `\end{document}` command (if you want it to be the last thing in the output document). Note that the `thebibliography` environment generates the section heading 'References' automatically (without any number being attached to it).

8.1.3 Title, Author and Date

The title is produced by the `\maketitle` command which, if it occurs at all in the input file, must be placed within the `document` environment. If the `\maketitle` command is used, then it has to be preceded by both `\title` and `\author` declarations. Optionally, it may also be preceded by a `\date` declaration; if this is omitted, then the current date is used. This appears, for example, as 'February 24, 1992'. Note that by default the title does *not* appear on a page by itself; if you do want the title, author and date information to be placed on a page all by itself, then choose the `titlepage` option to the `\documentclass` command. (This also makes the abstract, if one is present, appear on a separate page as well.)

The title itself occurs as an argument to the `\title` declaration. You can use the `\\` command within the argument to the `\title` declaration in order to force a line break. One or more `\thanks` commands can also appear within the argument to the `\title` declaration. These produce footnotes. Unlike normal footnotes, the markers produced are regarded as having zero width. This produces better looking output when the footnote marker is placed at the end of a line. If a `\thanks` command does not end a line, then it should be followed by a `\␣` command in order to insert some inter-word space.

The author or authors of the article occur as the argument to the `\author` declaration. If more than one author is included, then they should be separated by `\and` commands. Just as in the case of the `\title` declaration, you can use `\\` to force the end of a line and footnotes can be produced using the `\thanks` command.

The optional `\date` declaration can be used to produce a date of your choice (or, in fact, any other information). If this declaration is omitted, then the date on which you ran LaTeX on your input file is used as the date. Just as in the case of the `\title` declaration, you can use `\\` to force the end of a line and footnotes can be produced using the `\thanks` command.

A maximum of nine `\thanks` commands can occur in the arguments of the `\title`, `\author` and `\date` declarations. The footnotes produced are not indicated by numerical footnote marks, but by the following symbols *, †, ‡, §, ¶, ‖, **, †† and ‡‡.

8.1.4 Abstract

If you wish your document to have an abstract, then include this in an `abstract` environment. This should come within the `document` environment of your input file and usually the best place for it is just after the `\maketitle` command. Note that by default the first line of the abstract produced is indented. This paragraph indentation can be suppressed by using a `\noindent` command. By default the abstract produced

sectioning command	level number	in table of contents	numb- ered
\part	0	yes	yes
\section	1	yes	yes
\subsection	2	yes	yes
\subsubsection	3	yes	yes
\paragraph	4	no	no
\subparagraph	5	no	no

Table 8.1: Sectioning commands in the `article` document class.

does *not* appear on a page by itself, but by choosing the `titlepage` option to the \documentclass command you can force it to appear on a page by itself. An example of the use and placement of the `abstract` environment is shown in Fig. 8.1 on p. 84 above. The heading 'Abstract' is produced automatically. This appears in bold above the text of the abstract and it is centred horizontally. If you want a different heading to appear, then redefine the \abstractname command.

8.1.5 Sectioning Commands

The sectioning commands that are available in the `article` document class are \part, \section, \subsection, \subsubsection, \paragraph and \subparagraph. Associated with each sectioning command is a level number and this is used to determine whether or not the *heading* associated with a sectioning command occurs in the table of contents (if there is one) and whether or not the *heading* associated with the sectioning command that appears in the final document is numbered or not. (The level numbers for all the sectioning commands available in the `article` document class are shown in Table 8.1.) There are two counters that control these things, namely `tocdepth` and `secnumdepth`. All headings of sectional units with level numbers less than or equal to the value of the counter `tocdepth` will appear in the table of contents (if there is one) and all sectional units with level numbers less than or equal to the value of the `secnumdepth` counter are numbered. By default the value of both `tocdepth` and `secnumdepth` is 3 and the information in Table 8.1 relating to which sectioning commands are numbered and which headings appear in a table of contents applies to these default values.

You should not use a sectioning command with level number i (for $2 \le i \le 5$) if it is not preceded by a sectioning command with level number $i - 1$; though, of course, other sectioning commands with level number $i - 1$ may intervene as may arbitrary textual material and other LATEX commands. You can, however, use the \section command even if no \part command precedes it.

Associated with each sectioning command there is a counter whose name is the same as the name of its corresponding sectioning command except that it does not have an initial backslash character. For example, the counter associated with the

\section command is called section. At the start of an article all counters associated with sectioning commands are initialized to zero; they are incremented by their corresponding sectioning commands *before* the number of the section unit is produced. Sectioning commands with level number i (for $1 \leq i \leq 4$) reset all counters associated with sectioning commands with level numbers greater than i to zero when they are incremented. Note that this does not apply to \part; so, if the section before a \part command was numbered 8, then the first section following that occurrence of the \part command will be numbered 9.

The general format of the \section command is:

\section[*entry*]{*heading*}

(All sectioning commands behave in a similar fashion; so, although what I say here will be said about the \section command, it applies to all the sectioning commands.) If the optional argument *entry* is absent, then by default *heading* will appear in the table of contents if one is produced. If *entry* is present, then it will appear in the table of contents, but *heading* will appear in the document produced. If *entry* is present, then it is a moving argument; but if it is absent, *heading* is the moving argument. (For an explanation of what a moving argument is see section B.4.)

There is also a *-form of the \section command and it is often used in conjunction with an \addcontentsline command as follows:

\section*{*heading*}
\addcontentsline{toc}{section}{*heading*}

The effect of the \section* command is that the heading produced in the output document is neither numbered nor does it appear in the table of contents (if one is produced). The effect of the \addcontentsline command is to get the *heading* into the table of contents. (Note that it is section without an initial backslash that occurs as the second argument to the \addcontentsline command.) This combination of commands is used if you are producing a document with a table of contents in which sections are numbered but you want to include an unnumbered section such as a glossary or a single appendix.

The effect of an \appendix declaration is to alter the way in which sections are labelled. The first \section command following the \appendix declaration is labelled 'A', the next 'B', and so on. Note that the \appendix declaration does not take any arguments.

8.1.6   Labelling of Formulas, Figures and Tables

If you use the equation and eqnarray environments to generate equation numbers, then they are numbered consecutively throughout the output document starting at 1. If any figures occur in your document, they are numbered consecutively throughout the output document starting at 1. If any tables occur in your document, they are numbered consecutively throughout the output document starting at 1. Note that there can be an equation, a figure and a table all numbered 1, etc.

8.1.7   Running Heads

To begin with in this section I am assuming that the `twoside` document-class option has not been chosen as it complicates matters still further. As already mentioned the default page style for the `article` document class is `plain`, that is to say, it is as if the command `\pagestyle{plain}` had been included in the preamble of your input file. The effect of this is that the head region is empty and the foot region only contains the page number and that is centred.

If you want the head and foot regions to be empty throughout the output document, then you need to include the command `\pagestyle{empty}` in the preamble of your input file and you *also* need to include the command `\thispagestyle{empty}` in your input file inside the `document` environment and near to the beginning of that environment so that it is in force when LaTeX outputs the first page of your document.

If you choose the `headings` page style, that is to say, if you include the command `\pagestyle{headings}` in the preamble of your input file, then running heads are produced in the head region of the page. Normally, a running head will consist of a section number and heading, in that order and all in uppercase slanted type, starting at the left-hand edge of the head region and the page number in roman type flush right in the head region. If you have altered the value of the counter `secnumdepth` so that sections are not numbered, then neither will the section number appear in the running head; and if you have used the *-form of the `\section` command, then the *heading* argument will not appear in the head region.

If you want to put your own words into the running head, then you need to choose the `myheadings` option to the `\pagestyle` command and then you can use the `\markright{`*text*`}` command in the preamble to place *text* into the running head on all pages (except the first).

If you choose the `twoside` option to the `\documentclass` command and include the command `\pagestyle{headings}` in the preamble of your input file, then the running head on odd-numbered (right-handed) pages, except the first, will consist of the section and subsection numbers separated by a full stop and the subsection heading flush left in slanted type and the page number flush right in roman type; and on even-numbered (left-handed) pages the running head will consist of the page number flush left in roman type and flush right will appear the section number and heading in uppercase slanted type.

If you have altered the value of the counter `secnumdepth` so that either sections or subsections are not numbered, then neither will the suppressed number or numbers appear in the running head; and if you have used the *-form of either the `\section` or the `\subsection` command, then the corresponding *heading* will not appear in the running head.

If you want to put your own words into the running heads, then you need to choose the `myheadings` option to the `\pagestyle` command and then you can use the `\markboth{`*text₁*`}{`*text₂*`}` command to place *text₁* into the running head on even-numbered pages and *text₂* into the running head on odd-numbered pages.

8.2 The report Document Class

8.2.1 Introduction

The standard options to the report document class are as follows: at most one of 10pt (the default), 11pt or 12pt; at most one of letterpaper (the default), legalpaper, executivepaper, a4paper, a5paper or b5paper; at most one of final (the default) or draft; at most one of oneside (the default) or twoside; at most one of onecolumn (the default) or twocolumn; at most one of openright or openany (the default); and at most one of notitlepage or titlepage (the default). Furthermore, any or none of the following can occur in the argument *opt-list* of the \documentclass command: landscape, openbib, leqno and fleqn.

The report document class is similar to the article one in that most of the defaults are the same; one of the main differences is that the \chapter sectioning command is available. By default the output is formatted in the one-sided manner, but this can be altered by means of the twoside option to the \documentclass command. The default page style is plain, that is to say, the head is empty and the page number appears in the centre of the foot. If the headings page style is used, then the head contains the chapter name and page number, unless the twoside document class option has been used, when the head contains the chapter name and page number on even pages and the section name and page number on odd pages. This can be altered by using the myheadings option and associated commands.

If the \flushbottom declaration is included, then the height of the text on each output page will be the same—vertical blank space being added where necessary—but the default is as if the \raggedbottom declaration had been included. This allows the height of the text in the output to vary slightly from page to page. (If the twoside option is included, then the default becomes the \flushbottom declaration.) If the \maketitle command is present, usually just after the beginning of the document environment, then a separate title page is generated. As in the case of articles it has to be preceded by both \author and \title declarations and may be preceded by a \date declaration; \thanks commands can occur in the arguments of these as explained in subsection 8.1.3 above. If you wish to include an abstract, then the abstract environment should follow soon after the \maketitle command. The abstract will appear on a separate page.

Parts have a level number of -1 and chapters one of 0. The default value of the counter secnumdepth is 2. This means that all sectional units with level numbers less than or equal to 2 are numbered, that is to say, subsections and larger units. The default value of the counter tocdepth is 2. This means that all sectional units with level numbers less than or equal to 2 appear in the table of contents if there is one, that is to say, subsections and larger units. This information is summarized in Table 8.2. If the chapter before the \part command was 8, then the chapter number following it will be 9.

If you use the equation and eqnarray environments to generate equation numbers, then they are numbered consecutively throughout each chapter beginning with $X.1$, where X is the number of the chapter, and continuing with $X.2$, and so on. If any

sectioning command	level number	in table of contents	numb-ered
\part	−1	yes	yes
\chapter	0	yes	yes
\section	1	yes	yes
\subsection	2	yes	yes
\subsubsection	3	no	no
\paragraph	4	no	no
\subparagraph	5	no	no

Table 8.2: Sectioning commands in the **book** and **report** document classes.

figures occur in your document, they are numbered consecutively throughout each chapter beginning with $X.1$, where X is the number of the chapter, and continuing with $X.2$, and so on. If any tables occur in your document, they are numbered consecutively throughout each chapter beginning with $X.1$, where X is the number of the chapter, and continuing with $X.2$, and so on. Note that there can be an equation, a figure and a table all numbered $X.1$, etc. Note also that if an **equation** or **eqnarray** environment, figure or table occurs before any \chapter command, then X will be 0.

The effect of an \appendix declaration is to alter the way in which chapters are labelled. The first \chapter command following the \appendix declaration is labelled 'A', the next 'B', and so on. If your input file contains a **thebibliography** environment, then the chapter heading 'Bibliography' is generated (without any number being attached to it). If you want a different heading to appear, then redefine the \bibname command.

8.2.2 Root and Data Files

The **report** document class is usually used for quite lengthy documents and when working on such a document it is a good idea to split the input file into a number of separate input files. There are, no doubt, several ways in which this can be done, but the method presented is one that I have arrived at after several years of experimentation.

Imagine that you are toying with the idea of writing a book on logic and initially think that this will consist of six chapters; for each chapter you need a *root* and a *data* file. For example, in the case of Chapter 1 the root file could be called root01a.tex and the data file data01a.tex. The reason for using 01 as part of the base name rather than just simply 1 is that if you decide to have more than nine chapters and use an operating system that lists your files alphabetically, then using 01, etc., will result in, for example, root09a.tex being followed by root10a.tex; the reason for including the letter a as part of the base name is that sometimes you may want to split a large chapter into several input files and the root files for these could be called, for example, root01a.tex, root01b.tex, and so on, and the corresponding data files would then

```
%
% Your own definitions
% go here, where
% they are safe.
%
%
```

own.sty

```
\include{data01a}
\include{data02a}
\include{data03a}
\include{data04a}
\include{data05a}
\include{data06a}
```

common.tex

```
\documentclass{report}
\usepackage{own}
\includeonly{data01a}
\begin{document}
\input{common}
\end{document}
```

root01a.tex

```
\chapter{Introduction}
\typeout{Introduction}
%
To be written.
```

data01a.tex

$\vdots$

$\vdots$

```
\documentclass{report}
\usepackage{own}
\includeonly{data06a}
\begin{document}
\input{common}
\end{document}
```

root06a.tex

```
\chapter{Graph Proofs}
\typeout{Graph Proofs}
%
To be written.
```

data06a.tex

Figure 8.2: Splitting the input file.

be `data01a.tex`, `data01b.tex`, and so on.

The possible contents of six root and six data files are shown in Fig. 8.2; be careful not to include an `\end{document}` in any data file. The commands `\input`, `\include` and `\includeonly` are LaTeX's mechanism for allowing the input of a document to be split across several files. The `\include{`*file*`}` command is used in conjunction with

\includeonly{*file-list*} for producing only part of a large document whose content has been split into several input files. Note that the result of processing *file* will, if it appears at all, always start on a new page and it will terminate as if a \clearpage command had been included at the end of *file*.tex. The \includeonly{*file-list*} command can only occur in the preamble of your input file. The argument *file-list* is a list of zero or more extensionless filenames. If two or more are present, then they are separated by commas. (An item *file* in *file-list* refers to *file*.tex.) If *file* occurs in *file-list*, then the command \include{*file*} does not have to occur in the body of the input file. Only the text contained in a *file* that appears in *file-list* occurs in the output produced by LATEX, but that input is processed as if all the files had been processed as well and so, for example, cross-references between files work correctly. The \input{*file*} has the same effect as if the contents of the file *file* were present in this part of the input file. If *file* has no extension, then the file *file*.tex is included.

If you do decide to use this method for splitting a large document into several input files, then it is almost essential to have your own personal package as at least one command *has* to go there (if it is used at all), namely the \newcounter command. In any case, it is a very good idea to put all your definitions and declarations in a personal package, such as things like declarations that alter the size of the body region and definitions of your own commands and environments.

In order to get dvi files from the set-up described you need to run LATEX on each of the root files. It is most sensible to process the root files in chapter order beginning with root01a.tex. One of the minor drawbacks of this way of splitting your input is that you will need to process each root file at least *three* times in order to get any cross-referencing information correct.

When the work you are writing is nearing completion, you will need to produce a title page, a table of contents and other similar things for it. The easiest way to do this would be to create root00a.tex and data00a.tex files as shown in Fig. 8.3. You would then process the file root00a.tex at least twice in order to produce the additional material. The meanings of the commands in root00a.tex that have not been explained already are as follows:

\nofiles When LATEX is run a number of additional files are or may be created, namely the aux, glo, idx, lof, lot and toc files. (For example, if your original file is called *file*.tex, then the auxilary file is called *file*.aux.) If you include the \nofiles declaration in the preamble of your input file, the only place it can occur, then none of these additional files are written to. In particular, if any of them already exist, then they are not overwritten.

\makeindex This command can only occur in the preamble of an input file. It causes an idx file to be written or overwritten which contains the \indexentry commands generated by any \index commands that appear in your input file. A \nofiles declaration in the preamble suppresses the writing (or overwriting) of the idx file.

\pagenumbering{*num-style*} This global declaration specifies how page numbers will appear. The parameter *num-style* can be either arabic (for Arabic numerals),

```
\documentclass{report}
\usepackage{own}
\title{Logic}
\author{Antoni Diller}
\includeonly{data00a}
% \nofiles
\makeindex
\begin{document}
\pagenumbering{roman}
\maketitle
\tableofcontents
\listoffigures
\listoftables
\include{data00a}
\pagenumbering{arabic}
\input{common}
\end{document}
```

```
\chapter*{Preface}
\typeout{Preface}
\addcontentsline{toc}
{chapter}{Preface}
%
To be written.
%
\chapter*
{Acknowledgements}
\typeout
{Acknowledgements}
\addcontentsline{toc}
{chapter}
{Acknowledgements}
%
To be written.
%
```

root00a.tex

data00a.tex

Figure 8.3: The root00a.tex and data00a.tex files.

roman (for lowercase Roman numerals), Roman (for uppercase Roman numerals), alph (for lowercase letters) and Alph (for uppercase letters). The default value is arabic. (Note that the \pagenumbering global declaration redefines \thepage to be *num-style*{page}.)

\tableofcontents This command produces a table of contents at the place in the input file where it occurs. You need to run LaTeX at least twice to get a correct table of contents. It causes a toc file to be written or overwritten except if you have included a \nofiles command.

\listoffigures This command produces a list of figures at the place in the input file where it occurs. You need to run LaTeX at least twice to get a correct list of figures. It causes a lof file to be written or overwritten except if you have included a \nofiles command.

\listoftables This command produces a list of tables at the place in the input file where it occurs. You need to run LaTeX at least twice to get a correct list of tables. A new lot file is produced unless you include a \nofiles command.

There are no problems involved in combining this way of splitting your input file into several files with using either the thebibliography environment or BibTeX to produce a bibliography. If you want to use the `thebibliography` environment, then you just put it at the end of the data files, usually a bibliography comes just before the index, and that is all you have to do; `\cite` commands can occur in any data file. As usual, you will have to process all the root files at least twice, and maybe more times, in order to get the references correct.

Say you want to use B$_{\text{IB}}$T$_{\text{E}}$X to produce a bibliography and you have decided to make `data06a.tex` into the bibliography. You need to put a `\bibliographystyle` command in `root06.tex`; this goes inside the `document` environment before the `\input{common}` command. Furthermore, you need to put a `\bibliography` command in `data06a.tex`. If you are going to use `data06a.tex` as the bibliography, then you should make sure that it contains no `\chapter` or other sectioning commands. (I usually put my bibliography in a file called `data88a.tex` and the index in `data99a.tex`.) Note that you only need to run B$_{\text{IB}}$T$_{\text{E}}$X on the root file corresponding to the data file that contains the `\bibliography` command; after you have done that you still need to run L^{A}T$_{\text{E}}$X on all the root files at least two more times, that is to say, including the root file corresponding to the data file that contains the `\bibliography` command.

8.3　The `book` Document Class

The standard options to the `book` document class are as follows: at most one of `10pt` (the default), `11pt` or `12pt`; at most one of `letterpaper` (the default), `legalpaper`, `executivepaper`, `a4paper`, `a5paper` or `b5paper`; at most one of `final` (the default) or `draft`; at most one of `oneside` or `twoside` (the default); at most one of `onecolumn` (the default) or `twocolumn`; at most one of `openright` (the default) or `openany`; and at most one of `notitlepage` or `titlepage` (the default). Furthermore, any or none of the following can occur in *opt-list*: `landscape`, `openbib`, `leqno` and `fleqn`.

The `book` document class is almost the same as the `report` one, except that several of the defaults are different. The `twoside` option to the `\documentclass` command is the default and this formats the output in a form suitable for printing on both sides of a page. The default page style is `headings`, that is to say, the head contains the chapter name and page number on even pages and the section name and page number on odd pages. This can be altered by using the `myheadings` option and associated commands or by using the `plain` or `empty` options to the `\pagestyle` command.

If the `\raggedbottom` declaration is used, then the height of the text on each output page may vary slightly from page to page. The default, however, is the `\flushbottom` declaration which means that the height of the text on all pages is the same. If the `\maketitle` command is present, usually just after the beginning of the `document` environment, then a separate title page is generated. As in the case of articles it has to be preceded by both `\author` and `\title` declarations and may be preceded by a `\date` declaration; `\thanks` commands can occur in the arguments of these as explained in section 8.1.3 above. The `abstract` environment cannot be used in a `book`.

Level numbers of sectional units are the same as for the `report` option and are shown in Table 8.2 on p. 90; in particular, parts have a level number of -1 and chapters one of 0. If the chapter before the \part command was 8, then the chapter number following it will be 9. Because two-sided printing is the default each chapter will start on an odd-numbered page; this may result in a blank page being placed before new chapters. Furthermore, if you use the \part{*heading*} command, then the argument *heading* will always appear on an odd-numbered page; this may result in additional blank pages being placed immediately before and immediately after that page. The default value of the counter secnumdepth is 2. This means that all sectional units with level numbers less than or equal to 2 are numbered, that is to say, subsections and larger units. The default value of the counter tocdepth is 2. This means that all sectional units with level numbers less than or equal to 2 appear in the table of contents if there is one, that is to say, subsections and larger units. This information is summarized in Table 8.2.

If you use the equation and eqnarray environments to generate equation numbers, then they are numbered consecutively throughout each chapter beginning with $X.1$, where X is the number of the chapter, and continuing with $X.2$, and so on. If any figures occur in your document, they are numbered consecutively throughout each chapter beginning with $X.1$, where X is the number of the chapter, and continuing with $X.2$, and so on. If any tables occur in your document, they are numbered consecutively throughout each chapter beginning with $X.1$, where X is the number of the chapter, and continuing with $X.2$, and so on. Note that there can be an equation, a figure and a table all numbered $X.1$, etc. Note also that if an equation, eqnarray, figure or table environment occurs before any \chapter command, then X will be 0.

The effect of an \appendix declaration is to alter the way in which chapters are labelled. The first \chapter command following the \appendix declaration is labelled 'A', the next 'B', and so on.

The commands \frontmatter, \mainmatter and \backmatter are available in the book document class in order to help you with the large-scale organization of a book. The \frontmatter command causes pages to be numbered with lowercase Roman numerals and it redefines the \chapter command so that it does not produce a chapter number but the heading is included in the table of contents (if produced). The \mainmatter command resets the page counter and causes pages to be numbered with arabic numerals. The \backmatter command redefines the \chapter command so that it does not produce a chapter number but the heading is included in the table of contents (if produced).

8.4   The letter Document Class

The standard options to the letter document class are as follows: at most one of 10pt (the default), 11pt or 12pt; at most one of letterpaper (the default), legalpaper, executivepaper, a4paper, a5paper or b5paper; at most one of final (the default) or draft; and at most one of oneside (the default) or twoside. Furthermore, any or none of the following can occur in *opt-list*: landscape, leqno and fleqn.

The letter displayed in Fig. 8.4 was produced by means of the commands shown in Fig. 8.5. Note that the sample output shown in Fig. 8.4 only gives a rough idea of

27 Hudson Street,
Athens,
Wessex,
A26 7YY.

July 10, 1998

Dr Albert Grovenor,
'Appleblossom',
Whittington Green,
Hemlock.

Dear Albert,

Thank you very much for your letter of 30 June 1998 and the enclosed specimen. I carried out a full analysis—as you requested—but the results were so extraordinary that I can only give them to you in person.

Yours sincerely,

James Holmes

PS: I will be away on holiday until the 22nd.
cc: Mrs Dickens
  Prof. Cooper

Figure 8.4: Example of a letter formatted by LaTeX.

```
\documentclass[11pt]{letter}
\address{27 Hudson Street,\\
         Athens,\\
         Wessex,\\
         A26 7YY.}
\signature{James Holmes}
\begin{document}
%
\begin{letter}{Dr Albert Grovenor,\\
               'Appleblossom',\\
               Whittington Green,\\
               Hemlock.}
\opening{Dear Albert,}
Thank you very much for your letter of 30 June 1998 and the
enclosed specimen.  I carried out a full analysis---as you
requested---but the results were so extraordinary that I can
only give them to you in person.
\closing{Yours sincerely,}
\ps{PS: I will be away on holiday until the 22nd.}
\cc{Mrs Dickens \\ Prof.~Cooper}
\end{letter}
%
\end{document}
```

Figure 8.5: Example of a use of the letter environment.

what letters produced by LaTeX look like as it is not 'drawn' to scale; the positioning of the various units of the letter on the page is only an approximation of what appears on the actual LaTeX output.

In order to get LaTeX to format letters you have to choose the letter document class. The address of the letter's sender is declared in the preamble by means of the \address command and the sender's name is declared there by means of the \signature command; end-of-line commands can occur in the arguments of both of these declarations. You can, but do not have to, use a \date command in the preamble to declare a date; if you do not do so, then LaTeX automatically inserts into the output the date on which you processed your input file.

Inside the document environment each letter is produced by means of one letter environment. You can include several letter environments within the document environment of a single LaTeX input file. The name and address of the recipient of the letter is added as an argument to the command which opens the letter environment. The greeting is produced by the \opening command and the salutation by the \closing command. A postscript is produced by the \ps command and carbon copies are indicated by \cc. Enclosures can be indicated by the \encl command. Note that the \cc and \encl commands produce 'cc:' and 'encl:' in the final document, but the \ps command does not produce 'PS'.

Inside the letter environment most commands are available; though some, like the sectioning commands, which make no sense in a letter cannot be used. Note that paragraphs are not indented, but rather extra space is inserted between them.

The \makelabels command takes no arguments and has to be placed in the preamble of the input file (if it is used at all). It causes a list of all the recipient addresses to be produced on a new page following all the letters generated. These can be photocopied onto sticky labels, if so desired, or cut up and glued or sellotaped onto envelopes.

8.5   The slides Document Class

The slides document class can be used for producing the foils that are placed on an overhead projector. (The way to do this is to use LaTeX to produce paper versions of the slides and than photocopy these onto foils.) The standard options to the slides document class are as follows: at most one of letterpaper (the default), legalpaper, executivepaper, a4paper, a5paper or b5paper; at most one of final (the default) or draft; and at most one of notitlepage or titlepage (the default). Furthermore, any or none of the following can occur in *opt-list*: landscape, leqno, fleqn and clock. Note also that onecolumn can occur in *opt-list*, but twocolumn cannot.

Three environments are provided in order to produce slides, namely slide, overlay and note. The slide environment is used to produce a single slide. The first occurrence of this environment produces a slide numbered 1; the second occurrence produces a slide numbered 2; and so on. The overlay environment produces a slide that is meant to be placed over another one. If this environment follows a slide environment without any other overlay environments intervening, then the slide produced is numbered i–a, where i is the number of the slide produced by that slide environment. You can place several overlay environments between any two slide environments. The second one will be numbered i–b; the third i–c; and so on. The note environment produces a one-page note. The first note environment following a slide environment, which produced the slide numbered i, is numbered i–1; the second is numbered i–2; and so on.

The local declarations \invisible and \visible are available inside the three environments mentioned above. The \invisible declaration makes everything in its scope invisible and the \visible declaration makes everything in its scope visible.

The preamble commands \onlyslides and \onlynotes are available if you want to produce only some of the slides or only some of the notes from an input file. The command \onlyslides{*num-list*} has the effect that only the slides included in *num-list* will be produced. The argument *num-list* is a list of numerals or ranges, separated by commas, in ascending numerical order. For example, \onlyslides{2, 5, 8-11, 20} produces the slides indicated. The \onlynotes{*num-list*} command has the effect that only the notes to the slides included in *num-list* will be produced. The argument *num-list* is a list of numerals or ranges, separated by commas, in ascending numerical order. For example, \onlynotes{2, 5, 8-11, 20} produces the notes to the slides indicated.

If you use the clock document-class option, then the commands \settime and \addtime can be used to help you determine the length of a lecture or presentation that you intend to make. Neither of these two commands can occur inside any of the three environments unique to the slides document class and both of them take a single argument which is a non-negative whole number. This number represents a time in seconds. The \settime command assigns a value to an internal 'clock' and the \addtime command adds a number of seconds to this internal 'clock'. When you use the note environment, the time taken up to that point, in minutes, will be included in the note produced and the total time will be output on your terminal as you process your input file using LaTeX. Note that the time taken is rounded down to the nearest whole minute, so that 179 seconds, for example, is output as 2 minutes.

Chapter 9

Basic Mathematical Formatting

9.1 Introduction

As already mentioned, TEX was commissioned by the American Mathematical Society and one of its great strengths is its ability to correctly typeset mathematical formulas. When using TEX or LATEX to produce mathematical formulas you must never forget that the mathematics you write should be correctly punctuated. This is well expressed in Hart (1983), pp. 56–57:

> A mathematical formula or equation, whether occurring in the text or displayed, should be regarded as in every way an integral part of the sentence in which it occurs, and be punctuated accordingly. Thus, individual formulae may be separated by commas, groups by semicolons, and where a formula occurs at the end of a sentence it should be followed by a full point.

Most people naturally punctuate in-text mathematical formulas correctly; but many people when they first start using TEX or LATEX fail to correctly punctuate displayed formulas. These should be followed by a comma, semicolon or full stop as appropriate. For example, if you want to include the following formula in a document that you are writing:

$$\frac{d}{dx} \sinh^{-1} u = \frac{1}{\sqrt{u^2 + 1}} \frac{du}{dx},$$

then you must not forget the comma (or other appropriate punctuation mark) at the end. This displayed formula was produced by the following commands:

```
\[\frac{d}{dx} \sinh^{-1} u =
    \frac{1}{\sqrt{u^2 + 1}}\frac{du}{dx},\]
```

(The command \frac{*form*$_1$}{*form*$_2$} produces a fraction with numerator *form*$_1$ and denominator *form*$_2$, the command \sinh produces the unary function symbol 'sinh', the special character ^ produces superscripts and \sqrt{*form*} puts a square-root sign around *form*.) You should notice two things particularly about these commands. The first is that the comma that comes at the end of the mathematical formula is followed by the command \] that ends the environment used for displaying mathematical formulas. It would be wrong to put the comma *after* that command, because then the comma would not appear in the correct place. When typing in-text formulas, however, punctuation marks should come *after* the closing single dollar sign in order to ensure that the output looks correct.

The second thing that you should notice is that I did *not* punctuate the displayed LaTeX commands. This is because you, dear reader, may have thought that any punctuation mark used was part of the LaTeX input. If I had followed the LaTeX commands above with a full stop, then you might have thought that that full stop was part of the input you had to type in order to get LaTeX to produce the mathematical formula displayed above. The rule about punctuating *mathematical* formulas correctly does not apply to displayed material when there is a real possibility that any punctuation marks may be confused with the material being displayed. Thus, the rule does not apply to displayed computer programs or program fragments when it might not be obvious whether the punctuation mark involved is part of the program fragment being displayed or whether it is part of the sentence in whose scope the program fragment occurs. Similar considerations also apply to displayed chemical formulas.

9.2   Decorating Expressions

9.2.1   Introduction

People who use mathematical notation a lot like to decorate the symbols that they use in a variety of ways. In this section I explain how to get TeX to produce various kinds of accents, how to get it to underline and overline expressions and how to get it to produce subscripts, superscripts and limits. The simplest kind of decoration is the prime and to produce the primed version of a symbol you simply follow it with a single closing quotation mark; thus x' produces x'. This can be iterated; thus, to get the doubly primed expression x'' you need the input x''.

9.2.2   Accents

It is common in mathematical writing to decorate symbols, especially variables, with various sorts of accents. If you want TeX to produce, for example, the decorated symbol $\ddot{z}$, then you need to include in your input file the command $\ddot{z}$. TeX provides the following accents in maths mode:

output	input	output	input
$\acute{a}$	\acute{a}	$\dot{f}$	\dot{f}
$\bar{b}$	\bar{b}	$\grave{g}$	\grave{g}
$\breve{c}$	\breve{c}	$\hat{h}$	\hat{h}
$\check{d}$	\check{d}	$\tilde{\imath}$	\tilde\imath
$\ddot{e}$	\ddot{e}	$\vec{\jmath}$	\vec\jmath

This table also illustrates the use of the commands \imath and \jmath to produce a dotless letter 'i' and a dotless letter 'j', respectively, in maths mode. You should use these if you want to decorate either letter with an accent. (There are different TeX commands for producing accents over letters outside maths mode and these are explained on p. 21 above.)

All the above accents come in a single size and if you put any of them around an expression consisting of more than a single symbol, then TeX just centres the accent over the whole expression. Thus, the input $\tilde{x + y} = \hat{y + x}$ produces $\tilde{x + y} = \hat{y + x}$. However, TeX has two commands that produce accents that grow depending on the size of the expression that they decorate. These commands are \widehat and \widetilde and they each produce accents in three sizes:

output	input	output	input
$\widehat{k}$	\widehat{k}	$\widetilde{q}$	\widetilde{q}
$\widehat{lm}$	\widehat{lm}	$\widetilde{rs}$	\widetilde{rs}
$\widehat{nop}$	\widehat{nop}	$\widetilde{tuv}$	\widetilde{tuv}

Note that the commands \widehat and \widetilde do not produce accents of arbitrary size; they only produce the three sizes shown.

9.2.3 Underlining, Overlining and Related Decorations

TeX has a variety of methods of decorating expressions of any size. They are illustrated in the following table:

output	input
$\overline{\phi \land \psi}$	\overline{\phi \land \psi}
$\underline{\phi \land \psi}$	\underline{\phi \land \psi}
$\overrightarrow{\phi \land \psi}$	\overrightarrow{\phi \land \psi}
$\overleftarrow{\phi \land \psi}$	\overleftarrow{\phi \land \psi}
$\overbrace{\phi \land \psi}$	\overbrace{\phi \land \psi}
$\underbrace{\phi \land \psi}$	\underbrace{\phi \land \psi}

The command \underline can be used in any mode; the others can only be used in maths mode.

9.2.4   Subscripts and Superscripts

To produce a subscripted expression like x_i you include in your input file `$x_i$`. Braces are used to enclose an expression made up of several symbols that is to appear as a subscript. If no opening brace immediately follows the underline character, then only the next symbol is made into the subscript. Thus, `$x_\gamma,\delta$` produces x_γ, δ whereas `$x_{\gamma,\delta}$` produces $x_{\gamma,\delta}$. Superscripts are produced by the hat symbol `^`. Thus, `$x^3$` produces x^3. With suitable changes, what was said above concerning subscripts also holds for superscripts.

Formulas sometimes have both subscripts and superscripts. To get x_i^3 you need to put in your input file either `$x_i^3$` or `$x^3_i$`. When TeX produces a symbol which has both a subscript and a superscript the superscript is usually vertically above the subscript as in Γ_j^2 but this does not always happen. For example, in Γ_j^2 the subscript and superscript are not aligned vertically. In order to get such vertical alignment you need to type `$\mathit{\Gamma}{}_j^2$` which produces Γ_j^2. (The command `\mathit{text}` causes any letters, numerals or uppercase Greek letters that occur in *text* to be typeset in the italic style. If you have loaded the `amsmath` package, however, then any uppercase Greek letters occurring in the argument *text* are not typeset in the italic style. To get the italic uppercase Greek letters that are different from the corresponding upright ones when you are using `amsmath` you need the commands `\varGamma`, `\varDelta`, `\varTheta`, `\varLambda`, `\varXi`, `\varPi`, `\varSigma` `\varUpsilon`, `\varPhi`, `\varPsi` and `\varOmega`.)

The subscripts and superscripts that you attach to symbols can themselves have subscripts and superscripts. Thus, `$7^{x_i}$` produces 7^{x_i} and `$\Delta_{x^\ast}$` produces $\Delta_{x^\ast}$. Note that the symbols used for subscripts and superscripts are smaller that those used for in-text and displayed formulas. This holds for most symbols and not just for letters and numerals. Note, for example, the size of the two plus signs and the parentheses in the expression $(x + y)^{(x+y)}$. (Note also that the amount of space either side of the two plus signs is different.) If a subscript or superscript itself has a subscript or superscript, then that appears even smaller in the output; but additional subscripts or superscripts do not get smaller: TeX has just three different sizes of type available for typesetting mathematical formulas.

In addition, TeX has eight different ways in which it can typeset mathematics. These are known as *styles* and they are the normal and cramped versions of display, text, script and scriptscript style. The cramped versions are used for the denominators of fractions, expressions in square-root signs and similar things; in these places superscripts are not raised so high. Most users of LaTeX can forget the difference between the normal and cramped versions of these typesetting styles and I say very little about them in this book. Display style is used for formulas that do not appear in running text: text style is used for such formulas. Script style is used for first-order subscripts and superscripts and scriptscript style is used for higher-order subscripts and superscripts. To force TeX to use a different style than it would by default you can use the commands `\displaystyle`, `\textstyle`, `\scriptstyle` and `\scriptscriptstyle`. Thus,

`\[(x+y)^{\textstyle(x+y)}\]` produces

$$(x+y)^{(x+y)}.$$

Note that as well as using the same size of type for both the formula and superscript in this example the spacing around the plus signs is the same as well. In `\scriptstyle` and `\scriptscriptstyle` TEX has different rules to follow about spacing than in `\textstyle` and `\displaystyle`.

9.2.5 Combining Subscripts with \underbrace and \overbrace

A subscripted expression attached to the `\underbrace` command produces a label underneath it and a superscripted expression attached to the `\overbrace` command produces a label on top of it. For example, the following expression

$$\{ \overbrace{n \colon \mathbf{N}}^{\text{signature}} \underbrace{\mid \overbrace{n \ne 0 \land n \bmod 2 = 0}^{\text{formula}} \bullet \overbrace{n}^{\text{term}}}_{\text{set comprehension}} \},$$

(which is based on one that appears in Diller (1990), p. 28) was produced by the following commands:

```
\[\underbrace{\{
\overbrace{\mathstrut
  n \colon \mathbf{N}}^\mathrm{signature}
\mid
\overbrace{\mathstrut
  n \ne 0 \land n \bmod 2 = 0}^\mathrm{formula}
\bullet
\overbrace{\mathstrut n}^\mathrm{term}
\}}_\mathrm{set\ comprehension},\]
```

The plain TEX command `\mathstrut` produces an empty box in maths mode whose height is that of a parenthesis in the current type size; it is used here to ensure that the overbraces produced appear at the same height above the formulas over which they occur. The command `\mathbf{`*text*`}` causes any letters, numerals or uppercase Greek letters that occur in *text* to be typeset in the bold style and the command `\mathrm{`*text*`}` causes any letters, numerals or uppercase Greek letters that occur in *text* to be typeset in the Roman style. Note also the need for the command `\ ` in `\mathrm{set\ comprehension}`; this is needed because TEX is still in maths mode inside the braces and so spacing is done as it is usually done in maths mode.

9.2.6 Limits

Something that is quite common in some parts of mathematics is to place variables and more complicated expressions above and/or below other symbols. This happens, for example, in the following displayed formula:

$$\sum_{i=1}^{i=n} i^2 = \frac{n(n+1)(2n+1)}{6}.$$

Formulas like the $i=1$ and $i=n$ in this example I shall call *limits* for convenience. Limits are obtained using the same commands that produce subscripts and superscripts. Thus, the above formula was obtained by means of the following input:

```
\[\sum_{i = 1}^{i = n} i^2 = \frac{n (n + 1) (2n + 1)}{6}.\]
```

If I want to include the above formula as an in-text one, then I need to use these commands:

```
$\sum_{i = 1}^{i = n} i^2 = \frac{n (n + 1) (2n + 1)}{6}$.
```

The only things that have changed are that \[has been replaced by $ and \] by $ as well and the full stop has moved outside the closing single dollar sign whereas it was just before the command \] in the previous case. In-text the formula to find the sum of the first n positive whole numbers looks like this: $\sum_{i=1}^{i=n} i^2 = \frac{n(n+1)(2n+1)}{6}$. Note that the expression that was the limit above the summation sign in the displayed formula has become a superscript in the in-text formula and the expression that was the limit below the summation sign in the displayed formula has become a subscript in the in-text formula. A further difference is that the summation sign itself is smaller in the in-text formula than in the displayed formula. (Yet another difference is that the fraction has changed size as well.) There are a number of mathematical symbols that behave like this and a complete list can be found in section A.3.

In order to produce the following example of the differentiation of an integral:

$$\frac{d}{dx} \int_{\sin x}^{\cos x} e^t dt = \cos x e^{\sin x} + \sin x e^{\cos x},$$

you need to include the following commands in your input file:

```
\[\frac{d}{dx} \int_{\sin x}^{\cos x} e^t dt
= \cos x e^{\sin x} + \sin x e^{\cos x},\]
```

Some people may think that this formula looks better if the subscript and superscript to the integral sign appear as limits below and above it like this:

$$\frac{d}{dx} \int\limits_{\sin x}^{\cos x} e^t dt = \cos x e^{\sin x} + \sin x e^{\cos x}.$$

To obtain this the only change you need to make to the TeX commands displayed above is to replace \int_{\sin x}^{\cos x} with \int\limits_{\sin x}^{\cos x}. The command \limits, which comes *after* the command for the symbol that it is to act on, forces subscripted and superscripted expressions to appear as limits. It is most useful in display style but can also be used to force limits in text style. The related command \nolimits forces those expressions that would otherwise appear as upper limits to appear instead as subscripts and those expressions that would otherwise appear as lower limits to appear instead as superscripts. For example, the commands:

```
\[\sum\nolimits_{i = 1}^{i = n} i^3.\]
```

produce the following displayed formula:

$$\sum\nolimits_{i=1}^{i=n} i^3.$$

Both the commands \limits and \nolimits affect the placement of subscripts and superscripts in both display style and text style. There is also a \displaylimits command, however, which behaves like \limits in display style and \nolimits in text style.

9.3 Framing Formulas

Some people when writing a book or article like to put formulas or other sorts of information inside a frame. The following example of this is taken from Butkovskiy (1982), p. 51:

$$-\frac{d}{dx}\left[\tan x \cdot \frac{dQ(x)}{dx}\right] = f(x),$$

$$|Q(0)| < \infty, \qquad Q\left(\frac{\pi}{4}\right) = g_1, \qquad 0 \le x \le \frac{\pi}{4}.$$

This was produced by the following commands:

```
\newlength{\ii}
\setlength{\ii}{\textwidth}
\addtolength{\ii}{-2\fboxsep}
\addtolength{\ii}{-2\fboxrule}
\noindent
\fbox{%
\begin{minipage}{\ii}
\vspace{-\abovedisplayskip}
\[ - \frac{d}{dx}
\left[ \tan x \cdot \frac{dQ(x)}{dx} \right] = f(x), \]
\vspace{-\abovedisplayskip}
\[ \mathopen{\vert} Q(0) \mathclose{\vert} < \infty,\qquad
Q \left( \frac{\pi}{4} \right) = g_1,\qquad
0 \le x \le \frac{\pi}{4}. \]
\end{minipage}}
```

The purpose of the \newlength, \setlength and the two \addtolength commands is to ensure that the box produced with a frame around it is exactly as wide as the body of the page. The length parameter \textwidth contains the width of the body region and the length parameters \fboxsep and \fboxrule contain, respectively, the amount of space surrounding the box produced by processing the *text* argument of the \fbox command and the width of the line which makes up the frame. Note the presence of the \noindent command which ensures that the framed formulas are not indented and the comment character % following \fbox{ which ensures that no unnecessary space is inserted inside the framed box. If the first occurrence of the command \vspace{-\abovedisplayskip} was to be omitted, then there would be more space above the first formula in the box than there was below the last one. This is because the value of the rubber length parameter \abovedisplayskip is the additional amount of vertical space that is placed above a 'long' displayed formula. (See the entry in the glossary in Appendix C for more information.) Similarly, if the second occurrence of the command \vspace{-\abovedisplayskip} was to be omitted, then there would be too much space between the two groups of formulas.

9.4   Delimiters

A *delimiter* in TeX is a bracket-like symbol that can grow vertically and most delimiters do not have a maximum size. TeX has a large variety of delimiters. The following table shows the six basic types of delimiters that come in pairs:

output	input	name
(x, y)	`$(x, y)$`	parentheses
$\{x, y\}$	`$\{x, y\}$`	braces or
	`$\lbrace x, y\rbrace$`	curly brackets
$[x, y]$	`$[x, y]$`	brackets or
	`$\lbrack x, y\rbrack$`	square brackets
$\langle x, y\rangle$	`$\langle x, y\rangle$`	angle brackets
$\lceil x, y\rceil$	`$\lceil x, y\rceil$`	ceiling brackets
$\lfloor x, y\rfloor$	`$\lfloor x, y\rfloor$`	floor brackets

Note that angle brackets are *not* produced by the signs < and >. These produce the less-than and greater-than relation symbols. (There are contexts, however, where the signs < and > *can* take the place of the commands \langle and \rangle, respectively. They can do so, for example, following the commands \left and \right to be described below.) Braces are often used to represent sets when these are introduced either by enumeration or by abstraction as the following examples show:

$\{2, 3, 5, 7, 11\}$	`$\{2, 3, 5, 7, 11 \}$`
$\{x \mid x \le 100\}$	`$\{\, x \mid x \le 100 \, \}$`
$\{x : x \le 100\}$	`$\{\, x : x \le 100 \, \}$`

Note the presence of the command \, (which adds a thin amount of space) in the cases where sets are introduced by abstraction; this is the correct way of producing such expressions.

All the delimiters mentioned so far have—what Krieger and Schwarz (1989), p. 62, call—a *native size*; for example, typing \{ without qualification in maths mode (in either text or display style) will always produce an opening or left brace of the same size. Often in displayed mathematical formulas larger-sized delimiters are required. Not surprisingly, therefore, there is a mechanism in TeX for getting variable-sized delimiters in displayed formulas and its general format is:

$$\left cmd_1 \quad form \quad \right cmd_2$$

The arguments cmd_1 and cmd_2 must be commands that produce delimiters. What happens when TeX processes such a delimited expression is that, first, the formula *form* is processed and then delimiters of the correct size to fit around it are chosen automatically. For example, the commands:

```
\[\sum_{i = 1}^n i^3 = \left( \sum_{i = 1}^n i \right)^2.\]
```

produce the following displayed equation:

$$\sum_{i=1}^n i^3 = \left(\sum_{i=1}^n i \right)^2.$$

Note that both \left and \right have to be present, but a full stop can take the place of either cmd_1 or cmd_2 and that results in no output. The following example, from Morgan and Sanders (1989), p. 13, illustrates the use of the full stop to suppress the production of a delimiter:

$$\frac{xy^2}{2}\bigg|_{y=0}^{y=1} = \frac{x}{2},$$

```
\[\left. \frac{xy^2}{2}
\right\vert_{y=0}^{y=1}
= \frac{x}{2},\]
```

This example makes use of the command \vert. This and \Vert, when used by themselves, produce ordinary symbols, but when preceded by either \left or \right they become extensible delimiters. Similarly, the commands \uparrow, \Uparrow, \downarrow, \Downarrow, \updownarrow and \Updownarrow by themselves produce symbols for binary relations, but when preceded by either \left or \right they produce extensible delimiters.

The seven commands \lgroup, \rgroup, \lmoustache, \rmoustache, \arrowvert, \Arrowvert and \bracevert are different, however, in that they do not produce anything sensible when they occur by themselves, but they do produce extensible delimiters when preceded by either \left or \right.

Most of the delimiters known to TeX are shown in Table 9.1 and the commands that produce them are shown in Table 9.2. The local command \egarray used in Table 9.2 is defined as follows:

$$
\begin{pmatrix} 2 & 7 & 6 \\ 9 & 5 & 1 \\ 4 & 3 & 8 \end{pmatrix} \qquad \left\{ \begin{array}{ccc} 2 & 7 & 6 \\ 9 & 5 & 1 \\ 4 & 3 & 8 \end{array} \right\} \qquad \begin{bmatrix} 2 & 7 & 6 \\ 9 & 5 & 1 \\ 4 & 3 & 8 \end{bmatrix}
$$

$$
\left(\begin{array}{ccc} 2 & 7 & 6 \\ 9 & 5 & 1 \\ 4 & 3 & 8 \end{array} \right] \qquad \left[\begin{array}{ccc} 2 & 7 & 6 \\ 9 & 5 & 1 \\ 4 & 3 & 8 \end{array} \right| \qquad \left| \begin{array}{ccc} 2 & 7 & 6 \\ 9 & 5 & 1 \\ 4 & 3 & 8 \end{array} \right]
$$

$$
\left\uparrow \begin{array}{ccc} 2 & 7 & 6 \\ 9 & 5 & 1 \\ 4 & 3 & 8 \end{array} \right\Uparrow \qquad \left\Updownarrow \begin{array}{ccc} 2 & 7 & 6 \\ 9 & 5 & 1 \\ 4 & 3 & 8 \end{array} \right\Updownarrow \qquad \left| \begin{array}{ccc} 2 & 7 & 6 \\ 9 & 5 & 1 \\ 4 & 3 & 8 \end{array} \right\| \Downarrow
$$

$$
\left\{ \begin{array}{ccc} 2 & 7 & 6 \\ 9 & 5 & 1 \\ 4 & 3 & 8 \end{array} \right(\qquad \left\| \begin{array}{ccc} 2 & 7 & 6 \\ 9 & 5 & 1 \\ 4 & 3 & 8 \end{array} \right\| \qquad \left\| \begin{array}{ccc} 2 & 7 & 6 \\ 9 & 5 & 1 \\ 4 & 3 & 8 \end{array} \right\|
$$

Table 9.1: Delimiters in TeX (output).

```
\newcommand*{\egarray}{\begin{array}{ccc}
                2 & 7 & 6 \\
                9 & 5 & 1 \\
                4 & 3 & 8
                \end{array}}
```

The `array` environment that occurs in the definition of `\egarray` is explained in section 10.1 below.

The only delimiters not shown in Table 9.1 are those produced by the character / and the commands `\backslash`, `\langle`, `\rangle` and `\bracevert`. The first four of these are unusual in that they do have a maximum size. All 29 delimiters known to TeX and their most important properties are shown in Table 9.3. In the column headed 'commands' occur the various commands that produce delimiters in TeX. In the column headed 'kind' you will find the kind of symbol produced by the commands in the first column when they occur by themselves. In the three columns headed 'size' you can see whether or not the delimiters produced have a native size, a maximum size and a minimum size. The reason for the question mark in the 'native' column alongside `\arrowvert` and `\Arrowvert` is that, although Krieger and Schwarz (1989), pp. 61–62, say that the symbols produced by these two commands do not have a native size, they do produce sensible symbols when they occur by themselves in a formula.

Plain TeX also has a number of commands which increase the size of any delimiter they precede, namely `\big`, `\bigl`, `\bigm`, `\bigr`, `\Big`, `\Bigl`, `\Bigm`, `\Bigr`, `\bigg`,

```
\left(              \left\{              \left[
\egarray            \egarray             \egarray
\right)             \right\}             \right]



\left\lgroup        \left\lceil          \left\lfloor
\egarray            \egarray             \egarray
\right\rgroup       \right\rceil         \right\rfloor



\left\uparrow       \left\updownarrow    \left\downarrow
\egarray            \egarray             \egarray
\right\Uparrow      \right\Updownarrow   \right\Downarrow



\left\lmoustache    \left\arrowvert      \left\vert
\egarray            \egarray             \egarray
\right\rmoustache   \right\Arrowvert     \right\Vert
```

Table 9.2: Delimiters in TEX (input).

\biggl, \biggm, \biggr, \Bigg, \Biggl, \Biggm and \Biggr. Unlike \left and \right this \big family of commands always produces the same size of delimiter. If a bracket-like symbol has a native size, then a slightly larger opening or left version of that symbol can be produced by preceding it by the command \bigl and, similarly, a slightly larger closing or right version of that symbol can be produced by preceding it by the command \bigr. The following table illustrates these things with four of the commonest delimiters:

result	commands
$((x,y),(u,v))$	`$\bigl( (x, y), (u, v) \bigr)$`
$\{\{x,y\},\{u,v\}\}$	`$\bigl\{ \{x, y\}, \{u, v\}\bigr\}$`
$[[x,y],[u,v]]$	`$\bigl[ [x, y], [u, v] \bigr]$`
$\langle\langle x,y\rangle,\langle u,v\rangle\rangle$	`$\bigl< \langle x, y\rangle,`
	`\langle u, v\rangle \bigr>$`

The command \bigr[, for example, produces a right bracket slightly bigger than that produced by the symbol [by itself in maths mode. The command \Bigr[produces a right bracket 50% larger than \bigr[and \biggr[produces one two times the height of \bigr[and \Biggr[produces one two and a half times the size of \bigr[. Whereas \bigl*cmd* produces an opening symbol and \bigr*cmd* produces a closing symbol, \big*cmd* produces an ordinary symbol and \bigm*cmd* produces a relation

commands	kind	size		
		native	max	min
(, [, \{, \lfloor, \lceil	opening	yes	no	
\langle	opening	yes	yes	
),], \}, \rfloor, \rceil	closing	yes	no	
\rangle	closing	yes	yes	
/, \backslash	ordinary		yes	
\vert or |, \Vert or \\|	ordinary		no	
\uparrow, \Uparrow	relation		no	
\downarrow, \Downarrow	relation		no	
\updownarrow, \Updownarrow	relation		no	
\lgroup, \rgroup		no	no	\Big
\lmoustache, \rmoustache		no	no	\Big
\arrowvert, \Arrowvert		no?	no	
\bracevert		no	no	\big

Table 9.3: Properties of TEX's delimiters.

symbol (and this also applies to the other commands in this family). One situation in which you might want to produce a largish ordinary symbol occurs in the typesetting of some fractions. Sometimes the denominator and numerator of a fraction themselves consist of fractions. To produce such a fraction, for example, the following:

$$\frac{x+y}{x} \Big/ \frac{y}{x-y},$$

you need these commands

```
\[\frac{x+y}{x} \bigg/ \frac{y}{x-y},\]
```

One peculiarity of these commands is that they only work correctly when 10 point type is being used. In other words, \bigl\lceil, for example, will always produce the same size of opening ceiling bracket irrespective of the context in which it occurs and irrespective of the size of type being used. This family of commands is, however, redefined in the amsmath package so that they produce delimiters in increasing sizes no matter what size of type is being used.

9.5   Spacing in Mathematical Formulas

9.5.1   Introduction

If you look carefully at a mathematical formula like the following (which is taken from Ore (1988), p. 127):

$$x = 12 - 2y + t = 14 - 3t,$$

you will notice that the amount of space that occurs between a symbol for a binary relation (like the equals sign) and its operands is slightly larger than the amount of space that occurs between a symbol for a binary operation (like the plus sign) and its operands. In fact, TEX puts a thick amount of space between a symbol for a binary relation and its operands, if these are numerals or variables, and a medium amount of space between a symbol for a binary operation and its operands, again, if these are numerals or variables. A thick amount of space is normally five eighteenths of a quad and a medium amount of space is normally two ninths of a quad, where a quad is a horizontal amount of space one em wide. In the formula

$$\sin\theta = \sin(\theta + 2\pi)$$

TEX puts a thin amount of space, normally one sixth of a quad, between the function name 'sin' and its argument θ, but it puts no space between the function name and a following opening symbol.

In order to decide how much space to put between different sorts of symbol TEX partitions symbols into *kinds*; the most important of these are: ordinary symbols, unary operators, binary operators, binary relation symbols, opening symbols, closing symbols and punctuation marks. (Appendix A contains tables of symbols, arranged into their kinds, that are available in basic LaTEX and in the `latexsym` and `amssymb` packages.) For most users of LaTEX it is not important to know exactly how much space TEX puts after a closing symbol, say, when it is followed by a symbol for a binary operation. (If you do want to know, then look at the table in Knuth (1986a), p. 170.) It is useful, however, to know that mathematical symbols belonging to different kinds are treated differently by TEX. There are at least two reasons for this. The first is that there are a number of symbols which appear as if they belong to two different kinds. In TEX these would be produced by different commands. For example, both the commands `\mid` and `\vert` produce the symbol |, but `\mid` produces it as a symbol for a binary relation whereas `\vert` produces it as an ordinary symbol. If you use the wrong command, your output will not look right. The second reason for knowing that there are different kinds of symbol in TEX is if you are thinking of defining your own symbol for something. It is important that you define it as belonging to the correct kind for what it is supposed to do. (Information about how to define your own symbols can be found in Appendix A.)

As already mentioned, TEX can typeset formulas in eight different styles, namely the normal and cramped versions of display, text, script and scriptscript style. (The declarations `\displaystyle`, `\textstyle`, `\scriptstyle` and `\scriptscriptstyle` can be used to force what follows them to be typeset in the style that the name of the command suggests.) The amount of space used between symbols belonging to different kinds is different when they are typeset in script and scriptscript style from what it is when they are typeset in display and text style. For example, if you look at this formula:

$$\sum_{i=1}^{i=n} i = \frac{n(n+1)}{2},$$

you will notice that in the limits of the summation sign, which TEX treats like a

subscript and a superscript, no space has been inserted between the equals sign and
its operands.

9.5.2 Confusables

In books on English usage you will often find a section listing pairs of words that
are often confused. For example, the differences between the following pairs of words
might be explained: complementary/complimentary, principal/principle, shall/will,
stationary/stationery and so on. Here I do something similar for certain pairs of TeX's
commands for mathematical symbols.

\colon and :

The colon : in maths mode is not treated as a punctuation symbol. It is regarded as
being a symbol for a binary relation. One consequence of this is that the following
patterns of symbols are easy to generate:

$p:q::r:s$ `$p:q::r:s$`
$X := X + 7$ `$X := X + 7$`

If you want to use the colon as a punctuation symbol in maths mode, then you must
call it \colon. Note the difference in the following two formulas:

$f\colon X \to Y$ `$f \colon X \to Y$`
$f : X \to Y$ `$f : X \to Y$`

I used to think that the second of these was incorrect, as suggested in Knuth (1986a),
pp. 134 and 438, but now I am not so sure as in some contexts 'is of type' and 'is an
element of' are virtually synonymous.

\setminus and \backslash

The command \setminus produces a symbol for a binary relation which is used to
represent set difference, whereas \backslash produces an ordinary symbol used, for
example, to represent the double cosets of G by H or the fact that p divides n.

$\Gamma \setminus \Delta$ `$\Gamma \setminus \Delta$`
$G \backslash H$ `$G \backslash H$`
$p \backslash n$ `$p \backslash n$`

\mid and | or \vert

The command \mid produces the binary relation symbol |, whereas the command
\vert (or the symbol |) produces an ordinary symbol. Following \left or \right,
however, \vert and | produce a delimiter that can grow to any size.

\parallel and \| or \Vert

The command \parallel produces the binary relation symbol ∥, whereas the command \Vert (or the command \|) produces an ordinary symbol. Following \left or \right, however, \Vert and \| produce a delimiter that can grow to any size.

\langle and <

The command \langle produces an opening symbol (or left delimiter) that looks like ⟨, whereas < produces a symbol for a binary relation and should not be used for an opening angle bracket. After \left or \right, however, \langle and < can be used interchangeably and the result is a left angle bracket that is usually larger than that produced by \langle.

\rangle and >

The command \rangle produces a closing symbol (or right delimiter) that looks like ⟩, whereas > produces a symbol for a binary relation and should not be used for a closing angle bracket. After \left or \right, however, \rangle and > can be used interchangeably and the result is a right angle bracket that is usually larger than that produced by \rangle.

\perp and \bot

Both these commands produce a symbol that looks like ⊥, but \perp produces a binary relation symbol and \bot produces an ordinary symbol used, for example, to represent the least element of a partial order or lattice.

\dag and \dagger

The commands \dag and \dagger both produce the symbol †, but \dagger produces a binary operation symbol whereas \dag produces an ordinary symbol.

\ddag and \ddagger

The commands \ddag and \ddagger both produce the symbol ‡, but \ddagger produces a binary operation symbol whereas \ddag produces an ordinary symbol.

Chapter 10

More Mathematical Formatting

10.1 The array Environment

10.1.1 Introduction

The `array` environment is used for producing two-dimensional arrangements of mathematical material such as the following magic square:

11	16	15	56	61	60	47	52	51
18	14	10	63	59	55	54	50	46
13	12	17	58	57	62	49	48	53
74	79	78	38	43	42	2	7	6
81	77	73	45	41	37	9	5	1
76	75	80	40	39	44	4	3	8
29	34	33	20	25	24	65	70	69
36	32	28	27	23	19	72	68	64
31	30	35	22	21	26	67	66	71

In this section some of the ways in which the `array` environment can be used to produce a number of familiar mathematical structures are described. The `array` environment is very similar to the `tabular` environment described in section 5.3 and all the features of that environment also work with the `array` environment, so not all of them will be described again here. There are three main differences between these two environments. The first is that the `array` environment can only be used in maths mode and the entries in the array are themselves, by default, processed in maths mode. The second is that the box produced by an `array` environment has an axis. Associated with every mathematical expression and formula is an imaginary line, known as the *axis*, at the height at which a minus sign would go. The imaginary line is roughly half way between the top and bottom of the box produced by the `array` environment, but it can be altered. The general format of the `array` environment is:

$$\text{\\begin\{array\}} [pos] \{preamble\} \quad row\text{-}list \quad \text{\\end\{array\}}$$

The optional argument *pos* can be either c, t or b. The value c just emphasizes the default placement of the axis. If the value of *pos* is t, then the axis associated with the first row of the array becomes the axis of the whole array; whereas if the value of *pos* is b, then the axis associated with the last row of the array becomes the axis of the whole array. Sensible examples of this are difficult to think of, so here is a silly one:

$$
\begin{array}{c}
1 \ 2 \ 3 \\
4 \ 5 \ 6 \\
7 \ 8 \ 9
\end{array}
=
\begin{array}{c}
10 \ 11 \ 12 \\
13 \ 14 \ 15 \\
16 \ 17 \ 18
\end{array}
=
\begin{array}{c}
19 \ 20 \ 21 \\
22 \ 23 \ 24 \\
25 \ 26 \ 27
\end{array}
$$

This was produced by means of the following commands:

```
\[\begin{array}[t]{lll}
   1 &  2 &  3 \\  4 &  5 &  6 \\  7 &  8 &  9
\end{array}
= \begin{array}[c]{lll}
   10 & 11 & 12 \\ 13 & 14 & 15 \\ 16 & 17 & 18
\end{array}
= \begin{array}[b]{lll}
   19 & 20 & 21 \\ 22 & 23 & 24 \\ 25 & 26 & 27
\end{array}\]
```

The third difference between the `array` and `tabular` environments is that half the amount of horizontal space inserted between columns is given by the value of the length parameter `\arraycolsep` rather than `\tabcolsep`, which only works for the `tabular` and `tabular*` environments. The other style parameters, namely `\arrayrulewidth`, `\doublerulesep` and `\arraystretch`, have the same meaning that they have for the `tabular` and `tabular*` environments.

10.1.2 Matrices

The `array` environment can be used to produce matrices of various sorts. Consider, for example, the following matrix equation, which is based on equation (23.2) in Patterson and Rutherford (1965), p. 62:

$$
\begin{bmatrix}
y_1 \\
y_2 \\
\vdots \\
y_p
\end{bmatrix}
=
\begin{bmatrix}
a_{11} & a_{12} & \cdots & a_{1q} \\
a_{21} & a_{22} & \cdots & a_{2q} \\
\vdots & \vdots & \ddots & \vdots \\
a_{p1} & a_{p2} & \cdots & a_{pq}
\end{bmatrix}
\begin{bmatrix}
x_1 \\
x_2 \\
\vdots \\
x_q
\end{bmatrix}.
$$

It was produced by means of these commands:

```
\[\left[\begin{array}{c}
        y_1 \\ y_2 \\ \vdots \\ y_p
        \end{array}\right]
= \left[\begin{array}{cccc}
        a_{11} & a_{12} & \cdots & a_{1q} \\
        a_{21} & a_{22} & \cdots & a_{2q} \\
        \vdots & \vdots & \ddots & \vdots \\
        a_{p1} & a_{p2} & \cdots & a_{pq}
        \end{array}\right]
    \left[\begin{array}{c}
        x_1 \\ x_2 \\ \vdots \\ x_q
        \end{array}\right].\]
```

The commands \vdots, \cdots and \ddots are only available in maths mode and there they produce ellipses consisting of three vertical dots, three centred dots and three diagonal dots, respectively.

In the opening of the `array` environment there must always be a *preamble*. (Note that any valid `tabular` preamble is also a valid `array` preamble with the same meaning. So, everything I said about `tabular` preambles in section 5.3 is also correct for `array` preambles.) For example, \begin{array}{c} contains the single letter c as its preamble and in the command \begin{array}{cccc} the preamble is cccc. The single letter c in the preamble means that the array produced contains just a single column of entries and all the entries on all the rows are centred. In the case when the preamble is cccc this means that the array produced will consist of four columns of entries and entries in each column will be centred. In addition to c you can also use either l or r. The argument l means that the entries in that column will be typeset flush left and r means that they will be typeset flush right.

The actual rows of the array are separated by double backslashes \\, but it is a mistake to end the final row of the array with a double backslash (unless it is followed by a \hline or \cline command). Entries within rows are separated by ampersands. So, if your array has n columns, you will normally need $n-1$ ampersands, but the use of one or more \multicolumn commands may decrease the number of ampersands required.

10.1.3 Definition by Cases

The `array` environment can be used in order to typeset a definition by cases. The following example comes from Ore (1988), p. 293:

$$\lambda(2^\alpha) = 2^{\beta-2} \begin{cases} \beta = \alpha, & \text{when } \alpha \geq 3 \\ \beta = 3, & \text{when } \alpha = 2 \\ \beta = 2, & \text{when } \alpha = 1 \end{cases}$$

It was produced by means of the following LATEX commands:

```
\[\lambda (2^\alpha) = 2^{\beta-2}
```

```
\left\{\begin{array}{cl}
    \beta = \alpha, & \mbox{when $\alpha \geq 3$} \\
    \beta = 3, & \mbox{when $\alpha = 2$} \\
    \beta = 2, & \mbox{when $\alpha = 1$}
    \end{array}\right.\]
```

This same definition is produced using the `cases` environment, which is defined in the `amsmath` package, in section 11.5 below.

10.1.4   Tables of Values

The following is a table of the values of the function x^x:

x	0.1	0.2	0.3	0.4	0.5	0.6	0.7	0.8	0.9	1.0
x^x	0.794	0.725	0.697	0.693	0.707	0.736	0.779	0.837	0.910	1.0

It was produced by the following commands:

```
\[\setlength{\arraycolsep}{4pt}
\begin{array}{|l||*{10}{r@{.}l|}} \hline
x & 0 & 1 & 0 & 2 & 0 & 3 & 0 & 4 & 0 & 5 &
    0 & 6 & 0 & 7 & 0 & 8 & 0 & 9 & 1 & 0 \\ \hline
%
x^x & 0 & 794 & 0 & 725 & 0 & 697 & 0 & 693 & 0 & 707 &
    0 & 736 & 0 & 779 & 0 & 837 & 0 & 910 & 1 & 0 \\ \hline
\end{array}\]
```

The value of the rigid length parameter `\arraycolsep` is half the amount of horizontal space placed between the columns produced by the `array` environment. The presence of a vertical bar in the preamble produces a vertical line in the array produced and the expression *{*i*}{*pre*} is equivalent to *i* copies of *pre* where this is any legitimate combination of preamble commands. The @-expression @{.} that occurs in the preamble of the array above has the effect of inserting a full stop in every row. A further effect of @-expressions in general is that their presence removes space normally inserted between columns.

10.1.5   Lemmon-style Proofs

The `array` environment can be used to typeset logical proofs as presented in the widely-used book by Lemmon (1965). The following example comes from p. 16:

$$
\begin{array}{lll}
1   & (1) \quad P \to (Q \to R)   & \text{A} \\
2   & (2) \quad Q   & \text{A} \\
3   & (3) \quad P   & \text{A} \\
1,3   & (4) \quad Q \to R   & 1,3 \text{ MPP} \\
1,2,3   & (5) \quad R   & 2,4 \text{ MPP} \\
1,2   & (6) \quad P \to R   & 3,5 \text{ CP} \\
1   & (7) \quad Q \to (P \to R)   & 2,6 \text{ CP}
\end{array}
$$

This proof was produced by means of the following commands:

```
\[\newcommand*{cond}{\mathbin{\rightarrow}}
\begin{array}{lrll}
1        & (1) & P \cond (Q \cond R) & \mathrm{A} \\
2        & (2) & Q                    & \mathrm{A} \\
3        & (3) & P                    & \mathrm{A} \\
1, 3     & (4) & Q \cond R            & 1, 3\ \mathrm{MPP} \\
1, 2, 3  & (5) & R                    & 2, 4\ \mathrm{MPP} \\
1, 2     & (6) & P \cond R            & 3, 5\ \mathrm{CP} \\
1        & (7) & Q \cond (P \cond R) & 2, 6\ \mathrm{CP}
\end{array}\]
```

By itself the command `\rightarrow` produces a symbol for a binary relation, but
Lemmon uses it as a binary operator. The function of the command `\mathbin{`*exp*`}`
is to force LATEX to treat *exp* as a symbol for a binary operation. It is more fully
explained in section A.4 below.

10.1.6   The `\multicolumn` Command

The `\multicolumn` command was explained in connection with the `tabular` environment in subsection 5.3.2 above; it is very useful in putting lines inside a matrix and
two examples of that are given here. The following one comes from Munkres (1991),
p. 8:

$$C = \left[\begin{array}{cccccc} 1 & 0 & * & 0 & * & * \\ \hline 0 & 1 & * & 0 & * & * \\ 0 & 0 & 0 & 1 & * & * \\ 0 & 0 & 0 & 0 & 0 & 0 \end{array}\right].$$

It was produced by the following commands:

```
\[\newcommand*{\temp}{\multicolumn{1}{c|}{0}}
C = \left[
\begin{array}{cccccc}
1     & 0 & \ast  & 0 & \ast & \ast \\ \cline{1-1}
\temp & 1 & \ast  & 0 & \ast & \ast \\ \cline{2-3}
0     & 0 & \temp & 1 & \ast & \ast \\ \cline{4-6}
0     & 0 & 0     & 0 & 0    & 0
\end{array}
\right].\]
```

The next example is from p. 20 of Munkres (1991):

$$\det \left[\begin{array}{cccc} b & 0 & \dots & 0 \\ a_2 & & & \\ \vdots & & D & \\ a_n & & & \end{array}\right] = b(\det D).$$

It was produced by the following commands:

```
\[\newcommand*{\tempa}{\multicolumn{1}{|c}{}}
  \newcommand*{\tempb}{\multicolumn{1}{c|}{}}
%
\det \left[\begin{array}{cccc}
b      & 0      & \ldots & 0       \\ \cline{2-4}
a_2    & \tempa &        & \tempb \\
\vdots & \tempa & D      & \tempb \\
a_n    & \tempa &        & \tempb \\ \cline{2-4}
\end{array}\;\right] = b (\det D).\]
```

10.1.7   Program Fragments

The `array` environment can be used to produce program fragments like this:

$$
\Delta
\begin{cases}
\textbf{begin new } I; & \\
\left. \begin{array}{l} OUT := T[1]; \\ I := 1; \end{array} \right\} \Delta_1 & \\
\textbf{while } I \ne 10 \textbf{ do} & \\
\Delta_3 \begin{cases} I := I+1; \\ OUT := OUT + T[I] \end{cases} \Bigg\} \Delta_2 & \\
\textbf{end} &
\end{cases}
$$

The above program fragment was produced by means of the following commands:

```
\[\begin{array}{l}
  \mathbf{begin}\ \mathbf{new}\ I; \\
  \Delta \left\{
  \begin{array}{l}
    \left.
    \begin{array}{l}
      \mathit{OUT} := T\, [1]; \\
      I := 1;
    \end{array}
    \right\} \Delta_1 \\
    \left.
    \begin{array}{l}
      \mathbf{while}\ I \ne 10\ \mathbf{do} \\
      \Delta_3 \left\{
      \begin{array}{l}
        I := I + 1; \\
        \mathit{OUT} := \mathit{OUT} + T\, [I]
      \end{array}
      \end{array}
      \right.
    \end{array}
    \right\} \Delta_2
\end{array}
```

```
    \right. \\
    \mathbf{end}
\end{array}\]
```

The idea behind the construction of this can easily be illustrated by considering the innermost pair of labelled assignments, namely:

$$\Delta_3 \left\{ \begin{array}{l} I := I + 1; \\ OUT := OUT + T[I] \end{array} \right.$$

This was produced by the following commands:

```
\[\Delta_3 \left\{
\begin{array}{l}
I := I + 1; \\
\mathit{OUT} := \mathit{OUT} + T\, [I]
\end{array}
\right.\]
```

The idea here is very similar to the use of the `array` environment in order to produce matrices as explained in section 10.1.2 above. This `array` then becomes a single element in another instance of the `array` environment and so on till the program fragment is built up. The `tabbing` environment can also be used to typeset program fragments; see section 5.5 above for an example.

10.1.8   Text in Arrays

The following inference rules are based on the rules $\forall$-*elim* and $\forall$-*int* given on p. 118 of Diller (1990):

$\forall$-*elim* $\dfrac{\Gamma \vdash \forall x \colon X \bullet A}{\Gamma \vdash A[t/x]}$ Side condition: t is any term of the same type as x.

$\forall$-*int* $\dfrac{\Gamma \vdash A}{\Gamma \vdash \forall x \colon X \bullet A[x/a]}$ Side condition: x is a variable of type X and a a constant of the same type which does not occur in Γ.

(The idea of presenting inference rules in this way comes from Hindley and Seldin (1986); for example, this style of presentation occurs on p. 209.) The above arrangement of information was obtained by means of these commands:

```
\[\newcommand*{\tempa}{\begin{array}[t]{c}
\Gamma \vdash \forall x \colon X \bullet A \\ \hline
\Gamma \vdash A[t/x]
\end{array}}
\newcommand*{\tempb}{\begin{array}[t]{c}
\Gamma \vdash A \\ \hline
```

```
\Gamma \vdash \forall x \colon X \bullet A[x/a]
\end{array}}
\newcommand*{\tempc}{\underline{Side condition}:
$t$ is any term of the same type as $x$.}
\newcommand*{\tempd}{\underline{Side condition}:
$x$ is a variable of type $X$ and $a$ a constant
of the same type which does not occur in $\Gamma$.}
\begin{array}{lcp{2.5in}}
\allelim & \tempa & \tempc \\
& & \\
\allint  & \tempb & \tempd
\end{array}\]
```

The commands \allelim and \allint are defined like this:

```
\newcommand*{\allelim}{\mbox{$\forall$-\itshape elim}}
\newcommand*{\allint}{\mbox{$\forall$-\itshape int}}
```

10.1.9 Some Standard Derivatives

Some elementary calculus books contain lists of derivatives such as these:

$$\frac{d}{dx} \sin^{-1} u = \frac{1}{\sqrt{1 - u^2}} \frac{du}{dx}, \qquad \text{if } -\tfrac{\pi}{2} < \sin^{-1} u < \tfrac{\pi}{2},$$

$$\frac{d}{dx} \cos^{-1} u = \frac{-1}{\sqrt{1 - u^2}} \frac{du}{dx}, \qquad \text{if } 0 < \cos^{-1} u < \pi,$$

$$\frac{d}{dx} \tan^{-1} u = \frac{1}{1 + u^2} \frac{du}{dx}, \qquad \text{if } -\tfrac{\pi}{2} < \tan^{-1} u < \tfrac{\pi}{2}.$$

They were produced by means of the following commands:

```
\[\begin{array}{r@{\:=\:}l@{\qquad}l}
\dfrac{d}{dx} \sin^{-1} u
& \dfrac{1}{\sqrt{1 - u^2}} \dfrac{du}{dx},
& \mbox{if $- \frac{\pi}{2} < \sin^{-1}u < \frac{\pi}{2}$},
\\[4ex]
\dfrac{d}{dx} \cos^{-1} u
& \dfrac{-1}{\sqrt{1 - u^2}} \dfrac{du}{dx},
& \mbox{if $0 < \cos^{-1}u < \pi$},
\\[4ex]
\dfrac{d}{dx} \tan^{-1} u
& \dfrac{1}{1 + u^2} \dfrac{du}{dx},
& \mbox{if $- \frac{\pi}{2} < \tan^{-1}u < \frac{\pi}{2}$}.
\end{array}\]
```

The `array` environment is used here rather than the `eqnarray*` environment, to be described in the next section, because such a table of derivatives looks better if the side conditions are aligned as well as the equals signs. Note the use of the @-expression in the preamble to the `array` environment in order to insert space in every row produced. The command `\dfrac` is defined in the `amsmath` package; it produces a fraction in display style. It is useful even if you do not plan to use the `amsmath` package and can be defined like this:

```
\providecommand*{\dfrac}[2]{\displaystyle\frac{#1}{#2}}
```

It is a good idea to use the `\providecommand*` declaration here so that if you do load the `amsmath` package, before LaTeX encounters this declaration, then the `amsmath` version will be used.

10.2   Equation Arrays

10.2.1   Unlabelled Equation Arrays

The `eqnarray*` environment produces an equation array in which no line is labelled. The result is rather like using an `array` environment with preamble `rcl`, except that the expressions in the first and third columns are typeset in display style. (The expression in the second column is typeset in text style.) Additionally, the `\multicolumn` command cannot be used inside the `eqnarray*` environment.

The end of a row in the `eqnarray*` environment is indicated by the control symbol `\\` and the items in each of the three columns are separated by ampersands. There is no need for an end-of-line control symbol at the end of the final line. If added, then an extra blank line will be produced. To illustrate the use of the `eqnarray*` environment I will show you the LaTeX commands that can be used to produce the following equation array, which comes from Barnard and Neill (1996), p. 30:

$$
\begin{aligned}
ac & = & (b + hn)(d + kn) \\
& = & bd + hdn + bkn + hkn^2 \\
& = & bd + n(hd + bk + hkn).
\end{aligned}
$$

The above equation array was produced by means of the following commands:

```
\begin{eqnarray*}
ac & = & (b + hn) (d + kn) \\
   & = & bd + hdn + bkn + hkn^2 \\
   & = & bd + n (hd + bk + hkn).
\end{eqnarray*}
```

The `eqnarray*` environment has the peculiarity that quite a lot of space surrounds the symbol or symbols that appear in the central column. This can be irritating at times, but it does have its uses. Consider the following, from Barendregt (1992), p. 136:

$$
\begin{array}{rcl}
M \rightarrow_\beta N & \Rightarrow & \lambda \vdash M = N; \\
M \twoheadrightarrow_\beta N & \Rightarrow & \lambda \vdash M = N; \\
M =_\beta N & \Rightarrow & \lambda \vdash M = N.
\end{array}
$$

It was produced by means of the following commands:

```
\begin{eqnarray*}
\newcommand*{\temp}{\twoheadrightarrow}
M \rightarrow_\beta N & \Rightarrow & \lambda \vdash M = N; \\
M \temp_\beta N       & \Rightarrow & \lambda \vdash M = N; \\
M =_\beta N           & \Rightarrow & \lambda \vdash M = N.
\end{eqnarray*}
```

Here, the extra space around the central symbol $\Rightarrow$, produced by the `\Rightarrow` command, aids the understanding of the formulas involved. (Note that the symbol $\twoheadrightarrow$ is not available in standard LaTeX. In order to produce it you have to load the `amssymb` package.)

There are situations, however, in which the extra space is a positive hindrance to understanding the significance of the formulas involved. For example, the following is from MacLane and Birkhoff (1967), p. 39:

$$
\begin{array}{rcl}
m + n = \sigma^n(m) & = & \sigma^n(\sigma^m(0) = (\sigma^n \circ \sigma^m)(0) = (\sigma^m \circ \sigma^n)(0) \\
& = & \sigma^m(n) = n + m.
\end{array}
$$

It was produced by means of the following commands:

```
\begin{eqnarray*}
m + n = \sigma^n (m) & = & \sigma^n (\sigma^m (0) =
                           (\sigma^n \circ \sigma^m)(0) =
                           (\sigma^m \circ \sigma^n)(0) \\
                     & = & \sigma^m (n) = n + m.
\end{eqnarray*}
```

Here, the extra space is positively distracting, because it emphasizes two of the equals-signs when they are really all on a par. There is a better way of producing the above using the `align*` environment available in the `amsmath` package. This is described in the next chapter.

The `\lefteqn{`*form*`}` command can be used inside an `eqnarray` or an `eqnarray*` environment in order to produce a formula that LaTeX thinks is zero inches wide. The argument *form* is processed in display maths style. This is useful if you have a very long formula as in the following example:

$$
(x - y)(x + y)^6 =
$$
$$
x^7 + 5x^6 y + 9x^5 y^2 + 5x^4 y^3 - 5x^3 y^4 - 9x^2 y^5 - 5xy^6 - y^7.
$$

This was produced by means of the following commands:

```
\begin{eqnarray*}
\lefteqn{(x-y)(x+y)^6 =} \\   & &
x^7 + 5x^6y   + 9x^5y^2 + 5x^4y^3
    - 5x^3y^4 - 9x^2y^5 - 5xy^6 - y^7.
\end{eqnarray*}
```

10.2.2 Labelling Formulas

To produce a single displayed mathematical formula with a numerical label you need to use the **equation** environment. Thus, the labelled formula

$$(x + y)(x - y) = x^2 - y^2, \qquad\qquad (10.1)$$

was produced by the following commands

```
\begin{equation}
(x + y)(x - y) = x^2 - y^2,
\label{AA}
\end{equation}
```

Note that the label is generated automatically. It would still have been produced even if the **\label** command were not present. The function of the **\label** command is to enable you to refer to this formula from other parts of the document that you are writing. The general format of the **\label** command is **\label{***key***}**, where *key* is any sequence of letters, numerals and punctuation marks. Lowercase and uppercase letters are treated as being distinct, thus **aa** and **AA** are different keys. To refer to a labelled formula containing a **\label{***key***}** command you use a **\ref{***key***}** command. Thus, (**\ref{AA}**) produces '(10.1)'. Note that in referring to formulas labelled with a **\label** command using **\ref** you have to add the parentheses yourself; they are not produced automatically by LATEX. If you want to refer to the page on which this formula occurs, then use the **\pageref** command; for example, **p.~\pageref{AA}** produces 'p. 127'. The tilde inserts the normal amount of inter-word space, but it inhibits line-breaking.

By default the labels generated automatically by LATEX are placed on the extreme right-hand side of the output page. If you want the numerical labels to be placed on the extreme left-hand side of the output page instead, then you must use the **leqno** option to the **\documentclass** command.

In order to produce a number of displayed and numbered equations you can use the **eqnarray** environment. For example, the commands:

```
\begin{eqnarray}
(x + y + z)^2 & = & (x + y + z) (x + y + z), \label{BB} \\
& = & x^2 + 2xy + y^2 \nonumber \\
&   & \qquad \mbox{} + 2yz + z^2 + 2zx. \label{CC}
\end{eqnarray}
```

produce the following labelled series of displayed equations:

$$
\begin{aligned}
(x+y+z)^2 &= (x+y+z)(x+y+z), & (10.2)\\
&= x^2 + 2xy + y^2 \\
&\quad + 2yz + z^2 + 2zx. & (10.3)
\end{aligned}
$$

The \nonumber command inhibits the automatic production of a label on the line where it occurs.

Chapter 11

Introducing $\mathcal{AMS}$-LaTeX

11.1 Some Deficiencies of Basic LaTeX

The environments available in LaTeX for displaying mathematical formulas are fairly good, but they do have a number of deficiencies. Three of these are:

(1) The spacing around the symbol that occurs in the central column of an `eqnarray` or `eqnarray*` environment is greater than the usual spacing around that symbol (whatever it may be). This sometimes makes for strange-looking displays—especially when one of the symbols in the central column also occurs elsewhere on the same line.

(2) The labels produced by the `equation` and `eqnarray` environments are *numerical* labels and, although this is adequate for most purposes, sometimes it is useful to be able to attach a non-numerical label to a displayed formula. This can be done in basic LaTeX, but involves redefining the `\theequation` command and altering the value of the `equation` counter.

(3) Sometimes in a series of equations aligned on, say, the equals sign you want to insert a line of explanatory text and then carry on the series of equations *still* aligned on the equals sign. This is not possible in basic LaTeX.

Using the environments and commands available in the `amsmath` package it is possible to overcome these limitations of basic LaTeX. The purpose of this chapter is not to provide a comprehensive treatment of the `amsmath` package; it is rather to introduce a number of features of that package which allow you to produce several things that occur fairly commonly when typesetting mathematical material. Hopefully, this will whet your appetite so that you will want to find out more. Grätzer (1996) provides a thorough account of the `amsmath` and related packages. The `amsmath` package has had a chequered history and several changes of name; Grätzer (1996), pp. 379–382, chronicles these. Note that until fairly recently it was called `amstex`. Note also that the `amsmath` package is only one of the packages in the $\mathcal{AMS}$-LaTeX distribution; though it is the most important one. Other packages in that distribution include `amscd` (for producing commutative diagrams) and `amssymb` (for producing a wide variety of symbols). I say more about `amscd` in section 11.7 below and Appendix A contains details of the symbols that can be produced using the `amssymb` package.

11.2 The `align` and `align*` Environments

The `amsmath` package defines a number of environments for displaying several mathematical formulas. In this section I explain the `align` and `align*` environments and how they can be used to overcome the first of the three deficiencies of basic LATEX mentioned in section 11.1 above. The only difference between these two environments is that `align` automatically labels the formulas it typesets, whereas `align*` does not.

The following displayed equations represent a simple, but inefficient, bracket abstraction algorithm:

$$[x]\, x = \mathsf{I},$$
$$[x]\, e = \mathsf{K}\, e,$$
$$[x]\, Q\, R = \mathsf{S}\, ([x]\, Q)\, ([x]\, R).$$

Using the `align*` environment this can be produced by means of the following commands:

```
\begin{align*}
[x]\,x    & = \cI, \\
[x]\,e    & = \cK\,e, \\
[x]\,Q\,R & = \cS\,([x]\,Q)\,([x]\,R).
\end{align*}
```

The commands `\cI`, `\cK` and `\cS` used in this example, and the commands `\cB` and `\cC` which will be used later on in this chapter, are defined as follows:

```
\newcommand*{\cI}{\mbox{\textbf{\textsf{I}}}}
\newcommand*{\cK}{\mbox{\textbf{\textsf{K}}}}
\newcommand*{\cS}{\mbox{\textbf{\textsf{S}}}}
\newcommand*{\cB}{\mbox{\textbf{\textsf{B}}}}
\newcommand*{\cC}{\mbox{\textbf{\textsf{C}}}}
```

Combinators are usually represented in books and articles using an upright, bold, sans serif typeface, but unfortunately LATEX does not have such a typeface available in its mathematical fonts; that is why these definitions use the standard text fonts.

The `eqnarray` and `eqnarray*` environments both consist of three columns of formulas; the formulas in the first of these are typeset flush right, those in the second column are centred and those in the third are typeset flush left. The `align` and `align*` environments, by contrast, allow you to align formulas wherever you want (except within a subformula that LATEX has to process as a unit). The general format of the `align*` environment is:

```
\begin{align*}    row-list    \end{align*}
```

All the rows inside *row-list*, except the last, are terminated by \\ and each row looks like this:

$$form_1 \ \& \ form_2 \ \& \ \dots \ \& \ form_{2n}$$

Each formula *form$_i$* is processed in display maths style. The items *form$_i$* with odd subscripts are pushed to the right and those with even subscripts are pushed to the left. If ampersands are numbered from the left, then items on different rows are aligned at odd-numbered ampersands and even-numbered ones are used to separate columns. The resulting displayed formulas are evenly spaced out across the width of the body region. The following example illustrates most of the features of the `align*` environment:

$$\frac{d}{dx} \sin x = \cos x, \qquad\qquad \frac{d}{dx} \sinh x = \cosh x,$$

$$\frac{d}{dx} \cos x = -\sin x, \qquad\qquad \frac{d}{dx} \cosh x = \sinh x,$$

$$\frac{d}{dx} \tan x = \sec^2 x, \qquad\qquad \frac{d}{dx} \tanh x = \text{sech}^2 x.$$

These formulas were produced by means of the following commands:

```
\begin{align*}
\frac{d}{dx} \sin x  &=   \cos x,   &
\frac{d}{dx} \sinh x &=   \cosh x,  \\[0.25\baselineskip]
\frac{d}{dx} \cos x  &= - \sin x,   &
\frac{d}{dx} \cosh x &=   \sinh x,  \\[0.25\baselineskip]
\frac{d}{dx} \tan x  &=   \sec^2 x, &
\frac{d}{dx} \tanh x &=   \sech^2 x.
\end{align*}
```

The command \sech is neither defined in basic LaTeX nor in any of the $\mathcal{AMS}$-LaTeX packages; several ways of defining such a log-like operator are explained on p. 163 below.

The `amsmath` package also defines the `flalign` and `flalign*` environments; these are like `align` and `align*` except that the columns of formulas produced are spread out across the page so that the leftmost is set flush left and the rightmost is set flush right.

I will now show how the `align*` environment can be used to remedy the first deficiency of basic LaTeX mentioned in section 11.1 above. In Whitehead (1978), p. 535, there occurs the following series of equations:

$$h_1(\alpha) = h_2(\alpha) = 0 \qquad \textit{if } r \textit{ is odd};$$

$$2h_0(\alpha) = 0, \qquad 3h_1(\alpha) = 0, \qquad h_2(\alpha) = -h_1(\alpha) \qquad \textit{if } r \textit{ is even.}$$

In the book you are now reading this was produced by the following commands:

```
{\itshape
\begin{align*}
h_1 (\alpha) & = h_2 (\alpha) = 0 \qquad \text{if $r$ is odd}; \\
2h_0 (\alpha) & = 0, \qquad 3h_1 (\alpha)  = 0, \qquad
h_2 (\alpha)  = - h_1 (\alpha) \qquad \text{if $r$ is even}.
\end{align*}}
```

Using basic LaTeX's eqnarray* environment the appearance of this series of equations would be as follows:

$$\begin{aligned} h_1(\alpha) &= h_2(\alpha) = 0 & \text{if } r \text{ is odd;} \\ 2h_0(\alpha) &= 0, & 3h_1(\alpha) = 0, & & h_2(\alpha) = -h_1(\alpha) & \text{if } r \text{ is even.} \end{aligned}$$

It is possible to alter the default spacing around the central symbol in the eqnarray and eqnarray* environments, but if you decide to do this, then you have the further problem of having to decide what to alter it to. If you alter it to a thick amount of space, then it will look okay when the central column is occupied by binary *relations* but sometimes you will want binary *operations* to appear in the central column and then the spacing will look decidedly strange.

If you think that the issue of spacing is not very important, then you should consider how standard LaTeX could be used to display two or more mathematical formulas each of which contains several symbols for binary relations. The following is an example of such a case:

$$P \equiv P_0 \to P_1 \to \cdots \to P_u \equiv Q.$$
$$P \equiv P_0' \to P_1' \to \cdots \to P_v' \equiv Q.$$

The displayed formulas produced by the eqnarray* environment are such that your eyes are drawn to the two aligned equivalence signs on the right. These symbols are given undue prominence and that is distracting. Using the align* environment these two formulas would appear as:

$$P \equiv P_0 \to P_1 \to \cdots \to P_u \equiv Q.$$
$$P \equiv P_0' \to P_1' \to \cdots \to P_v' \equiv Q.$$

These were produced using the following commands, where \red has already been defined as being equivalent to \rightarrow:

```
\begin{align*}
P \equiv P_0  \red P_1  \red \cdots \red P_u  & \equiv Q. \\
P \equiv P'_0 \red P'_1 \red \cdots \red P'_v & \equiv Q.
\end{align*}
```

In the displayed formulas produced using the align* environment undue prominence is not given to the equivalence signs that appear on the right-hand sides of the formulas.

11.3 Non-numerical Labels

In this section I show how the second deficiency of basic LaTeX mentioned in section 11.1 above can be remedied by using commands and environments defined in the **amsmath** package. Sometimes you will want to give a label to a formula which is different from the numerical sequence that LaTeX generates automatically. For example, you may want to label the reduction rule for the combinator **S** by '(**S**)' like this:

$$\mathbf{S}\, f\, g\, x \rightarrow f\, x\,(g\, x). \tag{\textbf{S}}$$

In order to produce this you need the following commands:

```
\begin{equation} \tag{\cS}
\cS\,f\,g\,x \rightarrow f\,x\,(g\,x).
\end{equation}
```

To get several aligned and labelled formulas like this:

$$\mathbf{B}\, f\, g\, x \rightarrow f\,(g\, x), \tag{\textbf{B}}$$
$$\mathbf{C}\, f\, x\, y \rightarrow f\, y\, x. \tag{\textbf{C}}$$

you need the following commands:

```
\begin{align*}
\cB\,f\,g\,x & \rightarrow f\,(g\,x), \tag{\cB} \\
\cC\,f\,x\,y & \rightarrow f\,y\,x. \tag{\cC}
\end{align*}
```

The command `\tag{`*text*`}` can be used in any of the environments available in the **amsmath** package that produce displayed formulas. Its effect is to label a formula with *text*, which is processed in LR mode. The `\tag` command automatically puts parentheses around the label it produces; the `\tag*` command can be used to produce a label which is not enclosed in parentheses. Both the `\tag` and `\tag*` commands can be used in **amsmath**'s starred and unstarred environments. Neither of them increments the **equation** counter and you can refer to the labels they produce by means of a `\ref` command if you also use a `\label` command.

In the examples of the **align*** environment presented above to produce non-numerical labels there has been a symbol on which the equations have been aligned, namely →, but sometimes people want to label formulas or equations in which there is no convenient symbol to be used for alignment purposes. The **gather** and **gather*** environments can be used to achieve this. Consider, for example, the following collection of displayed formulas:

$$\Delta \vdash x : \sigma, \quad \text{if } x : \sigma \in \Delta, \tag{\textit{TAUT}}$$

$$\frac{\Delta \vdash M : \sigma \rightarrow \tau \quad \Delta \vdash N : \sigma}{\Delta \vdash MN : \tau}, \tag{\textit{COMB}}$$

$$\frac{\Delta_x \cup \{x : \sigma\} \vdash M : \tau}{\Delta \vdash \lambda x.M : \sigma \rightarrow \tau}. \tag{\textit{ABS}}$$

These were produced by means of the following commands:

```
\begin{gather}
\Delta \vdash x \colon \sigma, \qquad
  \text{if}\ x \colon \sigma \in \Delta,
  \tag{\textit{TAUT}} \\[0.5\baselineskip]
\frac{\Delta \vdash M \colon \sigma \fun \tau \qquad
  \Delta \vdash N \colon \sigma}{\Delta \vdash MN \colon \tau},
  \tag{\textit{COMB}} \\[0.5\baselineskip]
  \frac{\Delta_x \cup \{ x \colon \sigma \} \vdash M \colon \tau}
{\Delta \vdash \lambda x.M \colon \sigma \fun \tau}.
  \tag{\textit{ABS}}
\end{gather}
```

The \text command is defined in the amstext package (which is loaded automatically when you load the amsmath package); it is similar to the \mbox command except that when it is used in subscripts and superscripts the size of type used is one that is appropriate.

11.4 Explanatory Notes in Aligned Equations

In this section I show how the third deficiency of basic LATEX mentioned in section 11.1 above can be remedied by using the amsmath package. In order to show how a piece of explanatory text can be included between two displayed formulas without destroying the alignment between them I will make use of the following labelled tautology:

$$(P \lor Q) \land R \iff (P \land R) \lor (Q \land R). \tag{11.1}$$

This was produced by means of the following commands:

```
\begin{equation} \label{DD}
( P \lor Q ) \land R \iff ( P \land R ) \lor ( Q \land R ).
\end{equation}
```

The following sequence of formulas contains a piece of explanatory text:

$$
\begin{aligned}
x \in (U \cup V) \cap W &\iff (x \in U \cup V) \land x \in W, \\
&\iff (x \in U \lor x \in V) \land x \in W, \\
&\iff (x \in U \land x \in W) \lor (x \in V \land x \in W),
\end{aligned}
$$

which follows by using the tautology (11.1),

$$
\begin{aligned}
&\iff (x \in U \cap W) \lor (x \in V \cap W), \\
&\iff x \in (U \cap W) \cup (V \cap W),
\end{aligned}
$$

The aligned formulas just displayed, including the piece of explanatory text, were produced by means of the following commands:

```
\begin{align*}
x \in ( U \cup V ) \cap W
& \iff ( x \in U \cup V ) \land x \in W, \\
& \iff ( x \in U \lor x \in V ) \land x \in W, \\
& \iff ( x \in U \land x \in W ) \lor
      ( x \in V \land x \in W ), \\
\intertext{which follows by using the tautology (\ref{DD}),}
& \iff ( x \in U \cap W ) \lor ( x \in V \cap W ), \\
& \iff x \in ( U \cap W ) \cup ( V \cap W ),
\end{align*}
```

The `\intertext` command that is used here can occur inside any of the `amsmath` environments that produce several displayed formulas. It has to be placed after the `\\` command and no such command should follow it. You can, in fact, have more than one `\intertext` command inside the same environment.

11.5 Definition by Cases

In section 10.1.3 above I showed how a definition by cases could be produced in basic LaTeX by means of the `array` environment. The `amsmath` package includes a `cases` environment, which makes the production of such definitions very easy. In this section I show how it can be used to produce the same definition that was used as an example on p. 119 above. This comes from Ore (1988), p. 293:

$$\lambda(2^\alpha) = 2^{\beta-2} \begin{cases} \beta = \alpha, & \text{when } \alpha \geq 3 \\ \beta = 3, & \text{when } \alpha = 2 \\ \beta = 2, & \text{when } \alpha = 1 \end{cases}$$

This definition was produced by these commands:

```
\[\lambda (2^\alpha) = 2^{\beta - 2}
\begin{cases}
\beta = \alpha, & \text{when $\alpha \ge 3$} \\
\beta = 3,      & \text{when $\alpha = 2$} \\
\beta = 2,      & \text{when $\alpha = 1$}
\end{cases}\]
```

The general format of the `cases` environment is as follows:

```
\begin{cases}
form_{1,1}    &    form_{1,2}      \\
form_{2,1}    &    form_{2,2}      \\
   ⋮              ⋮          ⋮        ⋮
form_{n-1,1}  &    form_{n-1,2}   \\
form_{n,1}    &    form_{n,2}
\end{cases}
```

This produces a large left brace followed by the formulas $form_{i,1}$ (which are aligned on their left-hand sides) and then the formulas $form_{i,2}$ (again, aligned on their left-hand sides). Note that all the arguments $form_{i,j}$ are processed in maths mode and so, if you want some text, you need to use the \text command.

11.6   Fraction-like Structures

There are several ways in which you can produce a fraction in basic LaTeX. It is possible to use the slash symbol /. Whereas the symbols for addition (+), multiplication (×) and division (÷) are binary operations, TeX treats / as an ordinary symbol because when used to represent division it is normal typesetting practice *not* to put any extra space either side of it. Fractions involving a horizontal line are produced by the basic LaTeX \frac command. In many branches of mathematics, however, it is necessary to be able to produce other sorts of fraction-like notations. The amsmath package provides the \genfrac command which can produce a wide variety of fraction-like notations. Some of these are illustrated in the following table:

output	input
$\dfrac{x}{y}$	\genfrac{}{}{0pt}{}{x}{y}
$\dfrac{x}{y}$	\genfrac{}{}{}{}{x}{y}
$\dfrac{x}{y}$	\genfrac{}{}{2pt}{}{x}{y}
$\left[\dfrac{x}{y}\right]$	\genfrac{\lbrack}{\rbrack}{0pt}{}{x}{y}
$\left\{\dfrac{x}{y}\right\}$	\genfrac{\lbrace}{\rbrace}{0pt}{}{x}{y}

The general format of the \genfrac command is:

$$\genfrac\{cmd_1\}\{cmd_2\}\{len\}\{i\}\{form_1\}\{form_2\}$$

This command is only available if you are using the amsmath package and it can only be used in maths mode. It produces a fraction-like structure. The arguments cmd_1 and cmd_2 must be commands that produce delimiters; cmd_1 produces the delimiter that appears on the left of the generalized fraction and cmd_2 produces the one that appears on the right. The argument len determines the thickness of the line separating the numerator and the denominator of the fraction. The default is for a normal fraction line to be produced. The argument i determines the style in which the fraction will be produced. A value of 0 for i will produce a fraction in display style, a value of 1 will produce a fraction in text style, a value of 2 in script style and one of 3 in scriptscript style. The default is for the style to be determined by the context where \genfrac occurs. The argument *form*$_1$ produces the numerator and *form*$_2$ the denominator.

Although the \genfrac command is very useful for producing unusual fraction-like notations, its use is cumbersome for frequently occurring notations. The amsmath package provides the commands \dfrac, \tfrac, \binom, \dbinom and \tbinom for common notations. The equivalence of these, and the \frac command, to the more general \genfrac command is shown in the following table:

\frac{*form*$_1$}{*form*$_2$}   \genfrac{}{}{}{}{*form*$_1$}{*form*$_2$}
\dfrac{*form*$_1$}{*form*$_2$}   \genfrac{}{}{}{0}{*form*$_1$}{*form*$_2$}
\tfrac{*form*$_1$}{*form*$_2$}   \genfrac{}{}{}{1}{*form*$_1$}{*form*$_2$}
\binom{*form*$_1$}{*form*$_2$}   \genfrac{(}{)}{0pt}{}{*form*$_1$}{*form*$_2$}
\dbinom{*form*$_1$}{*form*$_2$}   \genfrac{(}{)}{0pt}{0}{*form*$_1$}{*form*$_2$}
\tbinom{*form*$_1$}{*form*$_2$}   \genfrac{(}{)}{0pt}{1}{*form*$_1$}{*form*$_2$}

The commands \binom, \dbinom and \tbinom are used for producing binomial coefficients. Consider, for example, the following equations:

$$(u+v)^n = \sum_{i=0}^{n} \binom{n}{i} u^{n-i} v^i,$$

where the value of the binomial coefficient $\binom{n}{i}$ is determined like this:

$$\binom{n}{i} = {}_nC_i = \frac{n!}{i!(n-i)!}.$$

These were produced by means of the following commands:

```
\begin{align*}
(u + v)^n    & = \sum^n_{i=0} \binom{n}{i} u^{n-i} v^i, \\
\intertext{where the value of the binomial coefficient
$\binom{n}{i}$ is determined like this:}
\binom{n}{i} & = {}_n C_i = \frac{n!}{i! (n-i)!}.
\end{align*}
```

This example provides another illustration of the use of the \intertext command.

One type of fraction that is difficult to produce using the commands mentioned so far is the continued fraction. The amsmath package also contains a \cfrac command for producing this type of fraction. I use it here to produce the formula from Ramanujan displayed in Chapter 1 and reproduced here:

$$\cfrac{1}{1+\cfrac{e^{-2\pi\sqrt{5}}}{1+\cfrac{e^{-4\pi\sqrt{5}}}{1+\cfrac{e^{-6\pi\sqrt{5}}}{1+\cdots}}}} = \left(\cfrac{\sqrt{5}}{1+\sqrt[5]{5^{3/4}\left(\frac{\sqrt{5}-1}{2}\right)^{5/2}-1}} - \frac{\sqrt{5}+1}{2} \right) e^{2\pi/\sqrt{5}}.$$

As well as illustrating the use of the `\cfrac` command I want to use this example to illustrate one way in which local definitions can be used in $\LaTeX$ to help in the production of complicated formulas. Using local definitions in this way decreases the chances of making a mistake in the process of working out what commands you need to use to produce a complex equation and they also help you to understand how the formula is constructed when you read your input file after a gap of several months or years and maybe want to make changes to it. The technique I am advocating is an application of what MacLennan (1987), p. 53, calls *the abstraction principle* and which he formulates as, 'Avoid requiring something to be stated more than once; factor out the recurring pattern.' If you look at Ramanujan's formula, you will notice that it contains the subformulas $e^{-2\pi\sqrt{5}}$, $e^{-4\pi\sqrt{5}}$ and $e^{-6\pi\sqrt{5}}$. These are the same except that where 2 occurs in the first, 4 occurs in the second and 6 occurs in the third. This pattern can be captured by means of a definition like this:

```
\newcommand*{\tempa}[1]{e^{-#1\pi\sqrt{5}}}
```

The three formulas discussed above can then be produced by means of the commands `\tempa{2}`, `\tempa{4}` and `\tempa{6}`. It is also a good idea to have a locally defined command produce the complicated formula that occurs in the denominator of the first fraction to the right of the equals sign. Putting all this together results in the following commands for producing Ramanujan's formula:

```
\[\newcommand*{\tempa}[1]{e^{-#1\pi\sqrt{5}}}
   \newcommand*{\tempb}{1+\sqrt[5]
      {5^{3/4}\left(\frac{\sqrt{5}-1}{2}\right)^{5/2}-1}}
%
\cfrac{1}
   {1 + \cfrac{\tempa{2}}
      {1 + \cfrac{\tempa{4}}
         {1 + \cfrac{\tempa{6}}
            {1 + \dotsb}}}}
= \left(
\frac{\sqrt{5}}{\tempb} - \frac{\sqrt{5} + 1}{2}
\right) e^{2\pi / \sqrt{5}}.\]
```

An alternative way of producing this, using more primitive $\TeX$ commands, is given in Borde (1992), p. 63, where it is equation (11).

11.7 Commutative Diagrams

Straightforward commutative diagrams can be produced by using commands that are defined in the `amscd` package. This is part of the $\mathcal{A}\mathcal{M}\mathcal{S}$-$\LaTeX$ distribution, but it can be used on its own as it is independent of the other packages in that distribution. The `amscd` package defines an environment called `CD`, which can only be used in maths mode, and a number of commands for producing extensible arrows and equals signs.

The following diagram, from MacLane and Birkhoff (1967), p. 65, was produced by using some of these commands:

$$
\begin{CD}
P @>f>> Q \\
@Vf'VV @VVgV \\
S @>>g'> R
\end{CD}
$$

In fact, it was produced by including the following in a LaTeX input file:

```
\[\begin{CD}
P            @>{f}>>      Q \\
@V{f'}VV                  @VV{g}V \\
S            @>>{g'}>     R
\end{CD}\]
```

Note that ampersands are not used inside the CD environment in order to separate the various components that make up a commutative diagram. This is because such diagrams have a regular structure. A simple commutative diagram can be thought of as being made up out of squares. The CD environment needs to be told what occurs at each of the four nodes and it also has to be informed about the symbols that make up each of the four edges of the square (or whether, in fact, there is empty space between any two of the nodes). The nodes are made up out of any symbols or expressions that can be produced by normal commands available in maths mode. The following commands are available inside the CD environment for producing the edges of a commutative diagram:

@(((produces a left arrow.

@(*form*((produces a left arrow with the expression *form* placed above the arrow; if a left parenthesis occurs in *form*, then *form* must be enclosed in braces.

@((*form*(produces a left arrow with the expression *form* placed below the arrow; if a left parenthesis occurs in *form*, then *form* must be enclosed in braces.

@))) produces a right arrow.

@)*form*)) produces a right arrow with the expression *form* placed above the arrow; if a right parenthesis occurs in *form*, then *form* must be enclosed in braces.

@))*form*) produces a right arrow with the expression *form* placed below the arrow; if a right parenthesis occurs in *form*, then *form* must be enclosed in braces.

@. is used to indicate that only blank space occurs between two of the nodes of the commutative diagram.

@<<< produces a left arrow.

@<*form*<< produces a left arrow with the expression *form* placed above the arrow; if a less-than sign occurs in *form*, then *form* must be enclosed in braces.

@<<*form*< produces a left arrow with the expression *form* placed below the arrow; if a less-than sign occurs in *form*, then *form* must be enclosed in braces.

@= is used to produce an extensible equals sign linking two nodes of the diagram horizontally.

@>>> produces a right arrow.

@>*form*>> produces a right arrow with the expression *form* placed above the arrow; if a greater-than sign occurs in *form*, then *form* must be enclosed in braces.

@>>*form*> produces a right arrow with the expression *form* placed below the arrow; if a greater-than sign occurs in *form*, then *form* must be enclosed in braces.

@\vert is used to produce an extensible equals sign linking two nodes of the commutative diagram vertically.

@| is used to produce an extensible equals sign linking two nodes of the commutative diagram vertically.

@AAA produces an up arrow.

@A*form*AA produces an up arrow with the expression *form* placed to the left of the arrow; if a capital letter A occurs in *form*, then *form* must be enclosed in braces.

@AA*form*A produces an up arrow with the expression *form* placed to the right of the arrow; if a capital letter A occurs in *form*, then *form* must be enclosed in braces.

@VVV produces a down arrow.

@V*form*VV produces a down arrow with the expression *form* placed to the left of the arrow; if a capital letter V occurs in *form*, then *form* must be enclosed in braces.

@VV*form*V produces a down arrow with the expression *form* placed to the right of the arrow; if a capital letter V occurs in *form*, then *form* must be enclosed in braces.

(Note that outside the CD environment extensible left and right arrows can be produced using the amsmath commands \xleftarrow and \xrightarrow.) Some of the above commands produce annotated arrows. In these cases it is not necessary to enclose *form* in braces, except in the situations explicitly mentioned, but there is no harm in doing this and it is a good idea to do this, as the general rule in LATEX, with only a small number of exceptions, is that arguments to commands are enclosed in braces or square brackets. The following diagram illustrates the effects of all the special commands that are available inside the CD environment. The only thing not illustrated in this diagram is the results produced by the commands that produce annotated arrows.

$$A \longleftarrow C \longrightarrow E \longleftarrow G$$

$$\uparrow \qquad \downarrow \qquad \| \qquad \|$$

$$B =\!\!=\!\!= D \qquad F \longrightarrow H$$

This diagram was produced by means of these commands:

```
\[\begin{CD}
A      @(((  C      @)))  E    @<<<  G \\
@AAA         @VVV         @|         @\vert \\
B      @=  D    @.  F  @>>>  H
\end{CD}\]
```

Note that each row inside the CD environment is terminated by a \\ command, but it would be a mistake to end the last row with this command.

To end this section I will show how the commands available inside the CD environment can be used to produce the following schema from Frege's letter to Husserl dated the 24th of May 1891 (Frege 1980, p. 63):

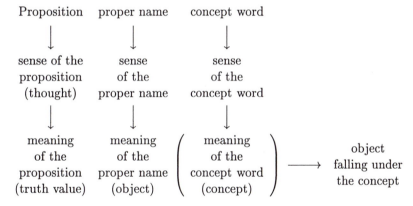

As well as illustrating an unusual application of the CD environment, I also want to use this example to illustrate one method of solving complicated typesetting problems using LaTeX and that is the technique of breaking the complex structure into a number of manageable components and then using local definitions to produce those elements. In effect, this method is just the application of a well-known technique of program design, namely the method of top-down stepwise development (though in this case there is only one step). To apply this problem-solving approach to Frege's schema it should be noted that it has the following general structure:

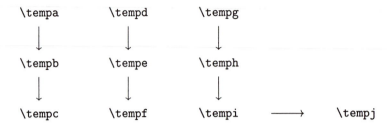

Given the information presented above about the way in which the CD environment works it is entirely straightforward to understand how such a diagram can be produced. The following commands suffice:

```
\[\begin{CD}
\tempa  @.  \tempd  @.  \tempg  @. \\
@VVV        @VVV        @VVV        \\
\tempb  @.  \tempe  @.  \temph  @. \\
@VVV        @VVV        @VVV        \\
\tempc  @.  \tempf  @.  \tempi  @>>>  \tempj
\end{CD}\]
```

The only thing that needs to be explained is how the nodes of Frege's schema are produced. That is to say, I need to tell you how to define the local commands \tempa, \tempb, ..., \tempi and \tempj. The best place to put the definitions of these local commands is between the commands \[and \begin{CD}. Their scope will then extend as far as the command \] that ends the display maths environment. These definitions are all very similar and so I will only give the definition of \tempb:

```
\newcommand*{\tempb}{\begin{array}{c}
                     \mbox{sense of the} \\
                     \mbox{proposition} \\
                     \mbox{(thought)}
                     \end{array}}
```

The large parentheses were produced by means of the commands \left(and \right), which were placed around the array environment but still inside the definiens of the local command \tempi.

Chapter 12

Simple Diagrams

12.1 Introduction

In this chapter I describe the `picture` environment in LaTeX. This is useful for producing fairly simple line drawings. In producing such diagrams using LaTeX you need to give the lengths of lines and also to specify positions in a Cartesian plane. Rather than using absolute units of length for this purpose, such as inches or centimetres, you use a relative unit of length within the `picture` environment and the magnitude of this is given by the `\unitlength` rigid length parameter. Thus, the command `\setlength{\unitlength}{1mm}` makes the unit of length in `picture` environments from that point on to be one millimetre. You do not, however, have to use the same unit of length in all your picture environments in a single document. You can give a new value to the `\unitlength` length parameter before each `picture` environment. You do not have to give the length in millimetres. Any LaTeX unit of length is acceptable. The default value for the unit of length is 1 point. That is to say, if you do not assign any value to the `\unitlength` length parameter, then the size of the unit that LaTeX uses is 1 point, where 1 inch = 72.27 points. (See section B.1 for a complete list of length units available in TeX.)

In order to produce the diagram shown in Fig. 12.1, which is based on one that occurs on p. 5 of Diller (1990), you need the following LaTeX commands:

```
\begin{center}
\setlength{\unitlength}{1mm}
\begin{picture}(110,50)(0,5)
\put(55,45){\makebox(0,0){formal methods}}
\put(20,5){\makebox(0,0){\framebox(37,9){formal specification}}}
\put(90,5){\makebox(0,0){\dashbox{1.5}(30,9){verified design}}}
\put(50,40){\line(-1,-1){30}}
\put(60,40){\line(1,-1){30}}
\end{picture}
\end{center}
```

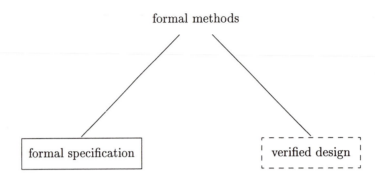

Figure 12.1: The branches of formal methods.

The `picture` environment that produced the diagram in Fig. 12.1 starts with the command:

```
\begin{picture}(110,50)(0,5)
```

The first argument to this opening command is mandatory and it represents the size of the box that LATEX produces. Thus, `(110,50)` indicates that the size of the box produced will be 110 units horizontally (that is to say, in the x direction) and 50 units vertically (that is to say, in the y direction). It is possible to draw lines outside of this area, but LATEX manipulates the box as if it were the size stipulated.

The second argument to the opening command, namely `(0,5)`, is optional and it indicates an offset. Normally, that is to say, when this second argument is omitted, the origin of the Cartesian plane on which pictures are to be drawn is at the bottom left-hand corner of the box that LATEX produces. However, if this second optional argument, say, (i, j), is present, then that bottom left-hand corner has coordinates (i, j). Thus, in this case the coordinates of the bottom left-hand corner of the box are $(0, 5)$; the coordinates of the bottom right-hand corner of the box are $(100, 5)$; the coordinates of the top left-hand corner of the box are $(0, 55)$; and the coordinates of the top right-hand corner of the box are $(110, 55)$. When devising the LATEX commands that you need to draw a picture, it is a good idea to either leave out the second (optional) argument or give it the value $(0, 0)$ (both of these alternatives have the same effect) and only to change it after you have completed your picture and want to position it precisely in relation to the context in which it occurs. This is often a trial-and-error process.

Only a small number of commands can be used inside the `picture` environment. Apart from declarations, the only commands that are allowed are `\put`, `\multiput`, `\bezier` and `\qbezier`. These commands are the only ones that draw lines and other shapes inside the `picture` environment. (Some packages define further commands that can be used inside the `picture` environment. For example, loading the `graphpap` package allows you to use the `\graphpaper` command inside the `picture` environment.) A number of additional declarations are also avaliable that alter the thickness of lines used inside the `picture` environment. These are `\thicklines`, `\thinlines` and `\linethickness`. The last of these takes a single parameter that must be a length.

The general format of the `\put` command is:

`\put`(*i, j*){*picture-object*}

This places the *picture-object* at the location in the picture whose *x*-coordinate is *i* and whose *y*-coordinate is *j*. Each picture object has a reference point associated with it and the coordinates (*i, j*) indicate the exact location of this reference point. (Almost anything can be considered as being a picture object, but certain things are used more frequently than others.) In the case of the commands that produced the picture in Fig. 12.1, the first three `\put` commands place text in the picture. The command

`\put(55,45){\makebox(0,0){formal methods}}`

contains as its picture object the component

`\makebox(0,0){formal methods}`

This is a LATEX command that makes a box which contains the text or symbols enclosed in braces; in this case the words 'formal methods'. The argument `(0,0)` indicates the size of the box produced. In this case the box has zero width and zero height. This has the consequence that the reference point is in the centre of the box that is produced when it has finished processing the text 'formal methods'. If the argument was (*i, j*), then a box of width *i* and height *j* would be produced with the reference point at the bottom left-hand corner of the box. The unit of length that is used is that specified by the last assignment to the `\unitlength` length parameter. Thus, the effect of the command

`\put(55,45){\makebox(0,0){formal methods}}`

is to place the text 'formal methods' in the picture at the position with coordinates (55, 45) in such a way that the centre of the box containing the text is placed at exactly this point.

The general format of the `\makebox` command, when used inside the `picture` environment, is:

`\makebox`(*i, j*) [*pos*] {*picture-object*}

(Note that the `\makebox` command, and the `\framebox` and `\savebox` commands to be described shortly, have a different form inside the `picture` environment from that which they have outside it; indeed, all three of them take different arguments inside the `picture` environment. For the use of these commands outside the `picture` environment see section 5.1.) The function of the optional argument *pos* to the `\makebox` command is to position the *picture-object* within the box produced by that command. If the argument *pos* is omitted, then the *picture-object* is centred within the box produced. The *pos* argument can take any of the values b, c, l, r, s and t or it can consist of two letters: one drawn from the set consisting of b, c and t and one drawn from the set consisting of c, l, r and s. Not all the possibilities are distinct; the various distinct options are:

b or bc or cb The *picture-object* is placed near the bottom of the box. It is mid way between the left and right edges of the box.

c or cc The *picture-object* is centred both horizontally and vertically.

l or cl or lc The *picture-object* is placed flush left inside the box produced. It is mid way between the top and bottom of the box.

r or cr or rc The *picture-object* is placed flush right inside the box produced. It is mid way between the top and bottom of the box.

s or cs or sc If the *picture-object* contains any rubber space, then it is stretched to fill the box produced horizontally and the *picture-object* is centred vertically.

t or tc or ct The *picture-object* is placed near the top of the box. It is mid way between the left and right edges of the box.

bl or lb The *picture-object* is positioned in the bottom left-hand corner of the box produced.

br or rb The *picture-object* is positioned in the bottom right-hand corner of the box produced.

bs or sb If the *picture-object* contains any rubber space, then it is stretched to fill the box produced horizontally and the *picture-object* is placed near the bottom of the box produced.

tl or lt The *picture-object* is positioned in the top left-hand corner of the box produced.

tr or rt The *picture-object* is positioned in the top right-hand corner of the box produced.

ts or st If the *picture-object* contains any rubber space, then it is stretched to fill the box produced horizontally and the *picture-object* is placed near the top of the box produced.

There are two commands that are closely related to the \makebox command, namely the \framebox and the \dashbox commands. The \framebox command has exactly the same arguments as the \makebox command. The only difference between them is that the \framebox command produces text with a rectangular box drawn around it. (Note that the length parameter \fboxsep has no effect inside the picture environment; no gap is ever left between the box produced and the frame.) The \dashbox command is similar except that it takes an extra argument. Its general format is:

\dashbox{*h*}(*i, j*) [*pos*] {*picture-object*}

The arguments (i, j), *pos* and *picture-object* are as for \makebox and \framebox. The command \dashbox produces text with a broken rectangular box drawn around it. The lengths of the dashes and spaces that make up the box are given by the argument h. When using \dashbox it is a good idea for the arguments i and j to be whole multiples of h. This makes the dashed box that is produced look better than it would otherwise do.

In the case of the picture in Fig. 12.1 the \framebox and \dashbox commands are themselves made into arguments for the \makebox command, which is then taken as the *picture-object* argument of a \put command, thus:

```
\put(20,5){\makebox(0,0){\framebox(37,9){formal specification}}}
\put(90,5){\makebox(0,0){\dashbox{1.5}(30,9){verified design}}}
```

The reason for this is that in both the \framebox and \dashbox command if the argument (i, j) has the value $(0, 0)$, then *no* line whatsoever is drawn around the box produced. Thus, in order to get a line you need non-zero values for both i and j in the argument (i, j). This, however, makes the box produced difficult to position precisely in the picture that is being drawn. Putting the \framebox and \dashbox commands inside a \makebox command, which is given $(0, 0)$ as one of *its* arguments, makes the resulting box easy to position because its reference point is in the centre of the box that is produced.

12.2   Straight Lines

The two sloping straight lines in Fig. 12.1 were produced by means of the commands:

```
\put(50,40){\line(-1,-1){30}}
\put(60,40){\line(1,-1){30}}
```

In order to produce a line in a picture you need a command with the following general format:

```
\put(i,j){\line(p,q){l}}
```

This draws a line one end of which starts at the point on the picture whose coordinates are given by the arguments (i, j). The coordinates (p, q) determine the slope of the line and the argument l determines its length. If we imagine the line that we want to draw being projected onto the x-axis, then the length of that projected line is l. (The picture in Fig. 12.2 should make this clearer.) The only exception to this occurs when we want to draw vertical lines when l gives the actual length of the line produced. This is because in this case the length of the projection of the line onto the x-axis is zero.

To produce a line with a particular slope you imagine how you would get back onto the line if you were only allowed to move horizontally and vertically. Thus, if you wanted to produce a line that was at 45° to the x-axis, you would have to move 1 unit horizontally and 1 unit vertically. The arguments p and q can be negative but they must be non-zero whole numbers without any common divisors (except -1 or $+1$) that

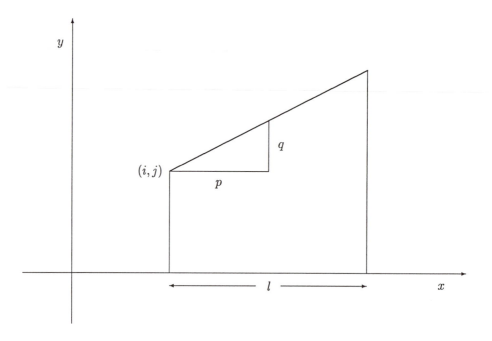

Figure 12.2: The arguments of the \put$(i,j)$\{\line$(p,q)${l}} command.

lie between -6 and $+6$ (and the values -6 and $+6$ are allowed). Assuming that p and q are both positive numbers, this is illustrated in the diagram in Fig. 12.2.

LATEX can produce lines in two thicknesses, namely thin and thick, and the default thickness of lines is the thin option. The lines in Fig. 12.1 are both thin. To get the thicker lines you need to include the declaration \thicklines. The scope of this can be made explicit by the use of curly braces. Alternatively, the use of the declaration \thinlines makes all lines from that point on to be thin.

Having explained all the commands relevant to the picture environment that produced the picture in Fig. 12.1 I just need to explain the occurrence of the center environment. This has the effect of centring the picture that it encloses on the page.

12.3   Disks and Circles

The diagram shown in Fig. 12.3, which comes from p. 164 of Diller (1990), was produced by the following LATEX commands:

```
\begin{center}
\setlength{\unitlength}{.3mm}
\begin{picture}(240,180)(0,0)
\put(70,20){\line(-1,3){50}}
\put(70,20){\line(1,1){150}}
```

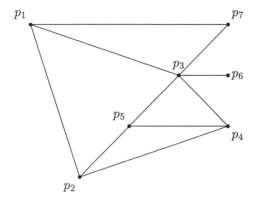

Figure 12.3: An example of a bill of materials.

```
\put(70,20){\line(3,1){150}}
\put(20,170){\line(1,0){200}}
\put(20,170){\line(3,-1){150}}
\put(120,70){\line(1,0){100}}
\put(170,120){\line(1,0){50}}
\put(170,120){\line(1,-1){50}}
%
\put(70,20){\circle*{3.7}}
\put(20,170){\circle*{3.7}}
\put(120,70){\circle*{3.7}}
\put(170,120){\circle*{3.7}}
\put(220,70){\circle*{3.7}}
\put(220,120){\circle*{3.7}}
\put(220,170){\circle*{3.7}}
%
\put(10,180){\makebox(0,0){$p_1$}}
\put(60,10){\makebox(0,0){$p_2$}}
\put(170,130){\makebox(0,0){$p_3$}}
\put(230,60){\makebox(0,0){$p_4$}}
\put(110,80){\makebox(0,0){$p_5$}}
\put(230,120){\makebox(0,0){$p_6$}}
\put(230,180){\makebox(0,0){$p_7$}}
\end{picture}
\end{center}
```

Most of these have been explained already. The filled in circles were produced by the
\circle* command. Thus, the filled in circle closest to the label p_1 was produced by
the command:

```
\put(20,170){\circle*{3.7}}
```

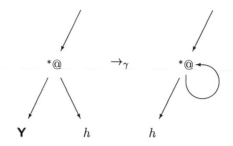

Figure 12.4: Graph-reduction of **Y** h.

This draws a solid circular disk whose diameter is 3.7 times the value of the rigid length parameter \unitlength. The centre of the disk is at the point whose coordinates are $(20, 170)$. There is also a LaTeX command for drawing circles that are not filled in. The general format of this command is:

\put$(i, j)${\circle{d}}

This places a circle of diameter d on the picture in such a way that its centre is at the point whose coordinates are (i, j). Note that LaTeX can only produce a very restricted class of circles and disks. The largest circle it can draw is 40 points (which is about half an inch) and the largest disk has a diameter of 15 points (which is about a fifth of an inch). Also, there are only a finite number of diameters available. If there is not one of exactly the size you specify, then LaTeX will use the one in its repertoire that is closest to the one you specify.

The label p_1 in Fig. 12.3 was produced by means of the command:

\put(10,180){\makebox(0,0){p_1}}

This illustrates how mathematical formulas can be positioned on a picture drawn by LaTeX.

12.4   Arrows and Ovals

The diagram that occurs in Fig. 12.4, which is based on Fig. 5.6 of Diller (1988), p. 77, was produced by means of the following commands:

```
\begin{center}
\setlength{\unitlength}{1mm}
\begin{picture}(60,40)(0,0)
\put(8,16){\vector(-1,-2){6}}
\put(12,16){\vector(1,-2){6}}
\put(18,36){\vector(-1,-2){6}}
\put(0,0){\makebox(0,0){\textsf{\textbf{Y}}}}
```

```
\put(20,0){\makebox(0,0){$h$}}
\put(10,20){\makebox(0,0){$^*@$}}
%
\put(30,20){\makebox(0,0){$\rightarrow_\gamma$}}
%
\put(48,16){\vector(-1,-2){6}}
\put(58,36){\vector(-1,-2){6}}
\put(55,15){\oval(10,10)[b]}
\put(55,15){\oval(10,10)[tr]}
\put(55,20){\vector(-1,0){2}}
\put(50,15){\line(0,1){2}}
\put(50,20){\makebox(0,0){$^*@$}}
\put(40,0){\makebox(0,0){$h$}}
\end{picture}
\end{center}
```

Two new features of LaTeX's `picture` environment are introduced in this example and they are the `\vector` and `\oval` commands. The first group of `\put` commands produce the graph to the left of the arrow $\rightarrow_\gamma$ in Fig. 12.4. For example, the command:

```
\put(18,36){\vector(-1,-2){6}}
```

draws an arrow which starts at the point with coordinates $(18, 36)$ and whose projection on the x-axis is 6 units long and whose slope is given by the argument $(-1, -2)$, that is to say, it goes one unit in the left direction for every two units it goes downwards. The arrowhead of an arrow drawn by the `\vector` command is always at the end of the arrow whose coordinates are *not* given by the first argument to the `\put` command. The only exception to this is for arrows of length 0, in which case just the arrowhead itself is drawn and it occurs at the position given by the first argument to the `\put` command. The slopes with which LaTeX can draw arrows is more restrictive than the slopes that lines can have. The numbers in the slope argument must be non-zero whole numbers between -4 and $+4$.

The graph on the right of the arrow $\rightarrow_\gamma$ in Fig. 12.4 is produced by the third group of `\put` commands in the `picture` environment. The `\oval` commands produce the circular part of the middle arrow. The `\oval` command in LaTeX produces oblongs with rounded corners. Its general format is:

```
\put(i,j){\oval(p,q)[part]}
```

This draws an oblong with smooth corners such that its centre is located at the point (i, j) and the oblong fits into a rectangle whose width is p units and whose height is q units. The optional *part* argument consists of a one- or two-letter code which indicates which part of the oblong is to be drawn. (If it is absent, the whole oblong is drawn.) A one-letter code draws half an oblong. Thus:

l The left half of the oblong is drawn.

t The top half of the oblong is drawn.

r The right half of the oblong is drawn.

b The bottom half of the oblong is drawn.

A two-letter code draws a quarter of an oblong. Only the following four combinations are meaningful:

tl The top left-hand quarter of the oval is drawn.

tr The top right-hand quarter of the oval is drawn.

br The bottom right-hand quarter of the oval is drawn.

bl The bottom left-hand quarter of the oval is drawn.

12.5   Saving and Reusing Boxes

Consider the following arrangement of circles:

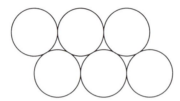

These circles were produced by means of the following commands:

```
\begin{center}
\begin{picture}(100,103.92)
\multiput(20,34.64)(40,0){3}{\circle{40}}
\multiput(0,69.28)(40,0){3}{\circle{40}}
\end{picture}
\end{center}
```

This illustrates the use of the \multiput command, the general format of which is:

$$\text{\textbackslash multiput}\,(i,j)\,(m,n)\,\{t\}\{picture\text{-}object\}$$

This is equivalent to the following t commands:

$$\text{\textbackslash put}\,(i,j)\,\{picture\text{-}object\}$$
$$\text{\textbackslash put}\,(i+m,j+n)\,\{picture\text{-}object\}$$
$$\text{\textbackslash put}\,(i+2m,j+2n)\,\{picture\text{-}object\}$$
$$\vdots$$
$$\text{\textbackslash put}\,(i+(t-1)m,j+(t-1)n)\,\{picture\text{-}object\}$$

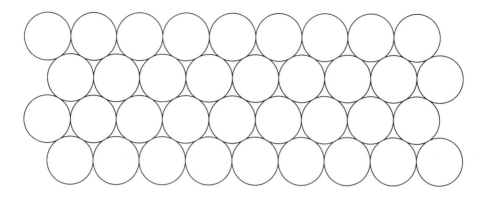

Figure 12.5: A pretty arrangement of circles.

LaTeX does not have a very large memory, so there is a maximum number of repetitions allowed and it is about 100.

One way of producing the arrangement of circles shown in Fig. 12.5 is by means of the following commands:

```
\newsavebox{\balls}
\savebox{\balls}(120,69.28){%
\begin{picture}(120,69.28)
\multiput(20,34.64)(40,0){3}{\circle{40}}
\multiput(0,69.28)(40,0){3}{\circle{40}}
\end{picture}}

\begin{picture}(340,173.2)
\multiput(0,0)(0,69.28){2}
        {\multiput(0,0)(120,0){3}{\usebox{\balls}}}
\end{picture}
```

The \newsavebox command here creates a *storage bin* called \balls. A storage bin is a region of memory that stores a box. It is a good idea to store boxes which require a lot of processing to produce and which you use several times in a document. If you use a macro rather than a stored box, then TeX will process it afresh each time it comes across it. The \savebox command here is similar to the \makebox command discussed earlier; it is processed in exactly the same way. Unlike the \makebox command, however, it does not produce anything that appears in the document that you are working on. Although it processes what is given to it as its argument, it puts the result into a storage bin. The general format of a \savebox command is:

```
\savebox{cmd}(i, j)[pos]{picture-object}
```

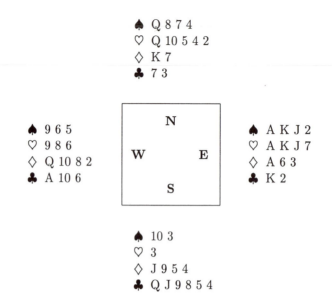

Figure 12.6: A contract bridge diagram.

The arguments (i, j), *pos* and *picture-object* have the same meaning as those of the \makebox command. The argument *cmd* is the name of a storage bin that must have been declared previously by a \newsavebox command and *cmd* must begin with a backslash. To print what is in a storage bin use the \usebox command. LaTeX has only a small amount of space at its disposal for storing boxes. If you need to store several boxes in a document, you can reclaim the space needed by, say, the \balls storage bin by means of the command \sbox{\balls}{}. The \sbox command is a variant of the \savebox command with no optional arguments.

12.6 Contract Bridge Diagrams

To produce the diagram shown in Fig. 1.3, and reproduced in Fig. 12.6, you first define the four hands in local commands \north, \east, \south and \west. These definitions are very similar to each other and so only that of \north is given here:

```
\newcommand*{\north}{%
\begin{tabular}{cl}
$\spadesuit$   & Q\,\,8\,\,7\,\,4 \\
$\heartsuit$   & Q\,\,10\,\,5\,\,4\,\,2 \\
$\diamondsuit$ & K\,\,7 \\
$\clubsuit$    & 7\,\,3
\end{tabular}}
```

The whole diagram shown in Fig. 12.6 is then produced by means of the following commands:

```
\begin{center}
\addtolength{\tabcolsep}{-1mm}
\setlength{\unitlength}{1mm}
\begin{picture}(90,90)
\put(30,30){\line(1,0){30}}
\put(30,30){\line(0,1){30}}
\put(60,60){\line(-1,0){30}}
\put(60,60){\line(0,-1){30}}
%
\put(45,55){\makebox(0,0){\bfseries N}}
\put(55,45){\makebox(0,0){\bfseries E}}
\put(45,35){\makebox(0,0){\bfseries S}}
\put(35,45){\makebox(0,0){\bfseries W}}
%
\put(32.5,75){\north}
\put(67.5,44){\east}
\put(32.5,12.5){\south}
\put(0,44){\west}
\addtolength{\tabcolsep}{1mm}
\end{picture}
\end{center}
```

12.7 Bézier Curves

It is also possible to get LaTeX to produce curves inside the `picture` environment such as this:

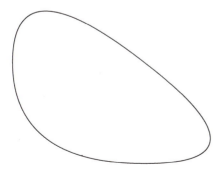

This closed curve is made up out of three pieces. It was produced by means of the following commands:

```
\begin{center}
\setlength{\unitlength}{1cm}
\begin{picture}(8,4.5)
\qbezier(0,3)(0,0)(4,0)
\qbezier(4,0)(8,0)(4,3)
\qbezier(4,3)(0,6)(0,3)
\end{picture}
\end{center}
```

The command \qbezier is used to produce curves. The general format of this command, and the closely related command \bezier, are as follows:

\bezier{*t*}(i_1, j_1) (i_2, j_2) (i_3, j_3)
\qbezier[*t*] (i_1, j_1) (i_2, j_2) (i_3, j_3)

Both of these commands produce a quadratic Bézier curve from the point whose co-ordinates are (i_1, j_1) to the point (i_3, j_3). The curve produced has the property that the line linking (i_1, j_1) and (i_2, j_2) is a tangent to it at the point (i_1, j_1) and the line linking (i_2, j_2) and (i_3, j_3) is a tangent to it at the point (i_3, j_3). The only difference between the \bezier and \qbezier commands is that the parameter t is mandatory in the \bezier command whereas it is optional in the \qbezier command. In both cases t is a positive number and it determines the number of points used to produce the curve. If it is absent in the \qbezier command, then enough points are chosen in order to produce a smooth curve. The maximum number of points that LaTeX can use is given by the value of the command \qbeziermax. The value of \qbeziermax can be changed by using the \renewcommand* command.

The following diagram reproduces the closed curve shown on p. 155 above. This time, however, it is drawn with the \thicklines declaration in force. Furthermore, the position of the control points is indicated. This should make clear how the \qbezier command works.

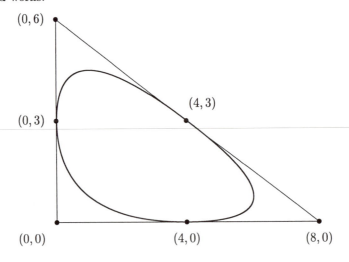

Appendix A

Mathematical Symbols

A.1 Introduction

There are several kinds or categories of mathematical symbols in TeX and the most important of these are: ordinary symbols, unary operators, binary operators, binary relation symbols, opening symbols, closing symbols and punctuation marks. In this appendix the symbols belonging to each of these categories are described in greater detail.

A.2 Ordinary Symbols

In maths mode as well as treating the 26 lowercase Roman letters a to z and the 26 uppercase Roman letters A to Z as ordinary symbols TeX also considers the following 18 characters to be ordinary symbols:

$$0 \quad 1 \quad 2 \quad 3 \quad 4 \quad 5 \quad 6 \quad 7 \quad 8 \quad 9 \quad ! \quad ? \quad . \quad | \quad / \quad ` \quad @ \quad "$$

To say that a character is an *ordinary symbol* means that TeX does not insert any extra space between that symbol and another ordinary symbol when these symbols occur next to each other (as Knuth (1986a), p. 132, explains). Note that the full stop is considered to be an ordinary symbol in maths mode and not a punctuation mark. This ensures that real numbers are correctly typeset in maths mode. Thus, $12.72 > x$ is produced by means of the input `$12.72 > x$`.

When any of the 52 lowercase and uppercase letters occur in maths mode, then they appear in maths italic font. This is slightly different from text italic. The letters themselves are slightly larger and the spacing is completely different. This comes out clearly in a word like 'effluent', which in text italic looks like *effluent*, but in maths italic appears as $effluent$. The reason for this is that mathematicians typically use single letters for the names of functions and variables and juxtaposition usually indicates multiplication. To get LaTeX to produce bold letters, upright letters, letters in a sans serif font and letters in typewriter font in maths mode you can use the commands `\mathbf`, `\mathrm`, `\mathsf` and `\mathtt`. The command `\mathit` is also provided to produce the maths italic font. Each of these commands take a single argument. It is also possible to use these commands to produce multi-letter identifiers that computer scientists like to use. Consider, for example, the following equation:

$$\textbf{effluent} = \text{effluent} = \mathsf{effluent} = \mathtt{effluent} = \mathit{effluent}.$$

This was produced by means of the following commands:

```
\[\mathbf{effluent} = \mathrm{effluent} = \mathsf{effluent} =
   \mathtt{effluent} = \mathit{effluent}.\]
```

One problem with using these commands to produce multi-letter identifiers, however, is that the arguments to these commands are processed in maths mode and so a hyphen, say, becomes a minus sign. Thus, `$\mathit{quasi-order}$` produces $quasi - order$.

It is possible to get LaTeX to produce Greek letters. TeX treats each of these as an ordinary symbol. The following table illustrates the commands involved:

α	\alpha	A	\mathrm{A}	A	A	A
β	\beta	B	\mathrm{B}	B	B	B
γ	\gamma	Γ	\Gamma	Γ	\mathit{\Gamma}	\varGamma
δ	\delta	Δ	\Delta	Δ	\mathit{\Delta}	\varDelta
ϵ	\epsilon	E	\mathrm{E}	E	E	E
ζ	\zeta	Z	\mathrm{Z}	Z	Z	Z
η	\eta	H	\mathrm{H}	H	H	H
θ	\theta	Θ	\Theta	Θ	\mathit{\Theta}	\varTheta
ι	\iota	I	\mathrm{I}	I	I	I
κ	\kappa	K	\mathrm{K}	K	K	K
λ	\lambda	Λ	\Lambda	Λ	\mathit{\Lambda}	\varLambda
μ	\mu	M	\mathrm{M}	M	M	M
ν	\nu	N	\mathrm{N}	N	N	N
ξ	\xi	Ξ	\Xi	Ξ	\mathit{\Xi}	\varXi
o	o	O	\mathrm{O}	O	O	O
π	\pi	Π	\Pi	Π	\mathit{\Pi}	\varPi
ρ	\rho	P	\mathrm{P}	P	P	P
σ	\sigma	Σ	\Sigma	Σ	\mathit{\Sigma}	\varSigma
τ	\tau	T	\mathrm{T}	T	T	T
υ	\upsilon	Υ	\Upsilon	Υ	\mathit{\Upsilon}	\varUpsilon
ϕ	\phi	Φ	\Phi	Φ	\mathit{\Phi}	\varPhi
χ	\chi	X	\mathrm{X}	X	X	X
ψ	\psi	Ψ	\Psi	Ψ	\mathit{\Psi}	\varPsi
ω	\omega	Ω	\Omega	Ω	\mathit{\Omega}	\varOmega

The first column shows the twenty-four lowercase letters of the Greek alphabet in their correct order. The second column shows the LaTeX commands which are used to produce the lowercase Greek letters. Note that omicron is produced by typing o in maths mode. The third column shows the twenty-four uppercase letters of the Greek alphabet and the fourth column shows the basic LaTeX commands which are needed to produce them. Note that by default upright versions of the uppercase Greek letters are produced (where these differ from their Roman equivalents); this is because these are the forms most commonly used in mathematics. The fifth column shows the italic versions of the uppercase Greek letters. How these are produced in basic LaTeX is shown in the sixth column and how they are produced if you are using the `amsmath` package is shown in the seventh column. Note that if you use the `amsmath` package $\mathit{\Gamma}$$, for example, produces Γ and not $\mathit{\Gamma}$.

Mathematicians also use variants of the lowercase Greek letters delta, epsilon, theta, pi, rho and phi. These are produced as follows:

∂	`\partial`	ϑ	`\vartheta`	ϱ	`\varrho`
ε	`\varepsilon`	ϖ	`\varpi`	φ	`\varphi`

Still another variant of epsilon, namely $\in$ produced by the command `\in`, is used for set membership, but TeX treats this as a relation and not an ordinary operator. TeX also contains the symbol ς, produced by typing `\varsigma`, but according to Knuth (1986a), p. 434, this and upsilon are not letters that are used by mathematicians. They are included in TeX in case someone wants to quote *short* Greek passages. The commands `\digamma` and `\varkappa` are available in the `amssymb` package; they produce $\digamma$ and $\varkappa$, respectively.

Basic LaTeX provides the command `\mathcal` for producing calligraphic letters. If you load the `eucal` package, the `\mathcal` command is redefined so that it produces letters belonging to the Euler Script alphabet. However, if you load the `eucal` package using the `mathscr` option, then the `\mathcal` command is not redefined and the Euler Script letters become available through the `\mathscr` command. To get blackboard bold letters you need to load the `amsfonts` package; this provides the command `\mathbb`. If you load either the `eufrak` or the `amsfonts` package, then you can use the `\mathfrak` command to produce letters from the Euler Fraktur alphabet. (These are the letters that mathematicians call *Gothic*.) The argument of the `\mathfrak` command can contain both lowercase and uppercase letters, whereas the others can only contain uppercase letters. The lowercase Gothic letters are shown in the following table:

$\mathfrak{a}$	`\mathfrak{a}`	$\mathfrak{j}$	`\mathfrak{j}`	$\mathfrak{s}$	`\mathfrak{s}`
$\mathfrak{b}$	`\mathfrak{b}`	$\mathfrak{k}$	`\mathfrak{k}`	$\mathfrak{t}$	`\mathfrak{t}`
$\mathfrak{c}$	`\mathfrak{c}`	$\mathfrak{l}$	`\mathfrak{l}`	$\mathfrak{u}$	`\mathfrak{u}`
$\mathfrak{d}$	`\mathfrak{d}`	$\mathfrak{m}$	`\mathfrak{m}`	$\mathfrak{v}$	`\mathfrak{v}`
$\mathfrak{e}$	`\mathfrak{e}`	$\mathfrak{n}$	`\mathfrak{n}`	$\mathfrak{w}$	`\mathfrak{w}`
$\mathfrak{f}$	`\mathfrak{f}`	$\mathfrak{o}$	`\mathfrak{o}`	$\mathfrak{x}$	`\mathfrak{x}`
$\mathfrak{g}$	`\mathfrak{g}`	$\mathfrak{p}$	`\mathfrak{p}`	$\mathfrak{y}$	`\mathfrak{y}`
$\mathfrak{h}$	`\mathfrak{h}`	$\mathfrak{q}$	`\mathfrak{q}`	$\mathfrak{z}$	`\mathfrak{z}`
$\mathfrak{i}$	`\mathfrak{i}`	$\mathfrak{r}$	`\mathfrak{r}`		

Ordinary calligraphic letters, Euler Script letters, blackboard bold letters and uppercase Gothic letters are shown in the following table:

$\mathcal{A}$	\mathcal{A}	$\mathscr{A}$	\mathscr{A}	$\mathbb{A}$	\mathbb{A}	$\mathfrak{A}$	\mathfrak{A}
$\mathcal{B}$	\mathcal{B}	$\mathscr{B}$	\mathscr{B}	$\mathbb{B}$	\mathbb{B}	$\mathfrak{B}$	\mathfrak{B}
$\mathcal{C}$	\mathcal{C}	$\mathscr{C}$	\mathscr{C}	$\mathbb{C}$	\mathbb{C}	$\mathfrak{C}$	\mathfrak{C}
$\mathcal{D}$	\mathcal{D}	$\mathscr{D}$	\mathscr{D}	$\mathbb{D}$	\mathbb{D}	$\mathfrak{D}$	\mathfrak{D}
$\mathcal{E}$	\mathcal{E}	$\mathscr{E}$	\mathscr{E}	$\mathbb{E}$	\mathbb{E}	$\mathfrak{E}$	\mathfrak{E}
$\mathcal{F}$	\mathcal{F}	$\mathscr{F}$	\mathscr{F}	$\mathbb{F}$	\mathbb{F}	$\mathfrak{F}$	\mathfrak{F}
$\mathcal{G}$	\mathcal{G}	$\mathscr{G}$	\mathscr{G}	$\mathbb{G}$	\mathbb{G}	$\mathfrak{G}$	\mathfrak{G}
$\mathcal{H}$	\mathcal{H}	$\mathscr{H}$	\mathscr{H}	$\mathbb{H}$	\mathbb{H}	$\mathfrak{H}$	\mathfrak{H}
$\mathcal{I}$	\mathcal{I}	$\mathscr{I}$	\mathscr{I}	$\mathbb{I}$	\mathbb{I}	$\mathfrak{I}$	\mathfrak{I}
$\mathcal{J}$	\mathcal{J}	$\mathscr{J}$	\mathscr{J}	$\mathbb{J}$	\mathbb{J}	$\mathfrak{J}$	\mathfrak{J}
$\mathcal{K}$	\mathcal{K}	$\mathscr{K}$	\mathscr{K}	$\mathbb{K}$	\mathbb{K}	$\mathfrak{K}$	\mathfrak{K}
$\mathcal{L}$	\mathcal{L}	$\mathscr{L}$	\mathscr{L}	$\mathbb{L}$	\mathbb{L}	$\mathfrak{L}$	\mathfrak{L}
$\mathcal{M}$	\mathcal{M}	$\mathscr{M}$	\mathscr{M}	$\mathbb{M}$	\mathbb{M}	$\mathfrak{M}$	\mathfrak{M}
$\mathcal{N}$	\mathcal{N}	$\mathscr{N}$	\mathscr{N}	$\mathbb{N}$	\mathbb{N}	$\mathfrak{N}$	\mathfrak{N}
$\mathcal{O}$	\mathcal{O}	$\mathscr{O}$	\mathscr{O}	$\mathbb{O}$	\mathbb{O}	$\mathfrak{O}$	\mathfrak{O}
$\mathcal{P}$	\mathcal{P}	$\mathscr{P}$	\mathscr{P}	$\mathbb{P}$	\mathbb{P}	$\mathfrak{P}$	\mathfrak{P}
$\mathcal{Q}$	\mathcal{Q}	$\mathscr{Q}$	\mathscr{Q}	$\mathbb{Q}$	\mathbb{Q}	$\mathfrak{Q}$	\mathfrak{Q}
$\mathcal{R}$	\mathcal{R}	$\mathscr{R}$	\mathscr{R}	$\mathbb{R}$	\mathbb{R}	$\mathfrak{R}$	\mathfrak{R}
$\mathcal{S}$	\mathcal{S}	$\mathscr{S}$	\mathscr{S}	$\mathbb{S}$	\mathbb{S}	$\mathfrak{S}$	\mathfrak{S}
$\mathcal{T}$	\mathcal{T}	$\mathscr{T}$	\mathscr{T}	$\mathbb{T}$	\mathbb{T}	$\mathfrak{T}$	\mathfrak{T}
$\mathcal{U}$	\mathcal{U}	$\mathscr{U}$	\mathscr{U}	$\mathbb{U}$	\mathbb{U}	$\mathfrak{U}$	\mathfrak{U}
$\mathcal{V}$	\mathcal{V}	$\mathscr{V}$	\mathscr{V}	$\mathbb{V}$	\mathbb{V}	$\mathfrak{V}$	\mathfrak{V}
$\mathcal{W}$	\mathcal{W}	$\mathscr{W}$	\mathscr{W}	$\mathbb{W}$	\mathbb{W}	$\mathfrak{W}$	\mathfrak{W}
$\mathcal{X}$	\mathcal{X}	$\mathscr{X}$	\mathscr{X}	$\mathbb{X}$	\mathbb{X}	$\mathfrak{X}$	\mathfrak{X}
$\mathcal{Y}$	\mathcal{Y}	$\mathscr{Y}$	\mathscr{Y}	$\mathbb{Y}$	\mathbb{Y}	$\mathfrak{Y}$	\mathfrak{Y}
$\mathcal{Z}$	\mathcal{Z}	$\mathscr{Z}$	\mathscr{Z}	$\mathbb{Z}$	\mathbb{Z}	$\mathfrak{Z}$	\mathfrak{Z}

To illustrate some of these letters, consider the following definition from Dummett (1977), p. 165:

$\mathscr{M}$ is *faithful* to $\mathscr{L} = \langle \mathbb{L}, \vdash_\mathscr{L} \rangle$ iff, for every Γ and A, if $\Gamma \vdash_\mathscr{L} A$, then $\Gamma \vDash_\mathscr{M} A$.

This definition was produced by means of the following commands:

```
\begin{quote}
$\mathscr{M}$ is \textit{faithful} to
$\mathscr{L} = \langle \mathbb{L}\,, \vdash_\mathscr{L} \rangle$
if{}f, for every $\Gamma$ and $A$,
if $\Gamma \vdash_\mathscr{L} A$,
then $\Gamma \vDash_\mathscr{M} A$.
\end{quote}
```

Note the use of the empty group {} to prevent a ligature being used in the output of 'iff'.

As well as treating all the letters discussed so far as ordinary symbols, TeX also treats a large number of other symbols as ordinary symbols. In fact it treats all the symbols in the following table as ordinary symbols:

∀	\forall[†]	#	\#[†]	∠	\angle[†]
∃	\exists[†]	%	\%[†]	⦦	\measuredangle[§]
∄	\nexists[§]	_	_[†]	⊲	\sphericalangle[§]
¬	\neg[†] or \lnot[†]	$	\$[†]	♠	\spadesuit[†]
⊤	\top[†]	&	\&[†]	♡	\heartsuit[†]
⊥	\bot[†]	ı	\imath[†]	◇	\diamondsuit[†]
∅	\emptyset[†]	ȷ	\jmath[†]	♣	\clubsuit[†]
∅	\varnothing[§]	ℓ	\ell[†]	◊	\lozenge[§]
∞	\infty[†]	℘	\wp[†]	◆	\blacklozenge[§]
ℵ	\aleph[†]	ℜ	\Re[†]	◇	\Diamond[¶]
ℶ	\beth[§]	ℑ	\Im[†]	△	\triangle[†]
ℷ	\gimel[§]	′	\prime[†]	△	\vartriangle[§]
ℸ	\daleth[§]	‵	\backprime[§]	▲	\blacktriangle[§]
ℏ	\hbar[†]	∇	\nabla[†]	▽	\triangledown[§]
ℏ	\hslash[§]	√	\surd[†]	▼	\blacktriangledown[§]
╱	\diagup[§]	♭	\flat[†]	□	\Box[¶]
/	/[†]	♯	\sharp[†]	□	\square[§]
|	|[†] or \vert[†]	♮	\natural[†]	■	\blacksquare[§]
‖	\\|[†] or \Vert[†]	ð	\eth[§]	∁	\complement[§]
\	\backslash[†]	★	\bigstar[§]	℧	\mho[§,¶]
╲	\diagdown[§]	Ⓢ	\circledS[§]	⅁	\Game[§]
𝕜	\Bbbk[§]	⅂	\Finv[§]	∂	\partial[†]
¶	\P[†]	†	\dag[†]	∫	\smallint[†]
§	\S[†]	‡	\ddag[†]	@	@[†]
!	![†]	?	?[†]	.	.[†]

The commands marked with † are available in basic LaTeX, those marked with ¶ require you to load the `latexsym` package and those marked with § require you to load the `amssymb` package. The symbol produced by the command \mho is available both in the `latexsym` and also in the `amssymb` package.

In order to force TeX to treat a symbol as an ordinary symbol you can use the command \mathord. Say, for example, that you wanted to use the symbol ∼ for negation and because you used it a lot you wanted to give it a sensible name. These two things could be achieved by means of the following definition:

```
\newcommand*{\lneg}{\mathord{\sim}}
```

Although the command \sim produces a symbol for a binary relation, the command \lneg produces an ordinary symbol. An alternative way in which to force TeX to treat something as an ordinary symbol is to enclose it in braces.

In section A.4, starting on p. 164, below I give a list of binary operators available in LaTeX; sometimes, however, such symbols are treated as ordinary symbols. This happens when they do not occur between two operands. For example, in the expression $x - y$ (produced by `$x - y$`) the minus sign is treated by TeX as being a binary operator, but in the expression $x = -y$ (produced by `$x = - y$`) the minus sign is treated as an ordinary symbol. This is true not only of $-$ and $+$; it is true of every binary operator (Knuth 1986a, p. 133).

Placed in front of delimiters, as explained in section 9.4 above, the commands `\big`, `\Big`, `\bigg` and `\Bigg` produce ordinary symbols.

A.3 Unary Operators

TeX contains a number of symbols for unary operations that come in two sizes; the larger size is used in display style and the smaller is used in text style. The following is a table of such so-called *large operators*:

$\bigcap$	`\bigcap`	$\bigvee$	`\bigvee`
$\bigcup$	`\bigcup`	$\bigwedge$	`\bigwedge`
$\bigodot$	`\bigodot`	$\coprod$	`\coprod`
$\bigoplus$	`\bigoplus`	$\int$	`\int`
$\bigotimes$	`\bigotimes`	$\oint$	`\oint`
$\bigsqcup$	`\bigsqcup`	$\prod$	`\prod`
$\biguplus$	`\biguplus`	$\sum$	`\sum`

When subscripts and superscripts are attached to a control word for a large operator in display style, then they appear under and over the symbol, respectively, as limits. For example, the commands `\[\sum_{i=1}^{i=n} i^2,\]` produce

$$\sum_{i=1}^{i=n} i^2,$$

whereas the commands `$\sum_{i=1}^{i=n} i^2$` produce $\sum_{i=1}^{i=n} i^2$ within text. That is to say, subscripts and superscripts attached to a control word for a large operator appear as subscripts and superscripts when processed in text style. Note that the size of the operator has altered as well.

Some unary functions used by mathematicians have names made up out of several letters, like 'sin'. These so-called *log-like operators* fall into two distinct categories depending on how subscripts and superscripts behave in display style. Subscripts and superscripts become limits in display style when attached to the following operators:

det	`\det`[†]	inj lim	`\injlim`[∞]	lim sup	`\limsup`[†]	Pr	`\Pr`[†]
gcd	`\gcd`[†]	lim	`\lim`[†]	max	`\max`[†]	proj lim	`\projlim`[∞]
inf	`\inf`[†]	lim inf	`\liminf`[†]	min	`\min`[†]	sup	`\sup`[†]

(The commands marked † are available in basic LaTeX, whereas those marked ∞ require the `amsmath` package.) In the next group of log-like symbols subscripts and superscripts appear as subscripts and superscripts when attached to these operators both in text style and display style:

arccos	\arccos[†]	coth	\coth[†]	lg	\lg[†]	tan	\tan[†]
arcsin	\arcsin[†]	csc	\csc[†]	ln	\ln[†]	tanh	\tanh[†]
arctan	\arctan[†]	deg	\deg[†]	log	\log[†]	$\varinjlim$	\varinjlim[∞]
arg	\arg[†]	dim	\dim[†]	sec	\sec[†]	$\varliminf$	\varliminf[∞]
cos	\cos[†]	exp	\exp[†]	sin	\sin[†]	$\varlimsup$	\varlimsup[∞]
cosh	\cosh[†]	hom	\hom[†]	sinh	\sinh[†]	$\varprojlim$	\varprojlim[∞]
cot	\cot[†]	ker	\ker[†]				

In order to define your own log-like function you have to decide how you want subscripts and superscripts to behave. There are three possibilities:

(1) You want subscripts and superscripts to appear as limits in display style, but you want them to appear as subscripts and superscripts in text style. In this case you should use the \displaylimits command in the following way:

   \newcommand*{\done}{\mathop{\mathrm{one}}\displaylimits}

If you use the amsopn package, then an alternative way to define the same sort of operator is by means of the \operatorname* command:

   \newcommand*{\done}{\operatorname*{one}}

Note that the operators defined in this way are typeset in upright, roman type. Alternatively, you could use the \DeclareMathOperator* command in your document's preamble or in a personal package, thus:

   \DeclareMathOperator*{\done}{one}

(2) You want subscripts and superscripts to appear as limits both in display style and in text style. In this case you should use the \limits command in this way:

   \newcommand*{\lone}{\mathop{\mathrm{one}}\limits}

(3) You want subscripts and superscripts to appear as subscripts and superscripts both in display style and in text style. In this case you should use the \nolimits command in this way:

   \newcommand*{\none}{\mathop{\mathrm{one}}\nolimits}

If you use the amsopn package, then an alternative way to define the same sort of operator is by means of the \operatorname command:

   \newcommand*{\none}{\operatorname{one}}

Note that the operators defined in this way are typeset in upright, roman type. Alternatively, you could use the \DeclareMathOperator command in your document's preamble or in a personal package, thus:

   \DeclareMathOperator{\none}{one}

A.4　Binary Operators

A binary operator is a symbol like + or ⊓. It makes a term out of two terms. It should be contrasted with a binary relation symbol like > or ⊒, since these make a formula out of two terms. This difference is reflected in how much space separates the operators from their arguments. In the case of a formula containing a symbol for a binary relation, like '$x > y$', there is a thick amount of separating space. This amount is represented by the command \; and is about five eighteenths of a quad. (A quad of space is one em wide.) In the case of a term containing a binary operator, like '$x + y$', there is a medium amount of separating space. This amount is represented by the command \: and is about two ninths of a quad. The following is a table of binary operators that are available in LaTeX 2_ε:

+	+[†]	·	\cdot[†]	∧	\wedge[†] or \land[†]
∔	\dotplus[§]	.	\centerdot[§]	Ā	\barwedge[§]
−	-[†]	•	\bullet[†]	Ā̄	\doublebarwedge[§]
±	\pm[†]	∘	\circ[†]	⋏	\curlywedge[§]
∓	\mp[†]	◯	\bigcirc[†]	∨	\vee[†] or \lor[†]
×	\times[†]	⊕	\oplus[†]	V̱	\veebar[§]
⋉	\ltimes[§]	⊖	\ominus[†]	⋎	\curlyvee[§]
⋊	\rtimes[§]	⊗	\otimes[†]	⊎	\uplus[†]
⋋	\leftthreetimes[§]	⊘	\oslash[†]	⊔	\sqcup[†]
⋌	\rightthreetimes[§]	⊙	\odot[†]	⊓	\sqcap[†]
÷	\div[†]	⊛	\circledast[§]	II	\amalg[†]
⋇	\divideontimes[§]	⊝	\circleddash[§]	⋄	\diamond[†]
mod	\bmod[†]	⊚	\circledcirc[§]	◁	\triangleleft[†]
*	\ast[†] or *[†]	⊞	\boxplus[§]	◁	\lhd[¶]
⋆	\star[†]	⊟	\boxminus[§]	⊴	\unlhd[¶]
∪	\cup[†]	⊠	\boxtimes[§]	▷	\triangleright[†]
⋓	\Cup[§]	⊡	\boxdot[§]	▷	\rhd[¶]
∩	\cap[†]	†	\dagger[†]	⊵	\unrhd[¶]
⋒	\Cap[§]	‡	\ddagger[†]	△	\bigtriangleup[†]
\	\setminus[†]	≀	\wr[†]	▽	\bigtriangledown[†]
╲	\smallsetminus[§]	⊤	\intercal[§]		

The symbols marked † are available in basic LaTeX, those marked ¶ require the latexsym package and those marked § require the amssymb package. Note that symbols for binary operations are treated as ordinary symbols when they do not occur between two operands (as explained on p. 161 above).

To define your own binary operator use the \mathbin command. Say you want to define the symbol ⧺ which some people, for example, Bird (1988), use for list concatenation. The way to do this is as follows:

```
\newcommand*{\con}{\mathbin{+\mkern-8mu+}}
```

The mu (maths unit) used here is a unit of length which can only be used in maths mode. (The equality 18 mu = 1 em is exact in TeX.)

A.5 Binary Relation Symbols

Commands marked with † in the following table of binary relation symbols are available in basic LaTeX; those marked with ¶ require the `latexsym` package and those marked § require the `amssymb` package. Note that the two commands `\sqsubset` and `\sqsupset` are available in the `latexsym` package and also in the `amssymb` package.

<	`<`†	>	`>`†	=	`=`†
≪	`\ll`†	≫	`\gg`†	≐	`\doteq`†
⋘	`\lll`§ or `\llless`§	⋙	`\ggg`§ or `\gggtr`§	≗	`\circeq`§
⩽	`\leqslant`§	⩾	`\geqslant`§	≖	`\eqcirc`§
≤	`\leq`† or `\le`†	≥	`\geq`† or `\ge`†	≓	`\risingdotseq`§
≦	`\leqq`§	≧	`\geqq`§	≒	`\doteqdot`§ or `\Doteq`§
⪇	`\eqslantless`§	⪈	`\eqslantgtr`§	≑	`\fallingdotseq`§
⋖	`\lessdot`§	⋗	`\gtrdot`§	≜	`\triangleq`§
≺	`\prec`†	≻	`\succ`†	≏	`\bumpeq`§
≼	`\preceq`†	≽	`\succeq`†	≎	`\Bumpeq`§
≼	`\preccurlyeq`§	≽	`\succcurlyeq`§	≡	`\equiv`†
⋞	`\curlyeqprec`§	⋟	`\curlyeqsucc`§	∼	`\sim`†
≲	`\lesssim`§	≳	`\gtrsim`§	∼	`\thicksim`§
⪅	`\lessapprox`§	⪆	`\gtrapprox`§	∽	`\backsim`§
≾	`\precsim`§	≿	`\succsim`§	≃	`\simeq`†
⪷	`\precapprox`§	⪸	`\succapprox`§	⋍	`\backsimeq`§
∈	`\in`†	∋	`\ni`† or `\owns`†	≅	`\cong`†
⊂	`\subset`†	⊃	`\supset`†	≈	`\approx`†
⋐	`\Subset`§	⋑	`\Supset`§	≈	`\thickapprox`§
⊆	`\subseteq`†	⊇	`\supseteq`†	≊	`\approxeq`§
⊆	`\subseteqq`§	⊇	`\supseteqq`§	◀	`\blacktriangleleft`§
⊏	`\sqsubset`§,¶	⊐	`\sqsupset`§,¶	◁	`\vartriangleleft`§
⊑	`\sqsubseteq`†	⊒	`\sqsupseteq`†	⊴	`\trianglelefteq`§
⌣	`\smile`†	⌢	`\frown`†	▶	`\blacktriangleright`§
⌣	`\smallsmile`§	⌢	`\smallfrown`§	▷	`\vartriangleright`§
∥	`\parallel`†	∣	`\mid`†	⊵	`\trianglerighteq`§
∥	`\shortparallel`§	∣	`\shortmid`§	⊥	`\perp`†
⊣	`\dashv`†	⬦	`\between`§	≍	`\asymp`†
⊢	`\vdash`†	⊩	`\Vdash`§	⫴	`\Vvdash`§
⊨	`\vDash`§	⋈	`\bowtie`†	∝	`\propto`†
⊨	`\models`†	⋈	`\Join`¶	∝	`\varpropto`§
∴	`\therefore`§	:	`:`†	∵	`\because`§
∍	`\backepsilon`§	⋔	`\pitchfork`§		

Note that `:` is treated by TeX as a binary relation symbol. This ensures the correct spacing in a construct like `$x := x + 1$`, which produces $x := x + 1$. In order to get the colon that is used to indicate the type of an object or function, see under punctuation symbols below. The following six symbols for binary relations are also available if you load the `amssymb` package:

$\lessgtr$	\lessgtr[§]	$\lesseqgtr$	\lesseqgtr[§]	$\lesseqqgtr$	\lesseqqgtr[§]
$\gtrless$	\gtrless[§]	$\gtreqless$	\gtreqless[§]	$\gtreqqless$	\gtreqqless[§]

To negate any relation symbol simply precede it by \not. Thus, $x \not\equiv y$ gives $x \not\equiv y$. This method does not always produce a symbol that looks correct; in the amssymb package there are defined quite a few commands for producing symbols for negated binary relations. The following table contains all the symbols in the first column of the table on p. 165 that have special negated versions:

$<$	<[†]	$\nless$	\nless[§]
$\leqslant$	\leqslant[§]	$\nleqslant$	\nleqslant[§]
$\leq$	\leq[†] or \le[†]	$\nleq$	\nleq[§]
		$\lneq$	\lneq[§]
$\leqq$	\leqq[§]	$\nleqq$	\nleqq[§]
		$\lneqq$	\lneqq[§]
		$\lvertneqq$	\lvertneqq[§]
$\prec$	\prec[§]	$\nprec$	\nprec[§]
$\preceq$	\preceq[§]	$\npreceq$	\npreceq[§]
		$\precneqq$	\precneqq[§]
$\lesssim$	\lesssim[§]	$\lnsim$	\lnsim[§]
$\lessapprox$	\lessapprox[§]	$\lnapprox$	\lnapprox[§]
$\precsim$	\precsim[§]	$\precnsim$	\precnsim[§]
$\precapprox$	\precapprox[§]	$\precnapprox$	\precnapprox[§]
$\in$	\in[†]	$\notin$	\notin[†]
$\subseteq$	\subseteq[†]	$\nsubseteq$	\nsubseteq[§]
		$\varsubsetneq$	\varsubsetneq[§]
		$\subsetneq$	\subsetneq[§]
$\subseteqq$	\subseteqq[§]	$\nsubseteqq$	\nsubseteqq[§]
		$\varsubsetneqq$	\varsubsetneqq[§]
		$\subsetneqq$	\subsetneqq[§]
$\parallel$	\parallel[†]	$\nparallel$	\nparallel[§]
$\shortparallel$	\shortparallel[§]	$\nshortparallel$	\nshortparallel[§]
$\vdash$	\vdash[†]	$\nvdash$	\nvdash[§]
$\vDash$	\vDash[§]	$\nvDash$	\nvDash[§]

The following table contains all the symbols that occur in the third column of the table on p. 165 that have special negated versions:

$>$	$>^\dagger$	$\ngtr$	\ngtr§
$\geqslant$	\geqslant§	$\ngeqslant$	\ngeqslant§
$\geq$	\geq† or \ge†	$\ngeq$	\ngeq§
		$\gneq$	\gneq§
$\geqq$	\geqq§	$\ngeqq$	\ngeqq§
		$\gneqq$	\gneqq§
		$\gvertneqq$	\gvertneqq§
$\succ$	\succ†	$\nsucc$	\nsucc§
$\succeq$	\succeq†	$\nsucceq$	\nsucceq§
		$\succneqq$	\succneqq§
$\gtrsim$	\gtrsim§	$\gnsim$	\gnsim§
$\gtrapprox$	\gtrapprox§	$\gnapprox$	\gnapprox§
$\succsim$	\succsim§	$\succnsim$	\succnsim§
$\succapprox$	\succapprox§	$\succnapprox$	\succnapprox§
$\supseteq$	\supseteq†	$\nsupseteq$	\nsupseteq§
		$\varsupsetneq$	\varsupsetneq§
		$\supsetneq$	\supsetneq§
$\supseteqq$	\supseteqq§	$\nsupseteqq$	\nsupseteqq§
		$\varsupsetneqq$	\varsupsetneqq§
		$\supsetneqq$	\supsetneqq§
$\mid$	\mid†	$\nmid$	\nmid§
$\shortmid$	\shortmid§	$\nshortmid$	\nshortmid§
$\Vdash$	\Vdash§	$\nVdash$	\nVdash§

The following table contains all the symbols that occur in the fifth column of the table on p. 165 that have special negated versions:

$=$	$=^\dagger$	$\neq$	\neq† or \ne†
$\sim$	\sim†	$\nsim$	\nsim§
$\cong$	\cong†	$\ncong$	\ncong§
$\vartriangleleft$	\vartriangleleft§	$\ntriangleleft$	\ntriangleleft§
$\trianglelefteq$	\trianglelefteq§	$\ntrianglelefteq$	\ntrianglelefteq§
$\vartriangleright$	\vartriangleright§	$\ntriangleright$	\ntriangleright§
$\trianglerighteq$	\trianglerighteq§	$\ntrianglerighteq$	\ntrianglerighteq§

In order to illustrate a few of LaTeX's relation symbols I will use a formula from Hindley and Seldin (1986), p. 139:

$$D_\infty \cong [D_\infty \to D_\infty].$$

This was produced by means of the following commands:

```
\[D_\infty \cong [D_\infty \to D_\infty].\]
```

The command \to here produces one of LaTeX's many arrow symbols. Mathematicians, logicians and computer scientists use a large number of these to stand for relations; the following are available in LaTeX:

↗	\nearrow[†]	↘	\searrow[†]
↙	\swarrow[†]	↖	\nwarrow[†]
←	\leftarrow[†] or \gets[†]	⟵	\longleftarrow[†]
⇐	\Leftarrow[†]	⟸	\Longleftarrow[†]
→	\rightarrow[†] or \to[†]	⟶	\longrightarrow[†]
⇒	\Rightarrow[†]	⟹	\Longrightarrow[†]
↔	\leftrightarrow[†]	⟷	\longleftrightarrow[†]
⇔	\Leftrightarrow[†]	⟺	\Longleftrightarrow[†]
↦	\mapsto[†]	⟼	\longmapsto[†]
↼	\leftharpoonup[†]	⇀	\rightharpoonup[†]
⇃	\downharpoonleft[§]	⇂	\downharpoonright[§]
⇁	\rightharpoondown[†]	↽	\lefhtharpoondown[†]
↾	\upharpoonright[§]	↿	\upharpoonleft[§]
⇈	\upuparrows[§]	⇊	\downdownarrows[§]
↩	\hookleftarrow[†]	↪	\hookrightarrow[†]
↢	\leftarrowtail[§]	↣	\rightarrowtail[§]
↞	\twoheadleftarrow[§]	↠	\twoheadrightarrow[§]
⇚	\Lleftarrow[§]	⇛	\Rrightarrow[§]
⇇	\leftleftarrows[§]	⇉	\rightrightarrows[§]
⇆	\leftrightarrows[§]	⇄	\rightleftarrows[§]
↝	\leadsto[¶]	⇝	\rightsquigarrow[§]
↭	\leftrightsquigarrow[§]	⇌	\rightleftharpoons[†]
⊸	\multimap[§]		

Those marked † in the above table are available in basic LaTeX; those marked ¶ require the `latexsym` package and those marked § require the `amssymb` package. Some of the above symbols have special negated versions; these are shown in the following table:

←	\leftarrow[†]	↚	\nleftarrow[§]
⇐	\Leftarrow[†]	⇍	\nLeftarrow[§]
↔	\leftrightarrow[†]	↮	\nleftrightarrow[§]
⇔	\Leftrightarrow[†]	⇎	\nLeftrightarrow[§]
→	\rightarrow[†]	↛	\nrightarrow[§]
⇒	\Rightarrow[†]	⇏	\nRightarrow[§]

The following six arrow symbols are different from those mentioned above:

↑	\uparrow[†]	↓	\downarrow[†]
⇑	\Uparrow[†]	⇓	\Downarrow[†]
↕	\updownarrow[†]	⇕	\Updownarrow[†]

When these six arrow symbols occur by themselves, TeX treats them as symbols for binary relations; but when preceded by \left, \right or any commands belonging to the \big family of commands, TEX treats them as belonging to the category that the qualifying command determines. If they are preceded by either \left or \right, then these commands produce either opening or closing symbols that can grow to any required size.

In order to define your own symbol for a binary relation you can use the \mathrel command. Say, for example, you want to use the symbol $\overline{\infty}$ for a relation. This can be achieved by defining \infbar as follows:

```
\newcommand*{\infbar}{\mathrel{\overline{\infty}}}
```

If you put $x \otimes z \infbar y$ in your input file, the output will be $x \otimes z \overline{\infty} y$.

Basic LATEX also contains the command \stackrel{*form*$_1$}{*form*$_2$} for producing symbols for binary relations: the argument *form*$_1$ is processed in script style and placed on top of *form*$_2$. For example, some people use the symbol $\stackrel{\wedge}{=}$ to indicate a definition. This can be defined as \ida as follows:

```
\newcommand*{\ida}{\stackrel{\wedge}{=}}
```

Placed in front of delimiters as explained in section 9.4 above the commands \bigm, \Bigm, \biggm and \Biggm produce symbols for binary relations.

A.6   Opening and Closing Symbols

Basic LATEX contains the following two groups of commands which, by themselves, are opening and closing symbols, respectively:

opening		closing	
(	(	)	)
[	[or \lbrack	]	] or \rbrack
{	\{ or \lbrace	}	\} or \rbrace
⟨	\langle	⟩	\rangle
⌊	\lfloor	⌋	\rfloor
⌈	\lceil	⌉	\rceil

Various other commands can be used to produce either opening or closing symbols if they occur in the right circumstances; see section 9.4 above for more information. The amssymb package also provides the commands \ulcorner and \llcorner to produce opening symbols and \urcorner and \lrcorner to produce closing symbols, but the size of these is fixed. They are all illustrated in the following example.

$$\ulcorner a + b - c = d \times e \urcorner \Rightarrow \llcorner b - c = (a \div d) \times e \lrcorner.$$

This was produced by means of the following commands:

```
\[\ulcorner a + b - c = d \times e \urcorner
  \Rightarrow
  \llcorner b - c = (a \div d) \times e \lrcorner.\]
```

The commands \mathopen and \mathclose can be used to force TEX to treat their arguments as opening and closing symbols, respectively, but the symbols produced are not extensible.

Placed in front of any of the delimiters the four commands \bigl, \Bigl, \biggl and \Biggl produce opening symbols and the four commands \bigr, \Bigr, \biggr and \Biggr produce closing symbols.

A.7   Punctuation Symbols

TEX treats a small number of symbols as punctuation marks in maths mode. When commas and semicolons occur in mathematical formulas TEX puts a thin space after them. It also does this for the colon when the command \colon is used. Notice the difference in spacing in the following:

$$f : x \rightarrow y, \qquad f : x \rightarrow y.$$

This was produced by means of the following commands:

```
\[f \colon x \rightarrow y, \qquad f : x \rightarrow y.\]
```

If you want to define your own punctuation mark, then you can use the \mathpunct command. For example, if you want to use the full stop as a punctuation mark in maths mode, then you could define a command \fullstop as \mathpunct{.} and use it appropriately.

Appendix B

Useful Notions

B.1 Lengths and Length Parameters

The following absolute length units are available in TeX: bp (big point), cc (cicero), cm (centimetre), dd (didot point), in (inch), mm (millimetre), pc (pica), pt (point) and sp (scaled point). The following conversions are exact, as Knuth (1986a), p. 57, states:

$$72 \text{ big points} = 1 \text{ inch,}$$
$$1 \text{ cicero} = 12 \text{ didot points,}$$
$$2.54 \text{ centimetres} = 1 \text{ inch,}$$
$$1157 \text{ didot points} = 1238 \text{ points,}$$
$$1 \text{ inch} = 72.27 \text{ points,}$$
$$10 \text{ millimetres} = 1 \text{ centimetre,}$$
$$1 \text{ pica} = 12 \text{ points,}$$
$$65536 \text{ scaled points} = 1 \text{ point.}$$

The scaled point is the dimension in terms of which TeX stores all lengths internally.

In addition to these absolute units of length, whose value does not depend on the current size of type, there are also three relative length units available, namely em, ex and mu (mathematical unit), the last of these is only available in maths mode. Traditionally, the em was the width of an uppercase letter 'M' and the ex was the height of a lowercase letter 'x', but in the fonts used by TeX these are just font-dependent units of length. In the Computer Modern fonts designed by Knuth the em-dash is always one em wide, the ten digits are each half an em wide and parentheses are one em high; furthermore, the letter 'x' is one ex high.

A *length parameter* is a length command whose value affects the appearance of the output produced by LaTeX. Length parameters are either *rigid* or *rubber*; a rubber one is one whose actual value depends on the context in which it occurs, whereas the value of a rigid length parameter is fixed and will neither stretch nor shrink. For example, the value of the rigid length parameter \textheight is the height of the body on the output page as produced by LaTeX. The following is a list of basic LaTeX's rigid length parameters:

\arraycolsep	\headsep	\marginparsep
\arrayrulewidth	\itemindent	\marginparwidth
\bibindent	\labelsep	\mathindent
\columnsep	\labelwidth	\oddsidemargin
\columnseprule	\leftmargin	\paperheight
\columnwidth	\leftmargini	\paperwidth
\doublerulesep	\leftmarginii	\parindent
\evensidemargin	\leftmarginiii	\rightmargin
\fboxrule	\leftmarginiv	\tabbingsep
\fboxsep	\leftmarginv	\tabcolsep
\footheight	\leftmarginvi	\textheight
\footnotesep	\linewidth	\textwidth
\footskip	\listparindent	\topmargin
\headheight	\marginparpush	\unitlength

In order to change one of these you need to use the \setlength command. You can either give one of these length parameters a definite value or you can give it a value depending on the value of some other length command; in the latter case you can multiply the length by a real number. The following illustrate these possibilities:

```
\setlength{\unitlength}{1mm}
\setlength{\rightmargin}{\leftmargin}
\setlength{\mathindent}{1.5\parindent}
```

You can also use the \addtolength command to alter the value of a rigid length parameter.

The following is a list of basic LaTeX's rubber length parameters:

\abovedisplayshortskip	\dbltextfloatsep	\partopsep
\abovedisplayskip	\floatsep	\textfloatsep
\baselineskip	\intextsep	\topsep
\belowdisplayshortskip	\itemsep	\topskip
\belowdisplayskip	\parsep	
\dblfloatsep	\parskip	

These can be altered by using the \setlength command just as the rigid length parameters can, but you have to tell TeX by how much the lengths involved can stretch and shrink. This is achieved by means of the following sort of assignment:

```
\setlength{\parskip}{12pt plus 4pt minus 2pt}
```

This means that the natural value of the rubber length parameter is 12 points, in TeXese this is known as *natural space*, but it can stretch or expand by up to 4 points and it can shrink or contract by up to 2 points. In assignments to rubber length parameters the plus and minus keywords and their associated lengths are optional; if either is omitted, then TeX assumes a zero point value.

B.2   Environments

There are 41 built-in environments in basic LaTeX though additional ones can be introduced by means of the \newenvironment*, \newenvironment and \newtheorem declarations and existing ones can be given new meanings by the \renewenvironment* and
\renewenvironment declarations. The following is a list of basic LaTeX's predefined
environments:

abstract	flushleft▽	sloppypar
array	flushright▽	tabbing
center▽	itemize▽	table
description▽	letter	table*
displaymath	list	tabular
document	lrbox	tabular*
enumerate▽	math	thebibliography▽
eqnarray	minipage	theindex
eqnarray*	note	titlepage
equation	overlay	trivlist
figure	picture	verbatim
figure*	quotation▽	verbatim*
filecontents	quote▽	verse▽
filecontents*	slide	

The general-purpose list environment, and its restricted trivlist version, are used
to define some of the other environments, namely the list-like ones which are marked
▽ in the above table.

B.3   Counters and Current \ref Values

A *counter* in LaTeX is an integer-valued variable and there are 23 built-in counters
though additional ones can be defined by means of the \newcounter global declaration (and sometimes using the \newtheorem command creates a new counter). The
following is a complete list of basic LaTeX's predefined counters:

bottomnumber	figure	subparagraph
chapter	footnote	subsection
dbltopnumber	mpfootnote	subsubsection
enumi	page	table
enumii	paragraph	tocdepth
enumiii	part	topnumber
enumiv	secnumdepth	totalnumber
equation	section	

Some of these counters are parameters that influence the placement of floats, namely
bottomnumber, dbltopnumber, topnumber and totalnumber. The counter tocdepth

controls what goes into the table of contents and `secnumdepth` influences the numbering of sectional units. The others are used for numbering various things and these numbers, except in the case of footnotes, can be used for cross-referencing purposes. The value of a counter can be output in various ways. For example, if *ctr* is a counter, then `\arabic{`*ctr*`}` outputs the value of *ctr* in the form of an Arabic numeral, whereas `\roman{`*ctr*`}` outputs its value in the form of a lowercase Roman numeral, `\Roman{`*ctr*`}` outputs its value in the form of an uppercase Roman numeral, `\alph{`*ctr*`}` and `\Alph{`*ctr*`}` output its value, but only if this lies between 1 and 26 inclusive, as a lowercase and uppercase letter, respectively. Corresponding to each counter *ctr* there is a command `\the`*ctr* which is the default text output associated with the counter. For example, the `page` counter keeps the current page number, but the output text that appears on the page is stored in the command `\thepage` whose default value is `\arabic{page}`. The textual output associated with LaTeX's predfined counters is not always in the form of an Arabic numeral as the examples in the following table show:

ctr	`\the`*ctr*
footnote	`\arabic{footnote}`
mpfootnote	`\alph{mpfootnote}`
page	`\arabic{page}`
part	`\Roman{part}`

Every `\label{`*key*`}` command writes a `\newlabel{`*key*`}{{`*text₁*`}{`*text₂*`}}` command to the `aux` file where *text₂* is the page number of the page on which `\label{`*key*`}` appeared and *text₁* depends on the context in which `\label{`*key*`}` appeared: inside an `enumerate` environment it is a label depending on how deeply nested the environment is; following a `\caption` command inside a `figure`, `figure*`, `table` or `table*` environment it is the figure or table label; inside an `equation` or `eqnarray` environment it is the label of the current formula; and elsewhere it is a label depending on some sectioning command. Note that in both the `book` and `report` document classes all these labels are preceded by the chapter number except those produced by the `enumerate` environment.

When you place a `\pageref{`*key*`}` command in your input, then *text₂* is output; and the presence of a `\ref{`*key*`}` command outputs *text₁*.

B.4   Moving Arguments and Fragile Commands

When your input file is being processed by LaTeX a number of files in addition to the `dvi` file are written (or overwritten) and some arguments to some LaTeX commands contain text and/or commands that are written to those additional files. For example, if your input file contains a `\makeindex` command and a number of `\index{`*text*`}` commands, then the *text* arguments will actually appear in the `idx` file that LaTeX writes. Such arguments are known as *moving* arguments. (There are also some cases in which a moving argument does not involve writing information to a file.) If a command has a moving argument, this information is included in the glossary contained in Appendix C.

LaTeX commands are either *fragile* or *robust*: a robust command is one that, if it appears in a moving argument, will be transferred to an additional file exactly as it occurs in that argument; however, in transferring a fragile command problems may occur but these can be avoided by preceding the fragile command with a \protect command.

Appendix C

Glossary

The order of non-alphanumeric characters in this glossary is determined by the order in which they occur in the following table (which is to be read from left to right):

␣	!	"	#	$	%	&	'	(	)	*
+	,	-	.	/	:	;	<	=	>	?
@	[	\	]	^	_	`	{	|	}	~

The escape character is regarded as invisible for the purposes of ordering (except that *name* follows *name*). Underlining is used to indicate that an argument to a command or environment is a moving one.

\\␣ This control symbol produces an inter-word space in both text modes. (Robust.)

\\! This control symbol produces a negative amount of thin horizontal space (normally about one sixth of a quad) in maths mode. (Robust.)

!` This control symbol produces the symbol ¡ in both text modes. The same symbol is also produced by the command \\textexclamdown. (Robust.)

\\"{*char*} This control symbol produces a diaeresis over the single character *char* in both text modes. For example, \\"{o} produces ö. (Robust.)

\# The special character # followed by a single digit indicates the place in a command or environment definition where an actual parameter is to go.

\\# This control symbol produces # in any mode. (Robust.)

$*form*$ This construct typesets *form* in maths mode and text style to produce an in-text formula. It can only occur in paragraph or LR mode and it is equivalent to both \\(*form*\\) and \\begin{math} *form* \\end{math}. (Robust.)

\\$ This control symbol produces $ in any mode. (Robust.)

% Everything that follows this special character to the next end-of-line character, including that character, is treated as a comment (and thus ignored) by TeX.

\\% This control symbol produces % in any mode. (Robust.)

& This special character is used in various environments to indicate vertical alignment.

\\& This control symbol produces & in any mode. (Robust.)

' In maths mode this character produces a prime, for example, x' produces x'. In paragraph and LR modes it produces a single closing quotation mark.

\\' Inside the `tabbing` environment this control symbol has a similar effect to that of the `\hfill` command except that it pushes text leftwards towards the imaginary alignment line numbered by the current value of *left-margin-tab*; it leaves a distance between that line and the text the value of which is given by the rigid length parameter `\tabbingsep`.

\\'{*char*} This control symbol produces an acute accent over the single character *char* in LR or paragraph mode, but *not* inside the `tabbing` environment. Thus, \\'{o} produces ó. To produce an acute accent inside the `tabbing` environment use \\a'{*char*}. (Robust.)

(x, y) The `picture` environment and several commands that can only be used inside it take arguments of this form. These arguments have several meanings. (1) The mandatory argument of the `picture` environment determines the size of the box that is going to be produced and the optional argument is an offset that is useful in positioning that box. (2) Various commands inside the `picture` environment require arguments that specify the position of a point. The location of such a point is given by its co-ordinates in a Cartesian co-ordinate system. (3) The `\line` and `\vector` commands use an argument of the form (x, y) in order to specify the slope of the line or arrow that is produced.

\\(*form*\\) This construct can only occur in LR or paragraph mode where it typesets *form* as an in-text mathematical formula in text style; it is equivalent to both `\begin{math}` *form* `\end{math}` and $form$. Both \\(and \\) are fragile.

\\) See \\(.

* This discretionary multiplication sign can only occur in maths mode where it indicates a place where a mathematical formula can be broken across lines; a multiplication sign × is inserted if the formula is broken across lines, but not otherwise.

*{*i*}{*pre*} This expression can only occur inside the *preamble* of an `array`, `tabular`, or `tabular*` environment. It is equivalent to *i* copies of *pre*, where *i* is any positive whole number and *pre* is any legitimate combination of preamble commands.

+ The plus sign produces the symbol + in all modes; in maths mode this is a binary operator.

\+ Inside the `tabbing` environment this control symbol increases the value of *left-tab-margin* by 1. (Fragile.)

\, This control symbol produces a thin amount of horizontal space (normally about one sixth of a quad) in all modes. Its value in maths mode is determined by the value of the command `\thinmuskip`. The preset value of this command is 3mu. (Robust.)

\- A single hyphen produces the binary operator $-$ in maths mode; in other modes it produces a hyphen. Use -- for an en-dash and --- for an em-dash in either paragraph or LR mode.

\- Except inside the `tabbing` environment this discretionary hyphen indicates a place in a word where TeX can end a line; if it does this, it inserts a hyphen.

\- Inside the `tabbing` environment this control symbol decreases the value of *left-tab-margin* by 1. (Fragile.)

-- In both text modes two hyphens next to each other, when neither the character preceding nor following them is itself a hyphen, produce an en-dash. An en-dash can also be produced by means of the command `\textendash`.

--- In both text modes three hyphens next to each other, which are neither preceded nor followed by a hyphen, produce an em-dash. An em-dash can also be produced by means of the command `\textemdash`.

\.{*char*} This control symbol produces a dot accent over the single character *char* in LR or paragraph mode. For example, \.{o} produces ȯ. (Robust.)

\/ This control symbol is the italic correction command which should be used whenever a change from an italic or slanted type to an upright one takes place.

: The colon produces the binary relation symbol : in maths mode. In both text modes it produces the colon as a punctuation mark. It should not be used for a punctuation mark in maths mode; for that use `\colon`.

\: This control symbol produces a medium amount of horizontal space (normally about two ninths of a quad) in maths mode. Its extent is determined by the value of the command `\medmuskip`. The preset value of this is 4mu plus 2mu minus 4mu. Note that in plain TeX this amount of space is indicated by the command \>. (Robust.)

\; This control symbol produces a thick amount of horizontal space (normally about five eighteenths of a quad) in maths mode. Its extent is determined by the value of the command `\thickmuskip` whose preset value is 5mu plus 5mu. (Robust.)

< The less-than sign produces the binary relation symbol $<$ in maths mode. It should *not* be used there for a left angle bracket; for that use `\langle`.

\< Inside the `tabbing` environment this control symbol undoes the effect of one previous \+ control symbol. (Fragile.)

= The equals sign produces the symbol = in all modes; in maths mode this is a binary relation symbol.

\= Inside the `tabbing` environment this control symbol sets tab positions. Note that any spaces following a \= control symbol are ignored by LATEX. (Fragile.)

\={*char*} This control symbol produces a macron accent over the single character *char* in LR or paragraph mode, but *not* inside the `tabbing` environment. (There use \a={*char*}.) Thus, \={o} produces ō. (Robust.)

> The greater-than sign produces the binary relation symbol > in maths mode. It should *not* be used there for a right angle bracket; for that use \rangle.

\> Inside the `tabbing` environment this control symbol is used to move to the next tab position. Note that any spaces following a \> control symbol are ignored by LATEX. Note also that in plain TEX this control symbol is used to produce a medium amount of space in maths mode. (Fragile.)

?' These two characters produce ¿ in paragraph or LR mode. The same symbol can also be produced by means of the command \textquestiondown. (Robust.)

\@ Placed before a colon, full stop, question mark or exclamation mark this control symbol makes the following space into one like that which normally follows these punctuation characters. (It is usually used between an uppercase letter and such a punctuation mark which actually does end a sentence.)

@(*form*$_1$(*form*$_2$(Inside the CD environment, defined in the `amscd` package, this command produces an extensible left arrow with the expression *form*$_1$ placed above the arrow and *form*$_2$ placed below it. (Either *form*$_1$ or *form*$_2$ or both of them can be absent.) If a left parenthesis occurs either in *form*$_1$ or in *form*$_2$, then the formula in question must be enclosed in braces. (It is a good idea, however, to always put braces around *form*$_1$ and *form*$_2$, if they are present.) To produce an extensible left arrow outside the CD environment, if you are using the `amsmath` package, use the \xleftarrow command.

@)*form*$_1$)*form*$_2$) Inside the CD environment, defined in the `amscd` package, this command produces an extensible right arrow with the expression *form*$_1$ placed above the arrow and *form*$_2$ placed below it. (Either *form*$_1$ or *form*$_2$ or both of them can be absent.) If a right parenthesis occurs either in *form*$_1$ or in *form*$_2$, then the formula in question must be enclosed in braces. (It is a good idea, however, to always put braces around *form*$_1$ and *form*$_2$, if they are present.) To produce an extensible right arrow outside the CD environment, if you are using the `amsmath` package, use the \xrightarrow command.

@. Inside the CD environment, defined in the `amscd` package, this command indicates that only blank space occurs between two nodes of the commutative diagram.

@<*form*$_1$<*form*$_2$< Inside the CD environment, defined in the `amscd` package, this command produces an extensible left arrow with the expression *form*$_1$ placed above the arrow and *form*$_2$ placed below it. (Either *form*$_1$ or *form*$_2$ or both of them can be absent.) If a less-than sign occurs either in *form*$_1$ or in *form*$_2$, then the formula in question must be enclosed in braces. (It is a good idea, however, to always put braces around *form*$_1$ and *form*$_2$, if they are present.) To produce an extensible left arrow outside the CD environment, if you are using the `amsmath` package, use the `\xleftarrow` command.

@= Inside the CD environment, defined in the `amscd` package, this command produces an extensible equals sign linking two nodes of the commutative diagram horizontally.

@>*form*$_1$>*form*$_2$> Inside the CD environment, defined in the `amscd` package, this command produces an extensible right arrow with the expression *form*$_1$ placed above the arrow and *form*$_2$ placed below it. (Either *form*$_1$ or *form*$_2$ or both of them can be absent.) If a greater-than sign occurs either in *form*$_1$ or in *form*$_2$, then the formula in question must be enclosed in braces. (It is a good idea, however, to always put braces around *form*$_1$ and *form*$_2$, if they are present.) To produce an extensible right arrow outside the CD environment, if you are using the `amsmath` package, use the `\xrightarrow` command.

@\vert Inside the CD environment, defined in the `amscd` package, this command produces an extensible equals sign linking two nodes of the commutative diagram vertically.

@{*text*} This so-called @-expression can only occur in the preamble of an `array`, `tabular` or `tabular*` environment; it places *text* in every row of the result. It removes any space that would normally be inserted in the row. The *text* argument is a moving one.

@| Inside the CD environment, defined in the `amscd` package, this command produces an extensible equals sign linking two nodes of the commutative diagram vertically.

@A*form*$_1$A*form*$_2$A Inside the CD environment, defined in the `amscd` package, this command produces an up arrow with the expression *form*$_1$ placed to the left of the arrow and the expression *form*$_2$ placed to the right of the arrow. (Either *form*$_1$ or *form*$_2$ or both of them can be absent.) If a capital letter A occurs either in *form*$_1$ or in *form*$_2$, then the formula in question must be enclosed in braces. It is a good idea, however, to always put braces around *form*.

\@listi This command is executed when a `list` environment occurring within the scope of no other `list` environment is opened. It is used to initialize a number of the length parameters affecting the appearance of the list.

\@listii This command is executed when a `list` environment which occurs within the scope of one other `list` environment is opened. It is used to initialize a number of the length parameters affecting the appearance of the list.

\@listiii This command is executed when a `list` environment which occurs within the scope of two other `list` environments is opened. It is used to initialize a number of the length parameters affecting the appearance of the list.

\@listiv This command is executed when a `list` environment which occurs within the scope of three other `list` environments is opened. It is used to initialize a number of the length parameters affecting the appearance of the list.

\@listv This command is executed when a `list` environment which occurs within the scope of four other `list` environments is opened. It is used to initialize a number of the length parameters affecting the appearance of the list.

\@listvi This command is executed when a `list` environment which occurs within the scope of five other `list` environments is opened. It is used to initialize a number of the length parameters affecting the appearance of the list.

@V*form*$_1$V*form*$_2$V Inside the CD environment, defined in the `amscd` package, this command produces a down arrow with the expression *form*$_1$ placed to the left of the arrow and the expression *form*$_2$ placed to the right of the arrow. (Either *form*$_1$ or *form*$_2$ or both of them can be absent.) If a capital letter V occurs either in *form*$_1$ or in *form*$_2$, then the formula in question must be enclosed in braces. It is a good idea, however, to always put braces around *form*.

[*arg*] Some LaTeX commands can have one or more optional arguments. When these are present, they have to be enclosed in square brackets. One exception is the optional argument to the `picture` environment which is enclosed in parentheses.

\[*form*\] This construct can only occur in paragraph mode and it there typesets *form* in maths mode and then makes it into a displayed equation centred on a line by itself *except* if the `fleqn` document-class option has been chosen. In that case the formula is indented from the left margin by the value of the `\mathindent` rigid length parameter. Note that \[*form*\] is equivalent to `\begin{displaymath}` *form* `\end{displaymath}`. Both \[and \] are fragile.

\\[*len*] This control symbol ends a line; if the optional argument *len* is present, *len* amount of vertical space is inserted between the current line and the next one. (Fragile.)

*[*len*] This command is like the \\[*len*] command except that the place where this command occurs will never be placed at the end of a page. (Fragile.)

\] See \[.

form$_1$^form$_2$ This construct makes *form*$_2$ into a superscript of *form*$_1$. If *form*$_2$ contains more than one symbol, then braces should be placed around it. The control sequence `\sp` can be used instead of the hat. Thus, *form*$_1$`\sp`*form*$_2$ is equivalent to *form*$_1$^*form*$_2$. (Robust.)

\^{*char*} This control symbol produces a circumflex accent over the single character *char* in LR or paragraph mode. Thus, \^{o} produces ô. (Robust.)

form$_1$*_form*$_2$ This construct makes *form*$_2$ into a subscript of *form*$_1$. If *form*$_2$ contains more than one symbol, then braces should be placed around it. The control sequence \sb can be used instead of the underline character. Thus, *form*$_1$\sb*form*$_2$ is equivalent to *form*$_1$*_form*$_2$. (Robust.)

_ This control symbol produces _ in any mode. (Robust.)

\' Inside the `tabbing` environment the effect of this control symbol is similar to that of \hfill in that it pushes any text that follows it rightwards as far as the prevailing right margin.

\'{*char*} This control symbol produces a grave accent over the character *char* in both text modes, but *not* inside the `tabbing` environment. (There use \a'{*char*}.) Thus, \'{o} produces ò. (Robust.)

{...} Braces are used in LATEX to group things together. They are used to enclose those arguments of a command that are mandatory. In maths mode an expression enclosed in braces is treated as an ordinary symbol. Braces also delimit the scope of local declarations.

\{ This control symbol produces a left brace { in all modes. In maths mode this is an opening symbol. There it can also be produced by means of the command \lbrace. (Robust.)

} See {.

\} This control symbol produces a right brace } in all modes. In maths mode this is a closing symbol. There it can also be produced by the command \rbrace. (Robust.)

~ This special character produces an inter-word space and inhibits line-breaking.

\~{*char*} This control symbol produces a tilde accent over the single character *char* in both text modes. For example, \~{o} produces õ. (Robust.)

10pt This is a document-class option. It ensures that the size of type being used is 10 point. Note that this option is the default in the `article`, `book`, `letter` and `report` document classes and that it has no effect in the `slides` document class. See also 11pt and 12pt.

11pt This is a document-class option. It ensures that the size of type being used is 11 point, rather than the default 10 point. Note that this option is not available in the `slides` document class. See also 10pt and 12pt.

12pt This is a document-class option. It ensures that the size of type being used is 12 point, rather than the default 10 point. Note that this option is not available in the `slides` document class. See also 10pt and 11pt.

\a'{*char*} This command is only available inside the `tabbing` environment where it produces an acute accent over the single character *char*. For example, \a'{g} produces ǵ. (Fragile.)

\a={*char*} This command is only available inside the `tabbing` environment where it produces a macron accent over the single character *char*. For example, \a={g} produces ḡ. (Fragile.)

\a'{*char*} This command is only available inside the `tabbing` environment where it produces a grave accent over the single character *char*. For example, \a'{g} produces g̀. (Fragile.)

a4paper This is a document-class option. Use it when you are producing a document that is going to be printed on A4-size paper, that is to say, paper whose size is 210 mm by 297 mm. See also a5paper, b5paper, executivepaper, legalpaper and letterpaper.

a5paper This is a document-class option. Use it when you are producing a document that is going to be printed on A5-size paper, that is to say, paper whose size is 148 mm by 210 mm. See also a4paper, b5paper, executivepaper, legalpaper and letterpaper.

\aa This command is available in both text modes for producing the lowercase Scandinavian letter 'å'. The command \r can be used to produce a circle accent over any letter. (Robust.)

\AA This command is available in both text modes for producing the uppercase Scandinavian letter 'Å'. The command \r can be used to produce a circle accent over any letter. (Robust.)

abbrv This is one of the possible options to the \bibliographystyle command. The entries in the bibliography are arranged alphabetically and each one is labelled by means of a number enclosed in square brackets, like [17]. The option takes its name from the fact that the names of authors, editors, months and journals are abbreviated. The other standard options are alpha, plain and unsrt.

\abovedisplayshortskip The value of this rubber length parameter is the additional amount of vertical space that is placed above a 'short' displayed formula (additional to the value of \baselineskip, that is to say), unless the fleqn option to the \documentclass command has been chosen. (If the fleqn option is used, then the extra amount of vertical space that is added is given by the value of \topsep.) A 'short' formula is one for which the distance labelled *e* in Fig. C.1 on p. 185 is greater than 2 em, where the length of em is determined by the size of type used in the paragraph preceding the formula. The value of this command is altered by certain declarations that change the size of type being used. (This is a primitive TEX command and these details are included for information only. They are, in any case, a simplification of what really happens. See Knuth

a	\abovedisplayskip + \baselineskip
b	\belowdisplayskip + \baselineskip
c	\abovedisplayshortskip + \baselineskip
d	\belowdisplayshortskip + \baselineskip
e	$\geq$ 2em

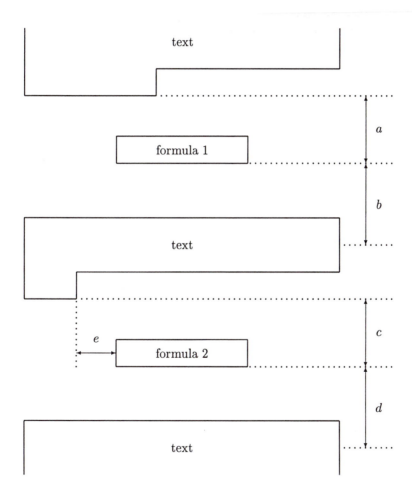

Figure C.1: 'Short' and 'long' displayed formulas.

(1986a), pp. 188–189, and Eijkhout (1992), pp. 202–203, for more information.) This is a robust command that must never be preceded by a \protect command.

\abovedisplayskip This command is a rubber length parameter; its value is the additional amount of vertical space that is placed above a 'long' displayed formula (additional to \baselineskip, that is to say), unless the fleqn option to the \documentclass command has been chosen. (If the fleqn option is used, then the extra amount of vertical space that is added is given by the value of \topsep.) A 'long' formula is one whose left-most point is to the left of the end of the last line of the paragraph preceding it or, if it is to the right of this point, the distance between those points is less than 2 em in the font used in the preceding paragraph. See Fig. C.1 on p. 185, where formula 1 is 'long' in this sense. The value of this command is altered by certain declarations that change the size of type being used. (This is a primitive TEX command and these details are included for information only. They are, in any case, a simplification of what really happens. See Knuth (1986a), pp. 188–189, and Eijkhout (1992), pp. 202–203, for more information.) This is a robust command that must never be preceded by a \protect command.

abstract This environment is used for producing abstracts in the **article** and **report** document classes; it is not defined in the **book** document class. It should be placed after the \maketitle command inside the **document** environment. By default the first line of the abstract is indented, but this indentation can be suppressed by using a \noindent command. The heading 'Abstract' is produced automatically. This appears in bold above the text of the abstract and it is centred horizontally. If you want a different heading to appear, then redefine the \abstractname command. If the **titlepage** option to the \documentclass command is selected, then the abstract environment starts a new page.

\abstractname When you use the **abstract** environment, the word 'Abstract' in bold appears centred horizontally on the page just before the text of your abstract. If you wish some other word to appear instead, then you need to redefine the \abstractname command.

\acute{*char*} This command produces an acute accent in maths mode. For example, $\acute{x}$ produces $\acute{x}$. (Robust.)

\addcontentsline{*ext*}{*sec-unit*}{*entry*} This command writes a \contentsline command to the file specified by the *ext* parameter which can be either **lof**, **lot** or **toc**. The argument *sec-unit* controls the nature of what is written: if *ext* is **lof**, then *sec-unit* must be **figure**; if *ext* is **lot**, then *sec-unit* must be **table**; if *ext* is **toc**, then *sec-unit* can be either **part**, **chapter** (but not in the **article** document class), **section**, **subsection**, **subsubsection**, **paragraph** or **subparagraph**. (Note that *sec-unit* is **section**, for example, and *not* \section.) The argument *entry*, which is a moving argument, is the actual text that will appear in the list of figures, list of tables or table of contents. If you want the number of a figure, table or sectional unit to occur in the appropriate list, then instead of just text appearing in *entry* you need to use a \numberline command. The following example illustrates this:

```
\addcontentsline{lof}{figure}
    {\protect\numberline{12.3}Cricket fielding positions.}
```

If *entry*, or the corresponding argument in \numberline, is too long, then you will get an error message telling you that the buffer size has been exceeded.

\address{*text*} This declaration can only occur in the **letter** document class. It is used for producing the address of the letter's sender. One or more \\ commands can occur within the argument *text* to force a new line.

\addtime{*i*} This command only makes sense in the **slides** document class when the **clock** document-class option is being used. It adds the value *i* to the internal 'clock' that is used by LaTeX to keep track of the length of time that a lecture or presentation is going to take. This command should not be placed inside a **slide**, **overlay** or **note** environment. See also \settime.

\addtocontents{*ext*}{*text*} This command writes *text* to the file specified by the *ext* argument which can be either **lof**, **lot** or **toc**. The moving argument *text* can contain formatting commands as well as ordinary text. If *text* is too long, then you will get a LaTeX buffer size exceeded error message.

\addtocounter{*ctr*}{*i*} This global declaration assigns to the counter *ctr* the result of adding *i* to the current value of *ctr*. See also \setcounter and **calc**. (Fragile.)

\addtolength{*cmd*}{*len*} This local declaration assigns to the length command *cmd*, which must begin with a backslash, the result of adding *len* to its current value. See also \setlength and **calc**. (Robust.)

\addvspace{*len*} This normally adds *len* amount of vertical space. However, two such commands in succession, like \addvspace{*len$_1$*}\addvspace{*len$_2$*} only add *len$_i$* amount of space, where *len$_i$* is the maximum of *len$_1$* and *len$_2$*. This command is used in the definition of many environments and results in the space surrounding nested environments being the same as the space above and below a single environment. (Fragile.)

\ae This command produces the lowercase vowel ligature 'æ' in both text modes. (Robust.)

\AE This command produces the uppercase vowel ligature 'Æ' in both text modes. (Robust.)

align This environment is only avaliable if you have loaded the **amsmath** package. It can only occur in paragraph mode and it is used for producing several displayed mathemtical formulas that are aligned in some way. Each displayed formula is automatically given a numerical label, but this can be suppressed by using a \notag command. The general format of the align environment is:

> \begin{align}   *row-list*   \end{align}

All the rows inside *row-list*, except the last, are terminated by \\ and each row looks like this:

> *form*$_1$ & *form*$_2$ & ...   & *form*$_{2n}$

Each formula *form*$_i$ is processed in display maths style. The items *form*$_i$ with odd subscripts are pushed to the right and those with even subscripts are pushed to the left. If ampersands are numbered from the left, then items on different rows are aligned at odd-numbered ampersands and even-numbered ones are used to separate columns. The resulting displayed formulas are evenly spaced out across the width of the body region. If you do not want a label to be attached to a particular row, then you need to include a \notag command before the command that terminates that row. This is \\ for all rows except the last when it is \end{align}. You can use a \tag or \tag* command to produce a label different from the default one and the \label command can be used for cross-referencing purposes.

align* This environment is defined in the amsmath package. It behaves just like the align environment except that it does not produce numerical labels. You can still, however, use the \tag and \tag* commands to produce your own labels.

alph This is one of the available options to the \pagenumbering global declaration. Page numbers appear as lowercase letters when it is used. The other available options are Alph, arabic, roman and Roman.

\alph{*ctr*} The value of the counter *ctr*, which must be a positive whole number less than 27, is output as a lowercase letter. (Robust.)

Alph This is one of the available options to the \pagenumbering global declaration. Page numbers appear as uppercase letters when it is used. The other available options are alph, arabic, roman and Roman.

\Alph{*ctr*} The value of the counter *ctr*, which must be a positive whole number less than 27, is output as an uppercase letter. (Robust.)

alpha This is one of the possible options to the \bibliographystyle command. The entries in the bibliography are arranged alphabetically and each one is labelled by means of a label made up out of the first three letters of the author's name and the last two digits of the year of publication. [Lak76] is an example. The other standard options are abbrv, plain and unsrt.

amsbsy This is one of the packages in the $\mathcal{AMS}$-LATEX distribution. It defines the commands \boldsymbol and \pmb which provide different sorts of bold symbols.

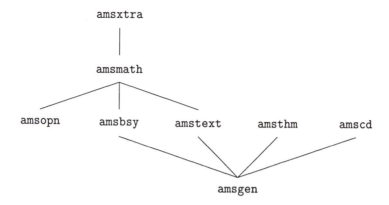

Figure C.2: Packages in the $\mathcal{AMS}$-LaTeX distribution.

amscd This package is part of the $\mathcal{AMS}$-LaTeX distribution, but it is independent of the other packages in that distribution and so it can be used even if none of the others are loaded. This package defines the CD environment and a number of commands that can be used inside it for the production of simple commutative diagrams. It is impossible, however, to use the CD environment to produce diagrams containing diagonal arrows. See section 11.7 for several examples of its use.

amsfonts Loading this package allows you to use the `\mathbb` and `\mathfrak` commands which produce blackboard bold and Gothic letters, respectively. This package is automatically loaded when you use the `amssymb` package.

amsgen This is one of the packages in the $\mathcal{AMS}$-LaTeX distribution. It is an auxiliary package used by `amsbsy`, `amstext`, `amsthm` and `amscd`.

amsmath This is the main package in the $\mathcal{AMS}$-LaTeX distribution. It defines a number of commands and environments that are useful in typesetting mathematics. Chapter 11 contains an introduction to some of its features and the package is fully described in Grätzer (1996). Fig. C.2 shows the relationship between the various packages in the $\mathcal{AMS}$-LaTeX distribution. A package in the diagram automatically loads every package below it to which it is linked by means of an arrow.

amsopn This is one of the packages in the $\mathcal{AMS}$-LaTeX distribution. It defines the following commands: `\operatorname`, `\operatorname*`, `\DeclareMathOperator` and `\DeclareMathOperator*`. These can all be used to define log-like operators as explained on p. 163.

amssymb Loading this package allows you to use a large number of commands that produce various kinds of mathematical symbols. See Appendix A for more information about these commands. If you use this package, then the `amsfonts` package is loaded automatically.

amstext This package defines the `\text` command. It is loaded automatically if you use the `amsmath` package.

amsthm This is one of the packages in the $\mathcal{A}_{\mathcal{M}}\mathcal{S}$-LaTeX distribution. It defines what in LaTeX are called *proclamations* or *theorem-like structures*; see Grätzer (1996), pp. 123–131, for details of what it can do.

amsxtra This is one of the packages in the $\mathcal{A}_{\mathcal{M}}\mathcal{S}$-LaTeX distribution. It defines a number of accents which are placed to the side of the characters they decorate.

\and This command can only occur in the argument of an `\author` declaration. It is used to separate the names of multiple authors.

\appendix This local declaration alters the way in which the sectional units of your document are numbered. In the `book` and `report` document classes chapters start being 'numbered' alphabetically and in the `article` document class sections start being 'numbered' alphabetically. It has no effect on the numbering of parts. Note that it takes no arguments.

\appendixname When a `\chapter` command occurs in an input file in the scope of an `\appendix` declaration, the word 'Appendix' is produced automatically by LaTeX and is placed at the front of the appendix. If you want some other word to appear instead, then you need to redefine the `\appendixname` command.

arabic This is one of the possible options to the `\pagenumbering` global declaration. Page numbers appear as Arabic numerals when it is used. The other available options are `alph`, `Alph`, `roman` and `Roman`.

\arabic{*ctr*} The value of the counter *ctr* is output as an Arabic numeral. (Robust.)

array This environment can only be used in maths mode where it produces a two-dimensional spatial arrangement of mathematical symbols. It is described in detail in section 10.1 above.

\arraycolsep The value of this rigid length parameter is half the amount of horizontal space left between the columns produced by an `array` environment. The corresponding parameter for the `tabular` and `tabular*` environments is `\tabcolsep`. It is a robust command that must not be preceded by a `\protect` command.

\arrayrulewidth The value of this rigid length parameter determines the width of the horizontal and vertical lines that can be produced by an `array`, `tabular` or `tabular*` environment. It is a robust command that must not be preceded by a `\protect` command.

\arraystretch This command has a value which is a floating-point number. It controls the amount of vertical space that occurs between the rows produced in an array, tabular or tabular* environment. The amount of vertical space used is given by the default value for this length multiplied by the value of \arraystretch. Its default value is 1 and changing it to 1.25, say, by the \renewcommand* declaration makes the rows produced one and a quarter times further apart.

article This is one of the five standard document classes available in LaTeX 2$_\varepsilon$. The standard options to it are: at most one of 10pt (the default), 11pt or 12pt; at most one of letterpaper (the default), legalpaper, executivepaper, a4paper, a5paper or b5paper; at most one of final (the default) or draft; at most one of oneside (the default) or twoside; at most one of onecolumn (the default) or twocolumn; and at most one of notitlepage (the default) or titlepage. Furthermore, any or none of the following can occur in *opt-list*: landscape, openbib, leqno and fleqn. Section 8.1 contains a lot more information about this document class.

\author{*text*} The author or authors of a document are declared by means of this command. If more than one author's name appears in *text*, then they should be separated by \and commands. You can use the \\ command inside *text* in order to force a line break and one or more \thanks commands can also appear in *text*. These produce footnotes whose markers are regarded as having zero width. If a \thanks command does not end a line, then it should be followed by a \␣ command in order to insert some inter-word space.

aux This is the file extension of the auxiliary file that LaTeX writes whenever you process an input file (except when a \nofiles command occurs in the preamble of that input file). This auxiliary file contains various pieces of information which are used for cross-referencing purposes and for the production of a table of contents, a list of figures and a list of tables. If your input file contains one or more \include commands, but does not contain an \includeonly command, then an auxiliary file will be written for each included file as well as the input file. If your input file contains one or more \include commands and also an \includeonly command, then the auxiliary files will only be written for the input file and the files listed in the argument of the \includeonly command. The cross-referencing information in an aux file, as well as the information used in producing the table of contents, can be printed out by running LaTeX on the lablst.tex file.

\b{*char*} This command produces a bar-under accent underneath *char* in both text modes. For example, \b{o} produces o̱. (Robust.)

b5paper This is a document-class option. Use it when you are producing a document that is going to be printed on B5-size paper, that is to say, paper whose size is 176 mm by 250 mm. See also a4paper, a5paper, executivepaper, legalpaper and letterpaper.

\backmatter This command is only available in the **book** document class. It redefines the **\chapter** command so that it does not produce a chapter number but the heading is included in the table of contents (if produced). See also **\frontmatter** and **\mainmatter**.

\bar{*char*} This command produces an accent in maths mode. Thus, **$\bar{x}$** produces $\bar{x}$. (Robust.)

\baselineskip This rubber length parameter is a primitive TeX command. The normal distance between the base lines of every two successive lines in a paragraph is given by the value of the parameter **\baselineskip** multiplied by the value of **\baselinestretch**. The value used for the entire paragraph is that which this command has when the end of the paragraph is reached. Although the value of this command can be a rubber length, Knuth says that giving it a rigid value produces a better looking page. Even when its value is a rigid length, the actual distance between the base lines of successive lines can vary if one of them contains a large symbol. See Knuth (1986a), pp. 78–79, for an account of what happens in those circumstances. Note that the value of **\baselineskip** is altered by declarations (like **\tiny** and **\large**) that change the size of type being used. (These details are included for information only. The value of **\baselineskip** is the responsibility of a document style's designer. If you really must alter the distance between base lines, for example, to produce the appearance of a double-spaced typewritten document, then alter the value of **\baselinestretch**.) This is a robust command that must not be preceded by a **\protect** command.

\baselinestretch The value of this command is a floating-point number and by default this is 1. The actual distance between the base lines of two successive lines in a paragraph is the value of **\baselineskip** multiplied by the value of **\baselinestretch**.

\batchmode If this command occurs in the prologue of your input file, that is to say, before the **\documentclass** command, then no messages are written to your terminal once it has been executed. (If a **\NeedsTeXFormat** command or one or more instances of the **filecontents** or **filecontents*** environments come before the **\batchmode** command, then any messages they generate are still written to the terminal.) The **log** file is still written, however. When this command is used TeX carries on processing as best it can even if errors occur.

bbl This is the file extension of a file written by BibTeX when it is run. It contains the LaTeX formatting commands that are actually used to produce the bibliography in your output; you can edit this file if you do not like any part of the output it produces. (In fact, the **bbl** file contains a **thebibliography** environment.) LaTeX reads the **bbl** file when it executes the **\bibliography** command in your input file and it produces the bibliography from the information that it finds there.

\begin{*env*} This command starts the *env* environment. (Fragile.)

\belowdisplayshortskip The value of this rubber length parameter is the additional vertical space that is placed below a 'short' displayed formula, unless the `fleqn` option to the \documentclass command has been chosen. See the entry for \abovedisplayshortskip for an explanation of what a 'short' formula is and see also Fig. C.1 on p. 185. This is a primitive TeX command and it is also a robust command that must not be preceded by a \protect command.

\belowdisplayskip The value of this rubber length parameter is the additional vertical space that is placed below a 'long' displayed formula, unless the `fleqn` option to the \documentclass command has been chosen. See the entry for \abovedisplayskip for an explanation of what a 'long' formula is and see also Fig. C.1 on p. 185. This is a primitive TeX command and it is also a robust command that must not be preceded by a \protect command.

\bezier{t}(i_1, j_1)(i_2, j_2)(i_3, j_3) This command can only be used inside the `picture` environment. It produces a quadratic Bézier curve from the point whose co-ordinates are (i_1, j_1) to the point (i_3, j_3). The curve produced has the property that the line linking (i_1, j_1) and (i_2, j_2) is a tangent to it at the point (i_1, j_1) and the line linking (i_2, j_2) and (i_3, j_3) is a tangent to it at the point (i_3, j_3). The mandatory argument t determines the number of points used to produce the curve. The value of the command \qbeziermax has no effect on the number of points used.

\bf This local declaration alters the style of the type being used. It selects a bold, upright, roman typeface. In LR and paragraph modes it is equivalent to the two declarations \normalfont\bfseries. (Robust.)

\bfseries This local declaration alters the series attribute of the type style being used to bold. It cannot be used in maths mode; the command \mathbf, which is not a declaration, should be used there. (Robust.)

bib This is the file extension of a file that contains one or more BibTeX bibliographic database entries.

\bibindent The value of this rigid length parameter, which can only be used if the `openbib` document-class option has been chosen, is the amount of indentation used for the second and subsequent lines of entries produced by the `thebibliography` environment. This is a robust command that must not be preceded by a \protect command.

\bibitem[*text*]{*key*} This command can only occur inside the `thebibliography` environment. The argument *key* is made up out of letters, numerals and punctuation marks other than a comma. It is used in a \cite command to refer to a work in the bibliography. If *text* is absent, then LaTeX generates a numerical label enclosed in square brackets like [31]; otherwise, if *text* is present, then [*text*] is used as the label. Note that *text*, if present, is a moving argument. (Fragile.)

\bibliography{*bib-file-list***}** If any \cite{*key*} commands occur in your input file, then B<small>IB</small>T_EX looks in the files listed in *bib-file-list* to see if an entry with key *key* occurs there. If it does, the bibliography produced will contain an entry produced from the data contained in the **bib** file. Only the base names of **bib** files occur in *bib-file-list* and multiple names are separated by commas.

\bibliographystyle{*bib-style***}** This command is used in conjunction with B<small>IB</small>T_EX and it determines how the bibliography in your output is going to look. Standard options for the *bib-style* argument are **abbrv**, **alpha**, **plain** and **unsrt**. (The default is **plain**.) Others, such as **agsm**, **dcu** or **kluwer**, which are used with the **harvard** package, may be available on your computer system.

\bibname If you use B<small>IB</small>T_EX or the **thebibliography** environment to produce a list of references in either the **report** or the **book** document classes, then L^AT_EX will automatically produce the unnumbered chapter heading 'Bibliography' for you. If you want your bibliography to be called something different, then you have to redefine the **\bibname** command.

\big*cmd* If you are using the **10pt** document-class option and *cmd* produces a delimiter, then **\big***cmd* produces an ordinary symbol which is slightly larger than the symbol produced by *cmd* on its own (which may or may not be an ordinary symbol). The symbol produced can still be used in an in-text formula. If you are using either the **11pt** or the **12pt** document-class option, then you need to load the **amsmath** package in order to get **\big** to work as described.

\Big*cmd* If you are using the **10pt** document-class option and *cmd* produces a delimiter, then **\Big***cmd* produces an ordinary symbol which is 50% bigger than the one produced by **\big***cmd*. If you are using either the **11pt** or the **12pt** document-class option, then you need to load the **amsmath** package in order to get **\Big** to work as described.

\bigg*cmd* If you are using the **10pt** document-class option and *cmd* produces a delimiter, then **\bigg***cmd* produces an ordinary symbol which is twice the size of the one produced by **\big***cmd*. If you are using either the **11pt** or the **12pt** document-class option, then you need to load the **amsmath** package in order to get **\bigg** to work as described.

\Bigg*cmd* If you are using the **10pt** document-class option and *cmd* produces a delimiter, then **\Bigg***cmd* produces an ordinary symbol which is two and a half times the size of the one produced by **\big***cmd*. If you are using either the **11pt** or the **12pt** document-class option, then you need to load the **amsmath** package in order to get **\Bigg** to work as described.

\biggl*cmd* If you are using the **10pt** document-class option and *cmd* produces a delimiter, then **\biggl***cmd* produces an opening symbol which is twice the size of the one produced by **\bigl***cmd*. If you are using the **11pt** or the **12pt** document-class option, then you need to load the **amsmath** package in order to get **\biggl** to work as described.

\Biggl*cmd* If you are using the 10pt document-class option and *cmd* produces a delimiter, then **\Biggl***cmd* produces an opening symbol which is two and a half times the size of the one produced by **\bigl***cmd*. If you are using either the 11pt or the 12pt document-class option, then you need to load the amsmath package in order to get **\Biggl** to work as described.

\biggm*cmd* If you are using the 10pt document-class option and *cmd* produces a delimiter, then **\biggm***cmd* produces a symbol for a binary relation which is twice the size of the one produced by **\bigm***cmd*. If you are using either the 11pt or the 12pt document-class option, then you need to load the amsmath package in order to get **\biggm** to work as described.

\Biggm*cmd* If you are using the 10pt document-class option and *cmd* produces a delimiter, then **\Biggm***cmd* produces a symbol for a binary relation which is two and a half times the size of the one produced by **\bigm***cmd*. If you are using either the 11pt or the 12pt document-class option, then you need to load the amsmath package in order to get **\Biggm** to work as described.

\biggr*cmd* If you are using the 10pt document-class option and *cmd* produces a delimiter, then **\biggr***cmd* produces a closing symbol which is twice the size of the one produced by **\bigr***cmd*. If you are using either the 11pt or the 12pt document-class option, then you need to load the amsmath package in order to get **\biggr** to work as described.

\Biggr*cmd* If you are using the 10pt document-class option and *cmd* produces a delimiter, then **\Biggr***cmd* produces a closing symbol which is two and a half times the size of the one produced by **\bigr***cmd*. If you are using either the 11pt or the 12pt document-class option, then you need to load the amsmath package in order to get **\Biggr** to work as described.

\bigl*cmd* If you are using the 10pt document-class option and *cmd* produces a delimiter, then **\bigl***cmd* produces an opening symbol which is slightly larger than the symbol produced by *cmd* on its own (which may or may not be an opening symbol). The resulting opening symbol is still acceptable, however, in an in-text formula. If you are using either the 11pt or the 12pt document-class option, then you need to load the amsmath package in order to get **\bigl** to work as described.

\Bigl*cmd* If you are using the 10pt document-class option and *cmd* produces a delimiter, then **\Bigl***cmd* produces an opening symbol which is 50% bigger than the one produced by **\bigl***cmd*. If you are using either the 11pt or the 12pt document-class option, then you need to load the amsmath package in order to get **\Bigl** to work as described.

\bigm*cmd* If you are using the 10pt document-class option and *cmd* produces a delimiter, then **\bigm***cmd* produces a symbol for a binary relation which is slightly larger than the one produced by *cmd* on its own (which may or may not be a symbol for a binary relation). The relation symbol produced is still acceptable, however, in an in-text formula. If you are using either the 11pt or the 12pt document-class option, then you need to load the amsmath package in order to get \bigm to work as described.

\Bigm*cmd* If you are using the 10pt document-class option and *cmd* produces a delimiter, then \Bigm*cmd* produces a symbol for a binary relation which is 50% bigger than the one produced by \bigm*cmd*. If you are using either the 11pt or the 12pt document-class option, then you need to load the amsmath package in order to get \Bigm to work as described.

\bigr*cmd* If you are using the 10pt document-class option and *cmd* produces a delimiter, then \bigr*cmd* produces a closing symbol which is slightly larger than the size of the symbol produced by *cmd* on its own (which may or may not be a closing symbol). The closing symbol produced is still acceptable, however, in an in-text formula. If you are using either the 11pt or the 12pt document-class option, then you need to load the amsmath package in order to get \bigr to work as described.

\Bigr*cmd* If you are using the 10pt document-class option and *cmd* produces a delimiter, then \Bigr*cmd* produces a closing symbol which is 50% bigger than the symbol produced by \bigr*cmd*. If you are using either the 11pt or the 12pt document-class option, then you need to load the amsmath package in order to get \Bigr to work as described.

\bigskip This command produces vertical space whose height is given by the value of \bigskipamount; it is defined as \vspace{\bigskipamount}. (Fragile.)

\bigskipamount The value of this rubber length command is 12pt plus 4pt minus 4pt. This value is the same whether you use the 10pt, 11pt or 12pt document-class option.

\binom{*form*$_1$}{*form*$_2$} This command, which is defined in the amsmath package, produces a binomial coefficient: *form*$_1$ appears above *form*$_2$ and both are enclosed in large parentheses. The size of the coefficient produced depends on whether \binom occurs as an in-text or a displayed formula. The commands \tbinom and \dbinom are also available; these force the coefficient to be typeset in textstyle and displaystyle, respectively.

blg This is the file extension of the log or transcript file that is written by BIBTEX when it is run; it contains all the information that appeared on your terminal when BIBTEX was processing your input file.

\boldmath This local declaration can only be used in LR or paragraph mode. Every mathematical expression in its scope is typeset in a bold style. See also \unboldmath. (Robust.)

`\boldsymbol{`*arg*`}` This command can only be used in maths mode and only if you have loaded the `amsbsy` package (and the AMS fonts are installed on your system). It produces its argument *arg* in bold. Note that *arg* can be a letter like 'A' or a command that produces a symbol like '`\equiv`'.

book This is one of the five standard document classes that is available in LATEX 2_ε. The standard options are as follows: at most one of `10pt` (the default), `11pt` or `12pt`; at most one of `letterpaper` (the default), `legalpaper`, `executivepaper`, `a4paper`, `a5paper` or `b5paper`; at most one of `final` (the default) or `draft`; at most one of `oneside` or `twoside` (the default); at most one of `onecolumn` (the default) or `twocolumn`; at most one of `openright` (the default) or `openany`; and at most one of `notitlepage` or `titlepage` (the default). Furthermore, any or none of the following can occur in *opt-list*: `landscape`, `openbib`, `leqno` and `fleqn`. Section 8.3 contains a lot more information about the book document class.

`\botfigrule` If a float is going to be placed at the bottom of a page, then the command `\botfigrule` determines what is to appear between the float and the text above it. By default, nothing appears, but by defining `\botfigrule` you can get LATEX to place a horizontal rule, say, there. Note that, if you do define `\botfigrule`, you must make sure that it does not add any extra vertical space between the float and the text above it. (Note that you need to *define* `\botfigrule` and not *redefine* it.) When a float is going to be placed at the bottom of a page, LATEX first puts `\textfloatsep` amount of vertical space below the text and then it executes `\botfigrule`. See also `\dblfigrule` and `\topfigrule`.

`\bottomfraction` The value of this command is a floating-point number between 0 and 1. Its value specifies how much of the bottom part of each text page can be used for floats. It can be altered by `\renewcommand*`. Its default value is 0.3. If the `twocolumn` document-class option has been chosen, the value of this command only affects single-column floats; there is no analogous command which applies to two-column floats.

bottomnumber The value of this counter is the maximum number of floats, that is to say, tables or figures, that can occur at the bottom of each text page. Its default value is 1. If the `twocolumn` document style option has been chosen, the value of this counter only affects single-column floats; there is no analogous command which applies to two-column floats.

bp This is a TEX keyword; it stands for *big point*, a unit of length, which exactly satisfies the equality 1 in = 72 bp. (Roughly, 1 bp = 0.0139 in = 0.35 mm = 1.004 pt.)

`\breve{`*char*`}` This command produces an accent in maths mode. Thus, `$\breve{x}$` produces $\breve{x}$. (Robust.)

bst This is the extension of a bibliography style file that is used by BibTeX. The information it contains controls the appearance of the bibliography produced. The base name of such a file is given as the argument to the `\bibliographystyle` command. Many bibliography style files have been written, but the only ones that are available in basic LaTeX are `abbrv.bst`, `alpha.bst`, `plain.bst` and `unsrt.bst`. A selection of other style files is to be found in Table 13.1 of Goossens, Mittelbach and Samarin (1994), pp. 377–378.

\c{*char*} This command produces a cedilla accent underneath the single character *char* in both text modes. For example, `\c{c}` produces ç. (Robust.)

calc This package, written by Kresten K. Thorup and Frank Jensen, redefines the commands `\setcounter`, `\addtocounter`, `\setlength` and `\addtolength` so that you can use expressions including the infix operators $+$, $-$, $*$ and $/$ in their second arguments. (Parentheses are used to group subexpressions.) In the case of `\setcounter` and `\addtocounter` the expressions can be made up out of integers, LaTeX's counters (in the form `\value{*ctr*}`) and TeX's integer registers (such as `\time`). In the case of `\setlength` and `\addtolength` lengths and length commands are allowed as well but the operators $+$ and $-$ must combine subexpressions both of which are lengths or both of which have an integer value and in the case of $*$ and $/$ the second argument can be an integer-valued expression when the first argument is a length. The `calc` package also provides the two commands `\real{*fpn*}` and `\ratio{*len*$_1$}{*len*$_2$}` (which is what you obtain when you divide *len*$_1$ by *len*$_2$). The redefinition of the four commands mentioned above has a small knock-on effect because several other commands are defined in terms of them. The most important of these are mentioned, for example, in the entry for `\depth`.

\caption{*heading*} This command can only occur inside a `figure`, `figure*`, `table` or `table*` environment. It produces a numbered caption. If you want to refer to a captioned figure or table, then you need to include a `\label` command either somewhere in *heading* or else following the `\caption` command but within the body of the environment. If a list of figures or a list of tables is produced by means of either the `\listoffigures` or the `\listoftables` command, then *heading* is the text that will appear in the list of figures or the list of tables produced. Note that *heading* is a moving argument so any fragile commands in it must be preceded by `\protect` commands. (Fragile.)

\caption[*entry*]{*heading*} This is the same as the `\caption{*heading*}` command, except that *entry* is the text that will appear in any list of tables or figures produced by a `\listoffigures` or the `\listoftables` command. In this form of the command *entry* is a moving argument but *heading* is not. (Fragile.)

cases This environment is only available if you have loaded the `amsmath` package. It can only be used in maths mode. It is used for typesetting a definition by cases and its general format is:

```
\begin{cases}
```
$form_{1,1}$ & $form_{1,2}$ \\
$form_{2,1}$ & $form_{2,2}$ \\
$\vdots$ $\vdots$ $\vdots$ $\vdots$
$form_{n-1,1}$ & $form_{n-1,2}$ \\
$form_{n,1}$ & $form_{n,2}$
```
\end{cases}
```

This produces a large left brace followed by the formulas $form_{i,1}$ (which are aligned on their left-hand sides) and then the formulas $form_{i,2}$ (again, aligned on their left-hand sides). Note that all the arguments $form_{i,j}$ are processed in maths mode and so, if you want some text, you need to use the \text command.

cc This is a TeX keyword; it stands for *cicero*, a unit of length, which exactly satisfies the equality 1 cc = 12 dd. (Roughly, 1 cc = 0.1777 in = 4.51 mm = 12.84 pt.)

\cc{*text*} This command can only occur inside the letter environment. It is used for listing any 'carbon copies'. LaTeX generates 'cc:' and *text* follows this. One or more \\ commands can occur in the argument *text* to force a new line.

\ccname When you use the \cc command in the letter environment, LaTeX automatically generates the text 'cc:' (including the colon). If you want some other expression to be generated, then you need to redefine the \ccname command. Note, however, that redefining \ccname has no effect on the colon; that will continue to be produced automatically.

CD This environment is defined in the amscd package. It can be used to produce simple commutative diagrams. The following commands, each of which has its own entry in this glossary, can be used inside the CD environment for producing extensible arrows and equals signs: @(((, @))), @<<<, @=, @>>>, @\vert, @|, @AAA and @VVV. (The command @. is used to indicate the absence of an arrow or an equals sign.) To produce extensible left and right arrows outside the CD environment use the \xleftarrow and \xrightarrow commands.

\cdots This command produces an ellipsis consisting of three 'centred' dots ($\cdots$) in maths mode. (Robust.)

center This environment is used for centring text (or any box). The command \\ can be used inside this environment in order to force the end of a line of text. Within this environment LaTeX is in paragraph mode. See section 4.5 for an example of its use.

\centering This local declaration causes the text (or box) in its scope to be centred in the body of a page. Note that the TeX command of the same name does something different; its original definition is available as \@centering.

\cfrac[*pos*]{*form*$_1$}{*form*$_2$} This command is defined in the amsmath package and can only be used in maths mode. It produces a continued fraction with numerator (top part) *form*$_1$ and denominator (bottom part) *form*$_2$. By default the numerator is centred, but by giving a value of l to *pos* you can force the numerator to be pushed to the left and by giving *pos* a value of r you can force the numerator to be pushed to the right. See also \frac, \tfrac, \dfrac and \genfrac.

chapter This counter is used to control the numbering of chapters. It is initialized to zero and incremented by the \chapter command before a number is generated. Values can be assigned to it by means of the \setcounter command. For example, if you want your first chapter to be numbered 0, include the command \setcounter{chapter}{-1} in the preamble of your input file.

\chapter[*entry*]{*heading*} A sectioning command which opens a new chapter. It is not available if the article document class is being used. If the report or book document class is being used, then chapters have level number 0. By default chapters are numbered automatically in those document classes. (This can be altered by changing the value of the counter secumndepth.) If the optional argument *entry* is absent, then by default *heading* will appear in the table of contents if one is produced. (This can be altered by changing the value of the counter tocdepth.) If *entry* is present, then it will appear in the table of contents but *heading* will appear in the body of the document produced. If *entry* is present, then it is a moving argument; but if it is absent, then *heading* is the moving argument. (Fragile.)

\chapter*{*heading*} A sectioning command which opens a new chapter which is neither numbered nor will it appear in the table of contents. (Fragile.)

\chaptername When a \chapter command occurs in an input file, then the word 'Chapter' is produced automatically by LaTeX and is placed at the front of the chapter. If you want some other word to appear instead, then you need to redefine the \chaptername command.

\check{*char*} This command produces an accent in maths mode. Thus, $\check{x}$ produces $\check{x}$. (Robust.)

\circle{*d*} This command can only occur as an argument to a \put or \multiput command inside a picture environment. Thus, \put(*i*, *j*){\circle{*d*}} places a circle of diameter *d* on the picture in such a way that its centre is at the point whose coordinates are (*i*, *j*). Note that LaTeX can only produce a very restricted class of circles. The largest circle it can draw is 40 points (which is about half an inch). Also, there are only a finite number of diameters available. If there is not one exactly the size you specify, then LaTeX will use the one in its repertoire that is closest to the one you specify. (Fragile.)

\circle*{*d*} This command is like **\circle{*d*}** except that the circle produced is a filled-in disk. Note that LATEX can only produce a very restricted class of disks. The largest disk it can produce has a diameter of 15 points (which is about a fifth of an inch). Also, there are only a finite number of diameters available. If there is not one exactly the size you specify, then LATEX will use the one in its repertoire that is closest to the one you specify. (Fragile.)

\cite[*text*]{*key-list*} This command is used for producing references to a bibliography produced by BIBTEX or done yourself. The argument *key-list* is a list of keys, separated by commas, that have been defined either in a **bib** file or a **thebibliography** environment. If *text* is present, it is added as an annotation to the reference. (Fragile.)

\cleardoublepage This command, which should only be used in paragraph mode, terminates the current paragraph and the current page. Any unfilled space is placed at the bottom of the page rather than between paragraphs even if you have used the **\flushbottom** declaration. All figures and tables in 'memory' are output. If two-sided printing is in effect, then the next page to have text on it will be a right-handed and odd-numbered one. If you are using the **twocolumn** document-class option, then the use of **\cleardoublepage** may cause the right-hand column to be entirely blank. (Fragile.)

\clearpage This command terminates the current paragraph and the current page. It can only be used in paragraph mode. Any unfilled space is placed at the bottom of the page rather than between paragraphs even if you have used the **\flushbottom** declaration. All figures and tables in 'memory' are output. If you are using the **twocolumn** document-class option, then the use of **\clearpage** may cause the right-hand column to be entirely blank. (Robust.)

\cline{*i-j*} This command is only available inside an **array**, **tabular** or **tabular*** environment. Whereas **\hline** produces a horizontal line across the entire width of the resulting table, this command only produces a line extending across columns *i* to *j* inclusive. Both *i* and *j* must be present, but they can be the same. It must come either after the command that opens the environment, after a **** command or after another **\cline** command.

clo Using a document-class option alters the appearance of the output produced when you process your input file using LATEX. Sometimes the commands that make these alterations are stored in a file whose extension is **clo**. For example, if you use the **11pt** document-class option to the **report** document class, then the file **size11.clo** is read in when your input file is processed.

clock This document-class option can only be used in the **slides** document class. When it has been chosen, the commands **\addtime** and **\settime** can be used to help you calculate the length of time that a lecture or presentation you make is going to take.

`\closing{`*text*`}` This command can only occur inside a `letter` environment. It is used for the message that occurs at the end of the letter. For example, *text* could be `Yours sincerely`.

`cls` This is the extension of a LATEX class file. When you give a value to the *doc-class* argument of the `\documentclass` command, then LATEX reads in the file *doc-class*`.cls` when processing your input file. The standard document classes are `article`, `report`, `book`, `letter` and `slides`, but there are several non-standard ones. The most important of these others are the three AMS document classes, namely `amsart`, `amsbook` and `amsproc`. See Chapter 8 of Grätzer (1996) for more information about these.

`cm` This is a TEX keyword; it stands for *centimetre*, a unit of length, which exactly satisfies the equality 1 in = 2.54 cm. (Roughly, 1 cm = 0.3937 in = 28.45 pt.)

`\columnsep` The value of this rigid length parameter is the width of the space between the two columns of text produced when you use the `twocolumn` document-class option. This is a robust command that must never be preceded by a `\protect` command.

`\columnseprule` The value of this rigid length parameter is the width of the vertical line that separates the two columns of text produced when you use the `twocolumn` document-class option. By default it has a value of 0 inches, that is to say, no visible rule is placed between the columns. This is a robust command that must never be preceded by a `\protect` command.

`\columnwidth` The value of this rigid length parameter is the width of a single column of text. It is calculated by LATEX from the values of `\textwidth` and `\columnsep`. It should only be used in order to determine the values of other length commands and it should not be altered.

`\contentsline{`*sec-unit*`}{`*entry*`}{`*p*`}` This command only occurs in the `lof`, `lot` and `toc` files that LATEX writes in appropriate circumstances. In the `lof` file *sec-unit* is `figure` and in the `lot` file it is `table`. In the `toc` file *sec-unit* can be either `part`, `chapter`, `section`, `subsection`, `subsubsection`, `paragraph` or `subparagraph`. (If you are producing a table of contents for an article, then *sec-unit* cannot take the value `chapter`.) The argument *entry* contains the text that is to appear in the list of figures, list of tables or table of contents. This text is usually preceded by a `\numberline{`*sec-num*`}` command which determines the indentation used in the formatting of the entry. The argument *p* is a page number.

`\contentsname` When you use the `\tableofcontents` command to get LATEX to produce a table of contents, the heading 'Contents' is generated automatically. If you want a different heading to be produced, then you need to redefine the `\contentsname` command.

\copyright This command produces the copyright symbol © in all modes. If used in maths mode, you get a LaTeX warning; but the symbol still gets produced. (Robust.)

\d{*char*} This command produces a dot-under accent underneath the single character *char* in both text modes. For example, \d{o} produces ọ. (Robust.)

\dag This command produces the dagger symbol † in all modes. (Robust.)

\dashbox{*h*}(*i*, *j*)[*pos*]{*picture-object*} This command can only appear inside the picture environment. It produces a box with a dashed frame drawn around it; the arguments have the same meaning as for the \makebox command, *q.v.*; except for *h* which is the length of the dashes and gaps that make up the frame. (Fragile.)

\date{*text*} In the article, report, book and slides document classes, this declaration is used to declare *text* to be the date of the document produced. If it is omitted, then the date on which you run LaTeX on your input file is used as the date of the document. You can use the \\ command inside *text* in order to force a line break and one or more \thanks commands can also appear in *text*. These produce footnotes whose markers are regarded as having zero width. If a \thanks command does not end a line, then it should be followed by a \⊔ command in order to insert some inter-word space. In the letter document class this declaration can be used in order to produce a date of your choice. One or more \\ commands can occur in *text*, but in this case no \thanks commands can occur in it.

\dbinom{*form*$_1$}{*form*$_2$} This command, which is defined in the amsmath package, produces a binomial coefficient which is typeset in displaystyle: *form*$_1$ appears above *form*$_2$ and both are enclosed in large parentheses. See also \binom and \tbinom.

\dblfigrule This command only has a meaning when the twocolumn document-class option is being used. When a double-column float is going to be placed at the top of a page, the command \dblfigrule determines what is to appear between the float and the text below it. By default, nothing appears, but by defining \dblfigrule you can get LaTeX to place a horizontal rule, say, there. Note that, if you do define \dblfigrule, you must make sure that it does not add any extra vertical space between the float and the text below it. (Note that you need to *define* \botfigrule and not *redefine* it.) When a double-column float is going to be placed at the top of a page, LaTeX first executes \dblfigrule and then it puts \dbltextfloatsep amount of vertical space before the text below it. If two or more double-column floats are going to appear at the top of a page, then what \dblfigrule produces only appears below the bottommost of those floats. This is true even if a single-column float is placed just underneath these double-column floats. See also \botfigrule and \topfigrule.

\dblfloatpagefraction The value of this command, which only does something if the `twocolumn` document-class option is being used, is a floating-point number between 0 and 1 which specifies the minimum amount of space that must be occupied by double-column floats on a floats-only page. For example, if its value is 0.6, then at least 60% of the page would have to be occupied by double-column floats. It can be altered by **\renewcommand***. Its default value is 0.5.

\dblfloatsep This is a rubber length parameter. If the `twocolumn` document-class option is being used, the value of this command affects the placement of two-column wide floats; it is the amount of vertical space that appears between two such floats on a page that contains both text and floats. It is a robust command that should not be preceded by a **\protect** command.

\dbltextfloatsep The value of this rubber length parameter only has an effect if the `twocolumn` document-class option has been chosen. Its value is the amount of vertical space left between a double-column float and the text either below or above it. It is a robust command that must not be preceded by a **\protect** command.

\dbltopfraction The value of this command only has an effect if the `twocolumn` document-class option has been chosen. Its value is a floating-point number between 0 and 1 which specifies how much of the top part of each text page can be used for double-column floats. It can be altered by **\renewcommand***. Its default value is 0.7.

dbltopnumber The value of this counter only has an effect if the `twocolumn` document class option has been chosen. Its value is the maximum number of two-column floats that can occur at the top of each text page. Its default value is 2.

dd This is a TeX keyword; it stands for *didot point*, a unit of length, which exactly satisfies the equality 1157 dd = 1238 pt. (Roughly, 1 dd = 0.0148 in = 0.376 mm = 1.07 pt.)

\ddag This command produces the double dagger symbol ‡ in all modes. (Robust.)

\ddot{*char*} This command produces an accent in maths mode. Thus, `$\ddot{x}$` produces $\ddot{x}$. (Robust.)

\ddots This command produces an ellipsis consisting of three diagonal dots in maths mode. (Robust.)

\DeclareMathOperator{*cmd*}{*text*} This preamble command is only available if you have loaded the `amsopn` package. It makes *cmd* into the name of a log-like function which appears as *text* in your document. Note that *text* is typeset in upright, roman type. Subscripts and superscripts attached to *cmd* appear as such in both text and display style.

`\DeclareMathOperator*{`*cmd*`}{`*text*`}` This preamble command is only available if you have loaded the `amsopn` package. It makes *cmd* into the name of a log-like function which appears as *text* in your document. Note that *text* is typeset in upright, roman type. Subscripts and superscripts attached to *cmd* appear as such in text, but as limits in display style.

`\depth` The general formats of the `\framebox`, `\makebox`, `\savebox`, `\raisebox` and `\parbox` commands and the `minipage` environment are as follows:

> `\framebox[`*len*`][`*pos*`]{`*text*`}`
> `\makebox[`*len*`][`*pos*`]{`*text*`}`
> `\savebox[`*len*`][`*pos*`]{`*text*`}`
> `\raisebox{`*len$_1$*`}[`*len$_2$*`][`*len$_3$*`]{`*text*`}`
> `\parbox[`*pos$_1$*`][`*len$_2$*`][`*pos$_2$*`]{`*len$_1$*`}{`*text*`}`
> `\begin{minipage}[`*pos$_1$*`][`*len$_2$*`][`*pos$_2$*`]{`*len$_1$*`}`
>   *text*
> `\end{minipage}`

It is possible for the `\depth` command to occur in the *len* argument of the `\framebox`, `\makebox` and `\savebox` commands, in the arguments *len$_1$*, *len$_2$* and *len$_3$* of the `\raisebox` command and in the argument *len$_2$* of the `\parbox` command and the `minipage` environment. The value of the length command `\depth` is the depth of the box obtained by typesetting the argument *text*. In the case of the `\framebox`, `\makebox`, `\savebox` and `\raisebox` commands *text* is processed in LR mode and in the case of the `\parbox` command and the `minipage` environment it is processed in paragraph mode. If you load the `calc` package, then you can use commands like `\framebox[\depth + 4mm]{`*text*`}`.

`description` This environment is usually used for making glossaries. An `\item[`*text*`]` command inside it produces *text* in bold type. See section 4.8 for some examples of its use.

`\dfrac{`*form$_1$*`}{`*form$_2$*`}` This command produces a fraction with numerator (top part) *form$_1$* and denominator (bottom part) *form$_2$* which is typeset in displaystyle. It is defined in the `amsmath` package and can only be used in maths mode. See also `\frac`, `\tfrac`, `\cfrac` and `\genfrac`.

`\displaylimits` The effect of *cmd*`\displaylimits_`*form$_1$*`^`*form$_2$* in display style (in maths mode) is to force *form$_1$* to appear as a limit below the symbol produced by *cmd* and to make *form$_2$* appear as a limit above it and in text style *form$_1$* appears as a subscript and *form$_2$* as a superscript. This is a primitive TEX command. See also `\limits` and `\nolimits`.

`displaymath` This environment is used for typesetting a mathematical formula so that it appears on a line by itself. The concise form `\[`*form*`\]` is also available. Inside this environment LATEX is in maths mode and display style.

\displaystyle This local declaration can only be used in maths mode. It forces
TeX to typeset formulas in display style, which is the default style for formulas
that occur on a line by themselves. This is a primitive TeX command. See also
\textstyle, \scriptstyle and \scriptscriptstyle. (Robust.)

doc In LaTeX 2.09 the file extension doc was used for a file which contained exactly
the same macros or commands as the corresponding sty file, but had more
explanatory material included in it as comments. The situation in LaTeX 2$_\varepsilon$ is
more complicated. See Chapter 14 of Goossens et al. (1994) for more information.

document This is the outermost environment in all input files.

\documentclass[*opt-list*]{*doc-class*}[*date*] This command comes between the *prologue* and the *preamble* of every LaTeX 2$_\varepsilon$ input file. The mandatory argument
doc-class specifies the document class. There are five standard document classes
and they are article, report, book, letter and slides. If present, the argument *opt-list* consists of one or more class options. No spaces should be included
in *opt-list* and if more than one option is included then commas should be used as
separators. What the possible candidates for inclusion in *opt-list* are depends on
the particular document class chosen. More information about possible options
is given in this glossary in the entries for the five standard document classes.
The optional argument *date* must have the format *year/month/day*, where *year*
consists of four digits and both *month* and *day* consist of two digits each. An example of the *date* parameter is 1998/03/11. A warning message will be printed
if the date of the class file specified is earlier than this.

\dot{*char*} This command produces an accent in maths mode. Thus, $\dot{x}$
produces $\dot{x}$. (Robust.)

\dotfill This command produces a row of dots that expands to fill all the available
space where it occurs; see Table C.1 on p. 207 for a picture of what it does.
(Robust)

\doublerulesep The value of this rigid length parameter is the distance that separates
two vertical lines produced by either a || expression in the *preamble* of an array,
tabular or tabular* environment or the distance between two horizontal lines
produced by two \hline commands. It is robust and must not be preceded by
a \protect command.

\downbracefill This command produces an upward pointing curly brace which expands to fill all the horizontal space available; see Table C.1 for a graphical
depiction of what it does.

draft Sometimes when your input file is being processed you get an overful hbox
error message and in the resulting output some text sticks out into the right-
hand margin. If you use this document-class option, then such pieces of text will
be marked with a black rectangle. See also final.

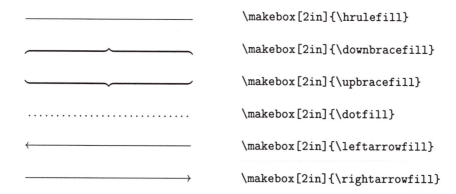

	`\makebox[2in]{\hrulefill}`
	`\makebox[2in]{\downbracefill}`
	`\makebox[2in]{\upbracefill}`
	`\makebox[2in]{\dotfill}`
	`\makebox[2in]{\leftarrowfill}`
	`\makebox[2in]{\rightarrowfill}`

Table C.1: Six `fill` commands.

dtx This is the extension of a LaTeX documented source file. If you run LaTeX on such a file, then the documentation for that file is produced.

dvi This is the file extension of the device independent file that is created when the corresponding `tex` file is processed by LaTeX.

em This is a font-dependent unit of length which is equal to the width of a quad. It used to be the width of a capital letter 'M', but that may or may not be the case nowadays. It is generally used for horizontal measurements. It is also the width of one `\quad`, twice the width of an `\enskip` or an `\enspace`, and half the width of a `\qquad`.

\em This local declaration is used in order to emphasize a piece of text. How it does this depends on the context in which it occurs. (Robust.)

\emph{*text*} This command emphasizes the phrase that is given to it as its argument *text*. The effect of the `\emph` command depends on the context in which it occurs. (Robust.)

empty This page-style option can be given as the argument to the `\pagestyle` and `\thispagestyle` declarations. The head and the foot of any page affected by those declarations are both left empty. The other three page-style options are `headings`, `myheadings` and `plain`.

\encl{*text*} This command can only occur inside a `letter` environment. It is used for listing any enclosures. LaTeX generates 'encl:' and *text* follows this. One or more `\\` commands can occur in the argument *text* to force a new line.

\enclname When you use the `\encl` command in the `letter` environment, LaTeX automatically generates the text 'encl:' (including the colon). If you want some other expression to be generated, then you need to redefine the `\enclname` command. Note, however, that redefining `\enclname` has no effect on the colon; that will continue to be produced automatically.

`\end{`*env*`}` A command used for ending the *env* environment. (Fragile.)

`\enlargethispage{`*len*`}` This command only affects the current page. It makes the height of the body region equal to the sum of the value of `\textheight` and *len*. The argument *len* can be negative. (Fragile.)

`\enlargethispage*{`*len*`}` This command is similar to `\enlargethispage` except that any rubber space in the page produced is squeezed as much as it can be.

`\enskip` This command produces horizontal space which is half an em wide in all modes. A line break can occur where this command appears. This is a plain TeX command.

`\enspace` This command produces horizontal space which is half an em wide in all modes. A line break cannot occur where this command appears. This is a plain TeX command.

`\ensuremath{`*form*`}` When this command occurs in either paragraph or LR mode, it is equivalent to `$`*form*`$`; but when it occurs in maths mode, it is equivalent to *form*. It is sometimes useful in definitions.

`enumerate` This environment is used to produce labelled lists. The nature of the labels depends on the level of nesting, but they are generated automatically when the `\item` command, without any arguments, is used. See section 4.7 for some examples of its use.

`enumi` This counter is used in the generation of the labels in an `enumerate` environment which does not appear inside another `enumerate` environment.

`enumii` This counter is used in the generation of the labels in an `enumerate` environment which is nested inside another one.

`enumiii` This counter is used in the generation of the labels in an `enumerate` environment which is nested inside two others.

`enumiv` This counter is used in the generation of the labels in an `enumerate` environment which is nested inside three others.

`eqnarray` This environment produces a collection of displayed equations each of which is numbered. (To suppress the numbering use the `eqnarray*` environment.) Inside this environment LaTeX is in maths mode. See section 10.2 for more information about how it works.

`eqnarray*` This environment is used for producing a collection of displayed equations none of which is labelled.

equation This counter is used by both the `equation` and the `eqnarray` environments in order to keep track of how it labels displayed formulas.

equation This environment produces a displayed mathematical formula with a numerical label generated automatically. In the `article` document class formulas are numbered consecutively throughout the output document starting with (1) and the labels are just single numbers. In the `report` and `book` document classes formulas are numbered consecutively throughout each chapter of the output document starting with $(X.1)$, where X is the number of the chapter, and all the labels are made up out of two numbers.

\errorstopmode This primitive TeX command makes TeX ask for user input when an error occurs; it is the default run mode. This is one of the few commands that can come before the `\documentclass` command in the input file.

eucal This package redefines the `\mathcal` command so that it produces letters belonging to the Euler Script alphabet. If you load the package using the `mathscr` option, then the `\mathcal` command is not redefined and letters in the Euler Script alphabet are available by using the `\mathscr` command.

eufrak This package defines the `\mathfrak` command that can be used to produce letters from the Euler Fraktur alphabet (mathematicians' Gothic letters).

\evensidemargin The value of this rigid length parameter affects the appearance of each even-numbered output page. On left-hand pages, if two-sided printing is in operation, the distance between the left-hand edge of the paper and the left-hand edge of the body is the sum of the value of `\evensidemargin` and one inch. (See Fig. C.4 on p. 260.) This is a robust command that must never be preceded by a `\protect` command.

ex This is a font-dependent unit of length which used to be equal to the height of a lowercase letter 'x', but that may or may not be the case nowadays. It is generally used for vertical measurements.

executivepaper This is a document-class option. Use it when you are producing a document that is going to be printed on paper which is 7.25 inches by 10.5 inches. See also `a4paper`, `a5paper`, `b5paper`, `legalpaper` and `letterpaper`.

\extracolsep{*len*} This length parameter that can only occur within the argument to an @-expression which occurs in the preamble of an `array`, `tabular` or `tabular*` environment. It has the effect of putting *len* amount of space to the left of all the following columns and this space is not suppressed by the presence of further @-expressions.

\fbox{*text*} This command produces $\boxed{text}$ in all modes, but not inside the `picture` environment, with *text* being processed in LR mode. The width of the lines is determined by the value of the `\fboxrule` length parameter and the width of the space separating the frame from the *text* is given by the value of the length parameter \fboxsep. Thus, the width of the resulting box is the width of the box produced after *text* has been processed plus twice the sum of the values of the length parameters \fboxrule and \fboxsep. (Robust.)

\fboxrule The value of this rigid length parameter is the width of the horizontal and vertical 'framing' rules produced by an \fbox or \framebox command, except inside the `picture` environment. Other commands control the width of lines produced in the `picture` environment.

\fboxsep The value of this rigid length parameter is the amount of space that separates the box produced by processing the *text* argument of an \fbox or \framebox command and the horizontal and vertical rules comprising the 'frame' that surrounds it, except inside the `picture` environment. Inside the `picture` environment no surrounding space is left.

fd This is the extension of a font definition file.

figure This counter is used in the numbering of floats created by the `figure` and `figure*` environments. It is only incremented if a \caption command has been included inside the environment.

figure This environment produces a float. If the `twocolumn` document-class option has been chosen, then the float produced is only one column wide and the b and h options for the *pos* argument are unavailable; otherwise, it behaves exactly like the `figure*` environment, *q.v.*

figure* This environment produces a float. If a \caption command is present inside it, the word 'Figure' and a numerical label are produced automatically. If you want a phrase other than 'Figure' to be produced, then redefine the \figurename command. If the `twocolumn` document-class option has been chosen, then the float produced is two columns wide. Its general format is:

\begin{figure*}[*pos*] *text* \end{figure*}

The *text* is processed in paragraph mode and a parbox of width \textwidth is produced. The optional argument *pos* is a sequence of between one and four different letters chosen from b, h, p and t. It affects the position where the float may appear as follows:

b The float may appear at the bottom of a text page.

h The float may be placed in the output in the same relative position to its neighbours as it occurs in the input.

p The float may appear on a floats-only page.

t The float may appear at the top of a text page.

The default value of *pos* is tbp. The character ! can also occur in the *pos* argument. This tells LaTeX to place the float as close as it can to the place where the environment that produced it occurs, but taking the other components of the *pos* argument into account. The \suppressfloats[*pos*] command ensures that no floats are placed on the current page. The optional argument *pos* can be either b or t. If it is b, then no floats will be placed at the bottom of the current page; and if it is t, then no floats will be placed at the top of the current page. If you use the ! character in the *pos* argument of either the figure or table environment, then that overrides the effect of any \suppressfloats command.

\figurename When you use the \caption command inside the figure and figure* environments, LaTeX produces a caption beginning with the word 'Figure'. If you want some other expression to be used instead, then you need to redefine the \figurename command.

filecontents This environment takes a single argument which is the name of a file including its extension. The body of the environment will become the contents of that file when the input file containing the environment is processed. Any number of filecontents environments can occur in the input file, but they must all precede the \documentclass command. When the input file is processed, LaTeX creates a file with the name given as argument to the filecontents environment (unless it already exists) and writes the body of the environment to that file. This environment is useful for sending documents to people at other locations. See also \listfiles.

filecontents* This environment behaves exactly like the filecontents environment except that any comments that occur in the body of the environment are not written to the external file (whose name is the same as the single argument that the environment takes). See also \listfiles.

\fill The natural length of this rubber length command is zero, but given the chance it will stretch as much as it can. It is used to define \hfill and \vfill. (Robust.)

final Sometimes when your input file is being processed you get an overful hbox error message and in the resulting output some text sticks out into the right-hand margin. If you use this document-class option, rather than draft, then such pieces of text will not be marked with a black rectangle. This option is the default in all five standard document classes.

fleqn This document-class option causes all displayed equations occurring within the \[and \] commands and also those occurring inside the displaymath, equation, eqnarray and eqnarray* environments to be indented from the left margin by a distance of \mathindent rather than being centred, as is the default.

\floatpagefraction The value of this command is a floating-point number between 0 and 1. Its value specifies the minimum amount of space that must be occupied by floats on a floats-only page. For example, if its value is 0.6, then at least 60% of the page would have to be occupied by floats. It can be altered by \renewcommand*. Its default value is 0.5. If the twocolumn document-class option has been chosen, the value of this command only affects single-column floats; for two-column floats see `\dblfloatpagefraction`.

`\floatsep` The value of this rubber length parameter is the amount of vertical space left between floats that appear on the same text page. If you are using the `twocolumn` document-class option, then the value of this command only affects single-column floats; for two-column floats see `\dblfloatsep`. This is a robust command that must not be preceded by a `\protect` command.

`\flushbottom` This local declaration has the effect of making the height of the text on a page the same on all pages. Extra space is added between paragraphs to achieve this when necessary. See also `\raggedbottom`.

`flushleft` This environment is used for producing paragraphs that are not right justified, but have a ragged right edge. See section 4.5 for an example of its use.

`flushright` This environment is used for producing paragraphs that are not left justified, but have a ragged left edge. See section 4.5 for an example of its use.

`fmt` This is the extension of a format file. The format file for LaTeX 2_ε is, for example, `latex.fmt` and for LaTeX 2.09 it is `lplain.fmt`. Format files are created by the `initex` program.

`\fnsymbol{`*ctr*`}` This command produces one of the following nine symbols depending on the value of the counter *ctr* (which must lie between 1 and 9 inclusive): ∗, †, ‡, §, ¶, ‖, ∗∗, †† and ‡‡. For example, the commands

> `\newcounter{stone}\setcounter{stone}{4}\fnsymbol{stone}`

produce §. (Robust.)

`\footheight` The value of this rigid length parameter is the height of the region containing the text in the foot of the page. See Fig. C.4 on p. 260. This is a robust command that must never be preceded by a `\protect` command.

`footnote` This counter is used for the numbering of footnotes. In the `book` and `report` document classes it is initialized to zero at the beginning of each chapter and in the `article` document class it is initialized to zero at the start of the document. It is incremented automatically by both the `\footnote` and `\footnotetext` commands before being used.

`\footnote[`*i*`]{`*text*`}` This command can be used either in paragraph mode or inside a `minipage` environment in order to produce a footnote. In paragraph mode, if the optional numerical argument *i* is missing, then the `footnote` counter is incremented and then used as the number of the footnote. This occurs as a superscript in the body of the page where the `\footnote` command occurs and also at the bottom of the body of the page where *text* also appears. If *i*, which must be a positive whole number, is present, then the counter `footnote` is left unaltered and i is used as the footnote number. Inside a `minipage` environment the footnote mark will appear as a letter and the *text* will appear in the bottom part of the box produced. If the number i is present, then the corresponding lowercase letter will be used as the footnote mark. Note that this LaTeX command is different from the plain TeX `\footnote` command. (Fragile.)

`\footnotemark[i]` This command can be used in any mode to produce a footnote mark which appears as a superscript in the body of the page but nowhere else. If i is absent, then the counter `footnote` is incremented by one and then that value is used as the footnote mark. If i, which must be a positive whole number, is present, then the counter `footnote` is left unaltered and i is used as the footnote mark. This command is usually used in conjunction with `\footnotetext`. (Fragile.)

`\footnoterule` Normally when a footnote appears on a page it is separated from the text above by a horizontal line or rule a third of the width of the page. This command produces that effect.

`\footnotesep` The value of this rigid length parameter minus the current length separating baselines gives the amount of space left between footnotes and also just below the horizontal line or rule generated by `\footnoterule`. This is a rigid length command that must not be preceded by a `\protect` command.

`\footnotesize` This local declaration alters the size of type being used. Usually the type size selected is just bigger than `\scriptsize` and just smaller than `\small`. In LaTeX 2.09 this declaration also selected the main text font being used, but this is no longer the case. It cannot be used in maths mode. (Fragile.)

`\footnotetext[i]{text}` This command can be used in any mode. It behaves exactly like `\footnote` except that no footnote mark appears in the body of the page marking the presence of a footnote. It is usually used in conjunction with `\footnotemark`. (Fragile.)

`\footskip` The value of this rigid length parameter is the distance between the bottom of the body and the bottom of the foot. See Fig. C.4 on p. 260. This is a robust command that must never be preceded by a `\protect` command.

`\frac{form₁}{form₂}` This command is only available in maths mode where it produces a fraction with numerator (top part) $form_1$ and denominator (bottom part) $form_2$. The `\genfrac` command available in the `amsmath` package can be used to provide a variety of fraction-like notations. (Robust.)

`\frame{picture-object}` This command, which is usually used inside the `picture` environment, puts a 'frame' made up out of vertical and horizontal lines around *picture-object* with no separating space. The bottom left-hand corner of the resulting box is the reference point. (Fragile.)

\framebox[*len*][*pos*]{*text*} Outside the `picture` environment this command processes *text* in LR mode and then 'frames' the result. If the arguemnt *len*, which must be a rigid length, is present, then it will determine the width of the box produced. The commands \depth, \height, \totalheight and \width can occur in *len*. The optional *pos* argument can be either c (the default), l, r or s. If it is c, then *text* is centred in the box produced. If it is l, then *text* is pushed left as far as it can go in the box produced. If it is r, then *text* is pushed right as far as it can be. If it is s and *text* contains stretchable space, then *text* will be stretched to fill the box produced. (Fragile.)

\framebox(*i, j*)[*pos*]{*picture-object*} This form of the \framebox command can only occur inside the `picture` environment. The parameters have the same meaning as for the \makebox command, *q.v.* The only difference between this command and \makebox is that this one produces text with a 'frame' made up out of vertical and horizontal lines surrounding it. (Fragile.)

\frenchspacing By default, TEX puts more than the normal amount of inter-word space after a colon, full stop, exclamation mark and question mark. When the \frenchspacing declaration is in force, however, TEX regards the space following these punctuation marks in exactly the same way that it treats a space between words. See also \nonfrenchspacing. (Fragile.)

\frontmatter This command is only available in the `book` document class. It causes pages to be numbered with lowercase Roman numerals and it redefines the \chapter command so that it does not produce a chapter number but the heading is included in the table of contents (if produced). See also \mainmatter and \backmatter.

\fussy This local declaration influences line breaking. When it is in force, and it is the default, text will sometimes stick out into the right-hand margin and a warning message will be displayed on your terminal. It affects the typesetting of any paragraph, if it is in force, when that paragraph ends.

gather This environment is only available if you have loaded the `amsmath` package. It is used for producing several displayed formulas; each such formula is centred and given a numerical label automatically. The \notag command can be used to suppress the production of a label on any particular line. The commands \\ and * are used inside the environment in order to separate formulas. One or more \intertext commands can occur inside the gather environment.

gather* This environment is only available if you have loaded the `amsmath` package. It is very similar to the gather environment; the only difference between them is that in the gather* environment the formulas produced are not labelled automatically. The commands \tag and \tag* can be used, however, to produce your own labels.

\genfrac{*cmd*₁}{*cmd*₂}{*len*}{*i*}{*form*₁}{*form*₂} This command is only available if you are using the amsmath package and it can only be used in maths mode. It produces a fraction-like structure. The arguments *cmd*₁ and *cmd*₂ must be commands that produce delimiters; *cmd*₁ produces the delimiter that appears on the left of the generalized fraction and *cmd*₂ produces the one that appears on the right. The argument *len* determines the thickness of the line separating the numerator and the denominator of the fraction. The default is for a normal fraction line to be produced. The argument *i* determines the style in which the fraction will be produced. A value of 0 for *i* will produce a fraction in display style, a value of 1 will produce a fraction in text style, a value of 2 in script style and one of 3 in scriptscript style. The default is for the style to be determined by the context where \genfrac occurs. The argument *form*₁ produces the numerator and *form*₂ the denominator.

glo This is the file extension of a file which is written if a \makeglossary command occurs in your input file (and a \nofiles command does not occur there). It contains a \glossaryentry{*text*}{*p*} command for every \glossary{*text*} command that occurs in your input file (and nothing else).

\glossary{*text*} This command causes the command \glossaryentry{*text*}{*p*} to be written to a glo file (if one is being written). Any characters can occur in *text* (but all braces, including \{ and \}, must come in matching pairs) unless the \glossary command occurs inside the argument of another command, when *text* can only include letters, numerals and punctuation marks. (Fragile.)

\glossaryentry{*text*}{*p*} This command can only occur in a glo file. It is written there automatically by LaTeX whenever a \glossary{*text*} command occurs in the input file. (This only happens if a \makeglossary command occurs in the preamble of your input file and a \nofiles command does not occur there.) The number *p* is the page number of the page in the output where \glossary{*text*} occurs.

\grave{*char*} This command produces an accent in maths mode. Thus, $\grave{x}$ produces $\grave{x}$. (Robust.)

\H{*char*} This command produces a long Hungarian umlaut over the single character *char* in LR or paragraph mode. For example, \H{o} produces ő. (Robust.)

harvard This package produces references in the Harvard style; it is fully described in section 6.5.

\hat{*char*} This command produces an accent in maths mode. Thus, $\hat{x}$ produces $\hat{x}$. (Robust.)

\hbox{*text*} This primitive TeX command makes a horizontal box; the individual components of the *text* argument are placed next to each other horizontally.

\headheight The value of this rigid length parameter affects the appearance of each output page. Its value is the height of the box containing the text in the head of the page. See Fig. C.4 on p. 260. This is a robust command that must never be preceded by a \protect command.

headings This page-style option can be given as the argument to the \pagestyle and \thispagestyle declarations. The document class determines what information goes into the head of the page; usually it is a sectional-unit heading, and the foot is left empty. It is the default page style for the book document class. The three other page-style options are empty, myheadings and plain.

\headsep The value of this rigid length parameter affects the appearance of each output page. Its value is the distance between the bottom of the head and the top of the body. See Fig. C.4 on p. 260. This is a robust command that must never be preceded by a \protect command.

\height The general formats of the \framebox, \makebox, \savebox, \raisebox and \parbox commands and the minipage environment are as follows:

> \framebox[*len*][*pos*]{*text*}
> \makebox[*len*][*pos*]{*text*}
> \savebox[*len*][*pos*]{*text*}
> \raisebox{*len*$_1$}[*len*$_2$][*len*$_3$]{*text*}
> \parbox[*pos*$_1$][*len*$_2$][*pos*$_2$]{*len*$_1$}{*text*}
> \begin{minipage}[*pos*$_1$][*len*$_2$][*pos*$_2$]{*len*$_1$}
>   *text*
> \end{minipage}

It is possible for the \height command to occur in the *len* argument of the commands \framebox, \makebox and \savebox, in the arguments *len*$_1$, *len*$_2$ and *len*$_3$ of the \raisebox command and in the argument *len*$_2$ of the \parbox command and the minipage environment. The value of the length command \height is the height of the box obtained by typesetting the argument *text*. In the case of the \framebox, \makebox, \savebox and \raisebox commands *text* is processed in LR mode and in the case of the \parbox command and the minipage environment it is processed in paragraph mode. If you load the calc package, then you can use commands like \framebox[\height + 4mm]{*text*}.

\hfill This is the same as \hspace{\fill}. (Robust.)

\hline This command is only available inside the array, tabular and tabular* environments. It produces a horizontal line across the entire width of the resulting table. It must come either after the command that opens the environment or after a \\ command.

\hrulefill This command produces a horizontal line or rule which expands to fill all the available space where it occurs. See Table C.1 on p. 207 for a picture of what it does. (Robust)

\hspace{*len*} This command produces *len* amount of horizontal space which disappears at a line break. (Robust.)

\hspace*{*len*} This command produces *len* amount of horizontal space which does not disappear at a line break. (Robust.)

\huge This local declaration alters the size of type being used. Usually the type size selected is just bigger than **\LARGE** and just smaller than **\Huge**. In LATEX 2.09 this declaration also selected the main text font being used, but this is no longer the case. It cannot be used in maths mode. (Fragile.)

\Huge This local declaration alters the size of type being used. Usually the type size selected is the largest available and is just bigger than **\huge**. In LATEX 2.09 this declaration also selected the main text font being used, but this is no longer the case. It cannot be used in maths mode. (Fragile.)

\hyphenation{*word-list*} This is a global declaration which tells TEX how the words that occur in *word-list* can be hyphenated; words in *word-list* are separated by spaces and hyphens in individual words indicate places where hyphenation is allowed. (Robust.)

\i This command produces a dotless letter 'ı' in paragraph and LR modes. (Robust.)

idx This is the file extension of the file that is written if a **\makeindex** command occurs in the preamble of your input file (and a **\nofiles** command does not occur there). It contains an **\indexentry{*text*}{*p*}** command for every **\index{*text*}** command that occurs in your input file (and nothing else).

ilg This is the extension of the log or transcript file that *MakeIndex* writes.

in This is a TEX keyword; it stands for *inch*, a unit of length, which exactly satisfies the equalities 1 in = 72.27 pt = 25.4 mm.

\include{*file*} This command is used in conjunction with **\includeonly{*file-list*}** for producing only part of a large document whose content has been split into several input files. Note that the result of processing *file* will, if it appears at all, always start on a new page and it will terminate as if a **\clearpage** command had been included at the end of *file*.**tex**. (Fragile.)

\includeonly{*file-list*} This command can only occur in the preamble of your input file. The argument *file-list* is a list of zero or more extensionless filenames; the comma is used as a separator. If *file* occurs in *file-list*, the output produced by LATEXwill contain the result of processing *file*.**tex**; otherwise it will not. (Fragile.)

ind This is the extension of a file that *MakeIndex* writes. It is used in the production of an index. It contains a **theindex** environment and it is read by the **\printindex** command that is defined in the **makeidx** package.

\indent This command forces the next line of text that LaTeX outputs to be indented by the amount that is the current value of the \parindent length parameter. See also \noindent. (Robust.)

\index{*text*} This command causes the command \indexentry{*text*}{*p*} to be written to an idx file (if one is being written to). Any characters can occur in *text* (but all braces, including \{ and \}, must come in matching pairs) unless the \index command occurs inside the argument of another command, when *text* can only include letters, numerals and punctuation marks. (Fragile.)

\indexentry{*text*}{*p*} This command can only occur in an idx file. It is written there automatically by LaTeX itself whenever an \index{*text*} command occurs in the input file. (This only happens if a \makeindex command occurs in the preamble of your input file and a \nofiles command does not occur there.) The number *p* is the page number of the page in the output where \index{*text*} occurs.

\indexname In the article document class the theindex environment places the index it produces into an unnumbered section headed 'Index' and in the report and book document classes the index produced is placed into an unnumbered chapter headed 'Index'. If you want a heading other than 'Index' to be generated, then you need to redefine the \indexname command.

\indexspace This command is used inside the theindex environment for producing extra vertical space. It is usually used to separate items beginning with different letters of the alphabet.

\input{*file*} This has the same effect as if the contents of the file *file* were present in this part of the input file. If *file* has no extension, then the file *file*.tex is included.

\intertext{*text*} This command is only available if you have loaded the amsmath package. Placed after a \\ or * command inside one of the amsmath environments for producing a number of displayed mathematical formulas it makes *text* into the explanatory text that occurs between two of the displayed formulas. Note that a \\ or * command should not follow the \intertext command and no command that starts a new paragraph can occur inside the argument *text*.

\intextsep The value of this rubber length parameter is the amount of vertical space placed above and below a float that occurs in the middle of a text page because the h location option has been chosen. This is a robust command that must not be preceded by a \protect command.

\invisible This local declaration is only available in the slides document class. Inside the slide, overlay and note environments it makes any text in its scope invisible. See also \visible.

ist This is the extension of an index style file that is used by the *MakeIndex* program. It contains information that controls the appearance of the index being produced.

See section 12.4 of Goossens, Mittelbach and Samarin (1994), pp. 357–364, for more information about `ist` files.

`\it` This local declaration alters the style of the type being used. It selects a medium, italic, roman typeface. In LR and paragraph modes it is equivalent to the two declarations `\normalfont\itshape`. (Robust.)

`\item[`*text*`]` This command can only occur inside a small number of environments, namely `enumerate`, `itemize`, `description`, `list`, `theindex` and `trivlist`. Although what it does differs slightly from environment to environment it always indicates the start of a new piece of information. Note that it is different from the plain TEX command of the same name. (Fragile.)

`\itemindent` The value of this rigid length parameter affects the appearance of the `list` environment as shown in Fig. C.3 on p. 225. This is a robust command that must not be preceded by a `\protect` command.

`itemize` This environment is used to produce labelled lists where the label does not, by default, change from one use of an `\item` command to another. See section 4.6 for an example of its use.

`\itemsep` The value of this rubber length parameter affects the appearance of the `list` environment as shown in Fig. C.3 on p. 225. This is a robust command that must not be preceded by a `\protect` command.

`\itshape` This local declaration alters the shape attribute of the current font to italic. It cannot be used in maths mode. (Robust.)

`\j` This command produces a dotless letter 'ȷ' in paragraph and LR modes. (Robust.)

`\jot` The value of this rigid length parameter is the amount of additional inter-row vertical space in an `eqnarray` or `eqnarray*` environment.

`\kill` This command can only occur inside the `tabbing` environment where it ensures that the row it terminates produces no output, but the values of any tab stops are retained. It also sets *next-tab-stop* to be the same as *left-margin-tab* and begins a new line.

`\l` This command produces a lowercase Polish letter 'ł' in both text modes. (Robust.)

`\L` This command produces an uppercase Polish letter 'Ł' in both text modes. (Robust.)

`\label{`*key*`}` This command is used for cross-referencing purposes. It associates *key*, which can only consist of letters, numerals and punctuation marks, with the current `\ref` value. Although fragile, this command does not have to be preceded by a `\protect` command when it occurs in the argument of a sectioning or a `\caption` command. If you use a lot of `\label` commands, you might forget which key labels what. Loading the `showlabels` package will cause keys to be printed in the margin of your output.

\labelenumi This command produces the label when an `enumerate` environment is used that does not occur inside another `enumerate` environment. It is initially defined to be \theenumi. (including the full stop), but can be redefined.

\labelenumii This command produces the label when an `enumerate` environment occurs inside one other `enumerate` environment. It is initially defined to be (\theenumii), including the parentheses, but can be redefined.

\labelenumiii This command produces the label when an `enumerate` environment is nested inside two other `enumerate` environments. It is initially defined to be \theenumiii. (including the full stop), but can be redefined.

\labelenumiv This command produces the label when an `enumerate` environment is nested inside three other `enumerate` environments. It is initially defined to be \theenumiv. (including the full stop), but can be redefined.

\labelitemi A command that holds the symbol used to label items in the outermost or top-level occurrence of an `itemize` environment. By default the symbol used is • (that is to say, the symbol produced by $\bullet$ but without any additional space that may be placed either side of it were it to be used in maths mode). A different symbol can be obtained by redefining the \labelitemi command.

\labelitemii This contains the symbol used to label the items of an `itemize` environment that occurs within one other `itemize` environment. By default the symbol used is –, that is to say, the symbol produced by ({\bfseries--}). A different symbol can be obtained by redefining the \labelitemii command.

\labelitemiii A command that holds the symbol used to label the items of an `itemize` environment that occurs within the scope of two other `itemize` environments. By default the symbol used is ∗ (that is to say, the symbol produced by $\ast$ but without any additional space that may be placed either side of it were it to be used in maths mode). A different symbol can be obtained by redefining the \labelitemiii command.

\labelitemiv This contains the symbol used to label the items of an `itemize` environment that occurs within the scope of three other `itemize` environments. By default the symbol used is · (that is to say, the symbol produced by $\cdot$ but without any additional space that may be placed either side of it were it to be used in maths mode). A different symbol can be obtained by redefining the \labelitemiv command.

\labelsep The value of this rigid length parameter affects the appearance of the `list` environment as shown in Fig. C.3 on p. 225. This is a robust command that must not be preceded by a \protect command.

\labelwidth The value of this rigid length parameter affects the appearance of the `list` environment as shown in Fig. C.3 on p. 225. This is a robust command that must not be preceded by a \protect command.

landscape This is a document-class option which is used when you want your output to be produced in landscape rather than portrait format.

\large This local declaration alters the size of type being used. Usually the type size selected is just bigger than **\normalsize** and just smaller than **\Large**. In LaTeX 2.09 this declaration also selected the main text font being used, but this is no longer the case. It cannot be used in maths mode. (Fragile.)

\Large This local declaration alters the size of type being used. Usually the type size selected is just bigger than **\large** and just smaller than **\LARGE**. In LaTeX 2.09 this declaration also selected the main text font being used, but this is no longer the case. It cannot be used in maths mode. (Fragile.)

\LARGE This local declaration alters the size of type being used. Usually the type size selected is just bigger than **\Large** and just smaller than **\huge**. In LaTeX 2.09 this declaration also selected the main text font being used, but this is no longer the case. It cannot be used in maths mode. (Fragile.)

\LaTeX This command produces the logo LaTeX.

\LaTeXe This command produces the logo LaTeX 2_ε.

latexsym There are eleven mathematical symbols available in basic LaTeX 2.09 which are no longer available in basic LaTeX 2_ε. These are the ordinary symbols produced by the commands **\Box**, **\Diamond** and **\mho**; the binary operators produced by **\lhd**, **\rhd**, **\unlhd** and **\unrhd**; and the binary relation symbols produced by **\Join**, **\leadsto**, **\sqsubset** and **\sqsupset**. In order to get all of these you need to load the **latexsym** package; the three symbols **\mho**, **\sqsubset** and **\sqsupset** are also available in the **amsssymb** package.

\ldots This command, which is available in all modes, produces an ellipsis (...) consisting of three 'low' dots. (Robust.)

\left*cmd₁ form* **\right***cmd₂* These commands are only available in maths mode and there only in display style. The formula *form* is processed and then delimiters are chosen of the correct size to fit around it. Both **\left** and **\right** have to be present, but a full stop can take the place of either *cmd₁* or *cmd₂* which results in no output. Both **\left** and **\right** are robust.

\leftarrowfill This command produces an arrow pointing left which expands to fill all the horizontal space available; see Table C.1 on p. 207 for a graphical depiction of what it does.

\lefteqn{*form***}** This command can only occur inside an **eqnarray** or **eqnarray*** environment. It is used for splitting long formulas that will not fit on a single line. The argument *form* is processed in maths display style.

\leftmargin The value of this rigid length parameter affects the horizontal distance between the left margin of the enclosing environment and the left margin of the current list environment as shown in Fig. C.3 on p. 225. If a list environment occurs within the scope of no other list environment, then by default \leftmargin is assigned the value \leftmargini; if a list environment occurs within the scope of one other list environment, then by default \leftmargin is assigned the value \leftmarginii; ...; if a list environment occurs within the scope of five other list environments, then by default \leftmargin is assigned the value \leftmarginvi; further nestings are not allowed. This is a robust command that must not be preceded by a \protect command.

\leftmargini The value of this rigid length parameter is used for setting the width of certain left margins, for example, in the list environment. See \leftmargin. This is a robust command that must not be preceded by a \protect command.

\leftmarginii The value of this rigid length parameter is used for setting the width of certain left margins, for example, in the list environment. See \leftmargin. This is a robust command that must not be preceded by a \protect command.

\leftmarginiii The value of this rigid length parameter is used for setting the width of certain left margins, for example, in the list environment. See \leftmargin. This is a robust command that must not be preceded by a \protect command.

\leftmarginiv The value of this rigid length parameter is used for setting the width of certain left margins, for example, in the list environment. See \leftmargin. This is a robust command that must not be preceded by a \protect command.

\leftmarginv The value of this rigid length parameter is used for setting the width of certain left margins, for example, in the list environment. See \leftmargin. This is a robust command that must not be preceded by a \protect command.

\leftmarginvi The value of this rigid length parameter is used for setting the width of certain left margins, for example, in the list environment. See \leftmargin. This is a robust command that must not be preceded by a \protect command.

legalpaper This is a document-class option. Use it when you are producing a document that is going to be printed on paper which is 8.5 inches by 14 inches. See also a4paper, a5paper, b5paper, executivepaper and letterpaper.

leqno This is a document-class option. By default formulas numbered automatically by LaTeX have their labels positioned on the right of the output page; including this option transfers them to the left of the page.

letter This is one of the five standard document classes that is available in LaTeX 2_ε. (The other four are article, book, report and slides.) The standard options are as follows: at most one of 10pt (the default), 11pt or 12pt; at most one of letterpaper (the default), legalpaper, executivepaper, a4paper, a5paper or b5paper; at most one of final (the default) or draft; and at most one of `oneside` (the default) or `twoside`. Furthermore, any or none of the following can occur in *opt-list*: `landscape`, `leqno` and `fleqn`. See section 8.4 for more information about this document class.

`letter` This environment can only occur when the `letter` document class is being used. It is used for producing letters. One or more `letter` environments can occur in the same input file. Its general format is:

> \begin{letter}{*text*₁}   *text*₂   \end{letter}

Note that *text*₁ here is a moving argument, so any fragile commands in it need to be preceded by a \protect command. This argument is used for the address of the recipient of the letter. One or more \\ commands can occur in *text*₁ in order to force a new line. Note also that *text*₁ is not an optional argument; you will get an error message if it is omitted. The argument *text*₂ contains the body of the letter. The whole `letter` environment is a moving argument.

`letterpaper` This is a document-class option. Use it when you are producing a document that is going to be printed on paper which is 8.5 inches by 11 inches. This is the default in all five standard document classes. See also `a4paper`, `a5paper`, `b5paper`, `executivepaper` and `legalpaper`.

\limits The effect of *cmd*\limits_*form*₁^*form*₂ in maths mode is to make *form*₁ appear as a limit underneath the symbol produced by *cmd* and *form*₂ to appear as a limit over it. This effect is produced in both text and display styles. It is not necessary for both *form*₁ and *form*₂ to be present. This is a primitive TeX command. See also \displaylimits and \nolimits.

\line(*p, q*){*l*} This command can only occur in the argument of a \put or \multiput command inside a `picture` environment. The command

> \put(*i, j*){\line(*p, q*){*l*}}

draws an arrow which starts at the point (*i, j*) and whose projection on the *x*-axis is *l* units. (The only exception to this occurs when you want to produce a vertical line, in which case *l* gives the actual length of the line produced.) The slope of the line is given by (*p, q*), that is to say, it goes *p* units in the *x* direction for every *q* units it goes in the *y* direction. Both *p* and *q* must be whole numbers between −6 and +6, inclusive, with no common divisor. Note that the LaTeX \line command is completely different from the plain TeX command of the same name. (Fragile.)

\linebreak[*i*] The optional numerical argument *i* can be either 0, 1, 2, 3, or 4. If it is absent or its value is 4, then the \linebreak command marks the position of the end of a line. The output is right justified, unless some other command or declaration has suppressed right justification, with the word that came before the \linebreak command occurring at the extreme right of the line on which it occurs. (This may cause an underfull \hbox warning message.) If the numerical argument i is 0, then TEX can end the line at that point, but the presence of the command neither encourages nor discourages this. If the numerical value of i is 1, 2 or 3, then this encourages TEX to make a line break at that point and the higher the number the stronger the encouragement. (Fragile.)

\linethickness{*len*} This local declaration affects the thickness of vertical and horizontal lines in a `picture` environment. It makes them *len* wide.

\linewidth The value of this rigid length parameter, which must never be altered, is the current width of lines. It is changed when certain environments, such as `quotation`, are used. Its value can be used to set the values of other length commands. This is a robust command that must not be preceded by a \protect command.

lis Usually the file extension of the log or transcript file written by LATEX is `log`, but on some operating systems `lis` is used.

list Usually the file extension of the log or transcript file written by LATEX is `log`, but on some operating systems `list` is used.

list This general-purpose environment is used for producing lists of information. Optionally, the items in the list can be labelled in a variety of ways. A number of parameters control the organization and appearance of the list; see Fig. C.3 on p. 225 for the effect of these. (The length parameter \parindent is also included in that diagram as this may influence the choice of values for some of the other parameters.) The general format of the `list` environment is:

\begin{list}{*text$_1$*}{*dec-list*}   *text$_2$*   \end{list}

The argument *text$_1$* is what will be generated by an \item command that does not have an optional argument. The argument *dec-list* is a sequence of assignments to some of the length parameters that appear in Fig. C.3 on p. 225; any length parameter that is not given a value in this way is initialized by an assignment in one of the commands @listi, ..., @listv or @listvi (the choice depends on the level of nesting) and one of these is executed before *dec-list*. The argument *text$_2$* is the information to be displayed; one or more \item commands can occur in *text$_2$*. Note that a \usecounter command can occcur in *dec-list* if you want the automatically generated labels to be numbered in an increasing sequence.

\listfiles This command can only occur in the preamble of a document. If included, it produces a list of (almost) all the files used in the processing of your input file. This information is written both to the terminal and to the `log` file. This information is useful if you are thinking of using either the `filecontents` or the `filecontents*` environment.

\listfigurename When you use the \listoffigures command to get LATEX to produce a list of figures for you, then the heading 'List of Figures' is generated

a	\topsep + \parskip or \topsep + \parskip + \partopsep		
b	\itemsep + \parsep	f	\leftmargin
c	\parsep	g	\listparindent
d	\labelwidth	h	\rightmargin
e	\labelsep	i	\parindent

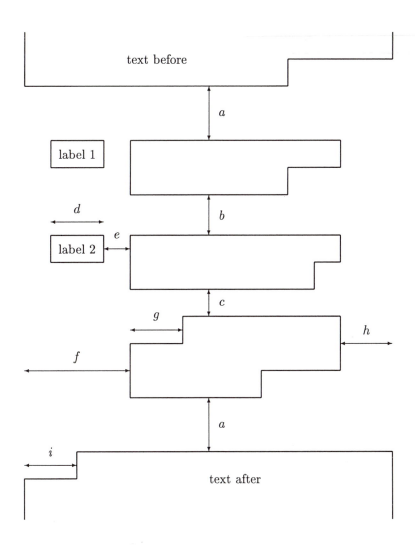

Figure C.3: Parameters of the list environment.

automatically. If you want a different heading to be produced, then you need to redefine the \listfigurename command.

\listtablename When you use the \listoftables command to get LaTeX to produce a list of tables for you, then the heading 'List of Tables' is generated automatically. If you want a different heading to be produced, then you need to redefine the \listtablename command.

\listoffigures This command produces a list of figures, made by occurrences of either the figure or the figure* environment in your input file, at the place in the input file where it occurs. A figure is only listed if a \caption command occurs in the scope of the environment that produced it. You need to run LaTeX at least twice to get a correct list of figures. The \listoffigures command causes a lof file to be written or overwritten except if you have included a \nofiles command in the preamble of your input file. The heading 'List of Figures' is generated automatically, but a different heading can be produced by redefining the \listfigurename command.

\listoftables This command produces a list of tables, made by occurrences of either the table or the table* environments in your inpur file, at the place in the input file where it occurs. A table is only listed if a \caption command occurs in the scope of the environment that produced it. You need to run LaTeX at least twice to get a correct list of tables. The \listoftables command causes a lot file to be written or overwritten except if you have included a \nofiles command in the preamble of your input file. The heading 'List of Tables' is generated automatically, but a different heading can be produced by redefining the \listtablename command.

\listparindent The value of this rigid length parameter affects the appearance of the list environment as shown in Fig. C.3 on p. 225. This is a robust command that must not be preceded by a \protect command.

lof This is the file extension of a file which is only created or overwritten if your input file contains a \listoffigures command (and does not contain a \nofiles command). The lof file contains the information necessary to produce a list of figures for your document. This information comes from every \caption command which occurs within the scope of a figure or figure* environment in your input file. The list of figures is produced by the \listoffigures command if a lof file exists when you process your input file.

log This is the extension of the transcript file that is created when you run LaTeX. It contains all the information that appeared on your terminal while LaTeX was running and also some additional information.

lot This is the file extension of a file which is only created or overwritten if your input file contains a \listoftables command (and does not contain a \nofiles command). The lot file contains the information necessary to produce a list of tables for your document. This information comes from every \caption command which occurs within a `table` or `table*` environment in your input file. The list of tables is produced by the \listoftables command if a `lot` file exists when you process your input file.

\lq The presence of this command in your input file has exactly the same effect as if a grave accent was there. In LR and paragraph modes it produces a single opening quotation mark. This can also be produced by means of the command \textquoteleft.

lrbox This environment is used for putting an LR box into a storage bin. Its general format is:

$$\text{\textbackslash begin\{lrbox\}\{}cmd\}\quad text\quad \text{\textbackslash end\{lrbox\}}$$

The argument *cmd* must be a command name beginning with an initial backslash that has been declared by means of a \newsavebox command and *text* is what is going to be put in the storage bin *cmd* after being processed. Note that any spaces at the beginning and end of *text* are removed before *text* is processed. The contents of the bin can be printed by means of the \usebox command.

ltx This is the extension of some of the files used by the `initex` program to produce `latex.fmt`. The main `ltx` file is `latex.ltx`.

\mainmatter This command is only available in the `book` document class. It resets the `page` counter and causes pages to be numbered with arabic numerals. See also \frontmatter and \backmatter.

\makebox[*len*][*pos*]{*text*} Outside the `picture` environment this command is like \framebox, *q.v.*, except that no 'frame' is produced. (Fragile.)

\makebox(*i, j*)[*pos*]{*picture-object*} This form of this command can only occur inside the `picture` environment. It is explained in section 12.1.

\makeglossary This command can only occur in the preamble of your input file. It causes a `glo` file to be written which contains the \glossaryentry commands generated by any \glossary commands that appear in your input file. A \nofiles declaration in the preamble suppresses the writing of the `glo` file.

makeidx Used in conjunction with the *MakeIndex* program this package largely automates the production of an index. See section 7.2 for more information about how to use it.

\makeindex This command can only occur in the preamble of your input file. It causes an `idx` file to be written which contains the \indexentry commands generated by any \index commands that appear in your input file. A \nofiles declaration in the preamble suppresses the writing of the `idx` file.

\makelabel{*text*} This command generates the label produced by the \item command using the *text* argument.

\makelabels This command takes no arguments and it can only occur in the preamble of a letter document class. It causes a list of all the recipient addresses to be produced on a new page following all the letters generated. These can be photocopied onto sticky labels if so desired.

\maketitle This command produces a title in the article, report, book and slides document classes. If you use the titlepage document-class option, then the title produced will appear on a page by itself; but if you use the notitlepage option, then this will not happen. The \maketitle command, if it occurs in the input file at all, must come within the document environment. If it is used, it must be preceded by both \title and \author declarations and may be preceded by a \date declaration.

\marginpar[*text₁*]{*text₂*} This command produce a marginal note. If the optional argument $text_1$ is absent, then $text_2$ will appear as a marginal note. If the optional argument $text_1$ is present, then $text_2$ will appear as a marginal note if the current location of marginal notes is in the right-hand margin and $text_1$ will appear as a marginal note if the current location of marginal notes is in the left-hand margin. The two local declarations \normalmarginpar and \reversemarginpar determine the placement of marginal notes. (Fragile.)

\marginparpush The value of this rigid length parameter affects the appearance of marginal notes on the output page. Its value is the minimum distance separating two successive marginal notes. This is a robust command that must never be preceded by a \protect command.

\marginparsep The value of this rigid length parameter affects the appearance of marginal notes on the output page. Its value is the distance between the outer edge of the body and the inner edge of marginal notes. When one-sided printing is in effect the default is that the outer edge of the body is the right one on all pages and the inner edge of marginal notes is the left one. When two-sided printing is in effect the default is that the outer edge of the body is the right one on odd pages and the left one on even pages and the inner edge of marginal notes is the left one on odd pages and the right one on even pages. These defaults can be altered by means of the \reversemarginpar declaration. This is a robust command that must never be preceded by a \protect command.

\marginparwidth The value of this rigid length parameter is the width of the parbox containing a marginal note. This is a robust command that must never be preceded by a \protect command.

\markboth{*text₁*}{*text₂*} Used in conjunction with the myheadings style option to either the \pagestyle or \thispagestyle declaration this command, in two-sided printing, makes $text_1$ into the running head on even-numbered pages and $text_2$ into the running head on odd-numbered pages. (Fragile.)

\markright{*text*} Used in conjunction with the `myheadings` style option to either the \pagestyle or \thispagestyle declaration this command, in one-sided printing, makes *text* into the running head on all pages except the first. (Fragile.)

math This environment is used for typesetting a mathematical formula so that it does not appear on a line by itself, that is to say, it is used for producing in-text formulas. The more concise forms \(*form*\) and $*form*$ are also available. Inside the math environment LaTeX is in maths mode and formulas are typeset in text style.

\mathbb{*exp*} To use this command you have to load the `amsfonts` package. If *exp* is an uppercase letter, then \mathbb{*exp*} produces *exp* in blackboard bold.

\mathbf{*exp*} This command causes any letters, numerals or uppercase Greek letters that occur in *exp* to be typeset in the bold style. It can only be used in maths mode. (Robust.)

\mathbin{*exp*} This command can only be used in maths mode. It makes LaTeX treat the expression *exp* as a symbol for a binary operation.

\mathcal{*exp*} This command causes *exp* to be typeset in the calligraphic style. The argument *exp* can only contain uppercase letters. It can only be used in maths mode. (Robust.)

\mathclose{*exp*} This command can only be used in maths mode. It makes LaTeX treat the expression *exp* as a closing symbol.

\mathfrak{*exp*} If you load either the `eufrak` or the `amsfonts` package, then you can use this command to produce letters from the Euler Fraktur alphabet. (These are the letters that mathematicians call *Gothic*.) The argument *exp* can contain both lowercase and uppercase letters.

\mathindent The value of this rigid length parameter is the distance by which displayed formulas are indented from the left-hand edge of the body of the page when the `fleqn` document-class option has been chosen. This is a robust command that must never be preceded by a \protect command.

\mathit{*exp*} This command causes any letters, numerals or uppercase Greek letters that occur in *exp* to be typeset in the italic style. It can only be used in maths mode. (Robust.)

\mathop{*exp*} This command can only be used in maths mode. It makes LaTeX treat the expression *exp* as a symbol for a unary, prefix operator.

\mathopen{*exp*} This command can only be used in maths mode. It makes LaTeX treat the expression *exp* as an opening symbol.

\mathord{*exp*} This command can only be used in maths mode. It makes LaTeX treat the expression *exp* as an ordinary symbol. Note that TeX treats any expression enclosed in braces an an ordinary symbol.

\mathpunct{*exp*} This command can only be used in maths mode. It makes LaTeX treat the expression *exp* as a punctuation mark.

\mathrel{*exp*} This command can only be used in maths mode. It makes LaTeX treat the expression *exp* as a symbol for a binary relation.

\mathrm{*exp*} This command causes any letters, numerals or uppercase Greek letters that occur in *exp* to be typeset in the Roman style. It can only be used in maths mode. (Robust.)

mathscr This is an option to the eucal package. If you use it, then the command \mathcal is not redefined and the \mathscr command produces uppercase letters in the Euler Script alphabet.

\mathscr{*exp*} Normally, the command \mathcal{*exp*}, where *exp* consists of uppercase letters, produces *exp* in the calligraphic script. However, if you load the eucal package, then \mathcal{*exp*} is redefined so that it produces *exp* in the Euler Script alphabet. If you load the eucal package with the mathscr option, then \mathcal is not redefined and the command \mathscr{*exp*} produces *exp* in the Euler Script alphabet. It can only be used in maths mode.

\mathsf{*exp*} This command causes any letters, numerals or uppercase Greek letters that occur in *exp* to be typeset in the sans serif style. It can only be used in maths mode. (Robust.)

\mathstrut This plain TeX command is only available in maths mode where it produces an invisible vertical rule the same height as a parenthesis but with no width.

\mathtt{*exp*} This command causes any letters, numerals or uppercase Greek letters that occur in *exp* to be typeset in the typewriter style. It can only be used in maths mode. (Robust.)

\mbox{*text*} This command can be used in any mode. The argument *text* is processed in LR mode and under no circumstances will the resulting box be broken across lines. If LaTeX is in either paragraph or LR mode when it encounters an \mbox command, then the processing of *text* is affected by the declarations in force at the place where the \mbox command occurred. If LaTeX is in maths mode when it encounters an \mbox command, then the processing of *text* is affected by the declarations in force at the place where LaTeX entered maths mode. For example, {\itshape when $17 > \mbox{age}$} produces *when* $17 > age$. (Robust.)

\mdseries This local declaration can only be used in LR or paragraph mode where it alters the series attribute of the current font to medium. (Robust.)

\medmuskip This is a primitive TeX length command which can only be used in maths mode and whose preset value is 4mu plus 2mu minus 4mu. It determines the length of the \: control symbol. See also \thinmuskip and \thickmuskip.

\medskip This command produces vertical space whose height is given by the value of \medskipamount; it is defined as \vspace{\medskipamount}. (Fragile.)

\medskipamount The value of this rubber length command is 6pt plus 2pt minus 2pt. This value is the same whether you use the 10pt, 11pt or 12pt document-class option.

minipage This environment is used for producing a parbox, that is to say, a box whose contents are processed in paragraph mode. Its general format is:

> \begin{minipage}[*pos*$_1$] [*len*$_2$] [*pos*$_2$]{*len*$_1$}
>   *text*
> \end{minipage}

The argument *len*$_1$ determines the width of the box that is produced; it must be a rigid length. The optional argument *pos*$_1$ can be used to determine the alignment of the box produced to the context in which it occurs. It can be either b, t or c (the default). If it is b, then usually what happens is that the base line of the bottom line in the box produced is aligned with the base line of the line where the minipage environment occurs; and if it is t, then usually what happens is that the base line of the top line in the box produced is aligned with the base line of the line where the minipage environment occurs. (Actually, it is the reference points of the two lines in question that are aligned.) If *pos*$_1$ is c or it is absent, then the box produced is centred vertically. If you want to use the optional *len*$_2$ argument, then you must also use the *pos*$_1$ argument. The argument *len*$_2$ determines the height of the box that is produced. The commands \width, \depth, \height and \totalheight can occur inside the argument *len*$_2$; these commands have values which are, respectively, the width, the depth, the height and the sum of the depth and the height of the box produced when *text* is processed in paragraph mode. If you use the calc package, you can substitute expressions like \height + 1cm for the *len*$_2$ argument. You can only use the *pos*$_2$ argument if *len*$_2$ is present. The optional argument *pos*$_2$ controls the alignment of the box produced as a result of processing *text* inside a box of width *len*$_1$ and height *len*$_2$. It can be either b, c, s or t. If it is b, then *text* is placed in the bottom of the larger box; if it is c, then it is centred in it; if it is s and *text* contains stretchable space, then it is stretched to fill all the vertical space available; and if it is t, it is put at the top of the larger box. If *pos*$_2$ is absent, then the value of *pos*$_1$ is used. The argument *text* can contain any of the list-like environments discussed in Chapter 4 and it can contain the tabular environment. The \footnote command can also occur in *text* and by default footnotes are indicated by means of lowercase letters starting with A. The counter mpfootnote is used for this purpose and not footnote, which is not incremented by the \footnote commands that occur inside the minipage environment.

minus *len* This TₑX keyword is used in assigning rubber length values; *len* represents the amount by which the natural value of the target length argument can shrink. See also **plus**.

\mkern*len* This primitive TₑX command is only available in maths mode where it generates *len* amount of space where *len* must be given in terms of the mathematical unit (**mu**). Whether the space is horizontal or vertical depends on the context where the command occurs.

mm This is a TₑX keyword; it stands for *millimetre*, a unit of length, which exactly satisfies the equality 10 mm = 1 cm. (Roughly, 1 mm = 0.03937 in = 2.845 pt.)

mpfootnote This counter is used for the numbering of footnotes inside the **minipage** environment. It is initialized to zero when the environment is opened. It is incremented automatically by both the **\footnote** and **\footnotetext** commands before being used. Although the value of this counter must be a positive whole number, it appears as the corresponding lowercase letter.

mu This is a TₑX keyword; it stands for *mathematical unit*; a font-dependent unit of length which can only be used in maths mode; 18 mu = 1 em, where the length of the em comes from the font in family 2 in the current style. (See, for example, Chapter 23 of Eijkhout (1992) for more information about this.)

\multicolumn{*i***}{***pre***}{***text***}** This command is used to produce material in a row of the **array**, **tabular** or **tabular*** environment in a way different from that specified in the preamble. The argument i is a positive whole number which indicates how many columns this command affects. The argument *pre* is similar to the preamble of the **array**, **tabular** or **tabular*** environment except that fewer expressions are allowed to occur in it and *text* is what is to appear. The argument *pre* must contain one and only one occurrence of either **l**, **r** or **c**; it can contain, but does not have to, one or more @-expressions and it can contain, but does not have to, one or more vertical line characters. A **\multicolumn** command must either begin a row or immediately follow an ampersand.

\multiput$(i, j)$**(m, n)**{*t*}{*picture-object*} This command can only occur inside the **picture** environment, where it is equivalent to the following t commands

$$\text{\textbackslash put}\,(i, j)\,\{picture\text{-}object\}$$
$$\text{\textbackslash put}\,(i + m, j + n)\,\{picture\text{-}object\}$$
$$\text{\textbackslash put}\,(i + 2m, j + 2n)\,\{picture\text{-}object\}$$
$$\vdots$$
$$\text{\textbackslash put}\,(i + (t - 1)m, j + (t - 1)n)\,\{picture\text{-}object\}$$

LATₑX does not have a very large memory, so there is a maximum number of repetitions allowed and it is about 100.

myheadings This is a page-style option to the \pagestyle and \thispagestyle local declarations which allows you to customize what information you want to appear in the head of the page. (The foot is left empty.) See \markboth and \markright for how to get information into the head. The other three page-style options are empty, headings and plain.

\NeedsTeXFormat{*format*}[*date*] This command can occur in the prologue of a LaTeX input file, but usually it occurs in a class file or package. Currently, the only value that the argument *format* can take is LaTeX2e, but other formats may become available. The optional argument *date* must have the format *year/month/day*, where *year* consists of four digits and both *month* and *day* consist of two digits each. An example of the *date* parameter is 1998/03/11. If the *format* has a release date earlier than *date*, then a warning message is given.

\newcommand{*cmd*}[*i*][*default*]{*definiens*} The effect of this local declaration is similar to that of \newcommand*. The difference between them only emerges if they are used to define commands that take one or more arguments. When \newcommand* is used to define such a command, its actual parameters cannot contain a command that creates a new paragraph; the actual parameters of a command defined by \newcommand can, however, contain such commands. (Fragile.)

\newcommand*{*cmd*}[*i*][*default*]{*definiens*} This local declaration is used to define commands. I will explain its use in three stages. First, I will say how it can be used to define a command which takes no arguments. Second, I will describe how it can be used to define a command which takes between one and nine arguments. Third, I will show how it can be used to define a command which takes arguments, the first of which has a default value. However it is used the argument *cmd* must begin with a backslash character and must not be the name of an existing command. Following the backslash in *cmd* there can be either a single non-alphanumeric character or a sequence of one or more letters (though this must not begin with the three letters end). (1) To define a command which takes no arguments you need to use the \newcommand* declaration in the form \newcommand*{*cmd*}{*definiens*}, where *definiens* can be any combination of text and/or LaTeX commands. Note that the braces that surround *definiens* do not delimit the scope of any local declarations that might occur in it when *cmd* is used. If you include any local declarations in *definiens* whose scope you want to be limited to *definiens*, then you need to include a pair of braces inside it. For example, \newcommand*{\Z}{{\bfseries Z}}. (2) To define a command which takes between one and nine arguments use the \newcommand* declaration in the form \newcommand*{*cmd*}[*i*]{*definiens*}, where *i* is a number between 1 and 9, inclusive. Inside *definiens* an occurrence of #*j* is replaced by the *j*th actual parameter when *cmd* is used. (When *cmd* is used, actual parameters have to be enclosed in braces.) Actual parameters cannot contain any commands which start a new paragraph. (Use \newcommand to define such commands.) (3) To define a command which takes arguments the first of which has a default value, use the \newcommand* declaration in the form \newcommand*{*cmd*}[*i*][*default*]{*definiens*}, where *default* is the default value of the first argument. (Fragile.)

\newcounter{*ctr*$_1$}[*ctr*$_2$] This global declaration makes *ctr*$_1$, which must consist entirely of letters and must not be the name of an existing counter, into a counter which is initialized to zero. The command \the*ctr*$_1$ is automatically defined to be \arabic{*ctr*$_1$}. This declaration cannot be used in a file whose name occurs as the argument to an \include command. It should only be used in the preamble of an input file. If *ctr*$_2$, which must be the name of an existing counter, is present, then *ctr*$_1$ is reset to zero whenever *ctr*$_2$ is incremented by either \stepcounter or \refstepcounter. (Fragile.)

\newenvironment{*env*}[*i*][*default*]{*definiens*$_1$}{*definiens*$_2$} This local declaration is very similar to \newenvironment*; the only difference between them is that if an environment requiring arguments is defined than the actual parameters, in the case of \newenvironment, can contain commands that start a new paragraph. (Fragile.)

\newenvironment*{*env*}[*i*][*default*]{*definiens*$_1$}{*definiens*$_2$} This local declaration is used to define a new environment. I will explain its use in three stages. First, I will say how it can be used to define an environment which takes no arguments. Second, I will describe how it can be used to define an environment which takes between one and nine arguments. Third, I will show how it can be used to define an environment which takes arguments, the first of which has a default value. However it is used every character in the argument *env*, which is the name of the environment being defined, except the last must be a letter; the last character can be * and if it is it cannot be the whole name of the environment. Furthermore, *env* must not be the name of an existing environment and *env* must not be the name of an existing command. (1) To define an environment which takes no arguments you need to use the \newenvironment* command in the form \newenvironment*{*env*}{*definiens*$_1$}{*definiens*$_2$}, where *definiens*$_1$ and *definiens*$_2$ are any legal combination of text and/or LaTeX commands. The argument *definiens*$_1$ is what will be executed when \begin{*env*} occurs in your input file and *definiens*$_2$ is what will be executed when \end{*env*} occurs in your input file. (2) To define an environment which takes between one and nine arguments use the \newenvironment* command in the form

\newenvironment*{*env*}[*i*]{*definiens*$_1$}{*definiens*$_2$}

where *i* is a number between 1 and 9, inclusive. Inside *definiens*$_1$ an occurrence of #*j* is replaced by the *j*th actual parameter when \begin{*env*}{*arg*$_1$}...{*arg*$_i$} occurs in your input file. Note that none of the actual parameters *arg*$_j$ can contain any commands that start a new paragraph. (Use \newenvironment to define such environments.) Note also that the #*j* cannot occur inside *definiens*$_2$. (3) To define an environment which takes arguments the first of which has a default value use the \newenvironment* command in the form

\newenvironment*{*env*}[*i*][*default*]{*definiens₁*}{*definiens₂*}

where *default* is the default value of the first argument. (Fragile.)

\newlength{*cmd*} This global declaration makes *cmd*, which must begin with a backslash and which must not have been defined previously, a rubber length command and initializes its value to zero points. If *cmd* is not undefined, you will get an error message. Values can be assigned to *cmd* by means of several commands including \setlength, \settodepth, \settoheight and \settowidth. For example, the local declaration

\setlength{*cmd*}{1in plus 0.3in minus 0.2in}

assigns to *cmd* a value which is a rubber length. (Fragile.)

\newline This command forces a line break at the place where it occurs. The resulting line is not right justified. It can only be used in paragraph mode and it should only be used inside a paragraph. (Fragile.)

\newpage This command forces the current paragraph and the current page to be terminated. If the twocolumn document-class option has been chosen, then this command terminates the current paragraph and the current column. (Robust.)

\newsavebox{*cmd*} This declares *cmd*, which must be a fresh command name beginning with a backslash, to be a storage bin. The declaration is global. The commands \savebox and \sbox and the lrbox environment are used to put a box into the bin and the \usebox command is used to print the contents of the bin. (Fragile.)

\newtheorem{*env₁*}[*env₂*]{*text*}[*ctr*] This global declaration defines *env₁* to be a new environment; the name *env₁* can only consist of letters and must not be the name of any existing counter or environment. At most one of the optional arguments *env₂* and *ctr* can be present. The argument *text* contains the word or phrase that will appear, by default in bold, whenever the environment *env₁* is used. If neither *env₂* nor *ctr* is present, then a counter also called *env₁* is created and each invocation of the environment *env₁* will produce output that is numbered consecutively and will start from 1. If *ctr*, which must be the name of a counter, is present, then a counter also called *env₁* is created and the numbers produced by a use of the environment *env₁* will look like $i.j$ where i is the value of *ctr* and j is the number of this particular invocation of the environment. If *env₂*, which must be the name of an environment created by an earlier \newtheorem declaration, is present, then invocations of both *env₁* and *env₂* will be numbered consecutively in the same numerical series. (Fragile.)

\nocite{*key-list*} This command is used for including items in a bibliography produced by BιBTeX that you do not actually refer to. The parameter *key-list* is a list of keys, separated by commas, that have been defined in a bib file; the corresponding entries are placed in the bibliography produced. To get a listing of everything in a `bib` file include a `\nocite{*}` command somewhere in the `document` environment. (Fragile.)

`\nofiles` When LaTeX is run a number of subsidiary files are or may be created, such as the `aux`, `glo`, `idx`, `lof`, `lot` and `toc` files. If you include the `\nofiles` declaration in the preamble of your input file, which is the only place it can occur, then the only files that are written are the `dvi` and `log` files.

`\noindent` Normally, paragraphs are indented slightly from the left edge of the body of text on a page. (The width of the indentation is given by the rigid length parameter `\parindent`.) This normal indentation can be suppressed by means of the `\noindent` command. It is useful sometimes, for example, right at the beginning of the `abstract` and `quotation` environments. See also `\indent`. (Robust.)

`\nolimits` The effect of cmd`\nolimits_`$form_1$`^`$form_2$ in maths mode is to make $form_1$ appear as a subscript to the symbol produced by cmd and $form_2$ to appear as a superscript to it. This effect is produced both in text and display style. It is not necessary for both $form_1$ and $form_2$ to be present. This is a primitive TeX command. See also `\displaylimits` and `\limits`.

`\nolinebreak[`i`]` The optional numerical argument i can be either 0, 1, 2, 3, or 4. If it is absent or its value is 4, then the `\nolinebreak` command marks a place which will under no circumstances be placed at the end of a line. If the numerical argument i is 0, then TeX can end the line at that point, but the presence of the command neither encourages nor discourages this. If the numerical value of i is 1, 2 or 3, then this discourages TeX from making a line break at that point and the higher the number the stronger the discouragement. (Fragile.)

`\nonfrenchspacing` By default TeX puts more space after certain punctuation marks, namely the colon, full stop, question mark and exclamation mark. Everything in the scope of the `\nonfrenchspacing` declaration is treated in this default manner. See also `\frenchspacing`. (Fragile.)

`\nonumber` This command can only occur inside the `eqnarray` environment where it prevents an equation number being produced for any row in which it occurs.

`\nonstopmode` This primitive TeX command ensures that the processing of your file will not stop if an error occurs, though an emergency stop will take place if user input is requested; it is one of the few commands that can come before the `\documentclass` command in the input file.

`\nopagebreak[`i`]` The optional numerical argument i can be either 0, 1, 2, 3, or 4. If it is absent or its value is 4, then the `\nolinebreak` command marks a place which will under no circumstances be placed at the end of a page. If the numerical argument i is 0, then TeX can end the page at that point, but the presence of the command neither encourages nor discourages this. If the numerical value of

i is 1, 2 or 3, then this discourages TEX from making a page break at that point and the higher the number the stronger the discouragement. If this command occurs inside a paragraph, then it applies to the point just below the line in which it is used. If the `twocolumn` document-class option has been chosen, then this command effects the ending of a column rather than that of a page. (Fragile.)

`\normalfont` Everything in the scope of this local declaration is typeset using the main text font of your document. By default this is a medium, upright, roman font and, again by default, LATEX uses the Computer Modern fonts that Donald Knuth designed. It is possible to get LATEX to use other fonts as explained in Chapter 11 of Goossens, Mittelbach and Samarin (1994). Note that this declaration cannot be used in maths mode. (Robust.)

`\normalmarginpar` This local declaration makes marginal notes appear in the default margin. See `\marginpar` to find out what the default margins are and `\reversemarginpar` for how to change this default.

`\normalsize` This local declaration alters the size of type being used. Usually the type size selected is just bigger than `\small` and just smaller than `\large`. In LATEX 2.09 this declaration also selected the main text font being used, but this is no longer the case. This declaration cannot be used in maths mode. (Fragile.)

`\not` This command is only available in maths mode where it is used to negate the following symbol by putting a slash through it. Thus, `\not\equiv` produces $\not\equiv$. The command `\notin` should be used to produce $\notin$ rather than `\not\in` because it looks better. Both `\neq` and `\ne` are alternative names for `\not=`. The `amssymb` package contains a large number of commands for producing a variety of negated binary relation symbols; see section A.5 for lists of these. (Robust.)

`\notag` This command can be used in any of the environments available in the `amsmath` package which produce displayed formulas that are labelled. The effect of the `\notag` command is to prevent a label being produced.

note This environment can only be used in the `slides` document class. It produces a one-page note. The first note environment following a `slide` environment, which produced the slide numbered i, is numbered i–1; the second is numbered i–2; and so on. See also `slide` and `overlay`.

notitlepage This is a document-class option. When it is in force, the title produced by the `\maketitle` command does not appear on a page by itself nor does any abstract produced by the `abstract` environment. Note that this option is not recognized by the `letter` document class and it is the default in the `article` class. See also `titlepage`.

`\numberline{`*sec-num*`}` This command can occur in the *entry* argument of the following two commands:

> \addcontentsline{*ext*}{*sec-unit*}{*entry*}
> \contentsline{*sec-unit*}{*entry*}{*p*}

The argument *sec-num* takes values like 2.3 or 14.2.8 and the effect of the \numberline command is to determine the indentation used when a list of figures, list of tables or a table of contents is produced by LaTeX. (Fragile.)

\o This command is only available in paragraph and LR modes where it produces the lowercase Scandinavian letter 'ø'. (Robust.)

\O This command is only available in paragraph and LR modes where it produces the uppercase Scandinavian letter 'Ø'. (Robust.)

\oddsidemargin The value of this rigid length parameter affects the appearance of the output page. On right-hand pages, if two-sided printing is in operation, and on all pages, if one-sided printing is in operation, the distance between the left-hand edge of the paper and the left-hand edge of the body is the sum of the value of \oddsidemargin and one inch. See Fig. C.4 on p. 260. This is a robust command that must never be preceded by a \protect command.

\oe This command produces the vowel ligature 'œ' in both text modes. (Robust.)

\OE This command produces the vowel ligature 'Œ' in both text modes. (Robust.)

onecolumn This is a document-class option which is not recognized by the letter document class (although the output produced when the letter document class is being used is in a single-column format). It ensures that only one column of text appears on each page produced. It is the default in all document classes. See also twocolumn.

\onecolumn This local declaration first starts a new page by executing \clearpage and then continues by typesetting the input in a one-column format. See also \twocolumn. (Fragile.)

oneside This is a document-class option which is not recognized by the slides document class. When it is in force no difference is made between odd-numbered and even-numbered pages. It is the default in the article, letter and report document classes. See also twoside.

\onlynotes{*num-list*} This command can only be used in the slides document class and if it is used it must be placed in the preamble of your input file. It has the effect that only the notes to the slides included in *num-list* will be produced. The argument *num-list* is a list of numerals or ranges, separated by commas, in ascending numerical order. For example, \onlynotes{2, 5, 8-11, 20} produces the notes to the slides indicated. See also \onlyslides.

\onlyslides{*num-list*} This command can only be used in the slides document class and if it is used it must be placed in the preamble of your input file. It has the effect that only the slides included in *num-list* will be produced. The argument *num-list* is a list of numerals or ranges, separated by commas, in ascending numerical order. For example, \onlyslides{2, 5, 8-11, 20} produces the slides indicated. See also \onlynotes.

openany This is a document-class option which is only available in the **book** and **report** document classes. (It is the default for the **report** document class.) It allows chapters to start on both odd-numbered and even-numbered pages. See also **openright**.

openbib This is a document-class option. Normally, when a bibliography is produced using the **thebibliography** environment the second and subsequent lines of each entry begin immediately below the start of the first line (with the label in the 'margin'). If you prefer the second and subsequent lines to be indented, then use this option. The rigid length parameter \bibindent controls the amount of indentation.

\opening{*text*} This command can only occur inside the **letter** environment. It is used for producing the salutation. Note that you must include the word **Dear** as part of *text* if you want this to appear in the letter produced.

openright This is a document-class option which is only available in the **book** and **report** document classes. (It is the default for the **book** document class.) It ensures that chapters start on an odd-numbered page. See also **openany**.

\operatorname{*text*} This command is defined in the **amsopn** package. It is used to define a log-like operator. The argument *text* is typeset in roman. Any subscripts or superscripts attached to the operator produced appear as subscripts or superscripts in both text style and display style.

\operatorname*{*text*} This command is defined in the **amsopn** package. It is used to define a log-like operator. The argument *text* is typeset in roman. Any subscripts or superscripts attached to the operator produced appear as subscripts or superscripts in text style, but as limits in display style.

\oval(*p*, *q*)[*part*] This command can only occur in the argument of a \put command or a \multiput command inside the **picture** environment; it is explained in section 12.4.

\overbrace{*form*} This command produces $\overbrace{form}$ in maths mode. In a displayed formula a superscript places a label over the brace. (Robust.)

overlay This environment can only be used in the **slides** document class. It produces a slide that is meant to be placed over another one. If this environment follows a **slide** environment without any other **overlay** environments intervening, then the slide produced is numbered i–a, where i is the number of the slide produced by that **slide** environment. You can place several **overlay** environments between any two `slide` environments. The second one will be numbered i–b; the third i–c; and so on. See also `slide` and `note`.

`\overleftarrow{`*form*`}` This command produces $\overleftarrow{form}$ in maths mode.

`\overline{`*form*`}` This command produces $\overline{form}$ in maths mode. (Robust.)

`\overrightarrow{`*form*`}` This command produces $\overrightarrow{form}$ in maths mode.

`p{`*len*`}` This expression can only occur within the *preamble* of an `array`, `tabular` or `tabular*` environment. Each entry in the column corresponding to this expression will be typeset in a parbox of width *len*, in effect, as if it were the argument *text* in a `\parbox[t]{`*len*`}{`*text*`}` command. As the command `\\` is used to separate rows in the `array`, `tabular` and `tabular*` environments, it can only occur within *text* in special circumstances, namely inside an environment like `array`, `minipage`, `tabular` or `tabular*`, inside the *text* argument of a `\parbox` or in the scope, which must be explicitly indicated with braces, of a `\centering`, `\raggedright` or `\raggedleft` declaration.

`\P` This command produces the 'paragraph' symbol ¶ in all modes. (Robust.)

`page` This counter contains the value of the *current* page. Unlike other counters it is incremented *after* the page number is generated. It is, therefore, initialized to one and not to zero.

`\pagebreak[`*i*`]` The optional numerical argument *i* can be either 0, 1, 2, 3, or 4. If it is absent or its value is 4, then the `\pagebreak` command marks the position of the end of a page. The output is right justified, unless some other command or declaration has suppressed right justification, with the word that came before the `\pagebreak` command occurring at the extreme right of the line on which it occurs. (This may cause an underfull `\hbox` warning message.) If the numerical argument *i* is 0, then TeX can end the page at that point, but the presence of the command neither encourages nor discourages this. If the numerical value of *i* is 1, 2 or 3, then this encourages TeX to make a page break at that point and the higher the number the stronger the encouragement. If the `twocolumn` document-class option is being used, then this command effects the ending of a column rather than that of a page. (Fragile.)

`\pagenumbering{`*num-style*`}` This global declaration specifies how page numbers will appear. The parameter *num-style* can be either `arabic` (for Arabic numerals), `roman` (for lowercase Roman numerals), `Roman` (for uppercase Roman numerals), `alph` (for lowercase letters) and `Alph` (for uppercase letters). The default value is `arabic`. This command redefines `\thepage` to be `\`*num-style*`{page}`. Whenever it is used, it resets the `page` counter to one. (Fragile.)

`\pageref{`*key*`}` This command is used for cross-referencing purposes. It produces as output the page number on which the corresponding `\label{`*key*`}` command occurred. (Fragile.)

\pagestyle{*page-style***}** This local declaration determines what goes into the head and foot regions of each page of the final output document. The argument *page-style* can be either `plain`, `empty`, `headings` or `myheadings`. (Fragile.)

\paperheight The value of this rigid length parameter is the height of the paper that your document is going to be printed on.

\paperwidth The value of this rigid length parameter is the width of the paper that your document is going to be printed on.

\par This command has the same effect as if you had left a blank line in your input file. (Robust.)

paragraph This counter is used to control the numbering of paragraphs. It is initialized to zero and incremented by the **\paragraph** command before a number is generated. Values can be assigned to it by means of the **\setcounter** command. The value of this counter is reset to zero by the **\chapter**, **\section**, **\subsection** and **\subsubsection** commands.

\paragraph[*entry***]{***heading***}** This sectioning command is used to start a new paragraph. Paragraphs have level number 4 in the `article`, `report` and `book` document classes. By default paragraphs are not numbered automatically in those document classes. (This can be altered by changing the value of the counter `secumndepth`.) By default *heading* will not appear in the table of contents if one is produced, but this can be altered by changing the value of the counter `tocdepth`. If paragraph headings do appear in the table of contents, then *heading* is used, unless the optional argument *entry* is present, when that is used instead. If *entry* is present, then it is a moving argument; but if it is absent, then *heading* is the moving argument. (Fragile.)

\paragraph*{*heading***}** This sectioning command is used to start a new paragraph which is neither numbered nor will it appear in the table of contents. (Fragile.)

\parbox[*pos$_1$***][***len$_2$***][***pos$_2$***]{***len$_1$***}{***text***}** This command is used for making a parbox, that is to say, a box whose contents are processed in paragraph mode. The argument *len$_1$* determines the width of the box that is produced; it must be a rigid length. The optional argument *pos$_1$* can be used to determine the alignment of the box produced to the context in which it occurs. It can be either `b`, `t` or `c` (the default). If it is `b`, then usually what happens is that the baseline of the bottom line in the box produced is aligned with the baseline of the line where the **\parbox** command occurs; and if it is `t`, then usually what happens is that the baseline of the top line in the box produced is aligned with the baseline of the line where the **\parbox** command occurs. (Actually, it is the reference points of the two lines in question that are aligned.) If *pos$_1$* is `c` or it is absent, then the box produced is centred vertically. If you want to use the optional *len$_2$* argument, then you must also use the *pos$_1$* argument. The argument *len$_2$* determines the height of the box that is produced. The commands

\width \depth, \height and \totalheight can occur inside the argument *len$_2$*; these commands have values which are, respectively, the width, the depth, the height and the sum of the depth and the height of the box produced when *text* is processed in paragraph mode. If you use the calc package, you can substitute arithmetical expressions like \height + 1cm for the *len$_2$* argument. You can only use the *pos$_2$* argument if *len$_2$* is present. The optional argument *pos$_2$* controls the alignment of the box produced by processing *text* inside a larger box of width *len$_1$* and height *len$_2$*. It can be either b, c, s or t. If it is b, then *text* is placed in the bottom of the larger box; if it is c, then it is centred in it; if it is s and *text* contains stretchable space, then it is stretched to fill all the vertical space available; and if it is t, it is put at the top of the larger box. If *pos$_2$* is absent, then the value of *pos$_1$* is used. The \parbox command is very similar to the minipage environment; the main difference between them is that you cannot use the \footnote command in the *text* argument of the \parbox command and if you intend to use the tabbing environment or the tabular environment or any of the list-like environments described in Chapter 4, then it is better to use the minipage environment. (Fragile.)

\parindent The value of this rigid length parameter is the width of the indentation at the beginning of a normal paragraph. In a parbox its value is set to zero inches. You can change its value, by means of the \setlength local declaration, anywhere. This is a robust command that must never be preceded by a \protect command.

\parsep This rubber length parameter determines the amount of vertical space that is placed between paragraphs of a single item within the list environment; see Fig. C.3 on p. 225 for a graphical depiction of what it does. It is a robust command that should not be preceded by a \protect command.

\parskip The value of this rubber length parameter is the additional vertical space that is inserted between consecutive paragraphs—additional, that is to say, to the amount of vertical space that normally separates consecutive lines within paragraphs; for this see \baselineskip. Note that \parskip is a rubber length whose natural value is zero inches. Its value can be changed anywhere, but it should always be a rubber or stretchable length. This is a robust command that must never be preceded by a \protect command.

part This counter is used to control the numbering of parts. It is initialized to zero and incremented by the \part command before a number is generated. Values can be assigned to it by means of the \setcounter command.

\part[*entry*]{*heading*} This sectioning command is used to start a new part. It can be used in the article, report and book document classes. Parts have level number 0 in the article document class, but in the report and book document classes they have level number −1. By default parts are numbered automatically in those document styles. (This can be altered by changing the value of the counter `secumndepth`.) If the optional argument *entry* is absent, then by default *heading* will appear in the table of contents if one is produced. (This can be altered by changing the value of the counter `tocdepth`.) If *entry* is present, then it will appear in the table of contents but *heading* will appear in the body of the document produced. If *entry* is present, then it is a moving argument; but if it is absent, then *heading* is a moving argument. (Fragile.)

`\part*{`*heading*`}` This sectioning command is used to start a new part which is neither numbered nor will it appear in the table of contents. (Fragile.)

`\partname` When you use the `\part` command, LATEX automatically generates the word 'Part'. If you want some other expression produced, then you need to redefine the `\partname` command.

`\partopsep` This is a rubber length parameter whose value is the additional vertical space added before and after a `list` environment if a blank line occurs just before the environment is opened. (The usual amount of vertical space that is placed in these two places is the sum of the values of `\topsep` and `\parskip`.) See Fig. C.3 on p. 225. This is a robust command that must not be preceded by a `\protect` command.

`pc` This is a TEX keyword; it stands for *pica*, a unit of length, which exactly satisfies the equality 1 pc = 12 pt. (Roughly, 1 pc = 0.166 in = 4.22 mm.)

`picture` This environment is used for producing simple line drawings. See Chapter 12 for full details of its use.

`plain` This page-style option can be given as the argument to the `\pagestyle` and `\thispagestyle` declarations. A page number is placed in the foot of the page and the head is left empty. It is the default page style for both the `article` and `report` document classes. The other standard options are `empty`, `headings` and `myheadings`.

`plain` This is a possible argument to the `\bibliographystyle` command. The bibliography produced is sorted alphabetically and labelled by numbers such as [17]. See also `abbrv`, `alpha` and `unsrt`.

`plus` *len* This TEX keyword is used in assigning rubber length values; *len* represents the amount by which the natural value of the target length parameter can stretch. See also `minus`.

`\pmb{`*arg*`}` This command can only be used in maths mode and only if you have loaded the `amsbsy` package. The argument *arg* is printed three times with the second and third printings being slightly displaced. Note that *arg* can be a letter like 'A' or a command that produces a symbol like '`\equiv`'; the result, however, is an ordinary symbol whatever the category of *arg*. Note also that the name of this command comes from the first letters of the words 'poor man's bold'.

\pmod{*exp***}** This command can only be used in maths mode where it produces a parenthesized 'modulo' expression. For example, $m_1 \equiv m_2 \pmod{n}$ produces $m_1 \equiv m_2 \pmod{n}$. (Robust.)

\poptabs This command is only available inside the **tabbing** environment where it restores the tab settings stored by a previous **\pushtabs** command. (Fragile.)

\pounds This command produces the pounds symbol £ in all modes. (Robust.)

\printindex This command is only available if you have loaded the **makeidx** package. It must be placed inside the **document** environment and it causes an index to be produced at that place after appropriate processing by LaTeX and *MakeIndex*. It does this by reading the **ind** file which has the same base name as the file in which it occurs.

\protect Every fragile command that occurs inside a moving argument must be preceded by this command. (Robust, of course.)

\providecommand{*cmd***}[***i***][***default***]{***definiens***}** The effect of this local declaration is similar to that of **\providecommand***. The difference between them only emerges if they are used to define commands that take one or more arguments. When **\providecommand*** is used to define such a command, its actual parameters cannot contain a command that creates a new paragraph; the actual parameters of a command defined by **\providecommand** can, however, contain such commands. (Fragile.)

\providecommand*{*cmd***}[***i***][***default***]{***definiens***}** The effect of this local declaration is very similar to that of **\newcommand***. If *cmd* is the name of an existing command, then **\providecommand*** will do nothing; but if *cmd* is not being used as the name of a command, **\providecommand*** will define it. (Fragile.)

\ps{*text***}** This command can only occur inside a **letter** environment. It is used to produce a postscript to a letter. Note that the letters 'PS' are *not* generated by LaTeX. Hence, there is no need for a separate **\pps** command.

pt This is a TeX keyword; it stands for *point*, a unit of length, which exactly satisfies the equality 1 in = 72.27 pt. (Roughly, 1 pt = 0.0138 in = 0.35 mm.)

\pushtabs This command is only available inside the **tabbing** environment where it saves the current tab settings (which can be restored by a **\poptabs** command). (Fragile.)

\put(*i, j***){***picture-object***}** This command can only occur inside the **picture** environment where it places the *picture-object* at the location in the picture whose *x*-coordinate is *i* and whose *y*-coordinate is *j*. Each picture object has a reference point associated with it and the coordinates (i, j) indicate the exact location of this reference point. (Almost anything can be considered as being a picture object, but certain things are used more frequently than others.)

\qbezier [*t*] (i_1, j_1) (i_2, j_2) (i_3, j_3) This command can only be used inside the `picture` environment. It produces a quadratic Bézier curve from the point whose coordinates are (i_1, j_1) to the point (i_3, j_3). The curve produced has the property that the line linking (i_1, j_1) and (i_2, j_2) is a tangent to it at the point (i_1, j_1) and the line linking (i_2, j_2) and (i_3, j_3) is a tangent to it at the point (i_3, j_3). The optional argument *t* determines the number of points used to produce the curve. If it is absent, then a smooth curve is produced. If the optional argument *t* is absent, then the maximum number of points that LaTeX can use is given by the value of the command \qbeziermax; otherwise, \qbeziermax has no effect. The value of \qbeziermax can be changed by using the \renewcommand* local declaration.

\qbeziermax If the optional argument of the \qbezier command is not present, then the maximum number of points that LaTeX can use in order to produce a curve is given by the value of \qbeziermax. Its default value is 500, but this can be changed by redefining \qbeziermax. Its value should always be, however, a positive whole number.

\qquad This plain TeX command produces horizontal space two ems wide in all modes.

\quad This plain TeX command produces one em of horizontal space in all modes.

quotation This environment is used for quotations. It can only occur in paragraph mode and inside the environment LaTeX is also in paragraph mode. The first line of every paragraph inside this environment is indented, but this can be suppressed by using a \noindent command. Vertical space between paragraphs is the same as normal. The left and right margins of the resulting parbox are indented from the normal margins by an equal amount. See section 4.3 for an example of its use.

quote This environment is used for short quotations. It can only be used in paragraph mode and inside the environment LaTeX is also in paragraph mode. The first line of a new paragraph is not indented but extra vertical space is inserted between paragraphs. The left and right margins of the resulting parbox are indented from the normal margins by an equal amount. See section 4.2 for an example of its use.

\r{*char*} This command produces a circle accent in both text modes. For example, \r{z} produces ż. (Robust.)

\raggedbottom This local declaration allows the height of the text on a page to vary slightly from page to page. The amount of vertical space that is inserted between paragraphs is kept constant. The alternative is the \flushbottom local declaration which makes every text page the same height by adding sufficient vertical space between paragraphs to achieve this. The \raggedbottom local declaration is in force by default in the `article`, `report` and `letter` document classes, except when the `twoside` document-class option is used.

\raggedleft This local declaration is used for producing paragraphs that are right justified, but not left justified. They thus have a ragged left edge.

\raggedright This local declaration is used for producing paragraphs that are left justified, but not right justified. They thus have a ragged right edge.

\raisebox{len_1}[len_2][len_3]{$text$} The effect of this command is that the argument *text* is processed in LR mode and the resulting box is raised a distance of len_1 above the current base line. If len_2 is present but len_3 is absent, then LATEX thinks a box extending a distance len_2 above the base line has been produced. If len_2 and len_3 are both present, then LATEX thinks a box extending a distance len_2 above the current base line and len_3 below it has been produced. Any of the commands **\depth**, **\height**, **\totalheight** and **\width** can occur in any of the arguments len_1, len_2 and len_3. (Fragile.)

\ratio{len_1}{len_2} This command is defined in the **calc** package and it can occur in the second argument of the **\setlength** and **\addtolength** commands if you load that package. It represents what you get when you divide len_1 by len_2.

\real{fpn} This command is defined in the **calc** package. The argument *fpn* must be a floating-point number. This command can occur in the second argument of the **\setlength** and **\addtolength** commands if you load **calc**.

\ref{key} This command is used for cross-referencing purposes. It produces as output the **\ref** value which was associated with *key* by a **\label{key}** command.

\refname If you use BIBTEX or the **thebibliography** environment to produce a list of references in the **article** document class, then LATEX will automatically produce the unnumbered section heading 'References' for you. If you want your list of references to be called something different, then you need to redefine the **\refname** command.

\refstepcounter{ctr} The effect of this command is to increase the value of the counter *ctr* by 1 and to reset all counters within it to zero. (If a counter ctr_1 is created by the **\newcounter{ctr_1}[ctr_2]** global declaration using the optional argument ctr_2, then ctr_1 is said to be within ctr_2.) Furthermore, the current **\ref** value is declared to be the text generated by **\the$ctr$**. The difference between this command and **\stepcounter** is that the latter command has no effect on the current **\ref** value.

\renewcommand{cmd}[i][$default$]{$definiens$} The effect of this local declaration is similar to that of **\renewcommand***. The difference between them only emerges if they are used to define commands that take one or more arguments. When **\renewcommand*** is used to define such a command, its actual parameters cannot contain a command that creates a new paragraph; the actual parameters of a command defined by **\renewcommand** can, however, contain such commands. (Fragile.)

\renewcommand*{*cmd***}[***i***]** **[***default***]{***definiens***}** The effect of this local declaration is very similar to that of **\newcommand***. If *cmd* is the name of an existing command, then **\newcommand*** will produce an error message; but **\renewcommand*** will redefine it. If *cmd* is not being used as the name of a command, then **\newcommand*** will define it; but **\renewcommand*** will produce an error message. (Fragile.)

\renewenvironment{*env***}[***i***]** **[***default***]{***definiens*₁**}{***definiens*₂**}** The effect of this local declaration is very similar to that of **\renewenvironment***; the only difference between them is that if an environment requiring arguments is defined then the actual parameters, in the case of **\renewenvironment**, can contain commands that start a new paragraph. (Fragile.)

\renewenvironment*{*env***}[***i***]** **[***default***]{***definiens*₁**}{***definiens*₂**}** The effect of this local declaration is very similar to that of **\newenvironment***; the only difference between them is that in the case of **\renewenvironment***, *env* must be the name of an already existing environment. (Fragile.)

report This is one of the five standard document classes available in LaTeX 2_ε. The standard options are as follows: at most one of 10pt (the default), 11pt or 12pt; at most one of letterpaper (the default), legalpaper, executivepaper, a4paper, a5paper or b5paper; at most one of final (the default) or draft; at most one of oneside (the default) or twoside; at most one of onecolumn (the default) or twocolumn; at most one of openright or openany (the default); and at most one of notitlepage or titlepage (the default). Furthermore, any or none of the following can occur in the argument *opt-list* of the \documentclass command: landscape, openbib, leqno and fleqn. See section 8.2 for more information.

\reversemarginpar This local declaration makes marginal notes appear in the opposite margin to the default one. See also \normalmarginpar and \marginpar.

\right See \left.

\rightarrowfill This command produces an arrow pointing right which expands to fill all the horizontal space available; see Table C.1 on p. 207 for a graphical depiction of what it does.

\rightmargin The value of this rigid length parameter affects the appearance of the list environment as shown in Fig. C.3 on p. 225. It is a robust command that must not be preceded by a \protect command.

\rm This local declaration alters the style of the type being used to a medium, upright, roman typeface. In LR and paragraph modes it is equivalent to the two declarations \normalfont\rmfamily. It can also be used in maths mode. (Robust.)

\rmfamily This local declaration can only be used in LR or paragraph mode where it alters the family attribute of the current font to roman. (Robust.)

roman   This is one of the available options to the \pagenumbering global declaration. Page numbers appear as lowercase Roman numerals when it is used.

\roman{*ctr*}   The effect of this command is that the value of the counter *ctr* is output as a lowercase Roman numeral. (Robust.)

Roman   This is one of the available options to the \pagenumbering global declaration. Page numbers appear as uppercase Roman numerals when it is used.

\Roman{*ctr*}   The effect of this command is that the value of the counter *ctr* is output as an uppercase Roman numeral. (Robust.)

\rq   The presence of this command in your input file has exactly the same effect as if an acute accent was there. In LR and paragraph modes it produces a single closing quotation mark. This can also be produced by means of the command \textquoteright. In maths mode \rq produces a prime. For example, $x\rq$ produces x'.

\rule[*len$_1$*]{*len$_2$*}{*len$_3$*}   This command produces a rectangular blob of width *len$_2$* and height *len$_3$* which is placed a distance of *len$_1$* above or below the current base line (depending on whether *len$_1$* is positive or negative). By default the value of *len$_1$* is zero millimetres. If either of *len$_2$* or *len$_3$* are given the value of zero points, then an invisible vertical or horizontal strut is produced. (Fragile.)

\samepage   This local declaration is used to get the material that occurs within its scope to appear on a single page. Within its scope a page break will not occur inside a paragraph or before or after a displayed mathematical formula. (Fragile.)

\S   This command produces the 'section' symbol § in all modes. (Robust.)

\savebox{*cmd*}[*len*][*pos*]{*text*}   Outside the picture environment this declaration processes *text* in LR mode and the resulting box is placed in the storage bin associated with *cmd*, which must begin with a backslash and must previously have been declared by means of the \newsavebox global declaration. The width of the box produced can be specified by means of the optional argument *len*, which must be a length. Any of the commands \depth, \height, \totalheight and \width can occur in *len*. If a width is specified, *text* is centred horizontally in the box produced; unless *pos* is give a value other than c. If *pos* is l, then *text* is placed next to the left edge of the box produced; if *pos* is r, then it is placed next to the right edge; and if *pos* is s and *text* contains some stretchable space, then *text* is stretched to fill the box produced. (Fragile.)

\savebox{*cmd*}(*i, j*)[*pos*]{*picture-object*}   This form of the \savebox command can only occur inside the picture environment. The parameters (*i, j*), *pos* and *picture-object* have exactly the same meaning as in the case of the version of the \makebox command that can occur inside the picture environment. The argument *cmd* is the name of the storage bin that must have been introduced previously by means of the \newsavebox global declaration and *cmd* must begin with an initial backslash. (Fragile.)

\sb This command, which can only occur in maths mode, is an alternative way to produce subscripts. Both x_{83} and $x\sb{83}$, for example, produce x_{83}.

\sbox{*cmd*}{*text*} Outside the picture environment this local declaration processes *text* in LR mode and the resulting box is placed in the storage bin associated with *cmd*, which must begin with a backslash and must previously have been declared by means of the \newsavebox global declaration. (Robust.)

\sc This local declaration alters the style of the type being used to a medium, small capitals, roman typeface. In LR and paragraph modes it is equivalent to the two local declarations \normalfont\scshape. (Robust.)

\scshape This local declaration can only be used in LR or paragraph mode where it alters the shape attribute of the current font to small capitals. (Robust.)

\scriptscriptstyle This local declaration can only be used in maths mode. It forces TEX to typeset formulas in scriptscript style which is the default for higher-order subscripts and superscripts. This is a primitive TEX command. See also \displaystyle, \textstyle and \scriptstyle. (Robust.)

\scriptsize This local declaration alters the size of type being used. Usually the type size selected is just bigger than \tiny and just smaller than \footnotesize. In LaTeX 2.09 this declaration also selected the main text font being used, but this is no longer the case. It cannot be used in maths mode. (Fragile.)

\scriptstyle This local declaration can only be used in maths mode. It forces TEX to typeset formulas in script style. This is the default style, for example, for subscripts and superscripts within in-text and displayed formulas. As well as causing a smaller size of type to be used, the spacing around symbols for relations and binary operators is different. This is a primitive TEX command. See also \displaystyle, \textstyle and \scriptscriptstyle. (Robust.)

\scrollmode This primitive TEX command ensures that the processing of your file will neither stop if an error occurs nor if user input is requested, though an emergency stop will take place if an attempt is made to \input a non-existent file. This is one of the few commands that can come before the \documentclass command in the input file.

secnumdepth The value of this counter controls which sectional units are numbered. All sectional units with level numbers less than or equal to the value in this counter are numbered. In the article document class the preset value of this counter is three and in the report and book document classes it is two.

section This counter is used to control the numbering of sections. It is initialized to zero and incremented by the \section command before a number is generated.

Values can be assigned to it by means of the `\setcounter` global declaration. In the case of the **report** and **book** document classes the value of the counter **section** is reset to zero by means of the `\chapter` command. Thus, the first section of Chapter X is $X.1$.

`\section[`*entry*`]{`*heading*`}` This sectioning command is used to start a new section. It can only be used in the **article**, **report** and **book** document classes. First, I will say what it does when the optional argument *entry* is absent and then I will say what happens when it is present. However it is used the level number of a section is always one. (1) In the **article** and **report** document classes the use of the command `\section{`*heading*`}` produces a numbered heading unless the value of the counter **secnumdepth** is less than one. (The preset value of the counter **secnumdepth** in the **article** document class is three and in the **report** document class it is two.) If you include the command `\pagestyle{headings}` in your input file, then the argument *heading* will appear in the running head of every even-numbered page in the **article** document class but in the **report** document class it will appear in the running head of every odd-numbered page except those that start a new chapter. If you produce a table of contents and the value of the counter **tocdepth** is greater than or equal to one, then *heading* will appear in it. (The preset value of the counter **tocdepth** in the **article** document class is three and in the **report** document class it is two.) In the **book** document class the use of the command `\section{`*heading*`}` is very similar to its use in the **report** document class. The only difference between them is that by default running heads are produced in the **book** document class. Note that *heading* is a moving argument. (2) The behaviour of the `\section[`*entry*`]{`*heading*`}` command is very similar to that of `\section{`*heading*`}`. The only difference between them is that *entry* is used in running heads and in the table of contents and it is *entry* and not *heading* that is the moving argument. Note that *heading* will still be used as the title of the section. (Fragile.)

`\section*{`*heading*`}` This sectioning command is used to start a new section. The heading produced is neither numbered nor will it appear in the table of contents. It is also the case that the **section** counter is not incremented. (Fragile.)

`\see` This command is defined in the **makeidx** package. If, for example, the command `\index{set|see{class}}` occurs in your input file, then the index produced by LaTeX and *MakeIndex* will contain the line

set, *see* class

To get an expression other than '*see*' to be produced you need to redefine the `\seename` command.

`\seename` The value of this command is the text placed into an index by means of the command `\see`, *q.v.*

`\setcounter{`*ctr*`}{`*i*`}` This global declaration assigns the value i to the counter *ctr*. See also `\addtocounter`. (Fragile.)

\setlength{*cmd*}{*len*} This local declaration assigns to the length command *cmd*, which must begin with a backslash, the value *len*. It can be used to assign both rigid and rubber lengths. See also \addtolength. (Robust.)

\settime{*i*} This command can only be used in the slides document class when the clock document-class option is being used. It assigns the value *i* to the internal 'clock' that is used by LaTeX to keep track of the length of time that a lecture or presentation is going to take. This command should not be placed inside a slide, overlay or note environment. See also \addtime.

\settodepth{*cmd*}{*text*} This local declaration assigns to the length command *cmd*, which must begin with a backslash, the natural depth of the box that is obtained by processing *text* in LR mode. (Robust.)

\settoheight{*cmd*}{*text*} This local declaration assigns to the length command *cmd*, which must begin with a backslash, the natural height of the box that is obtained by processing *text* in LR mode. (Robust.)

\settowidth{*cmd*}{*text*} This local declaration assigns to the length command *cmd*, which must begin with a backslash, the natural width of the box that is obtained by processing *text* in LR mode. (Robust.)

\sf This local declaration alters the style of the type being used to a medium, sans serif, upright typeface. In LR and paragraph modes it is equivalent to the two declarations \normalfont\sffamily. (Robust.)

\sffamily This local declaration can only be used in LR or paragraph mode where it alters the family attribute of the current font to sans serif. (Robust.)

\shortstack[*pos*]{*col*} This command is usually used to produce a piece of text running vertically down the page. Items in *col* are separated by \\ commands and *pos* can either be l (for positioning row items flush left), r (for positioning row items flush right) or the default c (for centring row items). If used in the picture environment, the reference point is at the bottom left-hand corner of the box produced. (Fragile.)

showlabels If you use lots of \label commands, it is easy to forget what you have labelled. Loading the showlabels package has the consequence that all the *key* arguments of the \label commands that you have used are printed in the margin of your document.

\signature{*text*} This local declaration can only occur in the letter document class. It is used for indicating that *text* is the sender of the letter. One or more \\ commands can occur within the argument *text* in order to force a new line.

\sl This local declaration alters the style of the type being used to a medium, slanted, roman typeface. In LR and paragraph modes it is equivalent to the two declarations \normalfont\slshape. (Robust.)

slide This environment can only be used in the **slides** document class. It is used to produce one slide. The first occurrence of this environment produces a slide numbered 1; the second occurrence produces a slide numbered 2; and so on. See also **overlay** and **note**.

slides This is one of the five standard document classes that is available in LaTeX 2_ε. The standard options are as follows: at most one of **letterpaper** (the default), **legalpaper**, **executivepaper**, **a4paper**, **a5paper** or **b5paper**; at most one of **final** (the default) or **draft**; and at most one of **notitlepage** or **titlepage** (the default). Furthermore, any or none of the following can occur in *opt-list*: **landscape**, **leqno**, **fleqn** and **clock**. Note also that **onecolumn** can occur in *opt-list*, but **twocolumn** cannot. See section 8.5 for more information.

\sloppy This local declaration influences line breaking. When it is in force text will rarely stick out into the right-hand margin, but a lot of space may be inserted between words. It affects the typesetting of any paragraph if it is in force when that paragraph ends.

sloppypar This environment typesets the material within it in paragraph mode with the **\sloppy** declaration in force.

\slshape This local declaration can only be used in LR or paragraph mode where it alters the shape attribute of the current font to slanted. (Robust.)

\small This local declaration alters the size of type being used. Usually the type size selected is just bigger than **\footnotesize** and just smaller than **\normalsize**. In LaTeX 2.09 this declaration also selected the main text font being used, but this is no longer the case. It cannot be used in maths mode. (Fragile.)

\smallskip This command produces a small amount of vertical space. It is defined as **\vspace{\smallskipamount}**. (Fragile.)

\smallskipamount The value of this rubber length command is **3pt plus 1pt minus 1pt**. It has this value whether you use the **10pt**, **11pt** or **12pt** document-class option.

sp This is a TeX keyword; it stands for *scaled point*, a unit of length used internally by TeX, which exactly satisfies the equality 1 pt $= 2^{16}$ sp ($= 65{,}536$ sp).

\sp This command, which can only occur in maths mode, is an alternative way to produce superscripts. Both x^{75} and $x\sp{75}$ produce x^{75}.

\space When used in the argument of the **\typeout** command, this command produces a single space on the terminal.

\sqrt[*n*]{*form*} This produces $\sqrt[n]{form}$, if n is present, and $\sqrt{form}$, if it is absent, in maths mode. (Fragile.)

\ss This command produces the German letter 'ß' in both text modes. (Robust.)

\SS This command is available in both text modes where it produces 'SS'.

\stackrel{*form₁*}{*form₂*} This command can only be used in maths mode where it produces a symbol for a binary relation in which *form₁* is placed over *form₂*. Note that *form₁* is processed in the same style as superscripts. For example, the input \$\stackrel{\wedge}{=}\$ produces $\stackrel{\wedge}{=}$. (Robust.)

\stepcounter{*ctr*} The effect of this command is to increase the value of the counter *ctr* by 1 and to reset all counters within it to zero. (If a counter *ctr₁* is created by the \newcounter{*ctr₁*}[*ctr₂*] global declaration using the optional argument *ctr₂*, then *ctr₁* is said to be within *ctr₂*.)

\stop When an error occurs one of the options available to you is to enter i\stop (without any spaces) and this terminates the processing of your input file.

\stretch{*fpn*} This is rubber length whose natural length is zero inches and whose stretchability is *fpn* times \fill, where *fpn* is a floating-point number which can be either positive or negative. (Robust.)

\strut This plain TₑX command is available in all modes where it produces an invisible vertical rule whose height is the value of \baselineskip and which has no width.

sty This is the file extension used by LATₑX packages. The reason why the extension sty is used is because in LATₑX 2.09 packages were called *style files*.

\subitem This command is used inside the theindex environment to produce an indented entry.

subparagraph This counter is used to control the numbering of subparagraphs. It is initialized to zero and incremented by the \subparagraph command before a number is generated. Values can be assigned to it by means of the \setcounter global declaration. The value of the counter subparagraph is reset to zero by the \chapter, \section, \subsection, \subsubsection and \paragraph commands.

\subparagraph[*entry*]{*heading*} This sectioning command is used to start a new subparagraph. Subparagraphs have level number 5 in the article, report and book document classes. By default subparagraphs are not numbered automatically in those document classes. (This can be altered by changing the value of the counter secnumdepth.) By default *heading* will not appear in the table of contents if one is produced, but this can be altered by changing the value of the counter tocdepth. If subparagraph headings do appear in the table of contents, then *heading* is used, unless the optional argument *entry* is present, when that is used instead. If *entry* is present, then it is a moving argument, but if it is absent, then *heading* is the moving argument. (Fragile.)

\subparagraph*{*heading*} This is a sectioning command which is used to start a new subparagraph which is neither numbered nor will its heading appear in any table of contents which may be produced. It is also the case that the `subparagraph` counter is not incremented. (Fragile.)

subsection This counter is used to control the numbering of subsections. It is initialized to zero and incremented by the `\subsection` command before a number is generated. Values can be assigned to it by means of the `\setcounter` global declaration. The value of the counter `subsection` is reset to zero by both the `\chapter` and `\section` commands.

\subsection[*entry*]{*heading*} This sectioning command is used to start a new subsection. Subsections have level number 2 in the `article`, `report` and `book` document classes. By default subsections are numbered automatically in those document classes. (This can be altered by changing the value of the counter `secnumdepth`.) If the optional argument *entry* is absent, then by default *heading* will appear in the table of contents if one is produced. (This can be altered by changing the value of the counter `tocdepth`.) If *entry* is present, then it will appear in the table of contents but *heading* will appear in the body of the document produced. If *entry* is present, then it is a moving argument, but if it is absent, then *heading* is the moving argument. (Fragile.)

\subsection*{*heading*} This sectioning command is used to start a new subsection which is neither numbered nor will it appear in the table of contents. It is also the case that the `subsection` counter is not incremented. (Fragile.)

\subsubitem This command is used inside the `theindex` environment to produce an entry which is indented more than one produced by the `\subitem` command.

subsubsection This counter is used to control the numbering of subsubsections. It is initialized to zero and incremented by the `\subsubsection` command before a number is generated. Values can be assigned to it by means of the `\setcounter` global declaration. The value of the counter `subsubsection` is reset to zero by the `\chapter`, `\section` and `\subsection` commands.

\subsubsection[*entry*]{*heading*} This sectioning command is used to start a new subsubsection. Subsubsections have level number 3 in the `article`, `report` and `book` document classes. By default subsubsections are numbered automatically in the `article` class, but they are not numbered automatically in the `report` or `book` classes. (This can be altered by changing the value of the counter `secumndepth`.) By default *heading* will appear in the table of contents in the `article` class if one is produced, but it will not appear in either the `report` or the `book` classes. (This can be altered by changing the value of the counter `tocdepth`.) If subsubsection headings do appear in the table of contents, then *heading* is used, unless the optional argument *entry* is present, when that is used instead. If *entry* is present, then it is a moving argument, but if it is absent, then *heading* is the moving argument. (Fragile.)

\subsubsection*{*heading*} This sectioning command is used to start a new subsubsection which is neither numbered nor will it appear in the table of contents. It is also the case that the subsubsection counter is not incremented. (Fragile.)

\suppressfloats[*pos*] This command ensures that no floats are placed on the current page. The optional argument *pos* can be either b or t. If it is b, then no floats will be placed at the bottom of the current page; and if it is t, then no floats will be placed at the top of the current page.

\symbol{*i*} This produces the character in the current font with number *i*. Thus, {\tt \symbol{92}char} produces \char. If *i* is preceded by ', it is considered to be an octal number and if by " then it is considered to be a hexadecimal number. (Robust.)

\t{*char₁ char₂*} This command produces a tie-after accent over the two characters *char₁* and *char₂* in LR or paragraph mode. For example, \t{ec} produces e͡c. (Robust.)

tabbing This environment is used for aligning information without the option of including either horizontal or vertical rules. See section 5.5 for more information.

\tabbingsep When the \' command is used inside the tabbing environment, text is pushed to the left and the value of this rigid length parameter is the distance left between the text and the left margin (or an appropriate tab position). This is a robust command that should never be preceded by a \protect command.

\tabcolsep The value of this rigid length parameter is half the amount of horizontal space left between the columns produced by a tabular or tabular* environment. When you use the array environment, this distance is given by the value of the rigid length parameter \arraycolsep. This is a robust command that must not be preceded by a \protect command.

table This counter is used in the numbering of floats created by the table and table* environments. It is only incremented if a \caption command has been included inside the environment.

table This environment produces a float. If a \caption command is present inside it, then the word 'Table' and a numerical label are produced automatically; otherwise, it behaves like the figure environment, *q.v.* If you want an expression other than 'Table' to be output, then redefine the \tablename command. If you are using the twocolumn document-class option, then the floats produced are only one column wide.

table* This environment is very similar to the table environment. The only difference between them is that if the twocolumn document-class option has been chosen, then the resulting float is two columns wide.

\tablename When you use the \caption command inside the table and table* environments, LaTeX produces a caption beginning with the word 'Table'. If you want some other expression to be used instead, then you need to redefine the \tablename command.

\tableofcontents This command produces a table of contents at the place in the input file where it occurs. You need to run LaTeX at least twice to get a correct table of contents. It also causes a toc file to be written unless you have included a \nofiles command in the preamble of your input file.

tabular The tabular environment can occur in any mode and its general format is:

> \begin{tabular}[*pos*]{*preamble*}
> *row-list*
> \end{tabular}

The optional *pos* argument controls the vertical positioning of the box produced. By default alignment is on the centre of the box, but a t option aligns on the top row and a b option aligns on the bottom row. The *preamble* specifies how the columns of the table are going to be formatted as explained in section 5.3.1. The *row-list* element consists of one or more *row* components which are separated by \\ commands. Each *row* will usually contain $i - 1$ ampersands where i is the number of columns that the table contains. (Note that if a row contains some \multicolumn commands, then fewer ampersands may be required.) Following a \\ command you can include one or more \hline commands. These produce horizontal lines. If two \hline commands occur next to one another, then the vertical space separating the lines produced by them is given by the rigid length parameter \doubleseprule. If you want a line to appear at the bottom of your table, then the final \hline command must be preceded by a \\ command, but the \\ command should be left out if not followed by a \hline command.

tabular* The general format of the tabular* environment is:

> \begin{tabular*}{*len*}[*pos*]{*preamble*}
> *row-list*
>
> \end{tabular*}

where *pos*, *preamble* and *row-list* are exactly as for the tabular environment, but *len* gives the width of the box produced. Care must be taken to ensure that the material placed in each row is exactly of this width; usually rubber length commands, like \hfill, are used to ensure this.

\tag{*text*} This command can be used in any of the environments available in the amsmath package which produce displayed formulas. Its effect is to label the formula with *text*, which is processed in LR mode. Parentheses are placed around *text*; if you want a label without parentheses, then use the \tag* command.

`\tag*{`*text*`}` This command is very similar to the `\tag` command; the only difference between them is that `\tag*` produces a label that is not enclosed in parentheses.

`\tbinom{`*form₁*`}{`*form₂*`}` This command, which is defined in the `amsmath` package, produces a binomial coefficient which is typeset in textstyle: $form_1$ appears above $form_2$ and both are enclosed in large parentheses. See also `\binom` and `\dbinom`.

`tex` This is the extension of a LaTeX input file.

`\TeX` This command produces the logo TeX.

`texlog` Usually the file extension of the log or transcript file written by LaTeX is `log`, but sometimes `texlog` is used.

`\text{`*text*`}` This command is defined in the `amstext` package (which is loaded automatically if you load `amsmath`). It is very like the `\mbox` command, except that when used in subscripts or superscripts in maths mode the size of type used is altered to one that is appropriate.

`\textbf{`*text*`}` This command can only be used in LR or paragraph mode where it typesets *text* using the family and shape attributes in force at the place where it occurs, but the series attribute used is bold. (Robust.)

`\textbullet` This command produces the symbol • in both text modes.

`\textcircled{`*char*`}` This command produces the letter *char* inside a circle in both text modes. Thus, `\textcircled{a}` produces ⓐ. The size of the circle is fixed and so trying `\textcircled{A}`, for example, does not produce a pleasing result. It is, however, possible to produce circled numerals and the best size of numeral to use is `\scriptsize`. Thus, `\textcircled{\scriptsize{7}}` produces ⑦.

`\textcompwordmark` This command can be used to prevent LaTeX producing a ligature. For example, `half\textcompwordmark␣life` produces 'halflife'. The same result can be produced by `half{\kern0pt}life`. Knuth (1986a), p. 306, discusses various ways of preventing TeX from producing ligatures and so does Eijkhout (1992), p. 37.

`\textemdash` This command produces the symbol — in both text modes. The same symbol can also be produced by three consecutive hyphens that are neither preceded nor followed by a hyphen.

`\textendash` This command produces the symbol – in both text modes. The same symbol can also be produced by two adjacent hyphens in your input file that are neither preceded nor followed by a hyphen.

`\textexclamdown` This command produces the symbol ¡ in both text modes. The same symbol can also be produced by putting the two characters !` in your input file

\textfloatsep When a float is put at the top or the bottom of a page, then the value of this rubber length parameter is the amount of vertical space left between it and the text either below or above it. If the `twocolumn` document-class option has been chosen, the value of this command only affects single-column floats; for two-column floats see `\dbltextfloatsep`. This is a robust command that must not be preceded by a `\protect` command.

\textfraction The value of this command is a floating-point number between 0 and 1 which represents the minimum amount of a text page, that is to say, one which contains both text and floats, that must be occupied by text. For example, if `\textfraction` is 0.6, then at least 60% of each text page must be occupied by things that are not floats. It can be altered by `\renewcommand*`. Its default value is 0.2.

\textheight The value of this rigid length parameter is the normal height of the body region of a page. See Fig. C.4 on p. 260. This is a robust command that must never be preceded by a `\protect` command.

\textit{*text***}** This command can only be used in LR or paragraph mode where it typesets *text* using the family and series attributes in force at the place where it occurs, but the shape attribute used is italic. (Robust.)

\textmd{*text***}** This command can only be used in LR or paragraph mode where it typesets *text* using the family and shape attributes in force at the place where it occurs, but the series attribute used is medium. (Robust.)

\textnormal{*text***}** This command typesets *text* using the family, series and shape attributes of the main text font of the document being processed. It cannot be used in maths mode. (Robust.)

\textperiodcentered This command produces the symbol · in both text modes.

\textquestiondown This command produces the symbol ¿ in both text modes. The same symbol can be produced by putting the two characters ?‘ in your input file

\textquotedblleft This command produces the symbol " in both text modes.

\textquotedblright This command produces the symbol " in both text modes.

\textquoteleft This command produces the symbol ' in both text modes.

\textquoteright This command produces the symbol ' in both text modes.

\textrm{*text***}** This command can only be used in LR or paragraph mode where it typesets *text* using the series and shape attributes in force at the place where it occurs, but the family attribute used is roman. (Robust.)

\textsc{*text***}** This command can only be used in LR or paragraph mode where it typesets *text* using the family and series attributes in force at the place where it occurs, but the shape attribute used is small capitals. (Robust.)

\textsf{*text*} This command can only be used in LR or paragraph mode where it typesets *text* using the series and shape attributes in force at the place where it occurs, but the family attribute used is sans serif. (Robust.)

\textsl{*text*} This command can only be used in LR or paragraph mode where it typesets *text* using the family and series attributes in force at the place where it occurs, but the shape attribute used is slanted. (Robust.)

\textstyle This local declaration can only be used in maths mode. It forces TEX to typeset formulas in text style. This is the default style for in-text formulas. It can be used in subscripts and superscripts, for example, in order to force the use of larger symbols and to force them to be typeset in text style. This is a primitive TEX command. See also \displaystyle, \scriptstyle and \scriptscriptstyle. (Robust.)

^{*text*} This command makes *text* into a superscript. It is formatted using the current text font rather than a maths font.

\texttt{*text*} In LR and paragraph mode this command typesets *text* using the series and shape attributes in force where it occurs, but the family attribute used is typewriter. (Robust.)

\textup{*text*} In LR and paragraph mode this command typesets *text* using the series and family attributes in force where it occurs, but the shape attribute used is upright. (Robust.)

\textvisiblespace This command produces the symbol ␣ in both text modes.

\textwidth The value of this rigid length parameter is the normal width of the body region of a page. See Fig. C.4 on p. 260. This is a robust command that must never be preceded by a \protect command.

\tfrac{*form*$_1$}{*form*$_2$} This command produces a fraction with numerator (top part) *form*$_1$ and denominator (bottom part) *form*$_2$ which is typeset in textstyle. It is defined in the amsmath package and can only be used in maths mode. See also \frac, \dfrac, \cfrac and \genfrac.

\thanks{*text*} This command can only occur inside the arguments of the \author, \date and \title declarations that are used by the \maketitle command. It is used to produce a footnote and *text* occurs as the footnote produced. The markers produced are regarded as having zero width. If a \thanks command does not end a line, then it should be followed by a \␣ command in order to insert some inter-word space. Too many \thanks commands, that is to say, more than nine, will cause a 'Counter too large' error message. Note that *text* is a moving argument.

\the*ctr* The \newcounter{*ctr*} command makes *ctr* into a counter, but in order for the value of *ctr* to be output it has to be converted into text, for example, by

a	\topmargin + 1 in	f	\footheight
b	\headheight	g	\oddsidemargin + 1 in
c	\headsep	g	\evensidemargin + 1 in
d	\textheight	h	\textwidth
e	\footskip − \footheight		

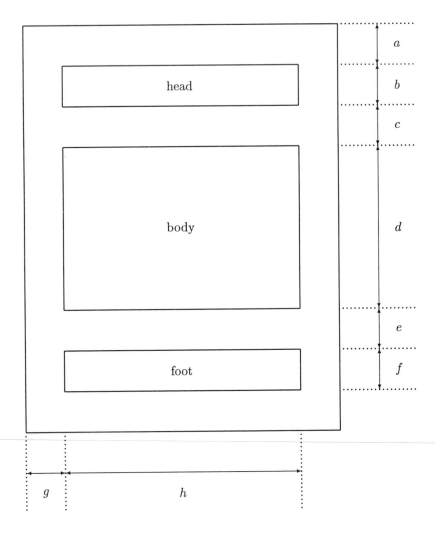

Figure C.4: Parameters affecting the appearance of the output page.

the \arabic or \Roman command. Whenever you introduce a new counter LaTeX automatically creates a new command \the*ctr* which produces text output and by default \the*ctr* is defined to be \arabic{*ctr*}. For example, the commands

```
\newcounter{ant}\setcounter{ant}{7}\theant
```

produce 7 and the commands

```
\setcounter{ant}{11}
\renewcommand*{\theant}{\Alph{ant}}
\theant
```

produce K. In the case of LaTeX's built-in counters what \the*ctr* produces varies widely; see section B.3 for more information. (Robust.)

thebibliography This environment is used for do-it-yourself bibliographies. How it works is explained in section 4.9.

theindex This environment is used for producing an index; the output appears in a two-column format. Inside the **theindex** environment the commands \item, \subitem and \subsubitem are used to format the index and the command \indexspace can be used to provide some vertical space. See section 7.1 for more information.

\thicklines This local declaration is used to select the thicker of the two standard thicknesses of lines and circles in the **picture** environment. (Robust.)

\thickmuskip This is a primitive TeX length command which can only be used in maths mode and whose preset value is 5mu plus 5mu. It determines the length of the \; control symbol. See also \thinmuskip and \medmuskip.

\thinlines This local declaration is used to select the thinner of the two standard thicknesses of lines and circles in the **picture** environment. (Robust.)

\thinmuskip This is a primitive TeX length command which can only be used in maths mode and whose preset value is 3mu. It determines the length of the \, control symbol. See also \medmuskip and \thickmuskip.

\thispagestyle{*page-style*} This global declaration is similar to \pagestyle, except that it only affects the current page. The parameter *page-style* can be either plain, empty, headings or myheadings. (Fragile.)

\tilde{*char*} This command produces an accent in maths mode. Thus, $\tilde{x}$ produces $\tilde{x}$. (Robust.)

\time This is a primitive TeX command which is an integer register. It contains the number of minutes that have elapsed since midnight. To output its value use the commands \the\time.

\tiny This local declaration alters the size of type being used. Usually the type size selected is the smallest available and just smaller than **\scriptsize**. In LATEX 2.09 this declaration also selected the main text font being used, but this is no longer the case. It cannot be used in maths mode. (Fragile.)

\title{*text***}** This local declaration can be used to declare *text* to be the title in the **article**, **report** and **book** document classes. (The actual title is produced by the **\maketitle** command inside the **document** environment.) You can use the **** command inside *text* in order to force a line break. One or more **\thanks** commands can also appear in *text*; these produce footnotes whose markers are regarded as having zero width. If a **\thanks** command does not end a line, then it should be followed by a **\␣** command in order to insert some inter-word space.

titlepage This is a document-class option. When it is in force, the title produced by the **\maketitle** command appears on a page by itself and, if the **abstract** environment is used, the abstract produced appears by itself on a separate page. Note that this option is not recognized by the **letter** document class and it is the default in the **book**, **report** and **slides** document classes. See also **notitlepage**.

titlepage This environment produces an empty page and ensures that the following page is numbered one. If you want anything to appear on the page produced, then you have to include text and/or LATEX commands in the body of the environment.

toc This is the file extension of a file which is only created or overwritten if your input file contains a **\tableofcontents** command (and does not contain a **\nofiles** command). The **toc** file contains the information necessary to produce a table of contents for your document. The information comes from all those sectioning commands in your input file whose level number is less than or equal to the value of the counter **tocdepth**. The table of contents is produced by the **\tableofcontents** command if a **toc** file exists when you process your input file.

tocdepth The value of this counter controls which sectional unit headings will appear in the table of contents, if there is one. All headings of sectional units with level numbers less than or equal to the value of this counter will appear in the table of contents. In the **article** document class the preset value of this counter is three and in the **report** and **book** document classes it is two.

\today This command causes the date of the day on which you created a **dvi** file from your input file to be included in that **dvi** file. The date is in the American format, for example, 'July 4, 1992'. (Robust.)

\topfigrule When a float is going to be placed at the top of a page, then the command **\topfigrule** determines what is to appear between the float and the text below it. By default, nothing appears, but by defining **\topfigrule** you can get LATEX to place a horizontal rule, say, there. Note that, if you do define **\topfigrule**, you must make sure that it does not add any extra vertical space between the float and the text below it. When a float is going to be placed at the top of a page, LaTeX first executes \topfigrule and then it puts \textfloatsep amount of vertical space below the float. (If the twocolumn document-class option is being used, the command \topfigrule only applies to single-column floats.) Note that if \topfigrule has been defined and two or more single-column floats appear on a page, then what \topfigrule produces only appears below the bottommost float. Note also that \topfigrule has to be *defined* and not *redefined*. See also \botfigrule and \dblfigrule.

\topfraction The value of this command is a floating-point number greater than zero and less than or equal to one. Its value specifies how much of the top part of each text page can be used for floats. It can be altered by \renewcommand*. Its default value is 0.7. If the twocolumn document-class option has been chosen, then the value of this command only affects single-column floats; for two-column floats see \dbltopfraction.

\topmargin The value of this rigid length parameter affects the appearance of each output page. The distance between the top edge of the paper and the top of the page's head is the sum of the value of \topmargin and one inch. See Fig. C.4 on p. 260. This robust command must not be preceded by a \protect command.

topnumber The value of this counter is the maximum number of floats, that is to say, tables or figures, that can occur at the top of each text page. Its default value is 2. If the twocolumn document-class option has been chosen, the value of this counter only affects single-column floats; for two-column floats see dbltopnumber.

\topsep The value of this rubber length parameter is used by the list environment to help determine the appearance and organization of the list generated. See Fig. C.3 on p. 225 for details of its effect. This is a robust command that must never be preceded by a \protect command.

\topskip The value of this rubber length parameter is the minimum distance between the top of the body region and the bottom of the first line of text. Its effect is rather like that of \baselineskip, except that it only affects the first line on the page. This robust command must not be preceded by a \protect command.

\totalheight The \framebox, \makebox, \savebox, \raisebox and \parbox commands and the minipage environment have the following general formats:

```
\framebox[len][pos]{text}
\makebox[len][pos]{text}
\savebox[len][pos]{text}
\raisebox{len₁}[len₂][len₃]{text}
\parbox[pos₁][len₂][pos₂]{len₁}{text}
\begin{minipage}[pos₁][len₂][pos₂]{len₁}
    text
\end{minipage}
```

The command \totalheight can occur in the *len* argument of the commands \framebox, \makebox and \savebox, in the arguments len_1, len_2 and len_3 of the \raisebox command and in the argument len_2 of the \parbox command and the minipage environment. The value of the length command \totalheight is the sum of the depth and the height of the box obtained by typesetting the argument *text*. In the case of the \framebox, \makebox, \savebox and \raisebox commands *text* is processed in LR mode and in the case of the \parbox command and the minipage environment it is processed in paragraph mode. If you load the calc package, then you can use arithmetical expressions like \totalheight + 4mm in those arguments where \totalheight can occur.

totalnumber The value of this counter is the maximum number of floats that can appear on a text page. Its default value is 3.

trivlist This environment is a restricted version of the list environment. It inherits the values of all parameters in force when the environment opens, except that \leftmargin, \labelwidth and \itemindent are set to zero inches and \parsep is set to the current value of \parskip.

\tt This local declaration alters the style of the type being used to a medium, upright, typewriter typeface. In LR and paragraph modes it is equivalent to the two declarations \normalfont\ttfamily. It can also be used in maths mode. (Robust.)

\ttfamily This local declaration can only be used in LR or paragraph mode where it alters the family attribute of the current font to typewriter. (Robust.)

twocolumn This is document-class option which makes two columns of text appear on every page. Note that this option is not recognized by the slides document class. See also onecolumn.

\twocolumn[*text*] This local declaration first starts a new page by executing the command \clearpage and then it typesets the following input in a two-column format. If the optional argument *text* is present, it is typeset as a single-column parbox that extends across the entire width of the text body. See also \onecolumn. (Fragile.)

twoside This is a document-class option. It causes odd- and even-numbered pages to be treated differently. For example, the default widths of the left margins on these pages are different and the moving heads on odd- and even-numbered pages are also different (if present at all). Note that this option is not recognized by the slides document class and it is the default option for the book document class. See also oneside.

\typein[*cmd*]{*text*} This command wites *text* to your terminal and it also writes it to the log file. After outputting *text* it stops the processing of your input file until you input something from your keyboard. This input must be terminated by a carriage return character. If *cmd* is absent, then your input is processed as if it occurred in your input file at the place where the \typein command occurs. If *cmd* is present, then it is defined or redefined to be what you input. (Fragile.)

\typeout{*text*} This command writes *text* to your terminal and it also writes it to the log file. The argument *text* is a moving one. Preceding a command name in *text* with \protect causes that command name to be output. A command name in *text* defined by either the \newcommand, \newcommand*, \providecommand, \providecommand*, \renewcommand or \renewcommand* local declaration is replaced by its definition. Use the command \space in the argument *text* to produce a space in the output. (Fragile.)

\u{*char*} This command produces a breve accent over the single character *char* in LR or paragraph mode. For example, \u{o} produces ŏ. (Robust.)

\unboldmath Every mathematcal formula in the scope of this local declaration, which can only occur in LR or paragraph mode, is typeset normally and not in bold. See also \boldmath. (Robust.)

\underbrace{*form*} This produces a horizontal brace under *form* in maths mode; in a displayed formula a subscript places a label below the brace. (Robust.)

\underline{*form*} This produces *form* in any mode. (Fragile.)

\unitlength The value of this rigid length parameter determines the length of the unit used for positioning and drawing picture objects in the picture environment. For example, placing the command \setlength{\unitlength}{1mm} just before a picture environment makes the unit of length one millimetre. Its default value is 1 point. This is a robust command which must never be preceded by a \protect command.

unsrt This is a possible argument to the \bibliographystyle command. The entries in the bibliography produced occur in the order of their first citation and are labelled by numbers like [31]. The other standard options are abbrv, alpha and plain.

\upbracefill This command produces a horizontal brace which expands to fill all the horizontal space available; see Table C.1 on p. 207 for a graphical depiction of what it does.

\upshape This local declaration can only be used in LR or paragraph mode where it alters the shape attribute of the current font to upright. (Robust.)

\usebox{*cmd*} This command outputs the contents of the storage bin *cmd*. (Robust.)

\usecounter{*ctr*} This local declaration can only occur in the *dec-list* argument to the list environment; it is used for numbering the items of a list automatically. (Fragile.)

\usepackage[*opt-list*]{*pack-list*}[*date*] This command can only occur in the preamble of a LaTeX 2_ε input file. It ensures that the packages listed in *pack-list* are loaded. The argument *pack-list* consists of the first names of one or more packages. If *pack-list* contains more than one item, then commas must be used as separators. If present, the argument *opt-list* consists of one or more package options. No spaces should be included in *opt-list* and if more than one option is included then commas should be used as separators. What the possible candidates for inclusion in *opt-list* are depends on the particular package chosen. If any options have been included in the \documentclass command, then they are taken to be options to any \usepackage commands that occur in the document preamble. The optional argument *date* must have the format *year/month/day*, where *year* consists of four digits and both *month* and *day* consist of two digits each. An example of the *date* parameter is 1998/03/11. If the release date of the package or packages requested is earlier than *date*, then you will get a warning message.

\v{*char*} This command produces a háček accent over the single character *char* in LR or paragraph mode. For example, \v{o} produces ǒ. (Robust.)

\value{*ctr*} This command is mainly used if you want to set the value of one counter equal to that of another; for example, \setcounter{war}{\value{equation}} has the result that the value of war is the same as that of equation. (The counter war must have been introduced previously by means of a \newcounter{war} global declaration.) This is a robust command which must never be preceded by a \protect command.

\vbox{*text*} This primitive TeX command produces a vertical box; if several things occur in *text*, then they are placed on top of one another.

\vdots This command is only available in maths mode where it produces an ellipsis consisting of three vertical dots. (Robust.)

\vec{*char*} This command produces an accent in maths mode. Thus, $\vec{x}$ produces $\vec{x}$. (Robust.)

\vector This command can only occur as the argument of a \put or \multiput command inside the picture environment. The commands

$$\put\,(i,j)\,\{\vector\,(p,q)\,\{l\}\}$$

draw an arrow which starts at the point (i, j) and whose projection on the x-axis is l units. (The only exception to this occurs when you want to produce a vertical line, in which case l gives the actual length of the line produced.) The slope of the line is given by (p, q), that is to say, it goes p units in the x direction for every q units it goes in the y direction. Both p and q must be whole numbers between -4 and $+4$, inclusive, with no common divisor. (Fragile.)

\verb*char text char* This outputs *text* in typewriter font exactly as it appears in your input file. The parameter *char* can be any single visible character, except a space or a letter or a *, that does not occur in *text*. A space between *char* and *text* or *text* and *char* appears in the output. No newline character should occur in *text*. A \verb command should not occur in the argument of any other command but it may occur in an environment.

\verb**char text char* This command is like the \verb command except that spaces in *text* appear as '␣' characters in the output.

verbatim This environment is used for producing text exactly as it appears in your input file using the typewriter style of type. Special characters and LaTeX commands do not have their usual meaning inside this environment. They are output as they appear, the only exception being the \end{verbatim} command. (Note that no space can occur between \end and {verbatim}.) This environment cannot occur in the argument to any other command, though it can occur inside another environment. See section 5.6 for an example of its use.

verbatim* This environment is similar to verbatim except that spaces in the input file appear as '␣' in the output document.

verse This environment can be used for displaying poetry. The left and right margins are indented by the same amount. Lines within a stanza are terminated by the \\ command and stanzas are separated by means of one or more blank lines. See section 4.4 for an example of its use.

\vfill This is just an abbreviation for \par\vspace{\fill}. (Fragile.)

\visible This local declaration is only available in the slides document class. Inside the slide, overlay and note environments it makes any text in its scope visible. See also \invisible.

\vline This command can only occur within an array, tabular or tabular* environment where it produces a vertical line whose height is that of the row in which it occurs. It can also occur in the argument of an @-expression. (Robust.)

\vspace{*len*} This command adds vertical space of height *len* in the output document unless a page break occurs within its 'scope'. If the \vspace command occurs in the middle of a paragraph, then the current line is finished before the space is added. (Fragile.)

\vspace*{*len*} This command is similar to \vspace{*len*} except that vertical space of height *len* is added even if a page break occurs within its 'scope'. (Fragile.)

\widehat This command produces an accent in maths mode which can vary in size. Its largest form appears in $\widehat{xyz}$ which produces $\widehat{xyz}$. (Robust.)

\widetilde This command produces an accent in maths mode which can vary in size. Its largest form appears in $\widetilde{xyz}$ which produces $\widetilde{xyz}$. (Robust.)

$$\xleftarrow[\text{form}_2]{\text{form}_1} \quad \xleftarrow[\text{form}_2]{\text{form}_1}$$

$$\xrightarrow[\text{form}_2]{\text{form}_1} \quad \xrightarrow[\text{form}_2]{\text{form}_1}$$

\xleftarrow[*form*₂]{*form*₁}

\xrightarrow[*form*₂]{*form*₁}

Figure C.5: Extensible left and right arrows.

\width The general formats of the \framebox, \makebox, \savebox, \raisebox and \parbox commands and the minipage environment are as follows:

```
\framebox[len][pos]{text}
\makebox[len][pos]{text}
\savebox[len][pos]{text}
\raisebox{len₁}[len₂][len₃]{text}
\parbox[pos₁][len₂][pos₂]{len₁}{text}
\begin{minipage}[pos₁][len₂][pos₂]{len₁}
    text
\end{minipage}
```

It is possible for the command \width to occur in the *len* argument of the commands \framebox, \makebox and \savebox, in the arguments len_1, len_2 and len_3 of the \raisebox command and in the argument len_2 of the \parbox command and the minipage environment. The value of the length command \width is the width of the box obtained by typesetting the argument *text*. In the case of the \framebox, \makebox, \savebox and \raisebox commands *text* is processed in LR mode and in the case of the \parbox command and the minipage environment it is processed in paragraph mode. If you load the calc package, then you can use commands like \framebox[\width + 4mm]{*text*}.

\xleftarrow[*form*₂]{*form*₁} This command is defined in the amsmath package; it produces an extensible left arrow with $form_1$ placed above it and $form_2$ placed below it. See Fig. C.5 for an illustration of how it works. Inside the CD environment use either the @(((or the @<<< command to produce an extensible left arrow.

\xrightarrow[*form*₂]{*form*₁} This command is defined in the amsmath package; it produces an extensible right arrow with $form_1$ placed above it and $form_2$ placed below it. See Fig. C.5 for an illustration of how it works. Inside the CD environment use either the @))) or the @>>> command to produce an extensible right arrow.

Appendix D

When Things go Wrong

D.1   Introduction

Things often do not go smoothly when LaTeX is processing your input file. When things go drastically wrong, the processing of your input file stops and you get an error message. This could either be produced by TeX or by LaTeX. Both kinds of error message begin with an exclamation mark, but those generated by LaTeX contain the words 'LaTeX Error:', whereas those generated by TeX do not have these additional words. Both kinds of error message give additional information about what the problem is; most of these are self-explanatory and it is a straightforward matter to correct the mistake. (In a small number of cases finding the source of the error may prove to be quite difficult.) After writing these various messages to your terminal, you will get a prompt beginning with a question mark. This tells you that the system is waiting for you to do something. I say more about LaTeX's error messages in section D.2 below and more about TeX's error messages in section D.3 below. If you ever get a prompt consisting of a single asterisk, then you have entered interactive mode. Typing \end{document} in response to this prompt should cause TeX to finish processing your file. If you ever get a prompt consisting of two asterisks, then TeX expects you to enter the name of an input file.

Sometimes something goes wrong when your input file is being processed, but the problem does not cause the processing to stop. In this case you get a warning message. These can come from a variety of sources, but most are produced by either TeX or LaTeX. Those that are generated by LaTeX contain the words 'LaTeX Warning:', whereas those that TeX produces do not contain these words. I say more about LaTeX's warning messages in section D.4 below and more about TeX's warning messages in section D.5 below.

D.2   LaTeX Error Messages

In order to illustrate what happens when you get a LaTeX error message replace the \noindent command in the file vamp.tex, displayed in Fig. 2.1 on p. 8 above, with \begin{center} and put an \end{centre} command just before the \end{document}

command. When you process the file, the processing will stop with the following
message being displayed on your terminal:

```
! LaTeX Error:
  \begin{center} on input line 6 ended by \end{centre}.

See the LaTeX manual or LaTeX Companion for explanation.
Type  H <return>  for immediate help.
 ...
l.25 \end{centre}
```

If you now type a letter e in response to the prompt, you should find yourself in
a text editor with the cursor positioned at the start of the line which caused the
problem. You can also type h in response to the prompt and then LaTeX or TeX will
usually give you additional information about what went wrong. Sometimes you may
experience difficulties in exiting LaTeX; in this case inputting i\stop in response to
the prompt should get you out. To illustrate another LaTeX error message change the
\begin{center} command to \begin{centre} and try processing your file again; you
should get something like this:

```
! LaTeX Error: Environment centre undefined.

See the LaTeX manual or LaTeX Companion for explanation.
Type  H <return>  for immediate help.
 ...
l.6 \begin{centre}
```

It is best to deal with errors one at a time as LaTeX and TeX errors have a tendency
to cause further errors which might disappear when the first error is corrected.

D.3   TeX Error Messages

In order to see what a TeX error message looks like change \begin{centre} into
\begin{center} and \end{centre} into \end{center without a final closing right
brace. If you process your file now, you will get the following error message:

```
Runaway argument?
{center \end {document}
! Paragraph ended before \end was complete.
<to be read again>
                    \par
l.27
```

Sometimes it is difficult to track down the source of this error message and you may
need to use the technique described in section D.6 below in order to find out what
caused this Runaway argument? error message.

D.4 LATEX Warning Messages

An example of a LATEX warning message that occurs very frequently when you use the
\label, \ref and \pageref commands is the following:

```
LaTeX Warning: Label(s) may have changed.
Rerun to get cross-references right on input line 20.
```

Fortunately, the problem that caused this message is very easy to deal with. All you
need to do is to process your file again.

D.5 TEX Warning Messages

Something that happens a lot when TEX is processing an input file is to get an Overfull
\hbox warning message. This sort of message looks something like this:

```
Overfull \hbox (6.54004pt too wide) in paragraph at lines 17--26
\OT1/cmr/m/n/10.95 sev-eral semi-military and re-li-gious
or-ders of knights then in existence---
```

This message tells you that while processing the paragraph that occupies lines 17 to
26 of your input file TEX was unable to properly right-justify the output and a bit of
text sticks out into the right-hand margin a distance of 6.54004 points (that is about a
tenth of an inch as 1 inch = 72.27 points). The command \OT1/cmr/m/n/10.95 tells
you that TEX is producing (roughly) 11 point roman type and what follows this is the
actual line whose end juts out into the right-hand margin. The single hyphens in this
are the places where TEX can hyphenate a word. The way to understand something like
\OT1/cmr/m/n/10.95 is to recall that a font in LATEX has three attributes in addition
to its size. The component cmr tells you the family that the type being used belongs to;
in this case it is Computer Modern Roman. The component m tells you the series the
type being used belongs to; in this case it is medium. The component n tells you the
shape of the type being used; in this case it is upright. The final component, namely
10.95, tells you the size of type being used. The component OT1 tells you the encoding
that is being used; in this case it indicates Donald Knuth's TEX text encoding. (The
letter O stands for 'obsolete'!) The general format of such commands is:

\encoding/family/series/shape/size

The correspondence between the letters used in such commands and the declarations
discussed in chapter 3 is given in the following table:

family		*series*		*shape*	
cmr	\rmfamily	bx	\bfseries	it	\itshape
cmss	\sffamily	m	\mdseries	sc	\scshape
cmtt	\ttfamily			sl	\slshape
				n	\upshape

By default, LaTeX uses the Computer Modern fonts designed by Donald Knuth. Thus, cmr stands for Computer Modern Roman, cmss for Computer Modern Sans Serif and cmtt for Computer Modern Typewriter. If you use some other collection of fonts, say, by loading the times package, then you will get other combinations of letters. More information can be found, for example, in section 8.5 of Kopka and Daly (1995), pp. 224–237.

D.6   When all else Fails

Sometimes you get an error or warning message the source of which is very difficult to track down. For example, it is often difficult to find the mistake that causes a TeX warning message such as:

```
(\end occurred inside a group at level 1)
```

Knowing that it was probably caused by a missing right brace does not often help you to track down the unmatched left brace. The best thing to do in such a case is to split your input file into two and process each half separately in order to see in which part of the file the error is in. (You cannot just split your input file into two; in the first part you need to include an \end{document} command and in the second part you need to include a \documentclass command, a preamble and a \begin{document} command.) If you have done this and still cannot find the error, then split the offending part into two again and carry on until the error can easily be located.

Appendix E

Differences

E.1 Introduction

In this appendix I explain the main differences between the old and new versions
of LaTeX. The most important difference is in the command that determines the
style or class of document that is going to be produced. Every LaTeX 2.09 input file
contains a \documentstyle command, whereas every LaTeX 2ε input file contains a
\documentclass command. The general formats of these two commands are:

> \documentstyle[*opt-list*]{*doc-style*}
> \documentclass[*opt-list*]{*doc-class*}[*date*]

(If the optional argument *date* is included, then you will get a warning message if
the release date of the document class you request is earlier than the one specified.)
LaTeX 2.09's document styles are replaced in LaTeX 2ε with document classes and there
are five standard ones of these, namely article, report, book, letter and slides.
In LaTeX 2.09 slides were produced with the help of a separate program called SLiTeX;
this is no longer the case in LaTeX 2ε.

In the \documentstyle command the optional argument *opt-list* contains a list
of options and/or base names of style files. For example, *opt-list* could contain the
option leqno. Normally, LaTeX puts equation numbers on the right-hand side of the
page, but if you choose the leqno document-style option, then LaTeX puts equation
numbers on the left-hand side of the page. But *opt-list* could also contain the name
of a style file, that is to say, a file consisting of a collection of macros for some specific
typesetting purpose. These two very different kinds of 'option' are clearly separated
in LaTeX 2ε. Style files are there renamed *packages* and a new command is used to
load them, namely \usepackage. For example, the following command could occur in
a LaTeX 2.09 input file:

> \documentstyle[twoside,11pt,makeidx,harvard]{report}

In LaTeX 2ε this would have to be replaced by:

> \documentclass[twoside,11pt]{report}
> \usepackage{makeidx,harvard}

If you make such changes to a LaTeX 2.09 input file, then it is very likely that it will be processed successfully by LaTeX 2ε. At worst, there will only be a handful of errors or warnings. Very few LaTeX 2.09 commands are unavailable in LaTeX 2ε, but LaTeX 2ε has a large number of new commands. (In fact, the only commands unknown to LaTeX 2ε are \documentstyle and \load.)

The \usepackage command itself can have options and any options given to the \documentclass command are passed on as options to any included packages. There are several new options available in LaTeX 2ε, but all the LaTeX 2.09 document-style options continue to work. The new options are 10pt, a4paper, a5paper, b5paper, executivepaper, legalpaper, letterpaper, final, landscape, oneside, openany, openright, notitlepage, onecolumn and clock (which only makes sense if you choose the slides document class). The provision of options like 10pt, letterpaper, final and onecolumn marks a feature of LaTeX 2ε which is that, if an optional argument has a default value, usually a value for that default is provided. For example, by default documents in LaTeX are typeset in 10 point type and in a single column, so the following two commands are fully equivalent:

```
\documentclass{report}
\documentclass[10pt,onecolumn]{report}
```

The latter, however, makes the type-size and the number of columns fully explicit.

E.2   Type-changing Declaration

One of the biggest changes between LaTeX 2.09 and LaTeX 2ε is the introduction of a large number of commands dealing with the way in which a font is chosen. In LaTeX 2ε a type style is seen as having three attributes, in addition to its size, namely its series, family and shape. Each attribute of a font can be altered independently of the others. The following local declarations are new to LaTeX 2ε: \bfseries, \mdseries, \rmfamily, \sffamily, \ttfamily, \itshape, \scshape, \slshape and \upshape. Corresponding to these declarations new commands have been introduced (each of which takes a single argument): \textbf, \textmd, \textrm, \textsf, \texttt, \textit, \textsc, \textsl and \textup. For example, \textbf{*text*} produces *text* in bold, but the family and shape of the type produced is determined by the context in which this command occurs. You can also use {\bfseries *text*} to produce *text* in bold. One advantage of using the parameterized commands over the declarations is that you do not have to worry about italic correction. LaTeX 2ε also contains the local declaration \normalfont and the command \textnormal; these produce output using the main text font of your document. The command \emph has also been added to correspond to the declaration \em.

The LaTeX 2.09 local declarations \bf, \rm, \sf, \tt, \it, \sc and \sl are still available in LaTeX 2ε, but their use is not encouraged. In both text modes the relation between the old and new declarations is shown in the following table:

```
\bf   \normalfont\bfseries
\it   \normalfont\itshape
\rm   \normalfont\rmfamily
\sc   \normalfont\scshape
\sf   \normalfont\sffamily
\sl   \normalfont\slshape
\tt   \normalfont\ttfamily
```

In LaTeX 2.09 the declarations \bf, \rm, \sf, \tt and \it could also be used in maths mode; they still can in LaTeX 2_ε, but it is much better to use the following new commands (each of which takes a single argument): \mathbf, \mathrm, \mathsf, \mathtt and \mathit.

LaTeX 2.09 had the strange feature that the declarations which were used to alter the size of type, like \LARGE, also selected the roman style of type; this is no longer the case. This means that \LARGE\bfseries and \bfseries\LARGE, for example, have exactly the same effect.

E.3   Increased Functionality

The functionality of the commands \newcommand and \renewcommand has been increased so that it is possible to define commands that can take a single optional argument and the command \providecommand has been added which does nothing if the command it is trying to define already exists but defines it if it does not exist. The three new commands \newcommand*, \renewcommand* and \providecommand* have been added; these are like the unstarred versions except that any arguments they take cannot contain any commands that start a new paragraph.

The functionality of the commands \newenvironment and \renewenvironment has been increased so that it is possible to define environments that can take a single optional argument and the new commands \newenvironment* and \renewenvironment* are available for defining environments which take arguments which do not contain any commands that start a new paragraph.

Quite a few improvements have been made to LaTeX's abilities to produce boxes. The general formats of the \framebox, \makebox and \savebox commands that are used outside the picture environment are as follows:

\framebox[*len*][*pos*]{*text*}
\makebox[*len*][*pos*]{*text*}
\savebox[*len*][*pos*]{*text*}

The entirely new commands \depth, \height, \totalheight and \width can occur in the *len* argument of these commands. (They can also occur in any of the length arguments of the \raisebox command.) In addition to the values l and r the *pos* argument can now take the values c and s; the value c just marks the default placement of the *text* argument (it is centred in the box produced) and the s argument stretches or shrinks any rubber space in *text* so that it exactly fills the box produced.

The values that the optional *pos* argument can take in the commands \framebox, \makebox, \savebox and \dashbox when they are used inside the `picture` environment have been extended. These commands have the following general formats:

> \framebox(*i,j*)[*pos*]{*picture-object*}
> \makebox(*i,j*)[*pos*]{*picture-object*}
> \savebox{*cmd*}(*i,j*)[*pos*]{*picture-object*}
> \dashbox{*h*}(*i,j*)[*pos*]{*picture-object*}

The *pos* argument can now take any of the values b, c, l, r, s and t or it can consist of two letters: one drawn from the set consisting of b, c and t and the other drawn from the set consisting of c, l, r and s.

The \parbox command and the `minipage` environment have been considerably improved. The general formats of these in LaTeX 2_ε are as follows:

> \parbox[*pos$_1$*][*len$_2$*][*pos$_2$*]{*len$_1$*}{*text*}
> \begin{minipage}[*pos$_1$*][*len$_2$*][*pos$_2$*]{*len$_1$*}   *text*   \end{minipage}

The arguments *len$_1$* and *pos$_1$* have the same meaning that they had in LaTeX 2.09 except that *pos$_1$* can take the additional values c and s; the new optional arguments *len$_2$* and *pos$_2$* relate to the height of the box produced. (The entirely new commands \depth, \height, \totalheight and \width can occur in *len$_2$*.)

The new environment `lrbox` is available in LaTeX 2_ε for putting a box into a storage bin and the commands \settodepth and \settoheight have been added to complement \settowidth.

The effect of the local declaration \boldmath has been extended in LaTeX 2_ε and the declarations \cal and \mit have been replaced with the commands \mathcal and \mathit, respectively. To help in the definition of commands that you may want to use in maths mode as well as in both text modes the command \ensuremath has been provided.

E.4   Entirely New Commands

The rigid length parameters \columnwidth, \paperheight and \paperwidth have been added in LaTeX 2_ε as have the \enlargethispage and \enlargethispage* commands; these latter two are useful when you are near to completing your document.

Several new commands have been added to LaTeX 2_ε in order to produce a number of symbols. All these symbols could be produced in other ways in LaTeX 2.09, but some could only be produced in maths mode and the others were not produced by means of an explicit command. The commands in question are shown in the following table:

\textbullet	\textperiodcentered	\textquoteleft
\textemdash	\textquestiondown	\textquoteright
\textendash	\textquotedblleft	\textvisiblespace.
\textexclamdown	\textquotedblright	

The new command \r produces a circle accent and \SS produces 'SS'. The command \textcircled puts its one argument in a little circle and \textsuperscript can be used to produce a superscript in a text font rather than a maths font. The command \textcompwordmark can be used to prevent a ligature being produced.

In the course of processing an input file LaTeX can produce a number of headings (and other phrases) automatically. For example, if you use the abstract environment, LaTeX automatically generates the heading 'Abstract'. In LaTeX 2_ε it is possible to alter the words and phrases that are thus generated. The following new commands have been introduced to enable this to be done:

\abstractname	\contentsname	\listtablename
\appendixname	\enclname	\partname
\bibname	\figurename	\refname
\ccname	\indexname	\tablename
\chaptername	\listfigurename	

LaTeX 2_ε provides a number of features to improve the placement and appearance of floats. The character ! can now appear in the optional *pos* argument of the figure, figure*, table and table* environments. This instructs LaTeX to place the float as close as it can be to the place where the environment that produced it occurs (but taking other components of the *pos* argument into account). The \suppressfloats command has also been added to help in the placement of floats. The commands \botfigrule, \dblfigrule and \topfigrule can be defined in order to place a rule, say, either below or above a float.

If you use the book document class, then LaTeX 2_ε provides the three commands \frontmatter, \mainmatter and \backmatter to help in the large-scale organization of your document.

In LaTeX 2.09 you could produce Bézier curves in the picture environment only if you used the bezier style file; basic LaTeX 2_ε provides the commands \bezier, \qbezier and \qbeziermax for use in the picture environment.

If you wanted to produce slides using LaTeX 2.09, then you had to use a special version of it called SLiTeX; but the production of slides has been incorporated into basic LaTeX 2_ε. You need to choose the slides document class and then you can use the slide, overlay and note environments in order to produce slides, overlays and notes to yourself. The following commands are also provided: \invisible, \visible, \onlyslides and \onlynotes. If you use the clock document-class option, then you can also use the \settime and \addtime commands.

To help you send LaTeX input files to other people LaTeX 2_ε provides the environments filecontents and filecontents*; these can be used to include any packages you use. The new command \listfiles can be used to inform you of what files are used in the processing of your input file. The command \NeedsTeXFormat can be used to emphasize the fact that your file is a LaTeX 2_ε input file and the command \LaTeXe produces the logo 'LaTeX 2_ε'.

Bibliography

Amis, M. (1985). *Money: A Suicide Note*, Penguin, Harmondsworth (Middlesex).

Barendregt, H. P. (1992). Lambda calculi with types, *in* S. Abramsky, D. M. Gabbay and T. S. E. Maibaum (eds), *Handbook of Logic in Computer Science, volume II, Background: Computational Structures*, Oxford University Press, Oxford, pp. 117–309.

Barnard, T. and Neill, H. (1996). *Mathematical Groups*, Teach Yourself Books, Hodder Headline, London.

Benson, D. J. (1991). *Representations and Cohomology: Basic Representation Theory of Finite Groups and Associative Algebras*, Vol. 1, Cambridge University Press, Cambridge. Cambridge Studies in Advanced Mathematics, vol. 30. Editorial board: D. J. H. Garling, D. Gorenstein, T. tom Dieck and P. Walters.

Bird, R. (1988). Lectures on constructive functional programming, *Technical Monograph PRG-69*, Programming Research Group, Oxford University Computing Laboratory.

Borde, A. (1992). *TEX by Example: A Beginner's Guide*, Academic Press, London.

Bride, M. (1995). *The Internet*, Teach Yourself Books, Hodder Headline, London.

Butkovskiy, A. G. (1982). *Green's Functions and Transfer Functions Handbook*, Ellis Horwood, Chichester. Translated from the Russian by L. W. Longdon.

Carroll, N. (1988). *Mystifying Movies: Fads and Fallacies in Contemporary Film Theory*, Columbia University Press, New York.

Carroll, N. (1990). *The Philosophy of Horror or Paradoxes of the Heart*, Routledge, New York and London.

Collin, P. H. (1997). *Dictionary of Printing and Publishing*, second edn, Peter Collin Publishing, Teddington (Middlesex).

Diller, A. (1988). *Compiling Functional Languages*, Wiley, Chichester.

Diller, A. (1990). *Z: An Introduction to Formal Methods*, first edn, Wiley, Chichester.

279

Diller, A. (1993). *LaTeX Line by Line: Tips and Techniques for Document Processing*, John Wiley & Sons, Chichester.

Dummett, M. (1977). *Elements of Intuitionism*, Oxford Logic Guides, general editor: Dana Scott, Oxford University Press, Oxford.

Eijkhout, V. (1992). *TeX by Topic: A TeXnician's Reference*, Addison-Wesley, Wokingham (England).

Euclid (1956). *The Thirteen Books of Euclid's Elements*, Vol. I, Introduction and Books I, II, second edn, Dover Publications, New York. Translated from the text of Heiberg with introduction and commentary by Sir Thomas L. Heath. Originally written about 300 BC.

Frege, G. (1980). *Philosophical and Mathematical Correspondence*, Basil Blackwell, Oxford. Edited by Gottfried Gabriel, Hans Hermes, Friedrich Kambartel, Christian Thiel and Albert Veraart. Abridged for the English edition by Brian McGuinness and translated by Hans Kaal.

Goossens, M., Mittelbach, F. and Samarin, A. (1994). *The LaTeX Companion*, Addison-Wesley, Wokingham (England).

Goossens, M., Rahtz, S. and Mittelbach, F. (1997). *The LaTeX Graphics Companion*, Addison Wesley Longman, Wokingham (England).

Grätzer, G. (1996). *Math into LaTeX: An Introduction to LaTeX and AMS-LaTeX*, Birkhäuser, Boston, Basel, Berlin.

Hart, H. (1983). *Hart's Rules for Compositors and Readers at the University Press Oxford*, 39th edn, Oxford University Press, Oxford. First published in 1893.

Heath, S. (1981). *Questions of Cinema*, Indiana University Press, Bloomington.

Hindley, J. R. and Seldin, J. P. (1986). *Introduction to Combinators and λ-calculus*, Cambridge University Press, Cambridge. London Mathematical Society Student Texts, vol. 1.

Hofstadter, D. R. (1979). *Gödel, Escher, Bach: An Eternal Golden Braid*, The Harvester Press, Hassocks (Sussex). Harvester Studies in Cognitive Science; general editor Margaret A. Boden.

Isaacs, A., Daintith, J. and Martin, E. (eds) (1991). *The Oxford Dictionary for Scientific Writers and Editors*, Oxford University Press, Oxford.

Knuth, D. E. (1986a). *The TeXbook*, Addison-Wesley, Wokingham (England).

Knuth, D. E. (1986b). *TeX: The Program*, Addison-Wesley, Wokingham (England).

Kopka, H. and Daly, P. W. (1995). *A Guide to LaTeX 2ε: Document Preparation for Beginners and Advanced Users*, second edn, Addison-Wesley, Harlow.

Krieger, J. and Schwarz, N. (1989). *Introduction to TEX*, Addison-Wesley, Wokingham (England).

Lamport, L. (1986). *LATEX: A Document Preparation System*, Addison-Wesley, Wokingham (England).

Lamport, L. (1994). *LATEX: A Document Preparation System: User's Guide and Reference Manual*, second edn, Addison-Wesley, Wokingham (England).

Lemmon, E. J. (1965). *Beginning Logic*, Nelson, London.

Littlewood, J. E. (1986). *Littlewood's Miscellany*, Cambridge University Press, Cambridge. Edited by B. Bollobás.

MacLane, S. and Birkhoff, G. (1967). *Algebra*, Collier–Macmillan, London.

MacLennan, B. J. (1987). *Principles of Programming Languages: Design, Evaluation, and Interpretation*, second edn, Holt, Rinehart and Winston, New York.

Morgan, C. and Sanders, J. W. (1989). Laws of the logical calculi, *Technical Monograph PRG–78*, Programming Research Group, Oxford University Computing Laboratory.

Munkres, J. R. (1991). *Analysis on Manifolds*, Addison-Wesley, Redwood City (California). This book was prepared using the TEX typesetting language.

Ore, O. (1988). *Number Theory and its History*, Dover, New York. First published in 1948.

Patterson, E. M. and Rutherford, D. E. (1965). *Elementary Abstract Algebra*, University Mathematical Texts (edited by Alexander C. Aitken and Daniel E. Rutherford), Oliver and Boyd, Edinburgh and Oxford.

Popper, K. R. (1975). *Objective Knowledge: An Evolutionary Approach*, Oxford University Press, London. Originally published in 1972.

Prawitz, D. (1965). *Natural Deduction: A Proof-theoretical Study*, Almqvist and Wiksell, Stockholm. Acta Universitatis Stockholmiensis; Stockholm Studies in Philosophy 3.

Quine, W. V. (1981). *Theories and Things*, Harvard University Press, Cambridge (Massachusetts) and London (England).

Quirk, R., Greenbaum, S., Leech, G. and Svartvik, J. (1985). *A Comprehensive Grammar of the English Language*, Longman, London and New York.

Spivak, M. (1986). *The Joy of TEX: A Gourmet Guide to Typesetting with the AMS-TEX Macro Package*, American Mathematical Society, Providence (Rhode Island).

Whitehead, G. W. (1978). *Elements of Homotopy Theory*, Springer-Verlag, New York.

Index

\␣, 28
! float placement, 59, 277
! (ordinary symbol), 161
!', 22
\", 21
special character, 9
\# (ordinary symbol), 54, 161
$ special character, 9, 10, 15, 106
\$, 10
\$ (ordinary symbol), 161
% special character, 9
\% (ordinary symbol), 161
& special character, 9, 10, 53
\&, 10
\& (ordinary symbol), 161
\', 21, 64
((opening symbol), 108, 111, 169
\(, 15
) (closing symbol), 108, 111, 169
\), 15
* (binary operator), 164
*-expression, 53, 120
+ (binary operator), 164
\+, 64
\,, 27, 28, 108
- (binary operator), 164
\-, 19, 64
. (ordinary symbol), 161
\., 21
/ (ordinary symbol), 110–112, 136, 161
\/, 8, 10, 11, 23, 25, 34
: (relation symbol), 114, 165, 170
\:, 124, 164
\;, 164
< (relation symbol), 115, 165, 166
= (relation symbol), 165, 167

\=, 21, 63, 65
> (relation symbol), 115, 164, 165, 167
\>, 63–65
? (ordinary symbol), 161
?', 22
@, 17
@ (ordinary symbol), 161
@-expression, 53, 55, 120, 124, 125
\@, 28
@AAA, 140
@VVV, 140
@(((, 139
@))), 139
@., 139
@<<<, 139
@=, 140
@>>>, 140
@\vert, 140
@|, 140
@article (BIBTEX), 68, 72
@booklet (BIBTEX), 68, 72
@book (BIBTEX), 67, 68, 70, 72, 73
@conference (BIBTEX), 68, 72, 73
@inbook (BIBTEX), 68, 72, 73
@incollection (BIBTEX), 68, 70, 72, 73
@inproceedings (BIBTEX), 68, 72, 73
@listi, 44
@listii, 44
@listiii, 44
@listiv, 44
@listv, 44
@listvi, 44
@manual (BIBTEX), 68, 72
@mastersthesis (BIBTEX), 68, 72
@misc (BIBTEX), 68, 72

@phdthesis (BIBTEX), 68, 72
@proceedings (BIBTEX), 68, 72, 73
@string (BIBTEX), 75
@techreport (BIBTEX), 68, 72
@unpublished (BIBTEX), 68, 72
[, 13
[(opening symbol), 169
\[, 15, 101, 106, 108, 111
\ special character, 9
\\, 33, 34, 53, 63–65, 85, 97, 119, 125, 130
], 13
] (closing symbol), 169
\], 15, 101, 106, 108, 111
^ special character, 9, 101, 104–106
\^, 21
_ special character, 9, 104–106
_ (ordinary symbol), 161
\', 21, 65
{ special character, 9, 13
\{ (opening symbol), 108, 111, 169
|, 53, 109, 114, 120
| (ordinary symbol), 161
\| (ordinary symbol), 115, 161
} special character, 9, 13
\} (closing symbol), 108, 111, 169
~ special character, 9, 28, 37
\~, 21
10pt document-class option, 13, 83, 89, 94, 95, 274
11pt document-class option, 8, 12, 83, 89, 94, 95, 273
11pt document-style option, 273
12pt document-class option, 13, 83, 89, 94, 95

\a', 65
\a=, 63
\a', 65
a4paper document-class option, 13, 83, 89, 94, 95, 98, 274
a5paper document-class option, 13, 83, 89, 94, 95, 98, 274
\aa, 22
\AA, 22

abbrv \bibliographystyle option, 76
\abovedisplayshortskip rubber length parameter, 172, 185
\abovedisplayskip rubber length parameter, 107, 108, 172, 185
abstract environment, 84, 85, 89, 173, 277
abstraction
    bracket, 130
    principle, ix, 138
\abstractname, 277
accents, 63, 65
    mathematical, 102
    text, 21
\acute, 102
acute accent, 21, 65, 102
\addcontentsline, 87, 93
address (BIBTEX), 67, 69, 72
address label, 98
\address, 97
\addtime, 99, 277
\addtocounter global declaration, 187
\addtolength, 25, 26, 45, 107, 155, 172
\ae, 22
\AE, 22
agsm
    \bibliographystyle option, 77, 78
    \citationstyle option, 78
\aleph (ordinary symbol), 161
Alice in Wonderland, 3, 25
align environment, 130
align* environment, 130–133, 135
\allelim (Diller), 123, 124
\allint (Diller), 123, 124
alph, 93
\alph, 174
Alph, 93
\Alph, 174
alpha \bibliographystyle option, 76, 77
\alpha (ordinary symbol), 53, 119, 158
alphabet
    Euler Fraktur, 159
    Euler Script, 159

\amalg (binary operator), 164
American Mathematical Society, 2, 101
Amis, Martin, 26
ampersand, 53, 119
AMS, 2, 101
amscd package, 129, 138–142
amsfonts package, 159
amsmath package, 104, 112, 120, 125, 129–138, 159, 162
amsopn package, 163
amssymb package, x, 113, 126, 129, 159, 161, 164–166, 168, 169
amstex package, 129
amstext package, 134
and (BibTeX), 74
and others (BibTeX), 74
\and, 85
angle brackets, 108
\angle (ordinary symbol), 161
annote (BibTeX), 69, 72
\appendix, 87, 90, 95
\appendixname, 277
\approx (relation symbol), 165
\approxeq (relation symbol), 165
apr (BibTeX), 71
arabic, 93
\arabic, 45, 174
\arccos (log-like operator), 163
\arcsin (log-like operator), 163
\arctan (log-like operator), 163
\arg (log-like operator), 163
argument
    mandatory, 13
    moving, 174
    optional, 13
    runaway
        error message, 270
array environment, 11, 58, 110, 111, 117–125, 142, 173
\arraycolsep rigid length parameter, 118, 120, 172
\arrayrulewidth rigid length parameter, 53, 118, 172
\arraystretch, 57, 58, 118

arrows, 150, 151
    extensible, 103
\arrowvert, 109, 111
\Arrowvert, 109, 111
article document class, 8, 12, 13, 16, 22, 29, 40, 79, 83–88, 273
article document style, 273
article.cls, 18
assignment, to length command, 172
\ast (binary operator), 36, 121, 164
asterisk prompt, 269
\asymp (relation symbol), 165
aug (BibTeX), 71
author (BibTeX), 67, 69, 72–74
\author, 8, 13, 85, 94
author–date system of references, 77
aux file, 8, 92, 174
auxiliary file, 8, 174
axiom, 41
axis, 117

b (bottom)
    float placement, 59
    oval-part specifier, 152
    positioning option, 52, 53, 118, 145, 146, 276
\b, 21
b5paper document-class option, 13, 83, 89, 94, 95, 98, 274
Bézier curves, 155–156, 277
\backepsilon (relation symbol), 165
\backmatter, 95, 277
\backprime (ordinary symbol), 161
\backsim (relation symbol), 165
\backsimeq (relation symbol), 165
\backslash (ordinary symbol), 10, 110, 111, 114, 161
\balls (Diller), 153, 154
\bar, 102
bar accent, 102
bar-under accent, 21
\barwedge (binary operator), 164
base line, 25
base name, 7

\baselineskip rubber length parameter, 25, 131, 134, 172

basic LaTeX, viii

\batchmode, 12

\Bbbk (ordinary symbol), 161

bbl file, 74

\because (relation symbol), 165

\begin, 10, 11

\belowdisplayshortskip rubber length parameter, 172, 185

\belowdisplayskip rubber length parameter, 172, 185

\beta (ordinary symbol), 119, 126, 158

\beth (ordinary symbol), 161

\between (relation symbol), 165

\bezier, 144, 156, 277

bezier style file, 277

\bf, 24, 274, 275

\bfseries, 22, 24, 36, 57, 271, 274, 275

bib file, 67, 75

\bibindent rigid length parameter, 172

\bibitem, 39–41

Biblical references, 28

bibliography, 40, 84

\bibliography, 75, 76, 78, 84, 94

\bibliographystyle, 75–78, 84, 94

\bibname, 40, 277

BibTeX, vii, 67–78, 84

bibtex operating system command, 77

\big, 110, 162, 169

\Big, 110, 162

big point, 171

\bigcap (large operator), 162

\bigcirc (binary operator), 164

\bigcup (large operator), 162

\bigg, 111, 112, 162

\Bigg, 111, 162

\biggl, 111, 170

\Biggl, 111, 170

\biggm, 111, 169

\Biggm, 111, 169

\biggr, 111, 170

\Biggr, 111, 170

\bigl, 110, 170

\Bigl, 110, 170

\bigm, 110, 169

\Bigm, 110, 169

\bigodot (large operator), 162

\bigoplus (large operator), 162

\bigotimes (large operator), 162

\bigr, 110, 170

\Bigr, 110, 170

\bigsqcup (large operator), 162

\bigstar (ordinary symbol), 161

\bigtriangledown (binary operator), 164

\bigtriangleup (binary operator), 164

\biguplus (large operator), 162

\bigvee (large operator), 162

\bigwedge (large operator), 162

bin, storage, 50, 153

binary operator, 113, 157, 164

binary relation symbol, 113, 157, 165–169

\binom, 137

binomial coefficient, 137

bjps (Diller), 75

blackboard bold letters, 159

\blacklozenge (ordinary symbol), 161

\blacksquare (ordinary symbol), 161

\blacktriangle (ordinary symbol), 161

\blacktriangledown (ordinary symbol), 161

\blacktriangleleft (relation symbol), 165

\blacktriangleright (relation symbol), 165

blank line, 7, 14

\bmod (binary operator), 105, 164

body of page, 16, 260

bold series, 22, 23, 271

\boldmath, 276

book document class, 12, 22, 29, 40, 79, 94–95, 174, 273, 277

book document style, 273

booktitle (BibTeX), 69, 72

\bot (ordinary symbol), 115, 161

\botfigrule, 277

\bottomfraction, 61, 62

`bottomnumber` counter, 60, 62, 173
`\bowtie` (relation symbol), 165
box, 15, 49–51, 152–154, 275
`\Box` (ordinary symbol), 161
`\boxdot` (binary operator), 164
`\boxminus` (binary operator), 164
`\boxplus` (binary operator), 164
`\boxtimes` (binary operator), 164
bp (big point), 171
braces, 108
    extensible, 103
    horizontal, 105
    use of, 13
`\bracevert`, 109–111
bracket abstraction, 130
brackets
    angle, 108
    ceiling, 108
    floor, 108
    square, 108
      meaning, 12
`\breve`, 102
breve accent, 21, 102
bridge, *see* contract bridge
`\bullet` (binary operator), 36, 105, 164
`\bumpeq` (relation symbol), 165
`\Bumpeq` (relation symbol), 165
bx (bold series), 271

c (centre) positioning option, 49, 50, 52,
    53, 118, 145, 146, 275, 276
`\c`, 8, 10, 21
`\cal`, 276
calc package, 198
calligraphic letters, 159
`\cap` (binary operator), 164
`\Cap` (binary operator), 164
`\caption`, 59, 60, 174
Carroll, Lewis, 3, 25
Carroll, Noël, 32
cases, definition by, 119, 135
`cases` environment, 120, 135
`\cB` (Diller), 130, 133
cc (cicero), 171
`\cc`, 97, 98

`\cC` (Diller), 130, 133
`\ccname`, 277
CD environment, 138–142
`\cdot` (binary operator), 36, 107, 164
`\cdots`, 119
cedilla accent, 21
ceiling brackets, 108
`center` environment, 31, 34, 35, 44, 51,
    53–55, 60, 143, 155, 173
`\centerdot` (binary operator), 164
`\centering`, 35
centimetre, 171
centring text and boxes, 34
`\cfrac`, 137, 138
chapter (BibTeX), 69, 72, 73
chapter counter, 173
`\chapter` sectioning command, 89, 90
`\chapter*` sectioning command, 93
`\chaptername`, 277
character
    escape, 10
    special, 9
`\check`, 102
check accent, 102
chemical formula, punctuation of, 102
`\chi` (ordinary symbol), 158
Christabel, 33
`\cI` (Diller), 130
cicero, 171
`\circ` (binary operator), 164
`\circeq` (relation symbol), 165
`\circle`, 150, 153
circle accent, 21, 277
`\circle*`, 149
`\circledast` (binary operator), 164
`\circledcirc` (binary operator), 164
`\circleddash` (binary operator), 164
`\circledS` (ordinary symbol), 161
circles, 148, 150
circumflex accent, 21
`\citationstyle`, 78
`\cite`, 40, 41, 67, 69, 75–78, 94
`\citeasnoun`, 78
`\cK` (Diller), 130

`\cleardoublepage`, 62

`\clearpage`, 62, 92

`\cline`, 55, 119, 121, 122

`clock` document-class option, 13, 98, 99, 274, 277

`\closing`, 97

closing symbol, 108, 113, 157, 169–170

`\clubsuit` (ordinary symbol), 161

cm (centimetre), 171

cmr (Computer Modern Roman), 271, 272

cmss (Computer Modern Sans Serif), 271, 272

cmtt (Computer Modern Typewriter), 271, 272

Coleridge, Samuel Taylor, 33

colon, 23, 28

`\colon` (punctuation symbol), 105, 114, 123, 170

`\columnsep` rigid length parameter, 62, 172

`\columnseprule` rigid length parameter, 62, 172

`\columnwidth` rigid length parameter, 62, 172, 276

command

   argument

      mandatory, 13

      optional, 13

      containing @, 17

      fragile, 174, 175

      length, 171, 172

      local

         example of, 56

         scope of, 58

   name

      misspelt error message, 18

   robust, 174, 175

   sectioning, 86

   user-defined, 16

comments in input file, 9

common (Diller), 42–44

common.tex (Diller), 91

commutative diagram, 4, 138

compatibility mode, viii

`\complement` (ordinary symbol), 161

Comprehensive TeX Archive Network, xii

Computer Modern fonts, 171

Computer Modern Roman, 272

Computer Modern Sans Serif, 272

Computer Modern Typewriter, 272

computer program

   formatting of, 65, 122

   punctuation of, 102

`\con` (Diller), 164

`\cond` (Diller), 121

confusables, 114

`\cong` (relation symbol), 165, 167

`\contentsname`, 277

contract bridge diagram, 4, 5, 154, 155

control

   sequence, 10

   symbol, 10

   word, 10

`\coprod` (large operator), 162

corollary, 41

correction, italic, 11, 23, 24

`\cos` (log-like operator), 106, 131, 163

`\cosh` (log-like operator), 131, 163

`\cot` (log-like operator), 163

`\coth` (log-like operator), 163

counter, 37, 173–174

   bottomnumber, 60, 62, 173

   built-in, 173

   chapter, 173

   dbltopnumber, 62, 173

   enumi, 37, 173

   enumii, 37, 173

   enumiii, 37, 173

   enumiv, 37, 173

   equation, 129, 133, 173

   figure, 173

   footnote, 29, 173, 174

   mpfootnote, 29, 173, 174

   page, 80, 173, 174

   paragraph, 173

   part, 173, 174

predefined, 173

secnumdepth, 86, 88, 89, 95, 173, 174

section, 87, 173

subparagraph, 173

subsection, 173

subsubsection, 173

table, 173

tocdepth, 86, 89, 95, 173, 174

topnumber, 60, 62, 173

totalnumber, 61, 62, 173

user-defined, 173

cross-referencing, 174

crossref (BibTeX), 69, 70, 72

\cS (Diller), 130, 133

\csc (log-like operator), 163

CTAN, viii, xii–xiii

\cup (binary operator), 164

\Cup (binary operator), 164

\curlyeqprec (relation symbol), 165

\curlyeqsucc (relation symbol), 165

\curlyvee (binary operator), 164

\curlywedge (binary operator), 164

curves, Bézier, 155–156, 277

\d, 21

\dag (ordinary symbol), 115, 161

\dagger (binary operator), 115, 164

\daleth (ordinary symbol), 161

dash

em, 26

en, 26

\dashbox, 143, 146, 147, 276

\dashv (relation symbol), 165

data00a.tex (Diller), 92, 93

data01a.tex (Diller), 90, 91

data01b.tex (Diller), 91

data06a.tex (Diller), 91, 94

data88a.tex (Diller), 94

data99a.tex (Diller), 94

\date, 13, 85, 94, 97

\dbinom, 137

\dblfigrule, 277

\dblfloatpagefraction, 63

\dblfloatsep rubber length parameter, 63, 172

\dbltextfloatsep rubber length parameter, 63, 172

\dbltopfraction, 62

dbltopnumber counter, 62, 173

dcu

\bibliographystyle option, 77, 78

\citationstyle option, 78

dd (didot point), 171

\dd (Diller), 45

\ddag (ordinary symbol), 115, 161

\ddagger (binary operator), 115, 164

\ddot, 102

\ddots, 119, 138

dec (BibTeX), 71

declaration, 11

global, 11, 17

local, 11, 17

scope, 11

type-changing, 24

type-size, 25

\DeclareMathOperator, 163

\DeclareMathOperator*, 163

definition

by cases, 119, 135

local, 56

definition (Diller), 41–44

\definition (Diller), 41

\deg (log-like operator), 163

delimiters, 108–112

extensible, 109

native size, 109

variable-size, 109

\delta (ordinary symbol), 158

\Delta (ordinary symbol), 158

\depth, 49, 52, 275, 276

description environment, 31, 38, 44, 82, 173

\det (log-like operator), 162

device independent file, 8, 174

\dfrac, 125, 137

diaeresis, 21, 102

\diagdown (ordinary symbol), 161

diagram
    commutative, 4, 138
    contract bridge, 4
\diagup (ordinary symbol), 161
\diamond (binary operator), 164
\Diamond (ordinary symbol), 161
\diamondsuit (ordinary symbol), 161
didot point, 171
\digamma (ordinary symbol), 159
\dim (log-like operator), 163
discretionary hyphen, 19
disks, 148, 150
display style, 15, 104, 113
displayed mathematical formula, 15
\displaylimits, 107, 163
displaymath environment, 15, 173
\displaystyle, 74, 104, 105, 113, 124,
    125, 138
\div (binary operator), 136, 164, 169
\divideontimes (binary operator), 164
document class
    article, 8, 12, 13, 16, 22, 29, 40,
        79, 83–88, 273
    book, 12, 22, 29, 40, 79, 94–95, 174,
        273, 277
    letter, 12, 22, 95–98, 273
    report, 12, 22, 29, 40, 79, 89–94,
        174, 273
    slides, 12, 98–99, 273, 274, 277
    standard, 12
document environment, 8, 10–13, 17, 83,
    173
document style
    article, 273
    book, 273
    letter, 273
    report, 273
document, logical structure, vii
document-class option
    10pt, 13, 83, 89, 94, 95, 274
    11pt, 8, 12, 83, 89, 94, 95, 273
    12pt, 13, 83, 89, 94, 95
    a4paper, 13, 83, 89, 94, 95, 98, 274
    a5paper, 13, 83, 89, 94, 95, 98, 274

b5paper, 13, 83, 89, 94, 95, 98, 274
clock, 13, 98, 99, 274, 277
draft, 13, 83, 89, 94, 95, 98
executivepaper, 13, 83, 89, 94, 95,
    98, 274
final, 13, 83, 89, 94, 95, 98, 274
fleqn, 13, 15, 83, 89, 94, 95, 98
landscape, 13, 83, 89, 94, 95, 98,
    274
legalpaper, 13, 83, 89, 94, 95, 98,
    274
leqno, 13, 83, 89, 94, 95, 98, 127
letterpaper, 13, 45, 83, 89, 94, 95,
    98, 274
notitlepage, 13, 83, 89, 94, 98,
    274
onecolumn, 13, 83, 89, 94, 98, 274
oneside, 13, 83, 89, 94, 95, 274
openany, 13, 89, 94, 274
openbib, 13, 83, 89, 94
openright, 13, 89, 94, 274
titlepage, 13, 83, 85, 86, 89, 94,
    98
twocolumn, 13, 58, 61, 83, 89, 94
twoside, 13, 83, 84, 88, 89, 94, 95,
    273
document-style option
    11pt, 273
    leqno, 273
    twoside, 273
\documentclass, 8, 12, 13, 15, 17, 45,
    83, 273, 274
\documentstyle, 273, 274
dollar sign, 15
\done (Diller), 163
\dot, 102
dot accent, 21, 102
dot-under accent, 21
\doteq (relation symbol), 165
\Doteq (relation symbol), 165
\doteqdot (relation symbol), 165
\dotfill, 49, 207
dotless 'i', 21, 102
dotless 'j', 21, 102

\dotplus (binary operator), 164

double quotation marks, 27

\doublebarwedge (binary operator), 164

\doublerulesep rigid length parameter, 53, 54, 118, 172

\downarrow (relation symbol), 109, 111, 168

\Downarrow (relation symbol), 109, 111, 168

\downbracefill, 207

\downdownarrows (relation symbol), 168

\downharpoonleft (relation symbol), 168

\downharpoonright (relation symbol), 168

draft document-class option, 13, 83, 89, 94, 95, 98

drawing, line, 143

dtx file, xiii

dvi file, 8, 92, 174

dvi2ps operating system command, 9

dvips operating system command, 9

dvitops operating system command, 9

edition (BIBTEX), 69, 72

editor (BIBTEX), 70, 72–74

\eg (Diller), 17

\Eg (Diller), 17

\egarray (Diller), 110

\ell (ordinary symbol), 161

ellipsis, 22

em, 171

em, 25, 65, 171

\em, 24, 274

em-dash, 26

em-rule, 26

emblematic verse, 3

\emph, 24, 274

emphasis, 24

empty group, 27, 160

empty \pagestyle option, 88

\emptyset (ordinary symbol), 161

en-dash, 26

en-rule, 26

\encl, 98

\enclname, 277

encoding, 271

\end, 10, 11

\enlargethispage, 276

\enlargethispage*, 276

\ensuremath, 276

entry (BIBTEX), 67

enumerate environment, 31, 36, 44, 173, 174

enumerated list, 36

enumi counter, 37, 173

enumii counter, 37, 173

enumiii counter, 37, 173

enumiv counter, 37, 173

environment, 10, 17, 173

   abstract, 84, 85, 89, 173, 277

   align, 130

   align*, 130–133, 135

   array, 11, 58, 110, 111, 117–125, 142, 173

   built-in, 173

   cases, 120, 135

   CD, 138–142

   center, 31, 34, 35, 44, 51, 53–55, 60, 143, 155, 173

   definition of, 47

   description, 31, 38, 44, 82, 173

   displaymath, 15, 173

   document, 8, 10–13, 17, 83, 173

   enumerate, 31, 36, 44, 173, 174

   eqnarray, 87, 89, 95, 127, 129, 130, 132, 173, 174

   eqnarray*, 125–127, 129, 130, 132, 173

   equation, 87, 89, 95, 127, 129, 133, 134, 173, 174

   figure, 58–63, 173, 174, 277

   figure*, 58, 173, 174, 277

   filecontents, 12, 173, 277

   filecontents*, 173, 277

   flalign, 131

   flalign*, 131

   flushleft, 31, 34, 35, 44, 173

   flushright, 31, 34, 35, 44, 46, 47, 173

gather, 133, 134
gather*, 133
general form, 11
itemize, 31, 35, 44, 173
letter, 97, 173
list, 31, 44–47, 173
list-like, 31, 52
    vertical space before, 35n
lrbox, 173, 276
math, 15, 173
minipage, 29, 45, 51–52, 107, 173,
    205, 216, 263, 268, 276
note, 98, 173, 277
overlay, 98, 173, 277
picture, x, 13, 14, 49, 143–156,
    173, 276, 277
predefined, 173
quotation, 10, 11, 17, 31, 32, 44,
    173
quote, 31, 32, 44, 66, 173
redefinition of, 47
slide, 98, 173, 277
sloppypar, 173
tabbing, 52, 63–65, 173
table, 58–63, 173, 174, 277
table*, 58, 173, 174, 277
tabular, 11, 52–58, 60, 117, 154,
    173
tabular*, 58, 173
thebibliography, 31, 39–41, 44, 67,
    85, 90, 94, 173
theindex, 79, 82, 173
titlepage, 173
trivlist, 31, 173
verbatim, 65–66, 173
verbatim*, 66, 173
verse, 31, 33, 44, 173
\epsilon (ordinary symbol), 158
\eqcirc (relation symbol), 165
eqnarray environment, 87, 89, 95, 127,
    129, 130, 132, 173, 174
eqnarray* environment, 125–127, 129,
    130, 132, 173
\eqslantgtr (relation symbol), 165

\eqslantless (relation symbol), 165
equation counter, 129, 133, 173
equation environment, 87, 89, 95, 127,
    129, 133, 134, 173, 174
\equiv (relation symbol), 165, 166
error, 269–272
    coping with, 18
    dealing with, 17
error message, 269
    buffer size exceeded, 187
    environment undefined, 270
    LaTeX, 269–270
    misspelt command name, 18
    runaway argument, 270
    TeX, 269–270
\errorstopmode, 12
escape character, 10
escape key, 10
\eta (ordinary symbol), 158
\eth (ordinary symbol), 161
eucal package, 159
Euclid, 41
Euler Fraktur alphabet, 159
Euler Script alphabet, 159
\evensidemargin rigid length parame-
    ter, 16, 83, 172, 260
ex, 171
ex, 171
examples of typesetting
    abstraction algorithm, 130
    article, 9, 14
    Bézier curves, 155, 156
    Biblical references, 28
    bibliography, 39, 40, 76, 78
    bill of materials, 149
    binomial coefficients, 137
    branches of formal methods, 144
    circles, 152
    commutative diagrams, 138–142
    computer program, 65, 122
    continued fraction, 2, 137
    contract bridge diagram, 5, 154
    definition by cases, 119, 135
    delimiters, 110

derivatives, 124, 131

equations, 125, 126, 131, 132

   labelled, 127, 128

float, 60

framed formula, 107

Frege's schema, 4, 141

glossary, 38

graph-reduction, 150

index, 79

letter, 96

limits, 105–107

list

   enumerated, 36, 37

   itemized, 35

logical proof, 120

matrix, 118, 121

minipage, 51

mouse's tale, 3, 25

musical references, 28

non-numerical labels, 133–134

poetry, 33

proclamation, 41–44

quotation, 11, 31–32

   marks, 27–28

set comprehension, 105

standard derivatives, 124

table of information, 52–58, 120

text

   aligned, 63–65

   centred, 34

   explanatory, 134

   framed, 49, 50

   ragged left, 34

   ragged right, 34

exclamation mark, 23, 28, 29

executivepaper document-class option, 13, 83, 89, 94, 95, 98, 274

\exists (ordinary symbol), 36, 54, 161

\exp (log-like operator), 163

extension, file, 7

\fallingdotseq (relation symbol), 165

family, 22, 271, 274

   roman, 22, 23

   sans serif, 22, 23

typewriter, 22, 23

\fbox, 50, 107

\fboxrule rigid length parameter, 49, 107, 172

\fboxsep rigid length parameter, 49, 107, 146, 172

feb (BibTeX), 71

field-name (BibTeX), 69

figure counter, 173

figure environment, 58–63, 173, 174, 277

figure* environment, 58, 173, 174, 277

figured verse, 3

\figurename, 59, 277

file

   aux, 8, 92, 174

   auxiliary, 8, 174

   bbl, 74

   bib, 67, 75

   device independent, 8, 174

   dtx, xiii

   dvi, 8, 92, 174

   extension, 7

   glo, 82, 92

   idx, 80, 82, 92, 174

   ilg, 81

   ind, 81

   input, 7, 83

      general structure, 12

      preamble, 13

   ist, 81

   list, 8

   lis, 8

   lof, 92, 93

   log, 8

   lot, 92, 93

   name, 7

   sty, xiii, 17

   style, viii

   texlog, 8

   tex, 8

   toc, 92, 93

   transcript, 8

   transfer protocol, xiii

`filecontents` environment, 12, 173, 277

`filecontents*` environment, 173, 277

`final` document-class option, 13, 83, 89, 94, 95, 98, 274

`\Finv` (ordinary symbol), 161

`flalign` environment, 131

`flalign*` environment, 131

`\flat` (ordinary symbol), 161

`fleqn` document-class option, 13, 15, 83, 89, 94, 95, 98

float, 58–63

    placement, 59, 173, 277

      !, 59, 277

      b (bottom), 59

      h (here), 59

      p (page), 59

      t (top), 59

`\floatpagefraction`, 61, 62

`\floatsep` rubber length parameter, 61, 63, 172

floor brackets, 108

`\flushbottom`, 84, 89, 94

`flushleft` environment, 31, 34, 35, 44, 173

`flushright` environment, 31, 34, 35, 44, 46, 47, 173

foot of page, 16, 260

`\footheight` rigid length parameter, 172, 260

footnote, 29

    author, 85

    date, 85

    inside `minipage`, 29

    placement of, 16

    title, 85

`\footnote`, 29, 51

footnote counter, 29, 173, 174

`\footnotemark`, 29

`\footnotesep` rigid length parameter, 172

`\footnotesize`, 25

`\footnotetext`, 29

`\footskip` rigid length parameter, 172, 260

`\forall` (ordinary symbol), 36, 54, 161

formula, mathematical, displayed, 15

`\frac`, 101, 106, 107, 109, 112, 125, 131, 136, 137

fractions, 136, 138

fragile command, 174, 175

`\framebox`, 49–51, 143, 145–147, 205, 216, 263, 268, 275, 276

framing formulas, 107

Frege, Gottlob, 4, 141

Frege's schema, ix, 4, 141

`\frenchspacing`, 29

`\frontmatter`, 95, 277

`\frown` (relation symbol), 165

ftp operating system command, xiii

full stop, 23, 28, 29

`\fullstop` (Diller), 170

`\Game` (ordinary symbol), 161

`\gamma` (ordinary symbol), 158

`\Gamma` (ordinary symbol), 158, 159

`gather` environment, 133, 134

`gather*` environment, 133

`\gcd` (log-like operator), 162

`\ge` (relation symbol), 165, 167

`\genfrac`, 136, 137

`\geq` (relation symbol), 119, 165, 167

`\geqq` (relation symbol), 165, 167

`\geqslant` (relation symbol), 165, 167

`\gets` (relation symbol), 168

`\gg` (relation symbol), 165

`\ggg` (relation symbol), 165

`\gggtr` (relation symbol), 165

`\gimel` (ordinary symbol), 161

glo file, 82, 92

global declaration, 11

    `\addtocounter`, 187

    `\hyphenation`, 19

    `\newcounter`, 45, 46, 92, 173

    `\newlength`, 45, 107

    `\newsavebox`, 50, 153

    `\newtheorem`, 31, 41–44, 173

    `\pagenumbering`, 92, 93

    `\setcounter`, 41

    `\thispagestyle`, 88

glossary, 38

\glossary, 82

\glossaryentry, 82

\gnapprox (relation symbol), 167

\gneq (relation symbol), 167

\gneqq (relation symbol), 167

\gnsim (relation symbol), 167

gnus, ix

Gothic letters, 159

\grave, 102

grave accent, 21, 65, 102

group, empty, 27, 160

grouping, 9

\gtrapprox (relation symbol), 165, 167

\gtrdot (relation symbol), 165

\gtreqless (relation symbol), 166

\gtreqqless (relation symbol), 166

\gtrless (relation symbol), 166

\gtrsim (relation symbol), 165, 167

\gvertneqq (relation symbol), 167

h (here) float placement, 59

\H, 21

háček accent, 21

Hallett, Michael, 39

harvard package, 77–78, 273

harvard style file, 273

Harvard system of references, 77

hat, 10

\hat, 102

hat accent, 102

\hbar (ordinary symbol), 161

head of page, 16, 260

head, running, 16, 88

\headheight rigid length parameter, 172, 260

headings \pagestyle option, 88

\headsep rigid length parameter, 172, 260

\heartsuit (ordinary symbol), 161

Heath, Stephen, 32

\height, 49, 52, 275, 276

\hfill, 45, 49, 64

'The Historical Dracula?', 9, 14

\hline, 53–55, 119

\hom (log-like operator), 163

\hookleftarrow (relation symbol), 168

\hookrightarrow (relation symbol), 168

horizontal rules, use of in this book, xii

howpublished (BibTeX), 70, 72

\hrulefill, 49, 207

\hslash (ordinary symbol), 161

\hspace*, 65

\huge, 25

\Huge, 25

Hungarian umlaut, 21

Husserl, Edmund, 4, 141

hyphen, 26

    discretionary, 19, 64

    use of, 27

hyphenation, 19

\hyphenation global declaration, 19

\i, 21

'i', dotless, 21, 102

\ida (Diller), 169

ide.bib (Diller), 69, 70

identifier, multi-letter, 158

idx file, 80, 82, 92, 174

idx.tex, 80

\ie (Diller), 17

\Ie (Diller), 17

iff, 160

ilg file, 81

\Im (ordinary symbol), 161

\imath (ordinary symbol), 102, 161

\implies (Diller), 37, 54, 55

in (inch), 12, 171

\in (relation symbol), 159, 165, 166

in-text mathematical formula, 15

inch, 12, 171

\include, 91

\includeonly, 91–93

ind file, 81

indentation, paragraph, suppression of, 14

index, 79–82

\index, 80–82, 92, 174

\indexentry, 80, 82, 92

\indexname, 79, 277

\indexspace, 79
\inf (log-like operator), 162
\infbar (Diller), 169
\infty (ordinary symbol), 107, 161, 167, 169
\injlim (log-like operator), 162
\input, 91–94
input file, 7, 83
    blank line in, 14
    comments in, 9
    general structure, 12
    preamble, 13
installing LaTeX, viii
institution (BibTeX), 70, 72
\int (large operator), 106, 162
interactive mode, 269
\intercal (binary operator), 164
Internet, xii
\intertext, 135, 137
\intextsep rubber length parameter, 61, 63, 172
\invisible, 98, 277
\iota (ordinary symbol), 158
Isaiah, 28
ist file, 81
it (italic shape), 271
\it, 24, 274, 275
italic
    correction, 11, 23, 24
    shape, 22, 23, 271
\item, 11, 35–38, 44, 45, 79
\itemindent rigid length parameter, 44, 172
itemize environment, 31, 35, 44, 173
itemized list, 35
\itemsep rubber length parameter, 172, 225
\itshape, 8, 11, 22, 24, 25, 34, 60, 271, 274, 275

'j', dotless, 21, 102
\j, 21
jan (BibTeX), 71
Jardine, Douglas, 66
Jensen, Frank, 198

\jmath (ordinary symbol), 102, 161
\Join (relation symbol), 165
journal (BibTeX), 70, 72
jul (BibTeX), 71
jun (BibTeX), 71

\kappa (ordinary symbol), 158
\ker (log-like operator), 163
kerning, 2
key, 40
key (BibTeX), 70, 72
\kill, 63, 65
kluwer \bibliographystyle option, 77, 78
Knuth, Donald, vii, 2, 171, 272

l (left)
    oval-part specifier, 151
    positioning option, 49, 50, 53, 145, 146, 275, 276
\l, 22
\L, 22
label
    address, 98
    inside description, 38
    inside enumerate, 36, 37
    inside itemize, 36
    inside thebibliography, 40
    non-numerical, 133
    out of sequence, 133
\label, 36, 37, 60, 127, 133, 134, 174, 271
label(s) may have changed warning message, 271
\labelitemi, 36
\labelitemii, 36
\labelitemiii, 36
\labelitemiv, 36
labelling mathematical formulas, 127
\labelsep rigid length parameter, 45, 172, 225
\labelwidth rigid length parameter, 44, 45, 172, 225
lablst.tex, 191
Lakatos, Imre, 39

\lambda (ordinary symbol), 119, 126, 158

\Lambda (ordinary symbol), 158

Lamport, Leslie, vii

\land (binary operator), 54, 105, 164

landscape document-class option, 13, 83, 89, 94, 95, 98, 274

\langle (opening symbol), 108, 110, 111, 115, 169

\large, 25

\Large, 25

\LARGE, 25, 275

large operator, 162

LaTeX
  basic, viii
  installation, viii

latex operating system command, 8

\LaTeXe, 277

latexsym package, x, 113, 161, 164, 165, 168, 221

\lbrace (opening symbol), 108, 111, 169

\lbrack (opening symbol), 108, 111, 169

\lceil (opening symbol), 108, 111, 169

\ldots, 22, 32, 34, 122

\le (relation symbol), 107, 108, 165, 166

le Carré, John, 38

\leadsto (relation symbol), 168

\left, 107, 109, 111, 119, 121–123, 142, 168, 169

left-margin-tab, 63

left-to-right mode, 14, 15

\leftarrow (relation symbol), 168

\Leftarrow (relation symbol), 168

\leftarrowfill, 207

\leftarrowtail (relation symbol), 168

\lefteqn, 127

\leftharpoondown (relation symbol), 168

\leftharpoonup (relation symbol), 168

\leftleftarrows (relation symbol), 168

\leftmargin rigid length parameter, 44–47, 172, 225

\leftmargini rigid length parameter, 172

\leftmarginii rigid length parameter, 172

\leftmarginiii rigid length parameter, 172

\leftmarginiv rigid length parameter, 172

\leftmarginv rigid length parameter, 172

\leftmarginvi rigid length parameter, 172

\leftrightarrow (relation symbol), 168

\Leftrightarrow (relation symbol), 168

\leftrightarrows (relation symbol), 168

\leftrightsquigarrow (relation symbol), 168

\leftthreetimes (binary operator), 164

legalpaper document-class option, 13, 83, 89, 94, 95, 98, 274

lemma, 41

length command, 171, 172

length parameter, 171
  rigid, 171
    assignment to, 172
  rubber, 171, 172
    assignment to, 172
    natural space of, 172

length unit, 171
  bp (big point), 171
  cc (cicero), 171
  cm (centimetre), 171
  dd (didot point), 171
  em, 171
  ex, 171
  in (inch), 12, 171
  mm (millimetre), 13, 171
  mu (mathematical unit), 171
  pc (pica), 171
  pt (point), 12, 171
  sp (scaled point), 171

\leq (relation symbol), 165, 166

leqno document-class option, 13, 83, 89, 94, 95, 98, 127

leqno document-style option, 273

\leqq (relation symbol), 165, 166

\leqslant (relation symbol), 165, 166
\lessapprox (relation symbol), 165, 166
\lessdot (relation symbol), 165
\lesseqgtr (relation symbol), 166
\lesseqqgtr (relation symbol), 166
\lessgtr (relation symbol), 166
\lesssim (relation symbol), 165, 166
letter document class, 12, 22, 95–98, 273
letter document style, 273
letter environment, 97, 173
letterpaper document-class option, 13, 45, 83, 89, 94, 95, 98, 274
letters
    blackboard bold, 159
    calligraphic, 159
    Euler Script, 159
    for posting, 95
    Gothic, 159
    Greek, 104, 158
    Roman, 157
level number, 86, 89, 90, 95
\lfloor (opening symbol), 108, 111, 169
\lg (log-like operator), 163
\lgroup, 109
\lhd (binary operator), 164
ligatures, ix, 1
    English, 1
    prevention, 160, 277
    vowel, 2, 21, 22
\lim (log-like operator), 162
\liminf (log-like operator), 162
limits, 105–107
\limits, 106, 163
\limsup (log-like operator), 162
line, 147
    base, 25
    drawing, 143
    vertical, 53
\line, 143, 147, 148, 155
\linebreak, 19
\linethickness, 145
\linewidth rigid length parameter, 172
lis file, 8

list
    enumerated, 36
    itemized, 35
list environment, 31, 44–47, 173
list file, 8
\listfigurename, 277
\listfiles, 277
\listoffigures, 60, 93
\listoftables, 60, 93
\listparindent rigid length parameter, 172, 225
\listtablename, 277
Littlewood, John, 46
\ll (relation symbol), 165
\llcorner (opening symbol), 169
\Lleftarrow (relation symbol), 168
\lll (relation symbol), 165
\llless (relation symbol), 165
\lmoustache, 109, 111
\ln (log-like operator), 163
\lnapprox (relation symbol), 166
\lneg (Diller), 161
\lneq (relation symbol), 166
\lneqq (relation symbol), 166
\lnot (ordinary symbol), 161
\lnsim (relation symbol), 166
\load, 274
local command, 56
local definition, 56
lof file, 92, 93
log file, 8
\log (log-like operator), 163
log-like operator, 162–163
\lone (Diller), 163
\longleftarrow (relation symbol), 168
\Longleftarrow (relation symbol), 168
\longleftrightarrow (relation symbol), 168
\Longleftrightarrow (relation symbol), 168
\longmapsto (relation symbol), 168
\longrightarrow (relation symbol), 168
\Longrightarrow (relation symbol), 168
\lor (binary operator), 36, 37, 54, 164

lot file, 92, 93
\lozenge (ordinary symbol), 161
lpm.tex (Diller), 84
LR mode, 14, 15
lrbox environment, 173
minipage environment, 276
\lrcorner (closing symbol), 169
\ltimes (binary operator), 164
\lvertneqq (relation symbol), 166

m (medium series), 271
macro, 16
macron accent, 21, 63
\mainmatter, 95, 277
\makebox, 50, 51, 143, 145, 147, 155, 205, 216, 263, 268, 275, 276
\makeglossary, 82
makeidx package, 80, 81, 273
makeidx style file, 273
MakeIndex, vii, 80–82
\makeindex, 80, 82, 92, 93, 174
\makelabels, 98
\maketitle, 8, 13, 18, 85, 89, 93
\mapsto (relation symbol), 168
mar (BIBTEX), 71
\marginpar, 61
\marginparpush rigid length parameter, 172
\marginparsep rigid length parameter, 172
\marginparwidth rigid length parameter, 172
\markboth, 88
\markright, 88
math environment, 15, 173
\mathbb, 159, 160
\mathbf, 105, 157, 158, 275
\mathbin, 37, 121, 164
\mathcal, 159, 276
\mathclose, 107, 170
mathematical formula
    displayed, 15
    in-text, 15
    labelling of, 127
    punctuation of, 15, 101

mathematical symbols
    binary operation, 113, 157, 164
    binary relation, 113, 157, 165–169
    bracket-like, 108
    closing, 108, 113, 157, 169–170
    large operator, 162
    log-like, 162–163
    opening, 108, 113, 157, 169–170
    ordinary, 113, 157–162
    punctuation, 157, 170
    unary operation, 113, 157
mathematical unit, 171
mathematics mode, 14
\mathfrak, 159
\mathindent rigid length parameter, 15, 172
\mathit, 53, 104, 157, 158, 275, 276
\mathop, 163
\mathopen, 107, 170
\mathord, 161
\mathpunct, 170
\mathrel, 169
\mathrm, 105, 121, 157, 158, 275
maths mode, 14, 15
    space in, 15
mathscr, 159
\mathscr, 159, 160
\mathsf, 157, 158, 275
\mathstrut, 105
\mathtt, 157, 158, 275
matrix, 118, 121
\max (log-like operator), 162
may (BIBTEX), 71
\mbox, 15, 50, 119, 124, 127
\mdseries, 22, 38, 271, 274
\measuredangle (ordinary symbol), 161
medium series, 22, 23, 271
medium space, 113, 164
message, error, 269
    LATEX, 269–270
    TEX, 269–270
\mho (ordinary symbol), 161
\mid (relation symbol), 105, 108, 113, 114, 165, 167

millimetre, 13, 171

\min (log-like operator), 162

minipage environment, 29, 45, 51–52, 107, 173, 205, 216, 263, 268, 276

minus, 172

minus sign, 26

misspelt command name error message, 18

\mit, 276

\mkern, 164

mm (millimetre), 13, 171

mode
    compatibility, viii
    interactive, 269
    left-to-right, 14, 15
    LR, 14, 15
    maths, 14, 15
        space in, 15
    paragraph, 14
    picture, 14
    processing, 14
    run, 12

\models (relation symbol), 165

month (BIBTEX), 70, 72

mouse's tale, 3, 25

moving argument, 174

\mp (binary operator), 164

mpfootnote counter, 29, 173, 174

mu (mathematical unit), 164, 171

\mu (ordinary symbol), 158

\multicolumn, 53–55, 60, 119, 121, 122

\multimap (relation symbol), 168

\multiput, 144, 152, 153

musical references, 28

myheadings \pagestyle option, 88

n (upright shape), 271

\nabla (ordinary symbol), 161

name
    environment, 11
    file, 7

native size, 109

\natural (ordinary symbol), 161

natural space, 172

\ncong (relation symbol), 167

\ne (relation symbol), 105, 167

\nearrow (relation symbol), 168

\NeedsTeXFormat, 277

\neg (ordinary symbol), 54, 161

\neq (relation symbol), 167

nested quotation marks, 27

\newcommand, 275

\newcommand*, 17, 22, 37, 55, 57, 121–123, 126, 138, 142, 154, 163, 164, 169, 275

\newcounter global declaration, 45, 46, 92, 173

\newenvironment, 47, 173, 275

\newenvironment*, 47, 173, 275

\newlabel, 174

\newlength global declaration, 45, 107

\newpage, 13, 61

\newsavebox global declaration, 50, 153

\newtheorem global declaration, 31, 41–44, 173

\nexists (ordinary symbol), 161

next-tab-stop, 63

\ngeq (relation symbol), 167

\ngeqq (relation symbol), 167

\ngeqslant (relation symbol), 167

\ngtr (relation symbol), 167

\ni (relation symbol), 165

\nleftarrow (relation symbol), 168

\nLeftarrow (relation symbol), 168

\nleftrightarrow (relation symbol), 168

\nLeftrightarrow (relation symbol), 168

\nleq (relation symbol), 166

\nleqq (relation symbol), 166

\nleqslant (relation symbol), 166

\nless (relation symbol), 166

\nmid (relation symbol), 167

\nocite, 75

\nofiles, 80, 92, 93

\noindent, 8, 10, 11, 14, 32, 85, 107

\nolimits, 106, 163

non-numerical labels, 133

\none (Diller), 163

\nonstopmode, 12

\nonumber, 127, 128
\normalfont, 24, 274, 275
\normalsize, 25
\not, 166
notational conventions, xi–xii
note (BibTeX), 67, 71, 72
note environment, 98, 173, 277
\notin (relation symbol), 166
notitlepage document-class option, 13, 83, 89, 94, 98, 274
nov (BibTeX), 71
\nparallel (relation symbol), 166
\nprec (relation symbol), 166
\npreceq (relation symbol), 166
\nrightarrow (relation symbol), 168
\nRightarrow (relation symbol), 168
\nshortmid (relation symbol), 167
\nshortparallel (relation symbol), 166
\nsim (relation symbol), 167
\nsubseteq (relation symbol), 166
\nsubseteqq (relation symbol), 166
\nsucc (relation symbol), 167
\nsucceq (relation symbol), 167
\nsupseteq (relation symbol), 167
\nsupseteqq (relation symbol), 167
\ntriangleleft (relation symbol), 167
\ntrianglelefteq (relation symbol), 167
\ntriangleright (relation symbol), 167
\ntrianglerighteq (relation symbol), 167
\nu (ordinary symbol), 158
number (BibTeX), 71–73
number, level, 86, 89, 90, 95
\nvdash (relation symbol), 166
\nvDash (relation symbol), 166
\nVdash (relation symbol), 167
\nwarrow (relation symbol), 168

\o, 22
\O, 22
oct (BibTeX), 71
\oddsidemargin rigid length parameter, 16, 172, 260
\odot (binary operator), 164
\oe, 22

\OE, 22
\oint (large operator), 162
\omega (ordinary symbol), 53, 158
\Omega (ordinary symbol), 158
omicron, 158
\ominus (binary operator), 164
\Once (Diller), 22, 23, 25
one-sided printing, 83
onecolumn document-class option, 13, 83, 89, 94, 98, 274
\onecolumn, 61
oneside document-class option, 13, 83, 89, 94, 95, 274
\onlynotes, 98, 277
\onlyslides, 98, 277
Open Society and its Enemies, The, 47
openany document-class option, 13, 89, 94, 274
openbib document-class option, 13, 83, 89, 94
\opening, 97
opening symbol, 108, 113, 157, 169–170
openright document-class option, 13, 89, 94, 274
operating system command
    bibtex, 77
    dvi2ps, 9
    dvips, 9
    dvitops, 9
    ftp, xiii
    latex, 8
operator
    binary, 164
    large, 162
    log-like, 162–163
    unary, 162–163
\operatorname, 163
\operatorname*, 163
\oplus (binary operator), 164
ordinary symbol, 113, 157–162
organization (BibTeX), 71, 72
\oslash (binary operator), 164
\OT1/cmr/m/n/10.95, 19, 271
\otimes (binary operator), 164, 169

\oval, 151
oval-part specifier
    b (bottom), 152
    l (left), 151
    r (right), 152
    t (top), 151
ovals, 150, 151
\overbrace, 103, 105
overfull \hbox warning message, 18, 271
overlay environment, 98, 173, 277
\overleftarrow, 103
\overline, 103, 169
overlining, 103
\overrightarrow, 103
own.sty (Diller), 17, 84, 91
\owns (relation symbol), 165

p (page) float placement, 59
p-expression, 57, 58
\P (ordinary symbol), 161
package, viii, 273
    amscd, 129, 138–142
    amsfonts, 159
    amsmath, 104, 112, 120, 125, 129–
        138, 159, 162
    amsopn, 163
    amssymb, x, 113, 126, 129, 159, 161,
        164–166, 168, 169
    amstext, 134
    amstex, 129
    calc, 198
    eucal, 159
    harvard, 77–78, 273
    latexsym, x, 113, 161, 164, 165,
        168, 221
    makeidx, 80, 81, 273
    obtaining, xii–xiii
    own, 17
    proof, xiii
    showlabels, 219, 251
    times, 272
page, appearance, 16, 260
page counter, 80, 173, 174
\pagebreak, 61

\pagenumbering global declaration, 92,
    93
\pageref, 37, 127, 174, 271
pages (BibTeX), 71–73
\pagestyle, 88
\paperheight rigid length parameter,
    172, 276
\paperwidth rigid length parameter, 172,
    276
\par, 14, 25, 35
paragraph
    indentation, 14, 26
        suppression of, 14
    mode, 14
    starting, 7, 14
paragraph counter, 173
\paragraph sectioning command, 86, 90
\parallel (relation symbol), 115, 165,
    166
parameter
    length, 171
        rigid, 171
        rubber, 171, 172
parbox, 51
\parbox, 51–52, 58, 205, 216, 263, 268,
    276
parentheses, 108
\parindent rigid length parameter, 14,
    25, 26, 172, 225
\parsep rubber length parameter, 44,
    172, 225
\parskip rubber length parameter, 14,
    25, 35, 44, 172, 225
part counter, 173, 174
\part sectioning command, 86, 90
\partial (ordinary symbol), 159, 161
\partname, 277
\partopsep rubber length parameter,
    35, 172, 225
Patashnik, Oren, 67
pc (pica), 171
Peirce's law, 36
\perp (relation symbol), 115, 165
\phi (ordinary symbol), 158

\Phi (ordinary symbol), 158
\pi (ordinary symbol), 107, 158
\Pi (ordinary symbol), 158
pica, 171
picture environment, x, 13, 14, 49, 143–156, 173, 276, 277
picture mode, 14
\pitchfork (relation symbol), 165
plain
 \bibliographystyle option, 76
 \pagestyle option, 88
plain TeX, vii
plus, 172
\pm (binary operator), 164
point, 12, 171
 big, 171
 didot, 171
 scaled, 171
pom.bib (Diller), 75, 84
popper (Diller), 47
Popper, Karl, 31, 47
\poptabs, 65
positioning option
 b (bottom), 52, 53, 118, 145, 146, 276
 c (centre), 49, 50, 52, 53, 118, 145, 146, 275, 276
 l (left), 49, 50, 53, 145, 146, 275, 276
 r (right), 49, 50, 53, 145, 146, 275, 276
 s (stretch), 49, 50, 52, 145, 146, 275, 276
 t (top), 52, 53, 118, 145, 146, 276
post (Diller), 42
PostScript, 9
postulate, 41
\Pr (log-like operator), 162
preamble, 53, 83
 array, 119
 input file, 13
 tabular, 119
\prec (relation symbol), 165, 166
\precapprox (relation symbol), 165, 166

\preccurlyeq (relation symbol), 165
\preceq (relation symbol), 165, 166
\precnapprox (relation symbol), 166
\precneqq (relation symbol), 166
\precnsim (relation symbol), 166
\precsim (relation symbol), 165, 166
\prime (ordinary symbol), 161
principle, abstraction, ix, 138
\printindex, 80, 81
printing
 one-sided, 83
 two-sided, 83, 88–89, 94–95, 172, 260, 264
proclamation, 41
\prod (large operator), 162
program, computer, formatting of, 65
\projlim (log-like operator), 162
prologue, 12, 83
prompt
 asterisk, 269
 question mark, 18, 269
 two asterisks, 269
proof, Lemmon-style, 120
proof package, xiii
proof trees, xiii
prop (Diller), 42–44
proposition, 41
\propto (relation symbol), 165
\protect, 175
\providecommand, 275
\providecommand*, 125, 275
\ps, 97, 98
\psi (ordinary symbol), 158
\Psi (ordinary symbol), 158
pt (point), 12, 171
publisher (BibTeX), 67, 71, 72
punctuation
 chemical formula, 102
 computer program, 102
 mathematical formulas, 15, 101
 mathematical symbols, 157, 170
\pushtabs, 65
\put, 143–145, 147, 149, 155

\qbezier, 144, 155, 156, 277

\qbeziermax, 156, 277
\qquad, 107, 124, 127, 170
quad, 113
question mark, 23, 28, 29
question-mark prompt, 18, 269
Quine, Willard Van Orman, 10
quotation, 10, 32
    marks
        double, 27
        nested, 27
        single, 27
        use of, 27, 28
quotation environment, 10, 11, 17, 31,
    32, 44, 173
quote environment, 31, 32, 44, 66, 173

r (right)
    oval-part specifier, 152
    positioning option, 49, 50, 53, 145,
        146, 275, 276
\r, 21, 277
ragged left text, 34
ragged right text, 34
\raggedbottom, 84, 89, 94
\raggedleft, 35
\raggedright, 35
\raisebox, 205, 216, 263, 268, 275
Ramanujan, Srinivasa, ix, 2, 137
\rangle (closing symbol), 108, 110, 111,
    115, 169
\rbrace (closing symbol), 108, 111, 169
\rbrack (closing symbol), 108, 111, 169
\rceil (closing symbol), 108, 111, 169
\Re (ordinary symbol), 161
\ref, 37, 127, 133, 174, 271
references
    Biblical, 28
    musical, 28
\refname, 40, 84, 277
\renewcommand, 275
\renewcommand*, 17, 58, 84, 275
\renewenvironment, 47, 173, 275
\renewenvironment*, 47, 173, 275
report document class, 12, 22, 29, 40,
    79, 89–94, 174, 273

report document style, 273
\rfloor (closing symbol), 108, 111, 169
\rgroup, 109
\rhd (binary operator), 164
\rho (ordinary symbol), 158
\right, 107, 109, 111, 119, 121–123,
    142, 168, 169
\rightarrow (relation symbol), 121, 133,
    168, 170
\Rightarrow (relation symbol), 36, 37,
    126, 168, 169
\rightarrowfill, 207
\rightarrowtail (relation symbol), 168
\rightharpoondown (relation symbol),
    168
\rightharpoonup (relation symbol), 168
\rightleftarrows (relation symbol), 168
\rightleftharpoons (relation symbol),
    168
\rightmargin rigid length parameter,
    46, 47, 172, 225
\rightrightarrows (relation symbol),
    168
\rightsquigarrow (relation symbol), 168
\rightthreetimes (binary operator), 164
rigid length command, 172
rigid length parameter
    \arraycolsep, 118, 120, 172
    \arrayrulewidth, 53, 118, 172
    assignment to, 172
    \bibindent, 172
    \columnseprule, 62, 172
    \columnsep, 62, 172
    \columnwidth, 62, 172, 276
    \doublerulesep, 53, 54, 118, 172
    \evensidemargin, 16, 83, 172, 260
    \fboxrule, 49, 107, 172
    \fboxsep, 49, 107, 146, 172
    \footheight, 172, 260
    \footnotesep, 172
    \footskip, 172, 260
    \headheight, 172, 260
    \headsep, 172, 260
    \itemindent, 44, 172

\labelsep, 45, 172, 225
\labelwidth, 44, 45, 172, 225
\leftmargini, 172
\leftmarginii, 172
\leftmarginiii, 172
\leftmarginiv, 172
\leftmarginv, 172
\leftmarginvi, 172
\leftmargin, 44–47, 172, 225
\linewidth, 172
\listparindent, 172, 225
\marginparpush, 172
\marginparsep, 172
\marginparwidth, 172
\mathindent, 15, 172
\oddsidemargin, 16, 172, 260
\paperheight, 172, 276
\paperwidth, 172, 276
\parindent, 14, 25, 26, 172, 225
\rightmargin, 46, 47, 172, 225
\tabbingsep, 65, 172
\tabcolsep, 53, 57, 58, 118, 155, 172
\textheight, 16, 171, 172, 260
\textwidth, 16, 45, 59, 62, 107, 172, 260
\topmargin, 16, 172, 260
\unitlength, 143, 155, 172
\risingdotseq (relation symbol), 165
\rm, 24, 274, 275
\rmfamily, 22, 24, 271, 274, 275
\rmoustache, 109, 111
robust command, 174, 175
roman, 93
roman family, 22, 23
\roman, 174
Roman, 93
\Roman, 174
root00a.tex (Diller), 92, 93
root01a.tex (Diller), 90, 91
root01b.tex (Diller), 91
root06a.tex (Diller), 91
\Rrightarrow (relation symbol), 168
\rtimes (binary operator), 164

rubber length parameter
    \abovedisplayshortskip, 172, 185
    \abovedisplayskip, 107, 108, 172, 185
    assignment to, 172
    \baselineskip, 25, 131, 134, 172
    \belowdisplayshortskip, 172, 185
    \belowdisplayskip, 172, 185
    \dblfloatsep, 63, 172
    \dbltextfloatsep, 63, 172
    \floatsep, 61, 63, 172
    \intextsep, 61, 63, 172
    \itemsep, 172, 225
    natural space of, 172
    \parsep, 44, 172, 225
    \parskip, 14, 25, 35, 44, 172, 225
    \partopsep, 35, 172, 225
    \textfloatsep, 61, 63, 172
    \topsep, 35, 172, 225
    \topskip, 172
\rule, 55, 58
runaway argument error message, 270
running head, 16, 88

s (stretch) positioning option, 49, 50, 52, 145, 146, 275, 276
\S (ordinary symbol), 161
sans serif family, 22, 23
\savebox, 50, 51, 145, 153, 154, 205, 216, 263, 268, 275, 276
\sbox, 50, 154
sc (small capitals shape), 271
\sc, 24, 274
scaled point, 171
schema, Frege's, ix, 4, 141
school (BibTeX), 71, 72
scope of a local declaration, 11
script style, 104, 113
scriptscript style, 104, 113
\scriptscriptstyle, 104, 105, 113
\scriptsize, 25
\scriptstyle, 104, 105, 113
\scrollmode, 12
\scshape, 22, 24, 271, 274, 275
\searrow (relation symbol), 168

\sec (log-like operator), 131, 163

secnumdepth counter, 86, 88, 89, 95, 173, 174

section counter, 87, 173

\section sectioning command, 86, 87, 90

\section* sectioning command, 87

sectioning command, 86, 87
  \chapter, 89, 90
  \chapter*, 93
  \paragraph, 86, 90
  \part, 86, 90
  \section, 86, 87, 90
  \section*, 87
  \subparagraph, 86, 90
  \subsection, 86, 90
  \subsubsection, 86, 90

\see, 81

\seename, 81

sep (BibTeX), 71

sequence, control, 10

\serial (Diller), 17

series, 22, 271, 274
  bold, 22, 23, 271
  medium, 22, 23, 271

series (BibTeX), 71, 72

\setcounter global declaration, 41

\setlength, 14, 16, 25, 26, 45–47, 53, 107, 143, 172

\setminus (binary operator), 114, 164

\settime, 99, 277

setting tabs, 63

\settodepth, 276

\settoheight, 276

\settowidth, 45, 276

\sf, 24, 274, 275

\sffamily, 22, 24, 38, 271, 274, 275

shape, 22, 271, 274
  italic, 22, 23, 271
  slanted, 22, 23, 271
  small capitals, 22, 23, 271
  upright, 22, 23, 271

\sharp (ordinary symbol), 161

\shortmid (relation symbol), 165, 167

\shortparallel (relation symbol), 165, 166

\shortstack, 55–58

showlabels package, 219, 251

\sigma (ordinary symbol), 158

\Sigma (ordinary symbol), 158

\signature, 97

\sim (relation symbol), 10, 161, 165, 167

\simeq (relation symbol), 165

\sin (log-like operator), 106, 131, 163

single quotation marks, 27

\sinh (log-like operator), 101, 131, 163

size11.clo, 18

sl (slanted shape), 271

\sl, 24, 274

slanted shape, 22, 23, 271

slide environment, 98, 173, 277

slides document class, 12, 98–99, 273, 274, 277

SliTeX, 273, 277

\sloppy, 19

sloppypar environment, 173

\slshape, 22, 24, 38, 271, 274, 275

\small, 25

small capitals shape, 22, 23, 271

\smallfrown (relation symbol), 165

\smallint (ordinary symbol), 161

\smallsetminus (binary operator), 164

\smallsmile (relation symbol), 165

\smile (relation symbol), 165

sp (scaled point), 171

space
  in maths mode, 15
  in text modes, 7, 10
  inter-word, 28, 85
  medium, 113, 164
  text modes, 28
  thick, 113, 164
  thin, 27, 28, 113
  vertical, 35

\spadesuit (ordinary symbol), 36, 161

special character, 9
  {, 9, 13

}, 9, 13

˜, 9, 28, 37

#, 9

$, 9, 10, 15, 106

%, 9

&, 9, 10, 53

\, 9

ˆ, 9, 101, 104–106

_, 9, 104–106

\sphericalangle (ordinary symbol), 161

\sqcap (binary operator), 164

\sqcup (binary operator), 164

\sqrt, 101, 124, 138

\sqsubset (relation symbol), 165

\sqsubseteq (relation symbol), 165

\sqsupset (relation symbol), 165

\sqsupseteq (relation symbol), 164, 165

\square (ordinary symbol), 161

square brackets, 13, 108

\ss, 22

\SS, 22, 277

\stackrel, 169

\star (binary operator), 164

\stop, 18, 270

storage bin, 50, 153

strut, 58

\strut, 138

sty file, xiii, 17

style, 104
    cramped, 104, 113
    display, 15, 104, 113
    normal, 104, 113
    script, 104, 113
    scriptscript, 104, 113
    text, 15, 104, 113

style file
    bezier, 277
    harvard, 273
    makeidx, 273

\subitem, 79

subparagraph counter, 173

\subparagraph sectioning command, 86, 90

subscript, 104, 105

subsection counter, 173

\subsection sectioning command, 86, 90

\subset (relation symbol), 165

\Subset (relation symbol), 165

\subseteq (relation symbol), 165, 166

\subseteqq (relation symbol), 165, 166

\subsetneq (relation symbol), 166

\subsetneqq (relation symbol), 166

\subsubitem, 79

subsubsection counter, 173

\subsubsection sectioning command, 86, 90

\succ (relation symbol), 165, 167

\succapprox (relation symbol), 165, 167

\succcurlyeq (relation symbol), 165

\succeq (relation symbol), 165, 167

\succnapprox (relation symbol), 167

\succneqq (relation symbol), 167

\succnsim (relation symbol), 167

\succsim (relation symbol), 165, 167

suffix, 7

\sum (large operator), 106, 107, 109, 162

\sup (log-like operator), 162

superscript, 101, 104, 105

\suppressfloats, 59, 277

\supset (relation symbol), 165

\Supset (relation symbol), 165

\supseteq (relation symbol), 165, 167

\supseteqq (relation symbol), 165, 167

\supsetneq (relation symbol), 167

\supsetneqq (relation symbol), 167

\surd (ordinary symbol), 161

\swarrow (relation symbol), 168

symbol, control, 10

t (top)
    float placement, 59
    oval-part specifier, 151
    positioning option, 52, 53, 118, 145, 146, 276

\t, 21

tabbing environment, 52, 63–65, 173

\tabbingsep rigid length parameter, 65, 172

\tabcolsep rigid length parameter, 53, 57, 58, 118, 155, 172

table counter, 173

table environment, 58–63, 173, 174, 277

table* environment, 58, 173, 174, 277

table of information, 52

\tablename, 59, 277

\tableofcontents, 93

tabs, setting, 63

tabular environment, 11, 52–58, 60, 117, 154, 173

tabular* environment, 58, 173

\tag, 133

\tag*, 133

tale, mouse's, 3, 25

\tan (log-like operator), 107, 131, 163

\tanh (log-like operator), 131, 163

Tatsuta, Makoto, xiii

\tau (ordinary symbol), 158

\tbinom, 137

termination of control word, 10

tex file, 8

texlog file, 8

text, modes, space, 28

text style, 15, 104, 113

\text, 132, 134, 136

\textbf, 23, 24, 274

\textbullet, 276

\textcircled, 277

\textcompwordmark, 277

\textemdash, 26, 276

\textendash, 26, 276

\textexclamdown, 22, 276

\textfloatsep rubber length parameter, 61, 63, 172

\textfraction, 61, 62

\textheight rigid length parameter, 16, 171, 172, 260

\textit, 8, 10, 12, 23, 24, 274

\textmd, 23, 24, 274

\textnormal, 24, 274

\textperiodcentered, 276

\textquestiondown, 22, 276

\textquotedblleft, 27, 276

\textquotedblright, 27, 276

\textquoteleft, 27, 276

\textquoteright, 27, 276

\textrm, 23, 24, 274

\textsc, 23, 24, 274

\textsf, 23, 24, 274

\textsl, 23, 24, 274

\textstyle, 104, 105, 113

\textsuperscript, 277

\texttt, 23, 24, 274

\textup, 23, 24, 274

\textvisiblespace, 276

\textwidth rigid length parameter, 16, 45, 59, 62, 107, 172, 260

\tfrac, 137

\thanks, 85

\the, 174

thebibliography environment, 31, 39–41, 44, 67, 85, 90, 94, 173

\theequation, 129

\thefootnote, 174

theindex environment, 79, 82, 173

\thempfootnote, 174

theorem, 41

theorem-like structure, 41

\thepage, 93, 174

\thepart, 174

\therefore (relation symbol), 165

\theta (ordinary symbol), 158

\Theta (ordinary symbol), 158

thick space, 113, 164

\thickapprox (relation symbol), 165

\thicklines, 145, 148

\thicksim (relation symbol), 165

thin space, 27, 28, 113

\thinlines, 145, 148

\thispagestyle global declaration, 88

Thorup, Kresten K., 198

tie-after accent, 21

tilde, 10, 37

\tilde, 102

tilde accent, 21, 102

times package, 272
\times (binary operator), 136, 164, 169
\tiny, 25
title (BibTeX), 67, 71, 72, 74
\title, 8, 13, 85, 94
titlepage document-class option, 13, 83, 85, 86, 89, 94, 98
titlepage environment, 173
\to (relation symbol), 114, 167, 168
toc file, 92, 93
tocdepth counter, 86, 89, 95, 173, 174
\top (ordinary symbol), 161
top-down stepwise development, ix, 141
\topfigrule, 277
\topfraction, 61, 62
\topmargin rigid length parameter, 16, 172, 260
topnumber counter, 60, 62, 173
\topsep rubber length parameter, 35, 172, 225
\topskip rubber length parameter, 172
\totalheight, 50, 52, 275, 276
totalnumber counter, 61, 62, 173
transcript file, 8
\triangle (ordinary symbol), 161
\triangledown (ordinary symbol), 161
\triangleleft (binary operator), 164
\trianglelefteq (relation symbol), 165, 167
\triangleq (relation symbol), 165
\triangleright (binary operator), 164
\trianglerighteq (relation symbol), 165, 167
trivlist environment, 31, 173
\tt, 24, 274, 275
\ttfamily, 22, 24, 38, 271, 274, 275
two asterisks prompt, 269
two-column output, 13, 61–63
\twocolumn, 61
twocolumn document-class option, 13, 58, 61, 83, 89, 94
\twoheadleftarrow (relation symbol), 168
\twoheadrightarrow, 126

\twoheadrightarrow (relation symbol), 168
twoside document-class option, 13, 83, 84, 88, 89, 94, 95, 273
twoside document-style option, 273
two-sided printing, 83, 88–89, 94–95, 172, 260, 264
type (BibTeX), 71, 72
type size, 12, 25
type style components, 22
\typeout, 91, 93
typewriter family, 22, 23
typewriter font, use of in this book, xi–xii

\u, 21
\ulcorner (opening symbol), 169
umlaut, 21
    Hungarian, 21
unary operator, 113, 157, 162–163
\underbrace, 103, 105
\underline, 103, 123
underlining, 103
unit, length, 171
unit, mathematical, 171
\unitlength rigid length parameter, 143, 155, 172
\unlhd (binary operator), 164
\unrhd (binary operator), 164
unsrt \bibliographystyle option, 76
\uparrow, 109, 111
\uparrow (relation symbol), 168
\Uparrow, 109, 111
\Uparrow (relation symbol), 168
\upbracefill, 207
\updownarrow, 109, 111
\updownarrow (relation symbol), 168
\Updownarrow, 109, 111
\Updownarrow (relation symbol), 168
\upharpoonleft (relation symbol), 168
\upharpoonright (relation symbol), 168
\uplus (binary operator), 164
upright shape, 22, 23, 271
\upshape, 22, 271, 274
\upsilon (ordinary symbol), 158

\Upsilon (ordinary symbol), 158
\upuparrows (relation symbol), 168
\urcorner (closing symbol), 169
\usebox, 50, 153, 154
\usecounter, 45
\usepackage, 17, 273, 274
user-defined command, 16

\v, 21
vamp.aux, 8
vamp.dvi, 8
vamp.log, 8
vamp.tex (Diller), 7–9, 12, 13, 18, 21
vamp2.tex (Diller), 13
\varDelta (ordinary symbol), 104, 158
\varepsilon (ordinary symbol), 159
\varGamma (ordinary symbol), 104, 158, 159
\varinjlim (log-like operator), 163
\varkappa (ordinary symbol), 159
\varLambda (ordinary symbol), 104, 158
\varliminf (log-like operator), 163
\varlimsup (log-like operator), 163
\varnothing (ordinary symbol), 161
\varOmega (ordinary symbol), 104, 158
\varphi (ordinary symbol), 159
\varPhi (ordinary symbol), 104, 158
\varpi (ordinary symbol), 159
\varPi (ordinary symbol), 104, 158
\varprojlim (log-like operator), 163
\varpropto (relation symbol), 165
\varPsi (ordinary symbol), 104, 158
\varrho (ordinary symbol), 159
\varsigma (ordinary symbol), 159
\varSigma (ordinary symbol), 104, 158
\varsubsetneq (relation symbol), 166
\varsubsetneqq (relation symbol), 166
\varsupsetneq (relation symbol), 167
\varsupsetneqq (relation symbol), 167
\vartheta (ordinary symbol), 159
\varTheta (ordinary symbol), 104, 158
\vartriangle (ordinary symbol), 161
\vartriangleleft (relation symbol), 165, 167

\vartriangleright (relation symbol), 165, 167
\varUpsilon (ordinary symbol), 104, 158
\varXi (ordinary symbol), 104, 158
\vdash (relation symbol), 36, 37, 126, 165, 166
\vDash (relation symbol), 165, 166
\Vdash (relation symbol), 165, 167
\vdots, 119, 122
\vec, 102
\vector, 151
vector accent, 102
\vee (binary operator), 164
\veebar (binary operator), 164
\verb, 66
verbatim environment, 65–66, 173
verbatim* environment, 66, 173
verse
    emblematic, 3
    figured, 3
verse environment, 31, 33, 44, 173
\vert (ordinary symbol), 107, 109, 111, 113, 114, 161
\Vert (ordinary symbol), 109, 111, 115, 161
\visible, 98, 277
volume (BiBTeX), 71–73
vowel ligatures, 2, 21, 22
\vspace, 107, 108
\Vvdash (relation symbol), 165

warning message, 269, 271–272
    \end occurred inside group, 272
    label(s) may have changed, 271
    LaTeX, 269, 271
    overfull \hbox, 18, 271
    TeX, 269, 271–272
\wedge (binary operator), 164, 169
\widehat, 103
\widetilde, 103
\width, 50, 52, 275, 276
Williams, Peter, 77
word, control, 10
\wp (ordinary symbol), 161
\wr (binary operator), 164

WYSIWYG, 7

\xi (ordinary symbol), 158
\Xi (ordinary symbol), 158
\xleftarrow, 140
\xrightarrow, 140

year (BIBTEX), 67, 71, 72

\zeta (ordinary symbol), 158

765122